LOCKHEED F-35

JOINT STRIKE FIGHTER

The Angle of Attack (AoA) achieved by the X-35A during
its flight test programme was 20 degrees. Not excessive,
but for such a short test programme quite impressive.
Copyright Lockheed Martin

LOCKHEED F-35

JOINT STRIKE FIGHTER

Design and Development of the International Aircraft

Gerard Keijsper

Pen & Sword
AVIATION

ACKNOWLEDGEMENTS

I would like to thank Dr. Luther Craig for his tireless effort and help, Eugene Golubkov for his material on the background of the AES and his invaluable friendship. John Kent and John Smith from Lockheed Martin for their help. Andy Bunce for his assistance and good humour. And last but certainly not least my family that had to spend a lot of time without me.

First published in Great Britain in 2007 by
Pen & Sword Aviation
An imprint of
Pen & Sword Books Ltd
47 Church Street
Barnsley
South Yorkshire
S70 2AS

Copyright © Gerard Keijsper, 2007

ISBN 978 1 84415 631 3

A CIP catalogue record for this book is
available from the British Library

Printed and bound in Singapore
By Kyodo Printing Co (Singapore) Pte Ltd

Pen & Sword Books Ltd incorporates the Imprints of Pen & Sword Aviation, Pen & Sword Maritime, Pen & Sword Military, Wharncliffe Local History, Pen & Sword Select, Pen & Sword Military Classics and Leo Cooper.

For a complete list of Pen & Sword titles please contact
PEN & SWORD BOOKS LIMITED
47 Church Street, Barnsley, South Yorkshire, S70 2AS, England
E-mail: enquiries@pen-and-sword.co.uk
Website: www.pen-and-sword.co.uk

CONTENTS

Another NASA proposition of a STOVL fighter. Note that the wing canard layout is similar to that of the Eurofighter, an aircraft still working toward operational capability in 2007. *NASA GRC.*

CHAPTER 1

HISTORY OF THE JSF PROGRAMME

The NATO studies that were being held during the fifties and sixties predicted that the airfields in Europe would be targets in the first wave of direct attacks by Soviet forces, making it impossible for regular aircraft to take off and land at these regular air force bases. The aircraft industry around the world was therefore charged to come up with proposals that would provide aircraft that would not require the highly vulnerable runways required by the fighters operational at that time. Many research projects started and most of them were unsuccessful. They included the Lockheed XFV-1 Salmon, the Mirage Balzac from France and the EWR VJ 101C from Germany to name but a few.

Many different technical approaches were tried, such as aircraft sitting on their tails and taking off vertically and transferring after take-off to horizontal flight. The major setback was that the pilot was lying on his back with his feet in the air and had therefore very bad visibility during landing – a major problem, especially during landing at sea. Other technologies that were tried were the tilt engines and the tilt wing. The tilt wing was in development for a transport for all US services: the Bell/Boeing V-22 Osprey.

Only Hawker from the UK with the Harrier and Yakovlev from Russia with the Yak-38 Forger succeeded in developing a Vertical Take-Off and Landing (VTOL) capable fighter. The Harrier and the Yak-38 Forger entered service, the latter with less commercial success

The Balzac has a rather low main landing gear giving it the right angle of attack for slow flight. The Balzac has the typical delta wing from Dassault. *Dassault.*

STOVL capability was deemed very important at the height of the cold war when everybody was looking into options to obtain this capability. A supersonic capability proved a bridge too far at the time. *Dassualt*

then the former. The Harrier was widely exported with the help of McDonnell Douglas, which adapted the Harrier for the United States Marine Corps (USMC) to become the biggest customer of the Harrier. The fact that the Harrier was subsonic made many experts expect the Harrier to be a sitting duck. The Harrier was developed from a design called the P1127, which evolved into the Kestrel and that again into the Harrier. A supersonic version was on the drawing board at the same time based around the BE.100 engine from Bristol Engines and was called the P1154 programme. But this programme was cancelled on 2 February 1965 in the same cancellation spree that hit the TSR2 programme four months later. The Harrier, however, quietened its critics during the Falklands war, where the Harrier proved itself against the supersonic Argentinean Air Force Dassault Mirage III. The Harrier, a design from the early sixties, was, however, getting to a respectable age and a new aircraft with supersonic capability was required.

On the basis of previous successful cooperation with the Harrier, the US Department of Defense (DoD) and the UK Ministry of Defence (MoD) joined in a research effort that was to lead to a Supersonic Short Take-Off and Vertical Landing (STOVL) Fighter (SSF) during 1983. This again resulted in a Memorandum of Understanding (MoU) being signed by the two parties in January 1986. Four powered-lift concepts were to be studied as options for the future SSF. The four options were:

- Advanced Vectored Thrust (AVT)
- Remote Augmented Lift System (RALS)
- Ejector Augmentor (EA)
- Hybrid Tandem Fan (HTF)

Through a joint project the US and the UK had its aviation industry working to come up with its best solution for each concept under study with the result that of all four options two studies had been completed. As the English industry base was not as large, British Aerospace and

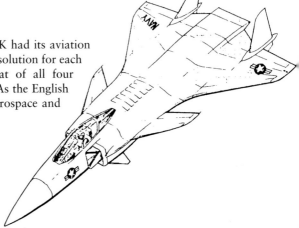

A drawing of the TF120 design. The vertical tails are canted inward and again the close coupled canard design. *NASA Ames*

The French effort in STOVL range of aircraft. Here can be seen the Balzac prototype. Note the different doors on top and on the bottom of the aircraft.
Dassualt.

Rolls-Royce performed all the studies. The US had the studies completed on a more competitive basis.

Vought worked on a tandem fanned V/STOL fighter aircraft designated the TF120, a delta-wing design with canards. The vertical tails spaced wide apart were canted inwards. General Dynamics was working on a design based on the ejector augmentation designated the E-7, the aircraft design based on its F-16. McDonnell Douglas was working on a further development of the proven concept of the Harrier but just like Rolls-Royce was continuing its research on PCB. Its aircraft was designated 279-3. Rockwell International was working on two different designs of which the major difference was the shape of the wing. The two designs had a dorsal intake which was hoped would reduce the Hot Gas Ingestion (HGI) problem. One major thing that the designs had in common was that weapon carriage was on the outside of the fighter, internal weapon bays had not yet become mandatory at this time. Stealth shape had as such not made an impact on the design of the V/STOL fighter.

Technical details of the different designs

Specification	General Dynamics E-7	McDonnell Douglas 279-3	Rockwell International baseline	Rockwell International Alternative	Vought TF120
Length	15.06 m 49.42 ft	17.07 m 56 ft	15.85 m 52 ft	15.85 m 52 ft	14.02 m 46 ft
wing span	9.88 m 32.40 ft	10.92 m 35.84 ft	9.60 m 31.50 ft	9.60 m 31.50 ft	8.53 m 28 ft
height	5.18 m 17 ft	5.29 m 17.34 ft	4.36 m 14.3 ft	4.36 m 14.3 ft	3.56 m 11.67 ft
Weights					
Structure	3848 kg 8494 lb	4351 kg 9592 lb	4143 kg 9133 lb	3916 kg 8633 lb	2442 kg 5384 lb
Propulsion	2573 kg 5672 lb	2003 kg 4415 lb	2437 kg 5373 lb	2475 kg 5456 lb	2553 kg 5629 lb
Systems and Equipment	1813 kg 3996 lb	2186 kg 4820 lb	1462 kg 3223 lb	1454 kg 3206 lb	1469 kg 3240 lb
Weight empty	8239 kg 18162 lb	8540 kg 18827 lb	8042 kg 17729 lb	7845 kg 17295 lb	6464 kg 14253 lb
Payload	449 kg 990 lb	665 kg* 1466 lb	544 kg 1200 lb	544 kg 1200 lb	754 kg 1662 lb
Fuel	5578 kg 12297 lb	4513 kg* 9950 lb	2559 kg 5641 lb	2427 kg 5350 lb	2846 kg 8480 lb
VTO gross weight	14640 kg* 32273 lb	13535 kg 29640 lb	11351 kg 25025 lb	11023 kg 24300 lb	11310 kg 24940 lb

Above: Here is a model in the 9 x 15 foot wind tunnel in 1990 under the ASTOVL programme. This model is from McDonnell Douglas and is seen during Hot Gas Ingestion tests. The model was called 279C. Note the Mirage-like inlets and big canard just behind the inlet. *NASA GRC*

Right: This was a McDonnell Douglas' 279-3C model evaluated at NASA in 1987. Several designs would pass through the wind tunnels of NASA to evaluate the different designs of the companies to find the future supersonic STOVL fighter. *NASA GRC*

A McDonnell Douglas design in the 9 x 15 feet wind tunnel at NASA Lewis for Hot Gas Ingestion tests, which was one of the biggest problems to be overcome. Note that the forebody was already adopting in similar shape to the X-35 design. *NASA GRC*

NASA Ames Research Center issued a Request for Proposals (RfP) in May 1986. For each of the propulsion systems it was planned that one contract would be awarded. The best out of the four would then be selected to build a technology demonstrator in the 1990/91 timeframe. The following teams were awarded the contracts by NASA Ames Research Center:

- McDonnell Douglas and Pratt & Whitney
- Grumman and General Electric (GE)
- General Dynamics and General Electric
- Lockheed and Pratt & Whitney/Rolls-Royce

Rolls-Royce's propulsion experience regarding VTOL goes back to 1953 when it demonstrated the Flying Bedstead with two vertically mounted Nene engines. Two years later the Rolls-Royce RB108 ran for the first time and it presented the first jet engine ever built as a direct lift unit. The French Dassault Barzac had eight Rolls-Royce RB108 lift engines installed. Experience from the RB108 was used for the development of the RB162, which ran for the first time in December 1961. The Rolls-Royce RB162 had been used in the Dassault IIIV. Rolls-Royce was such an authority in the field that it also cooperated with the Germans on lift cruise engines. Two engines were developed, the RB145 and the RB153. Furthermore the company's most successful project in the field was the Pegasus engine used in the Harrier. This was enough experience to welcome such a partner in the development of a future STOVL fighter.

Rolls-Royce initiated research in the field that it had most experience and that was with the variant of the BE.100 engine. At the time the company was still called Bristol Engines. The technology that was to provide supersonic capability was to be achieved by a technology called Plenum Chamber Burning (PCB). This technology involves basically a sort of combustor, called a plenum chamber, before the air goes through the vectoring nozzles, this giving the supersonic capability.

The Gas Couple Lift Fan (GCLF) had already been studied by General Electric in 1980s. General Electric considered that this was the best option for a future SSF. At the time there was no cooperation between the UK and the US. The US was trying to break the technological head start of the UK and the UK industry did not want to give this advantage away. The Shaft Driven Lift Fan (SDLF) was found to be heavier and the more compact option as opposed to the GCLF, which was lighter and bulkier. The GCLF would, however, be a more risky programme as the gas comes from the main engine at higher temperature, which would allow for the risk of Hot Gas Ingestion (HGI). With the SDLF this was not the case as all thrust provided by the lift fan would not be heated. All the above were found to provide insufficient power with the engines available at the time; the only hope was found in the new engines under development for the Advanced Tactical Fighter (ATF) programme. The YF119 and the YF120 engines had yet to prove themselves.

The US Marines decided they would replace all their current fighter aircraft with the Advanced Short Take-Off and Vertical Landing (ASTOVL) aircraft. The decision was made by 1987 and basically meant that both the AV-8B Harriers and the F-18 Hornets would be replaced by the ASTOVL, making the production run higher and as a result more interesting for the competing aircraft manufacturers.

After the Defense Advanced Research Projects Agency (DARPA) had seen to it that the *have blue programme* that led to the F-117 was successfully completed, it was considered that DARPA could help as well with the ASTOVL programme that had suffered lack of progress. So in early 1988 DARPA was requested to help the more or less stranded programme. DARPA, aiming to find out what the requirement would be for a future STOVL fighter, turned to the Navy for a list of requirements. Vice Admiral USN Deputy Chief of Naval Operations (Air Warfare) R.F. Dunn and USMC Lieutenant-General Deputy Chief of Staff of Aviation K.A. Smith sent their answer on 25 February. They included their Desired Operational Capabilities (DOC), stating that some of the requirements would not be compatible and that there would be some leeway for compromise in one or more areas.

DARPA was founded by a DoD directive on 7 February 1958 as ARPA. ARPA was to lead development projects for the DoD. A good fourteen years later on 23 March 1972 another directive from the DoD changed the name to DARPA. DARPA gave study contracts to General Dynamics, Lockheed Advanced Development Company (LADC) – the Skunk works, General Dynamics and McDonnell Douglas to research problems around Hot Gas Ingestion (HGI). Also, the power of the exhaust needed to lift the fighter would be so powerful that no one would be able to work around the aircraft during vertical landing (vertical take-off would not be used as it would use too much fuel and would require the services of already scarce refuelling aircraft). During operational missions the AV-8B Harriers were also using the short take-off capability instead of the vertical take-off capability.

All the results from these studies were to be evaluated by a team from both countries according to preset criteria. The most promising studies were:

• Shaft Driven Lift Fan (SDLF)

• Gas Coupled Lift Fan (GCLF)

• Ejector Augmentor (EA)

In the latter part of 1989 a joint US-Canadian STOVL programme was tested at NASA Ames Research Center. The programme was under the management of NASA and DARPA

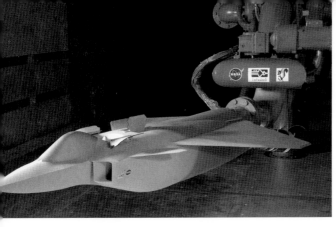

This forward fuselage model from Lockheed Martin showed that the canard was still under consideration. Otherwise the model still had the splitter plate inlets derived from the F-22. *NASA GRC*

on the US side and the Department of Industry, Science and Technology from the Canadian side. The E-7A model, which was an F-16XL lookalike with provision for thrust-augmenting ejectors, was tested for the first time in a 40 x 80 ft low-speed wind tunnel. The fact that the E-7A was an F-16XL lookalike was not that strange considering that it was a General Dynamics design. The ejector system was developed by de Havilland. The E-7A performed better then previous programmes, however the weight incurred by the ejector system was one problem that still had to be solved. Previous types that had researched this technology were the XV-4A and the XFV-12A. Propulsion was provided by the Rolls-Royce Spey 801 engine. The E-7A and its ejector system were supposed to be tested at the Outdoor Aerodynamic Research Facility (OARF).

A 9.2 per cent scale model designated 279-3C was tested during spring 1990 at the NASA Lewis Research Center in a 9 x 15 ft low-speed wind tunnel. The model represented a STOVL design from McDonnell Douglas and the research concerned HGI while the aircraft was in ground effects, which could be one of the major show-stoppers in the development of a supersonic STOVL fighter. HGI is divided into two categories – near field and far field HGI. Far field HGI occurs when the hot gas exhaust mixes with the air in front of the aircraft and a headwind would blow the hot air back in to the inlets. Near field is best described as when the forward and rearward propulsion exhausts disperse on the ground and meet each other to form a fountain. This fountain can hit the under surface of the fuselage of the aircraft and also go forward into the aircraft's inlet flow field.

Defense Secretary Dick Cheney reduced and delayed the four main acquisition programmes in April 1990. It remained to be seen if Congress would make further cuts. The ATF programme suffered the least. The ATF programme was delayed by two years but acquisition plans remained at 750 aircraft. The General Dynamics/McDonnell Douglas A-12 Avenger II was originally planned to have a production run of 858 aircraft but this was reduced to 620. The Northrop ATB B-2 programme with an original production plan of 132 was slashed to 75 flying wings. The last of the four programmes, the McDonnell Douglas C-17 Globemaster III, was also radically cut back. The original plan called for 210 C-17s. The new plan, however, accounted only for 120 aircraft.

Shortly after, the review and Dick Cheney's proposals were made public. The death bell sounded for the General Dynamics/McDonnell Douglas A-12 Avenger II in the form of news that the programme was delayed and over budget. Dick Cheney was embarrassed by this situation and ordered his people to look into the programme again and find out why this information had not come out during the review.

The Navy has had several projects to replace the Navy's A-6E aircraft. A programme that was the furthest developed and was still cancelled was the Advanced Tactical Aircraft (ATA) General Dynamics A-12 stealth attack wing, which was cancelled as a result of cost escalation and technical reasons. The ATA General Dynamics A-12 Avenger was cancelled on 7 January 1991, a little more than a year before the planned first flight of BuNo164519 in March 1992. The $4 billion spent on that programme resulted in a court case about the money spent and that had to be refunded, which was dragged out well into the next decade.

The Navy did, however, need a replacement for its A-6E so it started a new programme that was called the A-X and it also requested funds for upgrading the F/A-18C/D as a result of deficiencies found or expected in the near future in the F/A-18C/D and the Hornet 2000 study. All the Navy programmes had one thing in common and that was the requirement for two engines to give the crew a viable chance to return to the aircraft carrier if one failed.

The Navy was expected to issue a Request for Proposals (RfP) for the A-X programme after it had determined in March 1991 what the requirements were. At the beginning of July 1991 the Defense Acquisition Board (DAB) allowed the US Navy to conduct concept exploration studies for the A-X programme. However, the result of these studies and a cost and operational effectiveness analysis was required by the DAB prior to release of an RfP for the demonstration

This picture taken of a Lockheed model in 1996 shows that the decision to abolish the canard was taken relatively late in the programme. *NASA GRC*

and validation phase. On 28 August 1991 Naval Air Systems Command issued an RfP for concept exploration. Considering that weight and cost were the main reasons for cancellation of the General Dynamics/McDonnell Douglas A-12 Avenger II, it was inconsistent that there was no maximum weight requirement. It was, however, stated that a fighter/attack aircraft of more then 42,500 lb would be difficult to manipulate on ships.

The A-X programme was expected to be operational shortly in the new millennium. Five risk-reduction contracts were awarded by the US Navy for the A-X programme. The contracts for concept exploration and definition studies had been given to the following teams:

- McDonnell Douglas as the prime contractor teamed with LTV Aerospace (previously and afterwards called Vought), a new clean sheet programme.
- Grumman as prime contractor teamed with Boeing and Lockheed Advanced Development Company, a new clean sheet programme.
- Rockwell as prime contractor teamed with Lockheed Advanced Development Company as a subcontractor, a new clean sheet programme.
- Lockheed Aeronautical as prime contractor teamed with General Dynamics and Boeing studying a navalised version of the F-22.
- General Dynamics as prime contractor teamed with McDonnell Douglas and Northrop on a version of the A-12 design.

Around the same time the cooperation under the MoU between the UK's MoD and the US DoD expired but DARPA and the industry continued working on the ideas that they had developed.

During the summer of 1991 the Navy evaluated if the 2-D thrust vectoring/reversing technology should be incorporated in future fighter projects. Long before then the USAF started thinking about replacing the F-16 with a Multi Role Fighter (MRF). The F-16 would be past its twenty-year design life span and the F-22 was considered too expensive. In short, the USAF needed a cheap replacement, hence the MRF programme. Concept exploration and development was planned to begin by June 1992. The MRF was to have a price tag of $25 million apiece; this automatically required a high production rate and dictated a lightweight fighter. Early in 1992 USAF Chief of Staff General McPeak preferred the A-X to the MRF. He thought that the MRF could and should continue as both programmes were needed, but that the A-X was needed sooner than the MRF to replace aircraft such as General Dynamics F-111Fs, McDonnell Douglas F-15Es and the Lockheed F-117 Nighthawk. The funding for new aircraft types was difficult and it was deemed necessary that the A-X and the F-22 programme would have many main technologies such as engine and avionics in common. Another factor in the equation was the danger that if the McDonnell Douglas F/A-18E/F Super Hornet increased in cost, it could affect funding of the A-X programme. The USAF had the problem with the F-22 that the programme's cost increase could reduce funding for the MRF. The Navy's A-X programme had slowly developed into a joint Naval and USAF programme. The MRF, however, gained in urgency as the General Dynamics F-16 was thought to need replacement from 2005, as at that time F-16 production for the USAF was to end in 1993, although exports were thought to keep the production line open until 1997.

Plans called to split the MRF programme in two. One would be an update of the existing fighters, keeping them in production for longer and giving the second MRF programme more time. Programmes that required funding for the years to come were the McDonnell Douglas C-17 Globemaster III, Lockheed F-22, McDonnell Douglas F-18E/F Super Hornet, the A-X and the MRF. The Navy programme under the lead of DARPA somehow lost attention in all those budget quarrels.

The industry (British Aerospace and McDonnell Douglas) signed an agreement in early February 1992 to work together on the STOVL project and the same was done by the Navy and the Marines in the early summer of 1992. The need was anticipated for a Short Take-Off and Landing (STOL) version of the A-X. The cooperation between the UK and the US was renewed and DARPA took the lead and saw all the development work that had taken place before as phase one of the same programme. Phase two was to start now. The RfP was issued to the industry but it did not, however, call for two flying prototypes. Instead, it called for a risk-reduction effort and to aim at validating new technologies. The programme now led by DARPA, Navy, Marines and NASA would only pursue a flying prototype by 2001. Industry had to submit its proposals by 24 November 1992. DARPA planned to appoint two winning contractors in January 1993. To maintain cost at an acceptable level the empty weight of the design was not to exceed 24,000 lb. The maximum speed was to be Mach 1.8, which for a STOVL design was quite exceptional; only the STOVL Yak-141 Freestyle and the French Balzac prototypes had flown supersonic before. The other hard requirements set previously were eliminated, as they would only increase cost. The requirements basically dictated a single-engine fighter that would take the same or less space than the F/A-18 on the flight deck and have better manoeuvrability and agility then the F/A-18 and the AV-8B. The DARPA project was treated as an X-programme and the winning design would receive the designation X-32. The Navy was treating the programme as a technology demonstration programme. DARPA asserted that if the programme did not prove that a Supersonic STOVL Fighter SSF could be built cost effectively, it would not go any further than the technology demonstration programme.

Lockheed made a move to make its position on the market stronger by buying the General Dynamics Fort Worth division where the General Dynamics F-16 production line was situated. The Tactical Military Aircraft (TMA) unit, Fort Worth, was also a partner in the A-X programme with McDonnell Douglas on a 50/50 basis, which gave Lockheed a foot in an extra programme. General Dynamics also had a third share in the Lockheed F-22 programme; as a result Lockheed had bought a majority share in the F-22 programme. Lockheed had a second programme running within the A-X programme with Rockwell, and a third with Grumman and Boeing, giving Lockheed a 60 per cent chance of being part of the winning bidder team for the A-X programme.

In January 1993 USAF Secretary Donald Rice came up with a simple cost-reduction plan, which was to produce an MRF that was Navy-compatible or rather a Navy MRF that could be adapted for the USAF. The requirement should be set from the outset. It was questionable if the Navy could afford both the A-X and the F-18E/F Super Hornet programme. The A-X programme changed its name to A/F-X to describe a dual role, in an effort to save the programme. President Bill Clinton changed the name DARPA back to ARPA on 22 February 1993 and wanted ARPA to support technology programmes not only for defence purposes.

Two months later than expected, in March 1993, the winners of the DARPA-led Supersonic STOVL Fighter (SSF) programme, also known as the Advanced STOVL programme phase two, were announced. The winning teams were McDonnell Douglas in cooperation with General Electric and British Aerospace pursuing the Gas Coupled Lift Fan (GCLF) with a contract value of $27.7 million, and Lockheed in cooperation with Pratt & Whitney, Allison, Rolls-Royce and Hercules with a contract value of $32.9 million to pursue the Shaft Driven Lift Fan (SDLF) system. In fact, technology should be proven in phase two to make production of a manned prototype possible. Therefore, a Large Scale Powered Model (LSPM) had to be built by the two contenders to prove that the aircraft would be able to fly, or rather be capable of taking off and landing vertically. The winning design of these two proposals would be awarded a contract in 1995 for phase three, which would involve building two prototypes. DARPA was so optimistic about the possibilities that the GCLF and the SDLF had to offer that it would be able to replace besides the F/A-18 and the AV-8B the USAF's F-16s, as the lift fan would be removed and replaced by fuel tanks giving the fighter the required long range for the USAF. The GCLF would leave more space for internal fuel or systems than the SDLF as it would remove the ducting required and therefore the range increase could be very substantial, whereas the SDLF would only remove the shaft and the lift fan. The reasons for Lockheed to pursue the SDLF technology were threefold:

- The extra weight incurred by the lift fan and the shaft was insignificant compared with the extra thrust gained by this new technology.
- As the lift fan used no combustion the exhaust was colder, making the ground environment better suited for operations.
- STOVL thrust requirements can be disconnected from the main engine so that the engine is conventionally sized to the requirement of up-and-away thrust required for transonic acceleration.

The Navy, desperate to keep the A/F-X programme alive, was looking for another extension for the concept exploration phase of the A/F-X programme in early July 1993 as the previous extension would expire on 31 July 1993. To let the programme survive in the future as well, the Navy was looking into a technology demonstrator option.

In 1993 the US DoD had a bottom-up review, which came up with the obvious conclusion. The DoD could not afford both the Navy's programmes so it cancelled the A/F-X and recommended that the F/A-18E/F should proceed, although the success of this programme was seriously criticised by the General Accounting Office (GAO) in a report to be published in June 1996. By April 1993 the MRF and the A/F-X were scrapped. Another programme was, however, recommended to be initiated, the Joint Advanced Strike Technology (JAST) programme. This was, however, not an acquisition programme, it was a technology development programme. This gave it some protection from budget cuts as the savings from cutting the programme were limited.

The JAST programme's basis was that two versions of one aircraft could be built for the two services, i.e. the USAF and the US Navy. In history, every attempt to adopt an existing USAF fighter for the US Navy was unsuccessful. The last attempt to develop a joint service combat aircraft was the Tactical Fighter Experimental (TFX). The attempt was unsuccessful and entered service only with the USAF – the aircraft was the General Dynamics F-111 Aardvark. The US Navy cancelled its version and instead developed and bought the Grumman F-14 Tomcat. The USAF ended up with an aircraft heavier than it needed as it had incorporated from the outset some of the Navy's requirements, which made it heavier. Hence the remark of the USAF that it did not want the Navy to make the aircraft too heavy. However, as early as 1986 it was recognised by the Senate Armed Services Committee that the TFX programme was not a failure because of two services joining on one aircraft project, but that the problem was too many incompatible missions in one aircraft design. The Senate Armed Services Committee had tried to make the ATA and the ATF cross-service aircraft; in other words both types were to enter both USAF and US Navy services by linking this requirement to the funding of both projects for the fiscal year 1987.

The only two aircraft that were used by all three services were the McDonnell Douglas F-4 Phantom II and the Vought A-7 Corsair II LUFF (Little Ugly Fat Fella, the unofficial name used by the pilots). What those two aircraft had in common though was that they were both designed for carrier operations and were so successful that the USAF bought them as well. In short, now the idea was to design from the outset one plane that would have a standard airframe and specific equipment to fulfil specific service needs. In fact, there would be one production line for three variants of one aircraft. The JAST programme was to be conducted in three phases. In each phase special attention was to be given to propulsion, flight systems, structures, materials, avionics, supportability and lean manufacturing. Extra attention was paid during all those studies to keep development cost low. A good example of this was the engine, as the existing Pratt & Whitney F119 engine was further developed for the JAST programme. The JAST programme office was opened on 27 January 1994.

Although Boeing had lost out in the competition in the ASTOVL or Common Affordable Lightweight Fighter (CALF) programme as it was called, it had continued to work on a vertical lift propulsion system from its own funds. In March 1994 these efforts bore fruit and the US Congress provided more funds for ASTOVL technology development. Boeing therefore signed a contract with ARPA for US $32 million on 25 March 1994. Boeing and its industry partners Pratt & Whitney and Rolls-Royce would have twenty-six months to design and test their concept of direct lift STOVL. Boeing wanted to develop the direct lift system employed by the Harrier further as it is a proven concept and it was felt that it still had growth possibilities. In contrast with the other systems under development by Lockheed and McDonnell Douglas, this system would not need a lift fan or engine, which would save weight and scarce place for other hardware or systems. Boeing aimed during its CALF concept research to reduce STOVL dedicated technology to 5 per cent of the empty weight. It was hoped that this might make it attractive for the

Note that this model still has a similar canopy to the F/A-22 Raptor. Lockheed tried where possible to maintain commonality to decrease cost. *NASA GRC*

USAF to retain this technology to increase operational flexibility and commonality and thereby also reduce the overall cost as there would be no need for two different types on the production line. Pratt & Whitney as Boeing's partner automatically went with a further development of the YF-119 engine and Rolls-Royce was responsible for all the nozzle technology. STOVL technology was also studied in the newly started JAST programme but Boeing believed that the two programmes would eventually come together and that cost would be a major factor. Therefore, in order to prevent duplication Boeing did not treat the two programmes as separate efforts. Like the other contenders McDonnell Douglas and Lockheed, Boeing was to build as well an LSPM for phase two of the ASTOVL CALF programme. Under the JAST Concept Exploration programme a Broad Area Announcement (BAA) was issued in February 1994. On 6 May 1994 twelve contracts were signed under the BAA 94-1. The twelve contracts were awarded over four categories:

- Overall weapon system concept exploration
  Modular Multi-Service Airframe – Boeing Defense & Space at a value of $2.2 million
  Leveraging JAST affordability – Lockheed at a value of $2.0 million
  Joint Strike Warfare Concept – McDonnell Douglas at a value of $1.7 million
  Joint Strike Aircraft Concept Exploration – Northrop Grumman at a value of $0.7 million
  JAST affordability studies – Northrop Grumman at a value of $0.3 million
- Avionics
  Affordable next-generation avionics – Honeywell at a value of $0.1 million
  Sensor integration trade studies and architecture – Litton Amecom at a value of $0.5 million
  Affordable off-board architecture – McDonnell Douglas at a value of $0.6 million
- Weapons integration
  Cost effective weapons carriage options – Hughes Missiles at a value of $0.3 million
  Affordable Weapon Integration Study – McDonnell Douglas at a value of $0.7 million
- Virtual strike
  Virtual strike environment architecture – Cambridge Research at a value of $0.8 million
  Virtual strike environment – Northrop Grumman at a value of $0.5 million

On 28 June 1994, during a forum on JAST, US Deputy Defense Secretary John Deutch commented on the idea of combining ASTOVL and JAST into one programme. He thought the idea had more than merit. That same day the house appropriations committee also recommended the merging of the two programmes during 1995 rather than 1996. JAST programme director Brigadier General George Muellner wanted to delay the merging of the programmes so that he could strike a deal with ARPA about funding before ARPA could retire from the programme.

Northrop Grumman followed Boeing's path and about three months later in July 1994 by signing an agreement with ARPA to join the CALF programme. Northrop Grumman joined the programme with its own funds to increase its chances of getting a contract in the JAST programme, as that promised to be the most interesting programme financially for the company. Northrop Grumman was researching the option chosen by the Russians for their Yakovlev-designed STOVL aircraft, the Yak-38 Forger and Yak-141 Freestyle. Northrop Grumman teamed up with Pratt & Whitney and Rolls-Royce. At this stage the original winners of the second phase of the CALF programme had initiated production of their scale models of the CALF designs. Boeing was waiting for funding to proceed to that stage. Northrop Grumman did not have the resources for that and did not expect funding. Northrop Grumman saw that the biggest advantage of the Conventional Take-Off and Landing (CTOL) variant, which would not be fitted with the lift engine, would be its enormous fuel capacity – something also pursued by the McDonnell Douglas and Lockheed designs. Northrop Grumman did not plan to build an LSPM as it argued that its design would have no problem lifting off. One of the main reasons for having the LSPMs was the memory of the inability of the Rockwell XFV-12A to take off. This was to be prevented from happening again at all cost. The McDonnell Douglas/British Aerospace STOVL was tested in a variety of wind tunnels in 1994 and also at the BAe Warton wind tunnel.

By 10 August 1994 the UK and US signed an MoU for the development of a CALF aircraft to replace their Harrier and F-18. The UK committed $12 million to the second phase of the JAST programme. The decision to make a demonstration aircraft would be taken later during the year. The US part of the programme would be led by ARPA. The programme would have to use STOVL technology so that both the Harrier FR.2 and the AV-8B could be replaced. ARPA changed its name back to DARPA shortly after. Mission goals were set for the STOVL/CTOL CALF on 30 September 1994. The USMC and USAF were envisioned to replace their respective aircraft. To reduce costs the demonstrator aircraft should be able to be converted from the CTOL to the STOVL version.

Mission	Profile	Weapons	5% + 10 min sea level loiter fuel reserve goals
Deck-launched intercept	HI-HI	2 AIM 120 2 AIM 9X Gun	300 nm combat radius 1.5 Mach supercruise Bring back all weapons
Close Air Support (CAS)	LO-LO	4 Rockeye 2 AIM 9X Gun	200 nm combat radius
Air Defence/CAP	HI-HI	2 AIM 120 2 AIM 9X Gun	1 hour loiter at 400 nm Bring back all weapons
Interdiction	HI-MED-MED-HI	2 2000-lb JDAM 2 AIM 120 Gun	600 nm combat radius
Suppression of Enemy Air Defence (SEAD)	HI-LO-LO-HI	2 HARM 2 AIM 9X Gun	400 nm combat radius Bring back all weapons
Reconnaissance	HI-LO-LO-HI	RECCE package 2 AIM 9X	400 nm combat radius
Strike	HI-LO-LO-HI	2 2000-lb JDAM 2 AIM 120 Gun	Maximum combat radius (750 ft deck take-off)

The Concept Exploration phase confirmed that a single engine and single pilot concept was the most affordable option. The Navy for the first time accepted that it would have to agree to a single-engine aircraft. The Concept Definition and Design Research (CDDR) was the second phase, which ran from January 1995 to March 1996. On 2 September 1994 an RfP was issued for the CALF/JAST programme. Responses were due back on 4 November 1994 at the latest.

Although JAST was a joint programme and the first programme office director was a USAF general, there was a lot of bickering between the US Navy and the USAF. From the outset the main disagreement was that the US Navy issued all the contracts. The test facilities chosen from the outset were at Navy Air Station (NAS) Patuxent River. The Air Force Flight Test Center (AFFTC) at Edwards AFB offered its facilities as well to (JPD) USAF General Muellner and US Navy deputy programme director Craig Steidle. Both of them were flown in the F-16 Multi-Axis Thrust Vectoring (MATV) in 1994 to show what the AFFTC had to offer. The offer was finally accepted on 2 May 1995 and Edwards AFB AFFTC would be formally invited to participate in the programme.

The McDonnell Douglas team had completed its negotiations about work-share and other related matters with the signing of an MoU on 28 October 1994 and announced the fact a couple of days later on 1 November 1994. ARPA announced by the end of 1994 that the demonstrator that would be flown would be designated X-32A for the CTOL version and X-32B for the STOVL version.

For the CDDR phase twenty-six contracts were awarded. Of these, four were to aircraft producers. Twenty-four of these contracts were awarded on 22 December 1994. The JAST programme office had chosen these twenty-four proposals from a total of 150 proposals. The table below lists the contracts awarded.

Project	Contractor	Value
Advanced Survivability Model for Strike Warfare	Aerodyne Research Inc, Billerica, MA	$250,920
Spreadsheet Methodology for Tradeoff Analysis	ASI Systems International, Ridgecrest, CA	$346,553
JAST Multi-service Common Airframe	Boeing Defense and Space Group, Seattle, WA	$1,740,920
Tri-Service Weapon System Concept	Boeing Defense and Space Group, Seattle, WA	$27,614,120
Avionics Virtual Systems Engineering and Prototyping	Boeing Defense and Space Group, Seattle, WA	$2,288,774
Compare Performance of Proposed *SCI/RT* Mechanisms	D. Gustavson, Los Altos, CA	$50,000
Low Cost Nozzles for Enhanced Strike Effectiveness/Turbocooler Engine Demonstration for Flexible Thermal Management	GE Aircraft Engines, Cincinnati, OH	$3,657,288
Off-Board MS&A Concept Definition and Design Research	Geodynamics Corp, Colorado Springs, CO	$486,659

Wideband Integrated Forebody (*IFB*) Technology Maturation	Hughes Aircraft Co, El Segundo, CA	$1,310,174
JAST Secure Avionics Architecture Concept Development	Hughes Aircraft Co, El Segundo, CA	$291,980
Joint Strike Weapon System Concept Definition and Design Research	Lockheed Ft Worth Co, Ft Worth, TX	$19,900,000
Structurally Integrated Reconfigurable Multi-function Apertures (*SIRMA*) Study	Lockheed Ft Worth Co, Ft Worth, TX	$441,983
On-Board Off-Board Information Fusion	Lockheed Ft Worth Co., Ft Worth, TX	$2,016,004
JAST Affordable Modular EO/*IR* Sensor Subsystem	Martin Marietta Technologies, Inc, Electronics and Missiles, Orlando, FL	$535,755
Joint Strike Weapon System Concept Definition and Design Research	McDonnell Douglas Aerospace, St Louis, MO	$28,193,501
Joint Strike Weapon System Concept Definition and Design Research	Northrop Grumman Corp Advanced Technology and Development Center, Pico Rivera, CA	$24,085,919
Avionics Virtual Systems Engineering and Prototyping	Northrop Grumman Corp B-2 Division, Pico Rivera, CA	$2,125,190
JAST Propulsion System Demos/ JAST Maturing Technologies in an Engine Environment	Pratt & Whitney Government Engines and Space Propulsion, United Technologies Corp, West Palm Beach, FL	$5,448,143
RF Technology Maturation	Rockwell International Collins Avionics & Communications Division, Cedar Rapids, IA	$719,484
Fluidic Thrust Vectoring Nozzle Study	Rockwell International, Seal Beach, CA	$278,051
Avionics Virtual Systems Engineering and prototyping	Texas Instruments Inc Defense Systems & Electronics Group, Plano, TX	$2,464,392
Advanced Strike Integrated Diagnostics (*ASID*)	TRW Avionics and Surveillance Group, Beavercreek, OH	$2,004,219
Scaleable Multiprocessing System (*SMPS*)	Unisys Government Systems Group, Eagan, MN	$1,210,000
Affordable RF/*IF* Packaging	Westinghouse Electric Systems, Electronics Systems, Baltimore, MD	$314,943

The height of suspension could be altered in the Outdoor Aerodynamic Research Facility (OARF) so ground effects could be evaluated at different heights. *NASA Ames*

JAST was a joint Navy and USAF initiative but more money saving was to follow when it was discovered that the CALF programme, also a Navy programme under the management of DARPA, could easily be incorporated in the JAST programme. Lockheed had a model designated X-32 under the CALF programme that was thoroughly tested at NASA's Ames facilities. The model was tested in the Outdoor Aerodynamic Research Facility (OARF), and another smaller-scale model in the 80 by 120 ft subsonic wind tunnel during 1995. The wind-tunnel testing was initiated on the 1 February 1995 when the model was equipped with canards. This idea was then later also tested on the bigger model in October 1995.

DARPA director Gary Denman and General George Muellner, forced by Congress, agreed that it was mutually beneficial to merge the two programmes as they had similar goals. However, they had

This model was equipped with a complete STOVL propulsion system. The wind tunnel used at NASA Ames was 80ft by 120ft, one of the largest wind tunnels in the world. *NASA Ames*

The model being loaded into the wind tunnel, the large-scale powered model was 94% scale. *NASA Ames*

initially envisioned a merging of the two programmes after the risk-reduction phase had finished in the CALF programme in 1996.

As the ASTOVL/CALF would be integrated into the JAST programme the 1992 agreement between the UK and the US had to be altered. The UK MoD and US DoD officials met to sign a new MoU regarding the new JAST programme in early April 1995. The UK MoD expected to replace the Royal Navy's Sea Harrier F/A2 and fulfil Staff Target (air) 425 for a deep strike penetrator aircraft to eventually replace the Panavia Tornado GR4 or its upgrade depending on whether or not the JAST programme kept to its schedule.

Shortly after the contract had been awarded McDonnell Douglas and Northrop Grumman combined their efforts with British Aerospace. British Aerospace was allowed to join mainly because of its experience with the Harrier and its previous cooperation with McDonnell Douglas on the further development of the Harrier. Lockheed approached the problem differently; it contacted Yakovlev and its engineers as they had a long-

Here the model was tested with the four-poster tail in stead of the canard. Lockheed kept its options open until it had investigated all advantages and disadvantages. Canards have proven tricky to integrate with flight control systems as experienced with the Eurofighter and Gripen. *NASA Ames.*

The impressive scale of the wind tunnel facility at NASA Ames is given perspective by the people below. Note the open doors on the top side of the fuselage and the similarities with the F-22 design. *NASA Ames*

standing experience with Vertical/Short Take off and Landing (V/STOL) aircraft. Yakovlev had built the first V/STOL aircraft that could fly faster than the speed of sound, the Yak-141 Freestyle that stole the show together with its predecessor the Yak-38 Forger at Farnborough 1992. The two fighters were both equipped with a separate lift engine. Beside Yakovlev's propulsion expertise, Lockheed also had an interest in the ejection seat system as it could mean the difference between life and death.

Lockheed recognised that to survive on the decreasing defence market it had to become bigger. Buying over General Dynamics' Fort Worth division was the first step in this process. The second step was announced in March 1995. Lockheed merged with systems integrator Martin Marrieta, the merged entity was from then on called Lockheed Martin.

On 27 April 1995 Lockheed Advanced Development Company (the Skunk works) rolled out its LSPM before shipping it to NASA Ames in California. The LSPM was equipped with a Pratt & Whitney 100-220 engine. The main features were two dorsal intakes and canards following the European trend. One of the dorsal intakes showed the lift fan, which was connected by a shaft to the Pratt & Whitney 100-220 engine. The LSPM was manufactured from glass-reinforced-plastics and steel. Testing at the NASA OARF was expected to begin in June 1995.

Boeing, in a show of confidence, built its own test facilities in Tulalip, north of Everett, for its LSPM. The facility was expected to be complete by the end of the summer 1995 in time for the 94 per cent LSPM, which was to be tested before the year's end. Lockheed was not the only company to try to court British Aerospace for cooperation on its JAST design; Boeing was turned down as well. Boeing had discussions before with Lockheed but both companies did not want to give up their design so it was decided that they would resume talks about cooperation after the *down* select expected in 1996.

In May 1995 a house committee decided that the ASTOVL CALF programme should be integrated with the JAST programme. The Pentagon concurred that both programmes could be integrated at the end of phase two of the ASTOVL CALF programme. The committee had the opinion that the ASTOVL CALF programme should be a part of the JAST effort but DARPA, or ARPA as it was called during that time, should lead the research effort. Both programme offices were in talks with each other to address the committee's recommendations. The idea from the committee was basically to prevent funding two separate studies that were researching the same thing. The committee expected to save $51.7 million, which was requested for similar studies for DARPA's programme and the JAST programme. One thing was certain and that was that both programmes would be integrated by the time that phase three would be initiated. JAST was initiated for both the Navy and the USAF, and now it had to take into consideration the needs of the USMC. The JAST programme, not so far evolved yet, has had one major result from studies so far, which was that all airframe manufacturers consider commonality one of the main means of reducing cost. It is hoped that 70 to 90 per cent of commonality is achievable.

As the biggest experience in STOVL was in the UK it was obvious that British Aerospace was a valuable partner but as mentioned before it had chosen McDonnell Douglas but on an exclusive basis. Lockheed had very little or no experience in this field and therefore looked elsewhere. The only other company with the same amount of experience was to be found in Russia, the Yakovlev design bureau. The JAST programme office had no problem with the fact that Lockheed was going to a former state enemy company to obtain critical technology. State Department approval was needed and interim approval came by the end of June 1995. The only strange thing was that Yakovlev had only experience with the Lift Plus Lift Cruise (LPLC) configuration, which was under development by Northrop Grumman. Nevertheless, Lockheed believed that despite the technical difference between the two approaches Yakovlev could supply valuable assistance. However, the importance has been downplayed in several publications as an investment with minimum return.

McDonnell Douglas had teamed with British Aerospace and was later joined by Northrop Grumman. This was by some designated the dream team for the simple reason that all the STOVL and Navy aircraft experience was in one team. But the problems started during the second quarter of 1995 when the McDonnell Douglas team decided to change propulsion system, to continue with the LPLC. The LSPM with the Gas Coupled Lift Fan (GCLF) was nearly ready but was withdrawn from production. The ducting required for the GCLF would make the fuselage too bulky. The design of the airframe remained the same but the team went from a GCLF propulsion system to the LPLC propulsion system originally under study by team member Northrop Grumman. The change of propulsion system also made it possible to change the engine. Because no bleed air was required for the LPLC propulsion system a change was made to the F119 engine to reduce cost.

On 10 July 1995 the LSPM from Lockheed initiated testing at NASA Ames OARF. Hover tests were the first to evaluate the following side effects that STOVL fighters have to overcome:

- Airframe 'suck down'
- Hot Gas Ingestion
- Ground pressure
- Ground temperature

The combined thrust of the Pratt & Whitney 100-220 engine and the Allison Advanced Development Company lift fan is 75 kN (17,000 lb).

The Joint Initial Requirement Document (JIRD) was signed in 1995. The idea behind the JIRD was that it would give the option to adjust later the requirements, as operational requirements would change as well. It was, however, agreed that every change that was required would not increase the price unduly or other requirements would have to be lowered to balance the cost. In the first JIRD the main focus was on size, due to the weight-cost ratio, speed and stealth (survivability and maintainability). The Navy accepted a single-engine design and in that regard took a major step back in its requirements. The USAF, however, was not spared either. The USAF took a step back in the sense that it did not require a more manoeuvrable fighter than the F-16. The major advance had to be in stealth and survivability and here little or nothing was negotiable; only the price would be a driving force as the Joint Strike Fighter (JSF) was supposed to be affordable, meaning that the stealth facilities should be easily maintained. The red line through all requirement changes was that there were trades between cost and performance and that these were carried out in consultation with industry and the war fighters. The USMC needed a plane with a small logistic footprint and so was not really enthusiastic about LPLC as an extra engine meant increased maintenance requirements.

The separate technology development programmes' delays or progress could influence future inclusion or exclusion with cost as the main factor. Production expectations at that time were confidently high and as ever did not take into account future force and or budget reductions or any sharp rise in development cost as was noticed in the Engineering, Manufacturing and Demonstration (EMD) phase of the F-22 programme. The expected requirement from the USAF was 2036 JSFs, from the Marines 642 JSFs, from the Navy 300 JSFs and from the Royal Navy 60 JSFs, boosting total planned production to 3038 JSFs without any export. (The JAST and JSF was a joint US/UK programme from the outset.) This was reconfirmed on 20 December 1995 when an MoU was signed with regards to the Concept Demonstration Phase (CDP) of the programme.

By the end of October 1995 the McDonnell Douglas team revealed for the first time since

Note the striking commonality in the tail design compared to the YF-23. Furthermore the optimistic paint scheme that has by now almost died out of the services inventories. *Copyright McDonnell Douglas*

This was an early 'dream team' design. Note the tail is similar to the YF-23, furthermore this design still had canards. *Copyright McDonnell Douglas*

A top view of the large-scale powered model of the early Lockheed STOVL design, showing the hooks from which it will be lowered at the NASA Ames test facility. The photograph also provides a first view of the propulsion arrangement. A similarity with the vertical tail of the F-22 design can be noticed which later disappeared on the X-35 demonstrator aircraft. *Copyright Lockheed via NASA Ames*

altering its propulsion system its JAST proposal design. The new design was equipped with a 'lambda' shaped wing and a four-poster tail. The inlets were of the conventional type on the side of the fuselage under leading edge extensions. It was similar to its previous design as that part of the aircraft had gone through thorough wind-tunnel testing. A dorsal or F-16 intake were not an option for the simple reason that inlet and exhaust doors were required for the lift engine. A major concern with the LPLC system is ground erosion and Hot Gas Ingestion. These tests were performed at British Aerospace in England.

A draft RfP was released in December 1995 and the final request was due by the end of February 1996. Meanwhile, Lockheed had discovered that the canard configuration was not a good configuration for landing on an aircraft carrier. For this reason the canards were replaced by the normal tail stabiliser, making the Lockheed design a lookalike of a scaled-down F-22.

After wind-tunnel testing the McDonnell Douglas, Northrop Grumman and British Aerospace team changed the design of its JAST concept. The new design had a similar tail design to the unsuccessful Northrop/McDonnell Douglas YF-23, which also had stabilisers canted outward diagonally at 45 degrees. Control was to be enhanced by thrust vectoring. To reduce the risk of Hot Gas Ingestion two auxiliary dorsal air intakes were installed to function in the conversion flight regime. This was similar to Lockheed's design, which was equipped with one larger dorsal inlet for the main engine.

Lockheed felt that it was well ahead of its competitors as it had carried out major risk reduction tests at the NASA Ames OARF and the NASA 24 x 37 m wind tunnel since November 1995. The model had been taken up to 18° Angle of Attack (AoA) during 170 hours' of testing the propulsion system. The competitors had not reached the same risk-reduction level, especially the McDonnell Douglas team, which had changed propulsion system and airframe design so late in the programme.

The ARPA changed its name back to DARPA on 10 February 1996 under the administration of President Bill Clinton. Boeing announced on 1 September 1996 that it had come to an agreement to buy the Rockwell Aerospace and Defence units. Rockwell Aerospace's last two major projects were the B-1B Lancer and the international experimental X-31.

On 22 March 1996 the final and best offer RfP was issued. Two months later the JSF programme was changed from a technology development programme into an Acquisition CATegory I (ACAT I) programme. Although the JSF programme had acquired ACAT I status, the JSF office did not use the usual YF prefix used in previous programmes such as the ATF and the Light Weight Fighter (LWF) programmes. Instead, it continued using the X-32 designation, appointing that to Boeing and using the X-35 designation for the Lockheed Martin design, thereby maintaining a part of the experimental nature of the programme. X-aircraft are used to validate concepts and new technology and Y-aircraft are prototypes. For this reason the Preferred Weapon System Concept (PWSC) could develop further and integrate lessons from the CDP, reducing risk and cost. This could be used during the CDP phase when juggling funds might be more difficult. McDonnell Douglas had managed to accumulate 7500 hours' of wind-tunnel testing by the end of June 1996. According to McDonnell Douglas the 'near tailless' design had 40 per cent better turn performance in the up and away flight regime than the contemporary conventional fighters.

On 16 November 1996 both Boeing and Lockheed Martin were announced as winners and were to proceed to take part in the CDP. Both McDonnell Douglas and Northrop Grumman looked like being cut out of the manned fighter market for the next fifty years. One reason for McDonnell Douglas's elimination was the fact that the two-engine design was considered more prone to technological problems than the designs from Boeing and Lockheed Martin. Both Boeing and Lockheed Martin had performed major risk reduction around the propulsion system and were considered to deliver the best value for money. One problem that was already encountered very publicly in 1992 at the Farnborough Air Show was when the Yakovlev Yak-141 Freestyle was not permitted to perform a vertical take-off or landing. There were concerns that the lift engine would burn the runway because the engine exhaust was hot and could not be cooled. McDonnell Douglas, however, had been able to solve the problem according to its officials. Besides the technological risks, the lift engine was inducing a cost increase not only on the acquisition level but also for the Life Cycle Costs (LCC) for maintenance and fuel cost and spare parts. The purpose of the CDP is fourfold:

- To demonstrate commonality across the variants (CTOL, STOVL and CV – Carrier Version)

- To demonstrate commonality during the production process

- Each CDP participant should demonstrate their concept in flight for the STOVL version, ie propulsion, hover and the transition modes

- Each CDP participant should demonstrate their concept in flight for the CV version, mainly the low-speed carrier approach

The last of the 'dream team' design evolution. It was this design that was sent in as their end proposal. Note that the canard has disappeared from the design otherwise it has not altered much. *Copyright McDonnell Douglas*

Joint Strike Fighter
CTOL

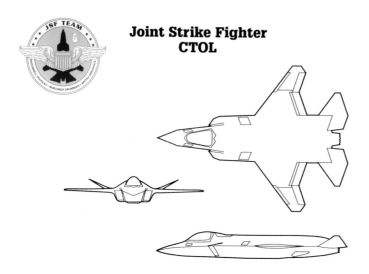

A three plan view of the CTOL proposal from the McDonnell Douglas, Northrop Grumman and BAe Systems team with the badge of the biggest customer - the USAF.
Copyright McDonnell Douglas

Joint Strike Fighter
CV

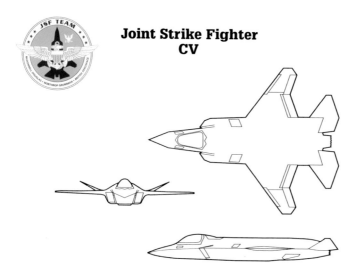

A three plan view of the CV proposal of the McDonnell Douglas, Northrop Grumman and BAe Systems team with the US Navy badge. *Copyright McDonnell Douglas*

Joint Strike Fighter
STOVL

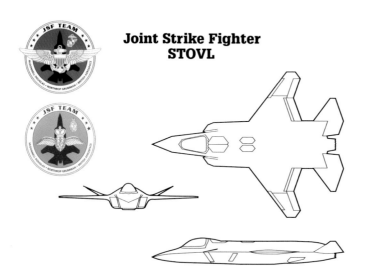

A three plan view of the STOVL proposal of the McDonnell Douglas, Northrop Grumman and BAe Systems team with the USMC and Royal Navy badges. Note that the dorsal inlets for both the vertical and main engines. The USMC did not like the idea of an additional engine
Copyright McDonnell Douglas

According to Lockheed Martin officials they planned to fly the first prototype, the CTOL demonstrator, in the latter part of first quarter of 2000, followed by the STOVL version two months later. The plan was to replace the wing on the CTOL demonstrator for the carrier demonstrator and equip it with a tail hook.

Lockheed Martin officials stated that a total of sixteen risk-reduction programmes were ongoing during the CDP. Some of them were under the JSF programme office technology maturation programmes, which had to be shared with Boeing, but others were geared to their proposal and kept confidential. Two of the risk-reduction development programmes that were at least acknowledged were the Signature Measurement Aircraft (SigMA) and the Cooperative Avionics Test Bed (CATB or CATBird), funded together with Northrop Grumman hence the word Cooperative. Simulations of assembly work was another part of the risk reduction and for this reason Lockheed Martin selected Computer Aided, Three-dimensional Interactive Application (CATIA) developed by Dassault Systèmes as the basis for its virtual development environment. CATIA is a system to support Computer Aided Design and Computer Aided Manufacturing (CAD/CAM) that Lockheed Martin hoped to initiate within the CDP to ensure low-cost development. Development costs were expected to go down by about 50 per cent and manufacturing costs by about 30 per cent.

The American Helicopter Society organised a symposium about the JSF in April 1997 where speakers from the US Navy and USAF expressed interest in the STOVL version. The USAF was interested in the STOVL version as a possible replacement for the A-10 Thunderbolt II. The US Navy, however, required a range of 600 nautical miles and it was doubtful that this requirement could be fulfilled by the STOVL version. Northrop Grumman announced its choice to join the Lockheed Martin team in the CDP phase of the programme after careful evaluation of both designs on 8 May 1997. British Aerospace was expected to make its choice between Boeing and Lockheed Martin shortly. On 15 May 1997 the Quadrennial *Defense Review (QDR)* was released. The QDR recommended that future acquisition would be reduced. The JSF programme was also affected. For the USAF the number of JSFs required went down to 1763 (a reduction of 273 aircraft). The 609 JSFs for the Marines was a reduction of 33 aircraft. Only the Navy came out without scratches; 480 JSFs were recommended instead of the original 300, an increase of 60 per cent. Some 230 of the Navy JSFs will be competed for by both the JSF and the F-18E/F. The JSF programme was not the only programme to suffer, the F-22 (F-22 at the time) acquisition programme had been reduced by almost 33 per cent. On 18 June 1997 at the Paris Air Show, le Bourget, it was announced that British Aerospace had decided to join the Lockheed Martin team. Meanwhile, Lockheed Martin completed its Initial Design Review (IDR) by the end of June 1997, allowing the company to proceed and initiate detailed design.

During the summer the AFFTC hired Lieutenant-Colonel Paul Smith as lead USAF JSF pilot. Lieutenant-Colonel Paul Smith had been working before for the JAST office but at Wright Patterson AFB. Lieutenant-Colonel Paul Smith had already in the early JAST programme stages expressed his eagerness to be involved in the flight-test programme. One of his tasks was to develop the Joint Test Force (JTF) concept. The concept was the idea of Joe Dowden, the head of the JSF site at the AFFTC. Lieutenant-Colonel Paul Smith further developed the concept and improved on it. The JTF concept was an innovative approach for the government to evaluate the testing to be done. Government pilots and engineers would be integrated into each contractor test team. The US Navy, however, did not like the JTF concept and it was ultimately Joint Program Director (JPD) USMC General Mike Hough in May 2000 that decided that the JTF concept was good and he installed Lieutenant-Colonel Paul Smith as the head of the JTF because he was the most senior person there. Originally the flight-testing had to begin by March 2000 but this decision was made two months later, which shows the delays caused by the bickering between the Navy and USAF. Lieutenant-

Colonel Paul Smith was assigned to the Lockheed Martin team as the government lead pilot and Commander Phil Yates was assigned to Boeing in a similar function. Both could communicate but only about lessons learned so that no technical information could spill over to another team.

By the end of 1997 a review of Lockheed Martin's PWSC was not only attended by US military officials but also by representatives of all the countries participating financially in the CDP, e.g. Denmark, the Netherlands, Norway and the UK.

The Final Design Review (FDR) started in July 1998 and continued through the summer months at the Lockheed Martin Skunk Works Palmdale facility and was completed by 2 October 1998. The FDR was split up in different areas. The different areas covered were:

- Air vehicle integration

- Flight sciences

- Mass properties

- Airframe structures

- Propulsion

- Vehicle Management Systems

- Integrated flight propulsion control

- Avionics

- Subsystems

- Crew station

- Reliability and maintainability

- Safety and flight test

Immediately after completion of the FDR Lockheed Martin rolled out a full-scale mock-up of its X-35 Concept Demonstration Aircraft (CDA).

British Aerospace announced on 30 November 1999 that it was to merge with Marconi Electronic Systems. The British Aerospace merger meant that it became not only an aircraft frame manufacturer but also a systems integrator. Thus the name was changed to BAE Systems.

The draft of the Joint Operational Requirement Document (JORD) was written in 1999 and was finally signed on 13 March 2000. Funding problems for the F-22 in 1999 could have altered the situation. Funding was being withheld and at that point USAF Chief of Staff General Michael Ryan almost brought the JSF programme to an early end. The US Congress had approved the Pentagon spending bill on 15 July 1999 but had excluded funds for the F-22 programme. The costs of the core technologies developed for the F-22 (passed on to the JSF) would now be carried by the JSF alone. This made the JSF too expensive and further requirements agreed upon by the USAF for the JSF were on the basis that there would be a Lockheed Martin F-22 to provide air superiority. The threat of not signing the JORD document, however, did not need to be put to the test as funds were reinstated, solving the problem. The Joint Requirement Oversight Council (JROC) validated the JORD on 11 April 2000 and it was again revalidated by the JROC on 18 October 2001, shortly before selection of the winner of the CDP. The Key Performance Parameters (KPP) that were agreed are shown in the table below.

KPP	USMC	USAF	USN	RN/RAF
Radio frequency signature		Very low observable		
Interoperability		Meet 100% of critical, top-level information exchange secure voice and data		
Combat radius	450 nm USMC profile	590 nm USAF profile	600 nm USN profile	450 nm UK profile
Sortie generation	4 surge 3 sustained	3 surge 2 sustained	3 surge 2 sustained	3 surge 2 sustained
Logistic footprint	< 8 C-17 equivalent loads (20 PAA)	< 8 C-17 equivalent loads	< 46,000 cu. ft 243 ST	< 21,000 cu. ft 102 ST
Mission reliability	95%	93%	95%	95%
STOVL mission performance				
Short Take-off distance	500 ft	N/A	N/A	450 ft ski jump
Vertical lift bring back capacity	2 x 1k JDAM 2 x AIM-120 reserve fuel			2 x 1k JDAM 2 x AIM-120 reserve fuel
Maximum approach speed	N/A	N/A	145 knots	N/A

A sign that the inventory was changing in the USAF was that the logistic footprint was no longer given in the Lockheed C-141 Starlifter as was the case with the ATF programme (F-22) and all previous fighter aircraft in the inventory. But now in Boeing (originally McDonnell Douglas) C-17 Globemaster IIIs. The maximum payload capacity of the C-17 is 170,900 lb whereas the payload of the C-141B was 90,200 lb. Logistic footprint means how many transports a squadron of twenty-four fighter aircraft needs to be able to operate independently for thirty days while maintaining wartime operation sortie rates. The interesting thing was that for the F-16 a logistic footprint was required of 14.6 C-141 Starlifters (90,200 lb multiplied by 14.6 equals 1,316,920 lb). The JSF should require fewer than eight C-17s, which translates into less than 1,367,200 lb. The JSF, although more modern, needs a bigger logistic footprint mainly due to the maintainability of the stealth features such as Radar Absorbing Material (RAM).

The Sortie Generation Rate (SGR) was an important figure because the more often an aircraft could fly a mission during a day the fewer aircraft were required. Mission reliability was an important feature to achieve high SGR. The F-16 had achieved with the first three production aircraft an 83 per cent mission reliability rate. This would not only have to be met but exceeded. In fact, the F-22 Raptor would be the aircraft it would be compared with as it would be the last aircraft to enter service.

Besides the funding problem mentioned earlier other things started to tarnish the reputation of the so far immaculately run programme. Delays in the development as well as software and hardware issues delayed the first flights of both contenders. Furthermore, the GAO stated in its reports that the main technologies were not advanced enough and therefore needed more time to mature. In short the GAO thought that the programme needed to be delayed. USAF acquisition chief Darleen Druyun did not concur and said delays in the STOVL flight programme could be taken into account as the scheduled contract award was not until May/June 2001. As to the GAO, according to Druyun, the task was not to get all the technologies matured so that there would no risk involved. The task that was part of the CDP was reducing risk to low or medium level, which would be achieved before the contract award of the EMD.

On 15 April 2000 a Request for Information was issued to both Boeing and Lockheed Martin. At this stage it was not sure if the contest was going to remain a winner takes all competition. It was according to some better to retain both companies as viable fighter aircraft manufacturers because in its original form the winner takes all also aptly named by USMC Gen Mike Hough as the bet your business contest had as a side effect that the winner would obtain a monopoly for the next generation fighter.

During the spring of 2000 another problem came up for JPD General Mike Hough. The US Senate and House delayed the funding of the JSF EMD phase, thus delaying the EMD phase. Down select was planned for 1 June 2001 followed by a 126-month long EMD phase with the first flight of the first prototype planned for early 2005. Delivery of the first production aircraft was due in 2008 with block 1 capability (block 1 capability offered AMRAAM and JDAM capability). The delay in funding would, however, have the effect that both teams would have to disband, which would have a disruptive effect as it was not certain if the same people could be put together again at a later stage.

The date for the return of proposals was set for 8 February 2001. Lockheed Martin announced on 7 February 2001 that it had handed over its proposal a day early. On 26 October 2001 the winner of the two teams was announced. The winner would go through to the EMD phase, a prize that was to be the biggest defence contract in history and for a long time to come.

The beauty and the beast, the question here is which is the beauty and which is the beast? *Copyright Lockheed Martin*

CHAPTER 2

THE BOEING DESIGN EFFORT

Boeing was in competition for DARPA's advanced STOVL programme, later called CALF. In March 1993 it lost out to McDonnell Douglas and Lockheed Martin. In agreement with DARPA it continued research with its own funds and this paid off as a little more than a year later Congress gave more money for lift propulsion research and DARPA signed an agreement with Boeing covering research for a direct lift propulsion. The direct lift propulsion system was also referred to as the super Harrier version. It is, however, strange that McDonnell Douglas and British Aerospace did not choose to pursue the route in which they had most experience, but DARPA was more interested in new technology that would have growth capacity and would increase knowledge such as the Gas Coupled Lift Fan (GCLF).

On 14 September 1995, Boeing initiated tests with its Large Scale Powered Model (LSPM) powered by a YF119 engine. The tests were held at a remote site 60 miles north of Seattle in Tulalip. The LSPM was built in a little more than fifteen months, which according to Boeing was a major engineering feat. The LSPM was a 94 per cent scale model of what Boeing envisioned as its Preferred Weapon System Concept (PWSC) at the time. The LSPM tests were mainly to prove the propulsion system in the vertical-landing mode. The model was more than 40 ft long and was over 45,000 lb as the construction material that was used was steel and aluminium.

For the Boeing design a high-fuel volume delta-wing was chosen from the outset during the CALF phase of the programme. The choice for a high-fuel volume delta-wing solved the problem of the increased range that was required, and it reduced the need for fuel tanks in the fuselage. The PWSC was expected to have approximately 2.5 times the range/payload of the current F-

Survivability evaluations were made using several models, including this full scale model. A problem was thought to be the exhaust reflection from the engine, as experienced with the Harrier. *Copyright Boeing*

16/F-18 types. The main fuselage would be used for the internal weapon bays and the inlet duct and engine. The inlet duct was already used on Boeing's Advanced Tactical Fighter (ATF) design proposal.

On 11 July 1996 Boeing submitted its proposal for its JSF design. Its proposal was based on data gained from 11,700 hours of tests performed with the LSPM, small-scale models and even full-scale models.

- The LSPM had been used for four months and was dedicated to HGI, ground effects, suck down, thermal and acoustic footprints.

- A full-scale model had been tested at Boeing's indoor radar range to prove Boeing's claims of a low Radar Cross Section (RCS).

- Small-scale models besides the LSPM were used for propulsion-related tests. The inlet design was verified and lift and exhaust systems were proven. Among these were the lift nozzles and the main nozzle.

- Three separate low-speed wind tunnels were used to test and prove low-speed aerodynamics.

- Six different wind tunnels in the US and the UK were used to test and prove high-speed aerodynamics.

- Four different wind tunnels were used for testing the CDA ability in the high AoA region (low speed up to 90 degrees' AoA and high speed 50 degrees' AoA).

- Weapon bay performance was also tested, mainly separation tests and the acoustic effects.

Boeing was awarded a $660-million JSF contract on 16 November 1996, starting with a fifty-one-month CDP. Boeing expected to fly its first CDA in mid-2000 according to the CDP contract. An important milestone for Boeing was an MoU that was signed on 20 January 1997 to cooperate with McDonnell Douglas on the JSF, which gave it access to

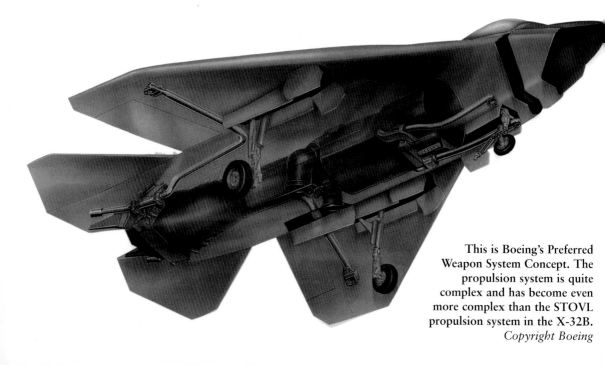

This is Boeing's Preferred Weapon System Concept. The propulsion system is quite complex and has become even more complex than the STOVL propulsion system in the X-32B.
Copyright Boeing

important experience from McDonnell Douglas in the AV-8 Harrier and the F/A-18 Hornet and F-4 Phantom II Navy fighters. The cooperation was unrelated to the merger plans with McDonnell Douglas. After the approval of the merger by the federal trade commission at the end of June 1997, approval from the European Union had to be waited for, which was due by the end of July 1997. On 4 August 1997 Boeing officially merged with McDonnell Douglas.

On 10 September 1997 Boeing had successfully passed the Initial Design Review (IDR). Boeing's IDR was a little over two months later than Lockheed Martin's. Boeing and the Joint Program Office (JPO) almost simultaneously had the Program Management Review (PMR) where the PWSC was also addressed as well as the CDA design, airframe subsystems, CDA weight and propulsion system integration.

On 5 February 1998 Boeing announced that the production of the two demonstrator aircraft would take place in Palmdale, California. The reason for this was that it is close to Edwards AFB and therefore it was the logical place as that was where the test flying would be held. People working on the JSF included current Boeing employees from Palmdale, Seattle, St Louis, Seal Beach (California) and Downey (California). This decision was not a reflection on where the future production line location would be situated. Boeing planned to use its first CDA, the X-32A, for demonstration of the CTOL and CV requirements for the USAF and US Navy, while using its second CDA, the X-32B, for STOVL requirements from the USMC and Royal Navy. The original goal from Boeing during the CALF programme to have 5 per cent difference between the STOVL and CTOL models had to be aborted at the time when the CV requirements were added. The new goal was, however, set at 85 per cent commonality but even this proved difficult and it was affecting the STOVL and CTOL performances so Boeing eased on that goal as well. Commonality was, however, still the aim but it was decided upon on a cost versus capability evaluation basis and the commonality achieved was in the high seventies.

On 8 July 1998 structural assembly of the first CDA started in St Louis Phantom works (previously McDonnell Douglas). When completed, the forward fuselage under assembly there was transferred to Palmdale for final assembly. The centre fuselage was assembled in Palmdale and work had commenced on 21 August 1998. Assembly work on the second forward fuselage was initiated on 23 September 1998, also in St Louis. All the assembly work had started ahead of schedule. The first single-unit wing skin for the X-32 had been delivered from Seattle to Palmdale by 4 November 1998. The single-unit wing skin, made from composites, weighs 742 lb and is placed on top of the wing. On 2 December 1998, Boeing stated that the FDR of its X-32 CDA was complete. At this stage it was clearly too late to change anything major on the CDA, however improvements and design changes were included in the still changing PWSC.

On 4 February 1999 Boeing presented a new PWSC. The design had now gained an aft horizontal tail unlike the CDA. The horizontal tail is important to increase control power during approach for landing on an aircraft carrier. As a result, the trailing edge of the main wing had to be modified as well. The wing's leading edge sweep remained unaltered just like the single-piece wing design with its high fuel capacity. The reason for retaining the leading edge sweep is twofold – good approach speed and stealth characteristics. Other changes included a lighter and stealthier aft swept chin inlet. The wing span remained the same. The vertical tail was also retained. The trapezoidal wing, meaning a wing having four sides with none parallel, replaced the earlier delta-wing design. The new designation of Boeing's PWSC was 373.

On 22 February 1999 Boeing announced that its cockpit avionics suite for the PWSC would include voice-recognition technology to ease the pilot's workload.

As with the F-22 programme, Boeing wanted to reduce the risk with the avionics system

Roll Nozzle

2D Thrust Vectoring
Cruise Nozzle

X-32B

F119 Derivative Engine

Aft Pitch-Yaw
Nozzles

Forward Pitch
Nozzles

Roll Nozzle

Jet Screen

Lift Nozzles

Common to All Variants

STOVL Unique

Boeing JSF X-32B Direct-Lift Propulsion System

Boeing aimed to keep commonality as high as possible. However, cost forced Boeing to leave the commonality goal of 95 per cent. As with Lockheed's X-35B, the X-32B required balancing lift posts in the wing. *Copyright Boeing*

and therefore tested the avionics in a Flying Test Bed (FTB). The FTB was a highly modified Boeing 737-200 and flew for the first time from Wichita on 26 March 1999. Preparations for the first flight of the Avionics Flying Laboratory (AFL), a term used instead of FTB by Boeing, started in April 1998. The actual modification work on the Boeing 737-200 was initiated in December 1998. The Boeing 737-200 was equipped with a stretched 48-inch nose and radome assembly. Further modifications were in the form of several antennas.

The forward fuselage assembly of the X-32A was completed on 26 March 1999. It was developed and assembled under cost, and more impressively under weight and ahead of schedule. The forward fuselage was shipped to Palmdale where on 1 April 1999 the final assembly was initiated when the forward fuselage was mated with the centre fuselage. On 13 June 1999 the wing was mated with the fuselage in six hours almost to complete the final assembly of the X-32A. The aircraft was now recognisable from the computer artist designs. A little bit more than two weeks later Boeing delivered the second forward fuselage on 29 June 1999 to Palmdale for the X-32B.

On 20 August 1999 the X-32A was almost complete when it was towed from the final assembly to undergo the structural tests required before the flight tests were to commence. A month later on 20 September 1999 the X-32B fuselage was also mated with its wing. The mating of the wing of the X-32B took only two-thirds of the time that it took to mate the wing of the X-32A. On 9 October 1999 thirty-four individual structure tests performed on the X-32A had been completed, meaning that the X-32A was structurally fit to go through its planned test-flight programme. The advantage of the high commonality was that the structural tests performed on the X-32A were also valid for the X-32B. During the last week of October 1999 Boeing underwent another PMR. During this PMR Boeing presented its

Final assembly of the X-32 underway. The second prototype took a significantly shorter time to assemble.
Copyright Boeing

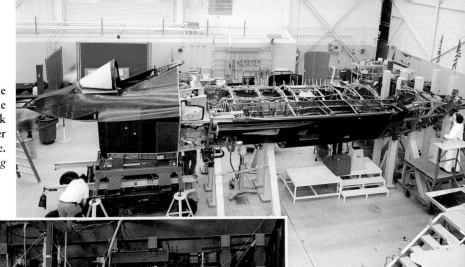

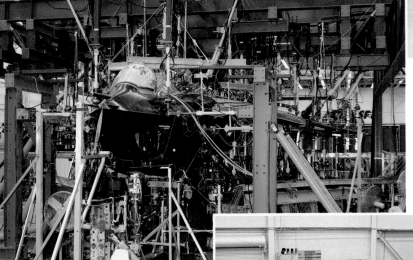

Structural tests were required prior to flight test. Here is one of the concept demonstrator aircraft, the X-32A, in the torture chamber.
Copyright Boeing

Boeing demonstrated lean manufacturing processes during the assembly of both X-32 Concept Demonstration Aircraft.
Copyright Boeing

Boeing's first X-32 on its unofficial roll-out without a paint job in 1999. It was on its way to structural tests that were required prior to flight testing. The high main landing gear is evident. Note that the inlet cowl is still missing.
Copyright Boeing

A view of the futuristic cockpit as it was foreseen by Boeing. A part of the avionics was besides this ground simulator and was also tested in a dedicated avionics flight test-bed. Interestingly, the Boeing team had also decided to opt for the side-stick. Beside the main displays, the layout of the smaller instruments can also be seen. The pilot is wearing the HMD that was to replace the HUD for the Boeing team. It was developed by BAe Systems. *Copyright Boeing*

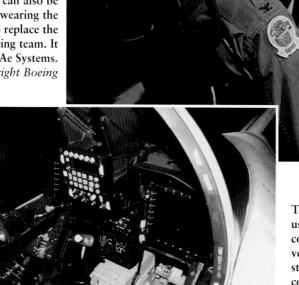

The cockpit of the X-32B. Boeing used the centre stick which is considered more conventional. A very modern cockpit by any standards but the operational cockpit would have been completely different. *Copyright Boeing*

latest update in its PWSC with designation 374.

On 14 December 1999 Boeing surprised everybody by rolling out both the X-32A and X-32B at once. The construction of the X-32B was initiated six months later than the X-32A, but it was finished only six weeks later than the X-32A – a gain of twenty weeks. According to Boeing this proved its commitment to lean manufacturing processes and cost reduction. The lean manufacturing processes had been tried out on a *black programme*. The aircraft from the *black programme* was called Bird of Prey. The Bird of Prey developed by McDonnell Douglas Phantom works (now Boeing) flew a total of thirty-two flights by three pilots between 1996 and 1999. The Bird of Prey was revealed from *the black world* by Boeing in October 2002.

On 7 March 2000, the X-32B completed its maximum power engine ground tests over the dedicated engine pit. The aircraft stands on a T-shaped grille, below which a pit is located to prevent HGI. The first flight of the X-32B planned for the third quarter of 2000 was, however, delayed to the fourth quarter of 2000 as a result of software and hardware development problems. At the time it was not clear what kind of effect a strike of engineering staff would have on the CDP for Boeing; the strike was ongoing since 9 February 2000 and lasted until 20 March 2000.

In the first ten days of April 2000 the X-32A was equipped with the engine that was to power it during test flights. Test engine YF004 is flight-rated and completed forty-five hours of acceptance testing prior to delivery. On 23 May 2000 the X-32A finished low- and

The Avionics Flying Laboratory was used not only for the avionics but also for the radar testing and was an integrated part of the risk reduction effort performed by Boeing. *Copyright Boeing*

medium-speed taxi testing. Low-speed taxi testing was at 30 knots and medium speed at 55 knots.

In mid-July 2000 Boeing equipped its X-32B with the engine that was to power it during its flight-test programme. Installing the flight-rated engine was a major milestone in the programme and Boeing proceeded with engine runs, the first phase of which was completed on 22 September 2000. Shortly before this on 17 August 2000 Boeing announced that it had chosen the Martin-Baker Mk.16 ejection seat for its PWSC. Other aircraft equipped with this Mk.16 seat are the fourth-generation fighters Dassault Rafale and Eurofighter Typhoon.

For the final test phase of Boeing's AFL a Synthetic Aperture Radar (SAR) was installed,

At the official roll-out Boeing achieved a first by presenting two prototypes at once. Many partner nations were invited to the occasion to show that it was truly an international programme. *Copyright Boeing*

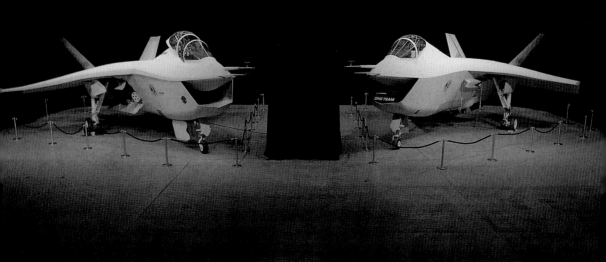

A view of the X-32B with the engine removed gives a good view of the nozzles. *Copyright Boeing*

The hover-pit tests were important safety features in the STOVL evaluation for each competitor. The hover-pit increased safety and unknowns could be evaluated more safely. *Copyright Boeing*

Ground tests beat predictions giving Boeing confidence for the flight test phase. Although many criticized the X-32B for having to remove the inlet lip (cowl) for the STOVL testing, it fulfilled all government requirements. *Copyright Boeing*

which was about 70 kg (150 lb) lighter than the previous radar tested in the AFL. The technical change-over took only eleven days according to Boeing officials. The Boeing 737 AFL role had been proving the on-board sensor fusion with the off-board data supply. On-board sensors include, besides the radar, a Targeting Forward Looking Infra Red (TFLIR) and Electronic Warfare (EW) systems. Off-board data can come from other fighters, J-STARS and AWACS. As the Boeing CDA are not equipped with the planned avionics they has to be proven aboard the AFL.

A difference of approach from Lockheed Martin was mainly that the X-32A, besides the USAF CTOL version, was also used to demonstrate the Navy CV requirements. The Boeing X-32A CTOL took off for its first flight on 18 September 2000, making it the first of the JSF CDA to fly. Fred Knox was the pilot during the first flight and he transferred the plane to Edwards AFB. Dennis 'Irish' O'Donoghue was the chase pilot during the first flight in an F-18 Hornet and from his plane he saw that there was a pink fluid escaping from the plane, which was leaving a trace over the fuselage. This was reason enough to shorten the flight. A minor hydraulic leak was the cause and the problem was solved quickly after landing. The second chase pilot, also in an F-18 Hornet, was Commander Philip Yates, the second pilot eventually to fly the X-32A on the fourth flight. A small problem was that during the first three flights Boeing had been unable to retract the Messier-Dowty landing gear. The Boeing's X-32A main landing gear retracted forward and the nose landing gear retracted aft. Boeing did not want to disrupt test-flying while solving the problem and therefore rearranged its test-flying programme and initiated flight-testing for the Navy (CV) version. The flight tests included Field Carrier Landing Practice (FCLP) and connected tests that had to be performed with the landing gear down and the US Navy pilot responsible (Philip 'Rowdy' Yates) for this role got to fly the fourth flight. The problem was solved shortly after the ninth flight and on 12 of October 2000 during the tenth flight, flown by Boeing pilot Fred Knox, the landing gear could be retracted for the first time.

On 24 October 2000 during a test flight Boeing's test pilot Dennis O'Donoghue saw a warning light come up in the cockpit of the X-32A,

Only the X-32A was equipped with a weapon bay. Neither the X-35 at this stage, or the X-32B had one. *Copyright Boeing*

notifying him that his landing brakes were not working. Suspecting a false alarm, he returned to Edwards AFB for a normal landing. Shortly after touch down he noticed that the brakes did not function so he took off again. Luckily the lakebeds located around Edwards AFB offered an easy way out without damaging the aircraft. Dennis O'Donoghue therefore landed the X-32A on a lakebed and let the aircraft roll to a standstill. The malfunction of the landing brakes turned out to be software related and part of a 'bigger problem'. The X-32A was grounded for the time being until the software problems were

The X-32A with landing gear extended over the desert near Edwards air force base. Boeing had more then their fair share of trouble during the X-32A flight test programme. They managed to accumulate 66 flights in just over a four and half months. *Copyright Boeing*

solved. The head start over Lockheed Martin was from this day diminishing as well, as Lockheed Martin performed its first flight with its X-35 demonstrator. The grounding had lasted for two weeks when Boeing officials hoped that the X-32A could return to flying duties by 10 November 2000. It took a bit longer, however, and it was not until 15 November 2000 that Commander Philip Yates took the X-32A for its first flight after the emergency landing. Five days later the X-32A and the X-35A met at Edwards AFB for a 'meet the press' session side by side.

On 2 December 2000 Boeing's X-32A completed the low-speed approach flight-testing that was required for the carrier variant. During this phase the X-32A flew ninety-seven approaches, including seventy-four landings and numerous wave offs. On 5 December 2000 the first two flights for up and away performance were flown. This was a new phase where

The probe and drogue system of aerial refuelling proved a bit of show stopper for Boeing although the X-32 qualified, it was considered safer to proceed flight testing without aerial refuelling, thus slowing the demonstration process for Boeing.
Copyright Boeing

A successful hook-up, although only prototypes are equipped with pitot heads, it can be rather dangerous when aerial refuelling as Boeing experienced with the X-32A.
Copyright Boeing

The instrumented AMRAAM can be seen in this view. The weapon bay would be at head height on the ground so that ground crew could easily manipulate the weapon. Easy access was one of the design requirements. *Copyright Boeing*

Boeing tested the aircraft to their own plans, with no guidelines from the JSF programme office. It would, however, include aerial refuelling and supersonic flight. The problems that had grounded the X-32A were now totally removed according to Boeing.

Three months after the first flight the X-32A performed its first air-to-air refuelling on 19 December 2000 behind a KC-10 tanker. The KC-10 Extender was provided by the 6th Air Refueling Squadron from Travis AFB. The KC-10 had been selected over the Marine Corps' C-130 tanker aircraft because the KC-10 is more stable, which proved to be an important requirement. The X-32 CDA are equipped with a Navy standard air-to-air refuelling probe, which extends from its hidden position in the fuselage. To prolong the individual test-flight duration it is imperative to be able to take fuel on board during flight. During the flight the drogue trailing the KC-10 tanker moved dangerously close to the pitots on the nose of the aircraft as a result of air turbulence. The pitots there for test purposes were in danger of being broken off by the drogue. This in itself would be bad but it would not result in the loss of the aircraft. However, the engine inlet just slightly aft, below the pitot, could with high probability choke on the pitot, killing the engine in the process. Luckily for Boeing this did not occur and the pilot, Commander Philip Yates, managed to put the probe into the drogue successfully. The drama of the flight, however, was not over as the fuel went everywhere except where it had to go. The pilot managed to disconnect safely and return to Edwards AFB. After evaluation of the flight data and the video images it was decided that it would be too dangerous to resume air-to-air refuelling and Boeing therefore could not extend the duration of its test flights and as a result the flight-test programme lasted longer than originally planned. During the last flight in the year 2000, on 21 December, the X-32A CDA, piloted by Lieutenant-Colonel Edward Cabrera, flew supersonic, copying the performance of the Lockheed Martin X-35A.

The X-32A taxiing. Note the huge flaps on the vertical tails. These were also to function as brakes, in similar fashion to the F-22.
Copyright Boeing

Prior to the first flight, the X-32A propulsion system was tested to its maximum power whilst restrained by chains. The afterburner gives a beautiful glow in the dark.
Copyright Boeing

On 10 January 2001 Boeing announced that a new phase in the test programme had been completed on 8 January when low- and medium-speed taxi tests with the X-32B were finished. High-speed taxi tests were due to follow quickly as they were the final ground tests prior to flight tests.

On 20 January 2001 the USMC test pilot Major Jeff 'Pigpen' Karnes flew for the first time in the X-32A and during that day he flew three times. After the CDP had finished he left the programme to return at a later date to become part of the Integrated Test Force (ITF) at Fort Worth.

On the sixty-first flight of the X-32A flown by Lieutenant-Colonel Edward Cabrera the weapon bays were opened and in them were an instrumented AMRAAM missile and JDAM. The test had multiple goals. The first goal was to demonstrate that it could fulfil the requirement. The second goal was to prove that the location of the weapon bays meant that the pilot could fly in such a way that he would not give himself away as he would use the weapon bay opposite the enemy radar. Even the opening of the weapon bay would have no effect on its radar reflection. The third aim was to test the acoustics. This was not required for the CDP but Boeing wanted to prove this capability. According to some sources it was even planned to fire the weapons from the aircraft in a similar fashion to the YF-22, but planned or not this did not happen.

The X-32A had its last flight on 3 February 2001 when it returned to Boeing's Palmdale facility. The sixty-sixth flight rounded off a highly successful test-flight programme. During the sixty-six flights six pilots had flown the demonstrator aircraft and the number of flight hours was 50.4 hours altogether.

On 29 March 2001 the second Boeing CDA, the X-32B, took off for its fifty-minute first flight in the hands of Dennis O'Donoghue. The flight included a conventional take-off and landing to ensure the flight quality before going into the risky part of flight-test envelope.

The X-32B seen here in flight. The doors that cover the lift nozzles show signs of exhaust residue. It is not clear what kind of effect the heat would have on the Radar Absorbing Materials around the nozzles. *Copyright Boeing*

The X-32B flown by Dennis O'Donoghue completed one major milestone on 13 April 2001 when the pilot during a fifty-eight-minute flight transitioned back and forth from normal cruise flight to vertical flight and back again to normal flight. Later during the same day Dennis O'Donoghue flew another fifty-two-minute flight during which forty minutes were flown in STOVL mode. For these flights the Boeing X-32B demonstrator was stripped of excessive weight. The inlet and the landing gear doors were removed. A secondary side effect of removing the frontal part of the inlet was that the X-32B could no longer fly supersonic. According to some experts the need to make weight reductions for the vertical flight

The X-32B on its first landing at Edwards AFB with Dennis R. 'Irish' O'Donoghue at the controls. He was Boeing's main test pilot for the STOVL tests.
Copyright Boeing

The X-32B during early flight testing at Edwards AFB. The aircraft was completed here including the inlet. In this version it was capable of flying supersonic. *Copyright Boeing*

demonstrations was one of the reasons why Boeing lost out in the down select.

From 4 May 2001 the X-32B undertook a cross-country flight from Edwards AFB to NAS Patuxent River. Because the X-32B was not qualified for air-to-air refuelling it took several days. The cross-country trip was carried out in several stages and due to the weather the transfer was somewhat delayed. The X-32B landed and refuelled at Luke AFB and departed the same day for Holloman AFB. On 6 May the X-32B flew to Altus AFB. Two days later the journey continued to Little Rock AFB. On 9 August the X-32B departed for Columbus AFB. On 10 May the X-32B was transferred to Shaw AFB. The X-32B arrived at Patuxent River on 11 May 2001 where the VX-23 had prepared the test ground.

As soon as the X-32B arrived at Patuxent River its flight-test programme was geared to proving the vertical landing capability. As NAS Patuxent River was at sea level things would be easier here. The aircraft was technically adjusted, which means that the landing gear doors and the inlet cowl were removed in an effort to save weight. The fear that the aircraft was too heavy was a real one but Boeing pointed out that its PWSC was lighter and would not incur this problem. Boeing did not want to have the embarrassment of a repeat of the old experimental STOVL planes that could not lift their own weight.

Flight-testing was resumed on 18 June 2001 at Patuxent River and the deceleration testing was initiated from that day. On the very next day the deceleration achieved was down to 90 knots. These tests continued with incremental steps reducing the speed and it was on 24 June that the milestones started to build up. On the forty-fourth flight-test pilot Dennis O'Donoghue performed the first Outside Ground Effect (OGE) stationary hover, followed on the same day with three more flights to evaluate the X-32B's STOVL handling qualities. This was just one day after the Lockheed Martin X-35 had achieved its first press up. At the end of the second flight on 27 June Dennis O'Donoghue performed the first vertical landing on the hover pit to reduce the ground effects. After the vertical landing on

Besides the inlet cowl that had to be removed, the landing gear doors were also removed. This was to reduce risk as Boeing had stated that its concept demonstration aircraft were overweight - but that the Preferred Weapon System Concept would eventually not have that problem. *Copyright Boeing*

Boeing performed STOVL conversion testing at Edwards AFB well above ground effect height. After it had made vertical landings at Patuxent river, the inlet cowl and landing gear doors were replaced to perform high-speed STOVL tests, again above ground effect height. *Copyright Boeing*

The X-32B lands at 90 knots, approaching the hover milestone in small but well set out steps, an accident at this phase in the program would kill Boeing's chances. *Copyright Boeing*

Athough many precautions were taken, during one landing, either just before or after touch-down, the engine of the X-32B experienced a pop stall. If it had occurred at a slightly higher altitude it could have had a very unfortunate effect on the aircraft and pilot. *Copyright Boeing*

the hover pit, data were quickly evaluated and it was decided to proceed with the test programme. Dennis O'Donoghue took off again and transferred from conventional flight again to hover to perform the first vertical landing on the landing pad. During this flight there was, however, a pop stall (when the engine stops as a result of HGI). Luckily it was about a second before touchdown but it prevented further testing that day. The X-32B's susceptibility to HGI during hover within ground effect prevented Boeing from trying a vertical take-off. There was, however, no requirement for a vertical take-off. Flight-testing was resumed on 30 June and on the first flight a second vertical landing was performed. The following day Boeing started testing another requirement and that was the short take-off. On the fourth flight of that day a short take-off demonstration was performed, which exceeded the requirements. Vertical landings were later performed by USMC Major Jeff 'Pigpen' Karnes (twice) on 3 July and Royal Navy pilot Lieutenant-Commander Paul Stone on 5 July. In answer to Lockheed Martin's X-mission, the Boeing X-32B flown by USMC Major Jeff Karnes executed a short takeoff, transitioned into conventional flight, broke the sound barrier, transitioned back to the STOVL mode in such manner that he was still airborne due to aerodynamic forces, and made a low-speed landing on the last day of flight test, 28 July 2001, a vertical landing was not risked.

In February 2001 Boeing submitted the final production PWSC of its CDA, which had the company designation model 375.

Although direct lift was already used in the Harrier the Boeing proposal was considered higher risk and was thought to have less growth capability. Boeing did not appeal the decision and conceded the victory to Lockheed Martin. George Muellner, the first JAST programme director, joined Boeing after retiring from the USAF and stated that Boeing had faired very well in the stealth evaluation compared with the Lockheed Martin design. During the CDP Boeing perceived that Lockheed Martin had an advantage in the stealth technology area.

The Boeing X-32 CDA played a significant part in the

The mobile Fresnel lens and landing system operator were required for Field Aircraft Carrier Landing Practice. *Copyright Boeing*

history of aviation. It was the first time that X-aircraft were connected with a production option. This was a good enough reason to have both aircraft transferred to museums. The X-32A stayed at the Air Force plant 42 in Palmdale. There it stayed until it was transported to the National Museum of the US Air Force in Dayton, Ohio. The wing, a single piece, was removed from the fuselage for transportation. The wing was then moved onto a specially designed carriage and then rolled onto a C-5A with the rest of the X-32A aircraft. The X-32A arrived at the museum on 9 April 2005. From that moment a team of Boeing and Museum restoration staff worked together for ten days assembling the aircraft. The final restoration phase was in the hands of the qualified museum restoration technicians.

The X-32B that completed its test programme at NAS Patuxent River stayed there. The X-32B was transferred to the museum on 31

The X-32A represented both the conventional land-based and carrier borne aircraft. *Copyright Boeing*

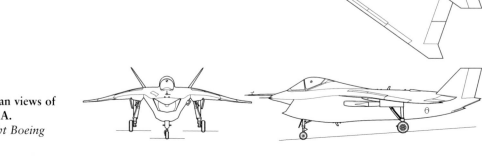

Three plan views of the X-32A.
Copyright Boeing

March 2005 and joined the X-35C that had been on display there since April 2003. The US Navy Patuxent River museum takes great pride that it is the only museum where both contenders can be admired.

Dimensions	Boeing X-32A CTOL/CV	Boeing X-32B STOVL	Lockheed Martin X-35A/B CTOL / STOVL	Lockheed Martin X-35C CV
Length	13.72 m 45 ft 0 in	13.33 m 43 ft 8.6 in	15.5 m 50 ft 9 in	15.5 m 50 ft 9 in
Height	4.06 m 13 ft 4 in	4.06 m 13 ft 4 in	4.8 m 15 ft 9 in	4.57 m 15 ft
Wingspan	10.97 m 36 ft 0 in	9.14 m 30 ft 0 in	10.05 m 33 ft 0 in	10.97 m 36 ft
Total flights	66	78	66 (27+39)	73
Total flight time	50.7 hours	43.3 hours	48.9 hours	58 hours
Number of vertical landings	n/a	6	27	n/a
Number of vertical take-offs	n/a	0	18	n/a

The X-32B is easily recognized by its clipped wings. Here it is seen over the sea in the Patuxent river area. *Copyright Boeing*

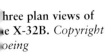

hree plan views of
e **X-32B.** *Copyright*
oeing

UK Government Test Pilot Paul Stone's Impressions
of the Boeing X-32

Paul Stone was the UK test pilot during the CDP on the Boeing X-32 aircraft. He was a graduate from the Empire Test Pilot School (ETPS). Prior to his participation in the JSF programme he was a Sea Harrier project pilot and the deputy Vector thrust Aircraft Advanced flight Control (VAAC) project pilot for the Defence Evaluation and Research Agency (DERA) Fast-Jet Test Squadron. His involvement in several STOVL projects made him the natural choice to become one of the British evaluation pilots, or as he said himself he was in the right place at the right time. Paul Stone, due to his involvement in the VAAC programme, was involved in the JSF programme from 1997.

He was also the Joint Combat Aircraft desk officer in the MoD. Paul Stone said that the Boeing team was very impressive and that it was like serving an apprenticeship with Fred Knox (Boeing JSF CTP) and Dennis O'Donoghue (Boeing STOVL Project Pilot). To prepare for the X-32 evaluation Paul Stone had about 750 hours' of development simulation, which did not incorporate any flying on the Boeing AFL. Paul Stone never flew on the AFL, although he undertook currency flying on the T-38 and F-18 while in the US.

Paul Stone flew in the X-32A for the first time on 16 December 2000; he was the fifth pilot to fly it. He flew a total of four flights (equalling about 3.9 hours) on the X-32A. His longest flight lasted about one and half hours. According to Paul Stone the X-32 flew just like the simulator, which is very important for digital flight controls – any deviations and you are exposing some significant problems with either the fidelity of the simulation or the flight control system. Paul Stone had more participation in the X-32B flight-test programme. Paul Stone's first flight on the X-32B was on 16 April 2001. It was one hour's duration and exactly four months after his first flight on the X-32A. It was the fifth flight of the X-32B and covered an array of flutter test points. During the same day he flew the X-32B once more to evaluate flying qualities.

Paul Stone flew two stages of the transit of the aircraft from Edwards AFB to NAS Patuxent River. After the transit the test flying was interrupted until 18 June. The day after, Paul Stone again took his place in the X-32B and performed STOVL handling quality tests. On his seventh flight on the X-32B, the second of the day, he performed the first semi-jetborne landing of the programme. On 17 July 2001 Paul Stone became the first pilot to take the X-32B to supersonic speed. Paul Stone was also the last pilot ever to fly the X-32B on 28 July 2001. He had flown twenty-two flights on the Boeing X-32B, accumulating 11.7 hours.

Comparing the Harrier with the X-32B, Paul Stone said that the latter aircraft felt much more stable and very flattering in the hover. The added envelope protection made semi-jetborne and jetborne manoeuvring much more carefree. In the cockpit the Harrier has situated beside the throttle one lever that has to be employed for moving the nozzles. If the pilot for any reason uses the wrong inceptor the effect could be fatal. Boeing had solved this problem by using a digital flight control system combined with a thumbwheel on the stick that replaced the nozzle lever. This made for very straightforward controls and was considered an interim step; the final solution would be a two-inceptor solution losing the direct nozzle control altogether. Boeing looked at the VAAC Harrier technology being developed but the technology was too immature to establish how close to the VAAC technology the final Boeing solution would be.

Describing the X-32, Paul Stone said that it performed like the best modern fighters. As he has flown the Eurofighter, F-18 Hornet, F-15 and F-16, he is most definitely qualified to make this statement and it gives credence to the X-32 design. In the STOVL environment it was a class better than the Harrier except the hover performance on the demonstrator was

The only foreigner to fly on the X-32 was Lt Cdr Paul Stone RN. The UK was the only Level One partner in the CDP phase but it is quite unheard of to allow a foreign pilot to fly a prototype aircraft so early in the programme.
Copyright Boeing

The UK government's test pilot for the X-32B programme, Lt. Cdr. Paul Stone RN, after his first vertical landing of the aircraft.
Copyright Boeing

lacking. Paul Stone was very impressed with the handling qualities in the STOVL regime. Beside the hover performance, the X-32B was susceptible to HGI. As Paul Stone described during one test flight, the engine surged in ground effect during one vertical landing due to hot gas re-circulating back into the engine intake. This was predicted to occur during landing with small angles of bank within ground effect situations, but repeated surge in ground effect would have a detrimental effect on the engine and require an intolerable inspection routine

However, this was a known fault with the X-32 configuration and there were plans to correct this in the PWSC. He concluded by saying that it would have been easy to train a pilot with a conventional fixed-wing background to fly the X-32B in semi-jetborne and hovering flight. It handled very predictably and was a joy to fly at all times. Paul Stone did not evaluate Boeing's PWSC simulator so unfortunately was not able to give any comments on improvements.

Some people thought that the relatively unconventional looks of the X-32 played a negative role in the selection between the Boeing and Lockheed demonstrators. However the main reason was that the potential development of the Boeing design was considered limited. *Copyright Boeing*

X-32A Flight Log

Flight	Date no.	Pilot	Flight duration (hours)	Company or force	Notes
1	18 Sept 2000	Fred Knox	0.3	Boeing	To Edwards AFB
2	23 Sept 2000	Fred Knox	0.8	Boeing	
3	26 Sept 2000	Fred Knox	0.8	Boeing	
4	28 Sept 2000	Cdr Philip Yates	0.8	US Navy	
5	03 Oct 2000	Dennis O'Donoghue	0.8	Boeing	
6	05 Oct 2000	Fred Knox	0.7	Boeing	
7	10 Oct 2000	Cdr Philip Yates	0.7	US Navy	
8	10 Oct 2000	Cdr Philip Yates	0.7	US Navy	
9	11 Oct 2000	Lt-Co Edward Cabrera	0.7	USAF	
10	12 Oct 2000	Fred Knox	0.8	Boeing	
11	12 Oct 2000	Fred Knox	0.4	Boeing	
12	12 Oct 2000	Cdr Philip Yates	0.4	US Navy	
13	13 Oct 2000	Cdr Philip Yates	0.8	US Navy	
14	13 Oct 2000	Cdr Philip Yates	0.4	US Navy	
15	24 Oct 2000	Cdr Philip Yates	0.7	US Navy	
16	24 Oct 2000	Cdr Philip Yates	0.3	US Navy	
17	24 Oct 2000	Dennis O'Donoghue	1.1	Boeing	
18	15 Nov 2000	Cdr Philip Yates	0.5	US Navy	
19	16 Nov 2000	Fred Knox	0.3	Boeing	
20	16 Nov 2000	Lt-Col Edward Cabrera	0.3	USAF	
21	17 Nov 2000	Cdr Philip Yates	0.4	US Navy	
22	18 Nov 2000	Cdr Philip Yates	0.5	US Navy	

23	29 Nov 2000	Fred Knox	0.7	Boeing
24	29 Nov 2000	Fred Knox	0.3	Boeing
25	30 Nov 2000	Cdr Philip Yates	0.3	US Navy
26	30 Nov 2000	Cdr Philip Yates	0.3	US Navy
27	30 Nov 2000	Cdr Philip Yates	0.3	US Navy
28	01 Dec 2000	Cdr Philip Yates	0.4	US Navy
29	01 Dec 2000	Cdr Philip Yates	0.4	US Navy
30	01 Dec 2000	Cdr Philip Yates	0.5	US Navy
31	01 Dec 2000	Fred Knox	0.4	Boeing
32	01 Dec 2000	Fred Knox	0.6	Boeing
33	02 Dec 2000	Cdr Philip Yates	0.4	US Navy
34	05 Dec 2000	Fred Knox	1.1	Boeing
35	05 Dec 2000	Lt-Col Edward Cabrera	1	USAF
36	07 Dec 2000	Lt-Col Edward Cabrera	1.4	USAF
37	07 Dec 2000	Lt-Col Edward Cabrera	1.4	USAF
38	08 Dec 2000	Dennis O'Donoghue	1.3	Boeing
39	08 Dec 2000	Dennis O'Donoghue	1	Boeing
40	14 Dec 2000	Fred Knox	1.1	Boeing
41	14 Dec 2000	Fred Knox	0.7	Boeing
42	16 Dec 2000	Lt-Col Edward Cabrera	1.1	USAF
43	16 Dec 2000	Lt-Col Edward Cabrera	1.1	USAF
44	16 Dec 2000	Lt-Cdr Paul Stone	0.8	UK Royal Navy
45	19 Dec 2000	Cdr Philip Yates	1	US Navy
46	20 Dec 2000	Cdr Philip Yates	1.2	US Navy
47	20 Dec 2000	Cdr Philip Yates	1.2	US Navy
48	20 Dec 2000	Major Jeff Karnes	0.9	USMC
49	21 Dec 2000	Lt-Col Edward Cabrera	1	USAF
50	05 Jan 2001	Fred Knox	1.1	Boeing
51	05 Jan 2001	Fred Knox	0.6	Boeing
52	16 Jan 2001	Lt-Col Edward Cabrera	1.1	USAF
53	16 Jan 2001	Lt-Col Edward Cabrera	1.2	USAF
54	17 Jan 2001	Cdr Philip Yates	0.7	US Navy
55	18 Jan 2001	Lt-Cdr Paul Stone	0.8	UK Royal Navy
56	19 Jan 2001	Dennis O'Donoghue	1	Boeing
57	20 Jan 2001	Major Jeff Karnes	1	USMC
58	20 Jan 2001	Major Jeff Karnes	0.8	USMC
59	20 Jan 2001	Major Jeff Karnes	0.4	USMC
60	22 Jan 2001	Cdr Philip Yates	0.9	US Navy
61	25 Jan 2001	Lt-Col Edward Cabrera	0.6	USAF

62	30 Jan 2001	Fred Knox	1.3	Boeing	
63	01 Feb 2001	Lt-Col Edward Cabrera	1.2	USAF	
64	02 Feb 2001	Lt-Cdr Paul Stone	1.5	UK Royal Navy	
65	02 Feb 2001	Lt-Cdr Paul Stone	0.8	UK Royal Navy	
66	3 Feb 2001	Fred Knox	0.7	Boeing	Back to Palmdale

X-32B Flight Log

Flight No.	Date	Pilot	Flight Duration (Hours)	Total Flight Time	Company or Force	Notes
1	29 Mar 2001	Dennis O'Donoghue	0.9	0.9	Boeing	Palmdale & EAFB
2	11 Apr 2001	Major Jeff Karnes	1	1.9	USMC	EAFB
3	13 Apr 2001	Dennis O'Donoghue	1	2.9	Boeing	1st Flow Switch
4	13 Apr 2001	Dennis O'Donoghue	0.9	3.8	Boeing	STOVL mode HQ
5	16 Apr 2001	Lt-Cdr Paul Stone	1	4.8	UK Royal Navy	Flutter
6	16 Apr 2001	Lt-Cdr Paul Stone	1	5.8	UK Royal Navy	FQ
7	20 Apr 2001	Lt-Col Edward Cabrera	0.6	6.4	USAF	Flutter
8	20 Apr 2001	Lt-Col Edward Cabrera	0.4	6.8	USAF	Flutter
9	23 Apr 2001	Fred Knox	1.2	8.0	Boeing	Flutter
10	23 Apr 2001	Fred Knox	1.3	9.3	Boeing	Flutter
11	23 Apr 2001	Fred Knox	1.2	10.5	Boeing	FQ
12	24 Apr 2001	Major Jeff Karnes	1.3	11.8	USMC	FQ
13	24 Apr 2001	Major Jeff Karnes	1.1	12.9	USMC	Flutter
14	2 May 2001	Lt-Cdr Paul Stone	1.2	14.1	UK Royal Navy	Flutter/FQ
15	4 May 2001	Dennis O'Donoghue	0.9	15.0	Boeing	Departure from Edwards AFB
16	4 May 2001	Dennis O'Donoghue	1.0	16.0	Boeing	Departure from Luke AFB
17	6 May 2001	Lt-Cdr Paul Stone	1	17.0	UK Royal Navy	Departure from Holloman AFB
18	8 May 2001	Lt-Cdr Paul Stone	1.1	18.0	UK Royal Navy	Departure from Altus
19	9 May 2001	Major Jeff Karnes	0.8	19.0	USMC	Departure from Little Rock AFB
20	10 May 2001	Major Jeff Karnes	1.2	20.2	USMC	Departure from Columbus AFB
21	11 May 2001	Major Jeff Karnes	1.2	21.3	USMC	Departure from Shaw AFB. Arrival at Patuxent River
22	18 June 2001	Dennis O'Donoghue	0.8	22.1	Boeing	STOVL HQ 10K
23	18 June 2001	Dennis O'Donoghue	0.6	22.7	Boeing	STOVL HQ 5K

24	18 June 2001	Dennis O'Donoghue	0.6	23.3	Boeing	STOVL HQ 1K
25	19 June 2001	Lt-Cdr Paul Stone	0.5	23.8	UK Royal Navy	STOVL HQ125
26	19 June 2001	Lt-Cdr Paul Stone	0.4	24.2	UK Royal Navy	STOVL HQ 110 /SL 125
27	19 June 2001	Lt-Cdr Paul Stone	0.3	24.5	UK Royal Navy	STOVL HQ 100/ SL 110
28	19 June 2001	Lt-Cdr Paul Stone	0.3	24.8	UK Royal Navy	STOVL HQ 90/ SL 100
29	20 June 2001	Major Jeff Karnes	0.4	25.2	USMC	STOVL BD 125 HQ
30	20 June 2001	Major Jeff Karnes	0.5	25.7	USMC	STOVL BD 110 HQ/SL 125
31	20 June 2001	Major Jeff Karnes	0.3	26.0	USMC	STOVL BD 90 HQ/SL 110
32	20 June 2001	Major Jeff Karnes	0.2	26.2	USMC	STOVL BD 80/SL 90
33	22 June 2001	Dennis O'Donoghue	0.3	26.5	Boeing	STOVL BD 80-70 HQ
34	22 June 2001	Dennis O'Donoghue	0.3	26.8	Boeing	STOVL HQ 80
35	22 June 2001	Dennis O'Donoghue	0.3	27.1	Boeing	STOVL HQ 60
36	22 June 2001	Dennis O'Donoghue	0.2	27.3	Boeing	SL 110
37	22 June 2001	Dennis O'Donoghue	0.2	27.5	Boeing	SL 80
38	23 June 2001	Lt-Cdr Paul Stone	0.3	27.8	UK Royal Navy	STOVL BD 60 HQ
39	23 June 2001	Lt-Cdr Paul Stone	0.2	28.0	UK Royal Navy	STOVL BD 50 HQ
40	23 June 2001	Lt-Cdr Paul Stone	0.3	28.3	UK Royal Navy	STOVL BD 50 HQ
41	23 June 2001	Lt-Cdr Paul Stone	0.2	28.5	UK Royal Navy	STOVL BD 60 HQ
42	23 June 2001	Lt-Cdr Paul Stone	0.2	28.7	UK Royal Navy	SL 70 KT
43	24 June 2001	Dennis O'Donoghue	0.2	28.9	Boeing	STOVL BD 40/SL 60
44	24 June 2001	Dennis O'Donoghue	0.2	29.1	Boeing	1st OGE Hover
45	24 June 2001	Dennis O'Donoghue	0.2	29.3	Boeing	Hover HQ
46	24 June 2001	Dennis O'Donoghue	0.3	29.6	Boeing	Hover HQ
47	24 June 2001	Dennis O'Donoghue	0.2	29.8	Boeing	Hover HQ
48	27 June 2001	Dennis O'Donoghue	0.2	30.0	Boeing	Hover HQ
49	27 June 2001	Dennis O'Donoghue	0.2	30.2	Boeing	1st VL pit
50	27 June 2001	Dennis O'Donoghue	0.2	30.4	Boeing	1st VL pad
51	30 June 2001	Dennis O'Donoghue	0.2	30.6	Boeing	VL pad
52	30 June 2001	Dennis O'Donoghue	0.4	31.0	Boeing	STOVL PERF
53	30 June 2001	Dennis O'Donoghue	0.4	31.4	Boeing	STOVL PERF
54	30 June 2001	Dennis O'Donoghue	0.2	31.6	Boeing	STOVL PERF
55	01 July 2001	Dennis O'Donoghue	0.3	31.9	Boeing	STOVL PERF
56	01 July 2001	Dennis O'Donoghue	0.1	32.0	Boeing	1st STO

57	01 July 2001	Dennis O'Donoghue	0.2	32.2	Boeing	2nd STO
58	01 July 2001	Dennis O'Donoghue	0.1	32.3	Boeing	STO 200 demo
59	03 July 2001	Major Jeff Karnes	0.2	32.5	USMC	STOVL HQ VL
60	03 July 2001	Major Jeff Karnes	0.2	32.7	USMC	STOVL HQ VL
61	03 July 2001	Lt-Cdr Paul Stone	0.2	32.9	UK Royal Navy	STOVL HQ
62	03 July 2001	Lt-Cdr Paul Stone	0.2	33.1	UK Royal Navy	STOVL HQ
63	04 July 2001	Lt-Cdr Paul Stone	0.2	33.3	UK Royal Navy	STOVL HQ
64	05 July 2001	Lt-Cdr Paul Stone	0.2	33.5	UK Royal Navy	STOVL HQ VL
65	15 July 2001	Major Jeff Karnes	1.1	34.6	USMC	0.95 flutter
66	15 July 2001	Major Jeff Karnes	0.9	35.5	USMC	0.95 flutter
67	17 July 2001	Lt-Cdr Paul Stone	0.8	36.3	UK Royal Navy	SS flutter
68	17 July 2001	Lt-Cdr Paul Stone	0.9	37.2	UK Royal Navy	Supersonic Mach 1.05
69	22 July 2001	Dennis O'Donoghue	1	38.2	Boeing	Nose survey
70	22 July 2001	Dennis O'Donoghue	0.7	38.9	Boeing	Nose survey
71	23 July 2001	Major Jeff Karnes	0.8	39.7	USMC	Cowl-on STOVL
72	24 July 2001	Lt-Cdr Paul Stone	0.5	40.2	UK Royal Navy	Cowl-On STOVL
73	26 July 2001	Major Jeff Karnes	0.3	40.5	USMC	Cowl-on STOVL
74	28 July 2001	Major Jeff Karnes	0.4	40.9	USMC	Cowl-on STOVL
75	28 July 2001	Major Jeff Karnes	0.8	41.7	USMC	SS flutter
76	28 July 2001	Major Jeff Karnes	0.2	41.9	USMC	Cowl-on STOVL
77	28 July 2001	Major Jeff Karnes	0.7	42.6	USMC	Cowl-on STOVL
78	28 July 2001	Lt-Cdr Paul Stone	0.7	43.3	UK Royal Navy	Supersonic dash

The two government pilot teams in front of their aircraft. The four pilots on the left were on the Boeing team. The four pilots on the right were on the Lockheed team. *Copyright Lockheed Martin*

CHAPTER 3

MILESTONES OF THE X-35A

Lockheed Martin completed the Initial Design Review (IDR) for its Concept Demonstration Aircraft (CDA) in the second week of June 1997. The IDR covered the CDA design, manufacturing plan, flight simulation plan, aircraft flight certification plan and the flight-test plan.

Lockheed Martin used the facilities at Arnold Engineering Development Center (AEDC) in Tennessee to refine the design of its Preferred Weapon System Concept (PWSC). A high-speed inlet/forebody was tested in the 16-ft transonic tunnel. It was one of the first tests with the new inlet design (a Diverterless Supersonic Inlet, DSI). The test results confirmed that the inlet design met or even exceeded requirements, providing the engine with a high-quality airflow. At NASA's Lewis Research Center (LeRC) similar tests were performed with a low-speed inlet/forebody model. The low-speed inlet/forebody model was evaluated in the 9-ft by 15-ft subsonic and the 8-ft by 6-ft supersonic wind tunnels. At this stage, early September 1997, Lockheed Martin expected to roll out the first of its two CDAs in 1999 still according

The first flight of the X-35, although later than its competitor, this was the start of a very aggressive flight test programme. *Copyright Lockheed Martin*

to schedule. The original plan was to fly the X-35 CTOL version first and after completing its flight programme the aircraft would be converted to the carrier version and then the second CDA was to be the designated STOVL test aircraft.

On 8 May 1999 the first of the two X-35 prototypes had completed their major structure assembly. The assembly work was on schedule for a planned first flight in the spring of 2000.

In early April 2000 the X-35A passed a flight-readiness review. It was now planned that the X-35A would have its maiden flight in June/July 2000 with the STOVL version (even more delayed as a result of engine integration problems) following in November or December at the latest.

The F119-611 engine was tested for the first time in the X-35A on 5 July 2000. On 24 August 2000 the engine in the X-35A was tested for the first time with full afterburner. Lockheed Martin's programme chief test pilot Tom 'Squid' Morgenfeld who used to be involved in test-flying the YF-22 and F-117 (bandit 101, meaning he was the 101st pilot to fly the F-117) performed the final taxi tests at the Lockheed Martin Aeronautics Company facilities in Palmdale, California, on 21 October 2000 in the X-35A. During these final tests the avionics, hydraulics, vehicle management displays, electrical systems and communication systems were all active. On 24 October, after final checks, Tom Morgenfeld took the X-35A for its first flight at 09.06 hours local time. The take-off run took just over 600 m (2000 ft), after which he flew the X-35A to 10,000 ft with the landing gear down. During the first flight, which lasted twenty-two minutes, there was no problem with retracting the landing gear and shortly before landing this was tried out. The main landing gear and the nose landing gear both retracted forward. The X-35A was transferred during its first flight to the USAF Flight Test Center at Edwards AFB.

As planned, on 3 November 2000 USAF Pilot Lt-Col Paul 'TP' Smith (TP stands for Tall Paul) became the first pilot from the service to fly the X-35A. Four days later, on his third flight in the X-35A, he tested the air-to-air refuelling capabilities and that flight was the X-35A's one until that time at two hours and fifty minutes. He hooked up with a KC-135 tanker from the 418th Flight Test Squadron (FTS).

BAE Systems had to wait until 18 November for its test pilot to make his first flight in

Before flight testing the X-35A underwent the usual ground tests, as shown here when restrained on a full afterburner test. *Copyright Lockheed Martin*

the X-35A, and during that day Simon Hargreaves made another flight. On the same day the UK's Royal Air Force's (RAF) test pilot Sqn Ldr Justin Paines became the sixth pilot to fly the X-35A. Two days later there was a 'meet the press' day when both prototypes and the test pilots of both teams were presented.

On 21 November 2000 Lockheed, again hoping to win the competition with an aggressive test programme as with the YF-22, let Tom Morgenfeld fly the X-35A at supersonic speed, ie Mach 1.05. The supersonic flight had been planned earlier but unspecified technical problems prevented it. It was not a requested requirement but was more a morale booster for the test team. A day later Tom Morgenfeld flew the X-35A back to Lockheed Martin Aeronautics Company's facilities in Palmdale, California, where the conversion from X-35A to X-35B could begin. The X-35A had flown twenty-seven times in thirty days. The X-35A had reached 20° AoA and an altitude of 34,000 ft.

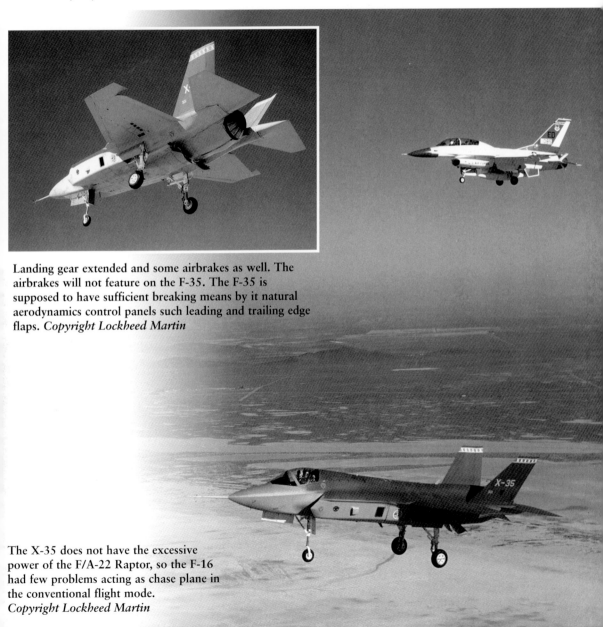

Landing gear extended and some airbrakes as well. The airbrakes will not feature on the F-35. The F-35 is supposed to have sufficient breaking means by it natural aerodynamics control panels such leading and trailing edge flaps. *Copyright Lockheed Martin*

The X-35 does not have the excessive power of the F/A-22 Raptor, so the F-16 had few problems acting as chase plane in the conventional flight mode. *Copyright Lockheed Martin*

Banking to starboard, the X-35A took to the sky like a fish to the water. *Copyright Lockheed Martin*

The directional three-bearing swivel nozzle can clearly be seen surrounding the jet exhaust on this stern shot of the X-35B.
Copyright Lockheed Martin

Unlike the European trend, the US still favours twin-tailed aircraft., the F-16 and the Harrier will eventually be replaced and then only the Gripen, Rafale and Typhoon will remain as single-tailed fighters within NATO. *Copyright Lockheed Martin.*

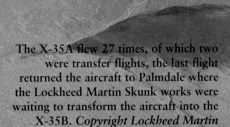

The X-35A flew 27 times, of which two were transfer flights, the last flight returned the aircraft to Palmdale where the Lockheed Martin Skunk works were waiting to transform the aircraft into the X-35B. *Copyright Lockheed Martin*

The KC-135 and the X-35A fly over the testing area near Edwards AFB. *Copyright Lockheed Martin*

Lockheed's JSF development programme was the first to use two aircraft for the initial trials that would then be modified as necessary to proceed to the next test phase. Usually prototypes end up in aviation museums.
Copyright Lockheed Martin

The F-16B is a two-seater fighter, a feature will disappear from the USAF when the F-16 and F-15 are replaced by the JSF and the F-22 Raptor. *Copyright Lockheed Martin*

X-35A Test Flights

Flight no.	Date	Pilot	Flight duration (hours)	Company or force	
1	24 Oct 2000	Tom Morgenfeld	0.5	Lockheed	1
2	27 Oct 2000	Tom Morgenfeld	0.3	Lockheed	
3	30 Oct 2000	Tom Morgenfeld	0.4	Lockheed	
4	02 Nov 2000	Tom Morgenfeld	0.7	Lockheed	
5	3 Nov 2000	Lt-Col Paul Smith	0.6	USAF	2
6	4 Nov 2000	Tom Morgenfeld	0.8	Lockheed	
7	5 Nov 2000	Lt-Col Paul Smith	0.8	USAF	
8	5 Nov 2000	Tom Morgenfeld	0.6	Lockheed	
9	6 Nov 2000	Tom Morgenfeld	0.6	Lockheed	
10	7 Nov 2000	Lt-Col Paul Smith	2.9	USAF	
11	9 Nov 2000	Tom Morgenfeld	1.4	Lockheed	
12	9 Nov 2000	Tom Morgenfeld	0.4	Lockheed	
13	10 Nov 2000	Art Tomassetti	0.8	US Marines	3
14	11 Nov 2000	Tom Morgenfeld	0.9	Lockheed	
15	12 Nov 2000	Lt-Col Paul Smith	1.8	USAF	
16	12 Nov 2000	Tom Morgenfeld	0.7	Lockheed	
17	14 Nov 2000	Lt-Col Paul Smith	1.9	USAF	
18	15 Nov 2000	Tom Morgenfeld	2.8	Lockheed	
19	15 Nov 2000	Joe Sweeney	0.6	Lockheed	4
20	18 Nov 2000	Simon Hargreaves	0.6	BAE Systems	5
21	18 Nov 2000	Simon Hargreaves	0.6	BAE Systems	
22	18 Nov 2000	Justin Paines	0.6	UK RAF	6
23	18 Nov 2000	Justin Paines	1.0	UK RAF	
24	21 Nov 2000	Tom Morgenfeld	1.4	Lockheed	
25	21 Nov 2000	Tom Morgenfeld	0.6	Lockheed	
26	22 Nov 2000	Lt-Col Paul Smith	2.5	USAF	
27	22 Nov 2000	Tom Morgenfeld	0.6	Lockheed	

Both X-35s in production at Palmdale. Boeing was also assembling their X-32 aircraft in Palmdale - almost next door. *Copyright Lockheed Martin*

CHAPTER 4

MILESTONES OF THE X-35B

As the X-35B used the same structure as the X-35A, it achieved its milestones earlier, but the transition basically started after 22 November 2000. The part of the flight-testing to be completed as the X-35B was seen as key to winning the contract. This flight demonstration would make or break Lockheed's chances. On 29 December 2000 a major milestone was passed in adapting the X-35A to the X-35B standard when the lift fan was installed. The engine was installed in less than three hours. This engine was used to facilitate STOVL although this particular engine would only be used for ground tests. The lift fan was produced by Rolls-Royce, previously known as Allison. Initial flight-testing would take place at Palmdale, then transfer to Edwards AFB, and to round off the testing it was planned to fly the F-35B to Patuxent River as well to demonstrate that it would function equally well at sea level, although that was considered easier.

On 23 February 2001 the X-35B started the hover pit testing. The pit is basically a tunnel covered by a grille in which the thrust of the engine flows. This prevents the aircraft from taking off and Hot Gas Ingestion (HGI), a major problem that Lockheed hoped it had solved. Other ground effects that had to be solved and could be show-stoppers were suck down and impingement. Suck down can happen when the exhaust joins the surrounding air and accelerates it. This causes a downward airflow around the aircraft and would pull it to the ground. The strength of the suck-down effect could not effectively be predicted, which was a concern. Impingement can happen when the exhaust of the aircraft is reflected from the ground

Mating of the forward fuselage to the aft fuselage of one of the X-35 aircraft in Palmdale. Production had come to a standstill when Lockheed Martin had to wait for a bulkhead. Luckily for Lockheed Martin the bulkhead finally arrived although very delayed. *Copyright Lockheed Martin*

back to the aircraft. This unbalances the aircraft, which so close to the ground can be very hazardous for the pilot. Another problem that it was considered could occur was ground erosion, similar to the problem encountered by the Yakovlev Yak-141. Ground erosion can be hazardous for the aircraft as it can create flying debris. Any damage to the aircraft from

The installation of the lift fan in progress. Lift fan installation required engine removal. The lift fan was installed in the aircraft after the X-35A had completed its demonstration programme.
Copyright Lockheed Martin

The lift fan is lowered into the hole behind the cockpit, both the X-35A and the X-35C had this hole behind the cockpit. So that Lockheed could switch in case of necessity. In fact originally it had planned to switch the X-35C around to the X-35B.
Copyright Lockheed Martin

The X-35B is restrained to the ground for propulsion tests. Note that the aircraft has not yet received its colourful tail painting, although it is clearly testing the STOVL propulsion system.
Lockheed Martin

whatever source would be highly undesirable as the test programme was very public and a crash would reduce the chances of the team to zero.

Prior to testing the actual aircraft a TAV-8B Harrier was used by the test pilots to fly over a hover pit as none of them had experience flying over one. The X-35B was securely fitted to the pit as a security so that it would not take off. The first test was carried out by pilot Simon Hargreaves from BAE Systems. During those tests that lasted little bit less than one month the engine and the lift fan were tested and performed well. HGI problems encountered on previous-generation STOVL aircraft were considered eliminated on 16 March 2001. From the initiation to completion of the hover pit testing twenty-six lift fan clutch engagements were performed. All twenty-six conversions from CTOL to STOVL (meaning lift fan engagements) were done at different Rotations Per Minute (RPM) levels; most importantly at high RPM level and at different lengths. A small auxiliary air intake behind the lift fan opened as well during transition and vertical flight to enable sufficient air to be fed to the main engine. The doors would be closed during conventional flight to maintain the clean aerodynamic and stealth features of the aircraft.

Vibration and noise levels in the cockpit were not significantly higher due to the lift fan. It was important to test these levels to predict any future noise and vibration reduction needs. On 17 April 2001 all the engine ground tests were completed. Tests performed after the hover pit were to check if the dynamic movement of the nozzle from CTOL to STOVL and back had any structural effects elsewhere in the aircraft. The day before, Rolls-Royce delivered the lift fan qualified for flight-testing to Lockheed Martin Palmdale. This made possible the transition from the ground-test lift fan to the airworthy lift fan. Lockheed Martin completed installation of the complete airworthy STOVL propulsion system on 12 May 2001. Simon Hargreaves started ground-testing of the airworthy propulsion system on 24 May 2001 after the JSF programme office completed on the two days before the Flight Readiness Review (FRR). During the ground tests on the pit the X-35B performed thirty-four clutch engagements prior to test-flying.

The X-35B with all doors open for STOVL operations. The aircraft started with 'press ups' prior to proceeding to normal up and away flight testing. *Crown Copyright*

The cold air from the lift fan prevents the hot gas from moving forward and entering the inlets. A problem which Boeing had not entirely solved. *Crown Copyright*

Flight envelope expansion was an issue that had to be resolved. For a conventional fighter there is enough experience and know-how for this not to be perceived as a problem but with STOVL aircraft it was a totally different issue. There was very little previous experience with successful STOVL flight-testing available but at least the most successful programme, the Harrier, was in-house technology as BAE Systems was a fully integrated partner. There were two ways of going about STOVL testing, one called the build down and the other called the build up. Build down is when one starts in conventional flight and slows down in small incremental steps to hover. Built up is the other way around, meaning one starts with a vertical take-off and in small incremental steps switches to wing-borne flight. It was decided to firstly evaluate the VTOL capability, or in other words the hover. When the hover was proven the other build down option would be used. This was thought to reduce the risk during the flight-test programme as the hover capability was already proven. The same aircraft had already proven the up and away flight envelope as the X-35A so for the following flight demonstrations Lockheed's team could concentrate immediately on the incremental slow-down flight part. For this part of the flight-test programme, the slow-down part, two different chase aircraft were used. One was the previously mentioned TAV-8B, BuNo 163191, on loan from NAS China Lake (the same aircraft that was previously used for the Integrated Helmet Audio Visual System (IHAVS) programme in support of the JAST programme in 1995/6) and the other was a Beech T-34 Mentor (S/N 819) on loan from NASA. The T-34 Mentor was flown by Gordon Fullerton and Dana Purifoy from NASA during those chase flights.

On 23 June 2001 the X-35B lifted from the ground vertically for the first time with BAE Systems pilot Simon Hargreaves at the controls. Simon Hargreaves was the lead test pilot on the

The F-16, although a highly capable fighter, could only remain close during the conventional flight programme. For the STOVL flight tests the TAV-8B was used as the chase aircraft. *Crown Copyright*

Here the lift fan can be seen clearly seen in operation with all the system doors open above the lakebeds around Edwards. The doors to the lift fan on the production aircraft will be back hinged. *Crown Copyright*

X-35B; this was quite unusual as it was mainly a US project. Lockheed was the lead contractor, however, experience and the team members' involvement had their influence so for the first time in an American fighter the first flight was flown by an English pilot. The flight lasted only a few seconds and was, as with many of the following flights, above a hover pit. Simon Hargreaves repeated the feat the next day, this time holding the aircraft for thirty-five seconds at 25 ft before landing it smoothly. Vertical take-off was considered a risk and it was not a requirement. Even if it was a requirement the amount of fuel used during vertical take-offs would have a disadvantageous effect on the mission range. US Marine pilot Major Art 'Turbo' Tomassetti became the second pilot to fly the X-35B on 29 June 2001 when he made three vertical flights. A day later UK RAF pilot Justin Paines made his first and second vertical flights in the X-35B. After eleven vertical lift-offs and landings the X-35B was transferred to Edwards AFB on 3 July 2001. Simon Hargreaves was the pilot during this short flight. As soon as the aircraft was at Edwards AFB the testing was geared to transitioning from normal flight to hover. The fact that the stage from hover to landing had already been profusely tested during the short testing period at Palmdale would make the stage after that so much easier.

On Monday 9 July the X-35B achieved its first milestone in preparation for its full-capability demonstration, which was planned at a later stage. Simon Hargreaves engaged the lift fan during flight and then disengaged it again to proceed to supersonic flight, reaching Mach 1.08. The lift fan can be engaged at any power setting according to Lockheed. The milestone was of importance as it proved that the aircraft had no problems with either extreme of the flight envelope. A week later, on Monday 16 July, Simon Hargreaves took the X-35B for a short take-off and after that landed vertically at Edwards AFB. It was the first time that the short take-off had been combined with a vertical landing. During the weekend the test team had been testing

The short take-off demonstrated. Note that the auxiliary doors open inwards and the doors to the lift fan open outwards. *Crown Copyright*

Short take-off was part of the so called 'Mission X' as seen here. It would be followed by a level supersonic dash and a vertical landing; according to Lockheed, the X-35B was the first aircraft ever to perform this feat. *Crown Copyright*

The X-35B with all the doors open for a good view of the lift fan from above. *Team JSF*

Lockheed Martin's X-35B had the same aerodynamics features as the X-35A, this helped the test programme as Lockheed had already completed up and away testing. *Crown Copyright*

short take-offs with slow landings, both with the lift fan engaged, which had provided confidence for this step. All flights, including the milestone flights since the arrival of the X-35B, had been flown by Simon Hargreaves until Monday 16 July.

From that moment Simon Hargreaves was given a break. It was the turn of USMC test pilot Major Art Tomassetti to make a first in aviation history on Friday 20 July 2001 as he was the first pilot to make a short take-off using the lift fan. He then proceeded to level flight and achieved supersonic speed during level flight. After the supersonic dash he landed back at Edwards AFB vertically, performing exactly the mission profile it was anticipated the Preferred Weapon System Concept (PWSC) had to fulfil. To prove that it was no accident Lockheed repeated the feat but this time with Simon Hargreaves at the controls on Thursday 26 July 2001. This was a feat that Boeing could not do with its X-32B demonstrator as a result of the weight problem encountered.

The X-35B flew a total of thirty-nine flights in forty-five days from 23 June to 6 August 2001, accounting for 21.5 flight hours. The last flight was also the longest flight as test pilot Tom Morgenfeld had to make up for the fact that he flew only twice in the X-35B so he flew the two longest flights, totalling 6.4 hours. In total seventeen vertical take-offs and fourteen short take-offs were executed. Six short landings and twenty-seven vertical landings were performed during those flights. Two flights, called mission X (because they contained a short take-off, a level supersonic dash and a vertical landing) were performed, demonstrating the X-35B could fulfil the requirements set. According to Lockheed Martin it was the first aircraft to perform such a feat. This means that during their talks with Yakovlev it was mentioned that this was not achieved during the flight-test programme of the Yak-141. The French VTOL programmes had achieved Mach 2 but had not been able to combine the short take-off with a level supersonic dash and then conversion to vertical landing in one mission. The X-35B was flown by only four pilots – two English (twenty-eight flights) and two Americans (eleven flights). During the entire flight-test programme of the X-35B Lockheed performed fifty-nine clutch engagements in the aircraft. Of those, fourteen were made in flight-reducing risk. Another five clutch engagements were made by the propulsion system removed from the aircraft. The conversion from normal to vertical flight by engaging the clutch will take ten seconds. This time is taken up by opening the doors and spinning up the lift fan.

A front view of the X-35B in hover showing the bulkiness of the aircraft. Compared with the AV-8B, the F-35B should be capable of carrying twice the payload of the AV-8B. The range should also be 1.8 times that of the AV-8B - impressive improvements over the Legacy aircraft. *Copyright Lockheed Martin*

A vertical landing in wet conditions had to be simulated because of the desert environment. *Copyright Lockheed Martin*

X-35B Flight Tests

Flight no.	Date	Pilot	Flight duration (hours)	Company or force	Notes
1	23 June 2001	Simon Hargreaves	0.1	BAE Systems	
2	24 June 2001	Simon Hargreaves	0.1	BAE Systems	
3	24 June 2001	Simon Hargreaves	0.1	BAE Systems	
4	25 June 2001	Simon Hargreaves	0.1	BAE Systems	
5	27 June 2001	Simon Hargreaves	0.2	BAE Systems	
6	27 June 2001	Simon Hargreaves	0.1	BAE Systems	
7	29 June 2001	Art Tomassetti	0.1	US Marines	
8	29 June 2001	Art Tomassetti	0.1	US Marines	
9	29 June 2001	Simon Hargreaves	0.1	BAE Systems	
10	30 June 2001	Justin Paines	0.2	UK RAF	
11	30 June 2001	Justin Paines	0.2	UK RAF	
12	03 July 2001	Simon Hargreaves	0.5	BAE Systems	
13	07 July 2001	Simon Hargreaves	0.3	BAE Systems	
14	09 July 2001	Simon Hargreaves	1.4	BAE Systems	
15	11 July 2001	Simon Hargreaves	0.5	BAE Systems	
16	11 July 2001	Simon Hargreaves	0.5	BAE Systems	
17	13 July 2001	Simon Hargreaves	0.5	BAE Systems	
18	13 July 2001	Simon Hargreaves	0.5	BAE Systems	
19	13 July 2001	Simon Hargreaves	0.3	BAE Systems	
20	15 July 2001	Simon Hargreaves	0.4	BAE Systems	
21	16 July 2001	Simon Hargreaves	0.3	BAE Systems	
22	16 July 2001	Simon Hargreaves	0.2	BAE Systems	
23	19 July 2001	Justin Paines	1.1	UK RAF	
24	19 July 2001	Justin Paines	0.3	UK RAF	
25	20 July 2001	Art Tomassetti	0.4	US Marines	Mission X
26	20 July 2001	Art Tomassetti	0.6	US Marines	
27	21 July 2001	Justin Paines	0.7	UK RAF	
28	21 July 2001	Justin Paines	0.7	UK RAF	
29	21 July 2001	Justin Paines	0.6	UK RAF	

It is at this point, just before touch down, that engine failure can have catastrophic effects on pilot and aircraft. Other mechanical failures are similarly catastrophic, enough reason to look into the Russian Automatic Ejection System. *Copyright Lockheed Martin*

The X-35B during mid-flight transition. All the doors open prior to engaging the lift fan and when the lift fan is engaged the 3-bearing swivel nozzle moves to the required angle. *Copyright Lockheed Martin*

30	23 July 2001	Art Tomassetti	0.4	US Marines	
31	23 July 2001	Art Tomassetti	0.5	US Marines	
32	26 July 2001	Simon Hargreaves	1.1	BAE Systems	Mission X
33	26 July 2001	Simon Hargreaves	0.3	BAE Systems	
34	26 July 2001	Tom Morgenfeld	2.7	Lockheed	
35	29 July 2001	Justin Paines	0.3	UK RAF	
36	30 July 2001	Art Tomassetti	0.2	US Marines	
37	30 July 2001	Art Tomassetti	0.7	US Marines	
38	30 July 2001	Art Tomassetti	0.4	US Marines	
39	06 Aug 2001	Tom Morgenfeld	3.7	Lockheed	

The X-35B during a vertical landing, here one has a relatively good view on the tail nozzle that forms the stern lift on the STOVL propulsion system. *Copyright Lockheed Martin*

CHAPTER 5

MILESTONES OF THE X-35C

Although the X-35C was the second of the Lockheed demonstrators to fly, it was the first aircraft to be built. Every aircraft has to undergo structural testing to allow it to perform test flights. For this purpose there are normally dedicated structural test items. However, for such a short technology demonstration programme it would be too expensive to have such a dedicated structural aircraft. The norm for structural testing is up to 150 per cent of the predicted air loads. For the JSF CDA, however, the first structure was tested up to loads of 100 per cent, which would allow the aircraft to fly safely up to 80 per cent of the predicted air loads. The first aircraft structure was therefore used for the structural load testing, which is why construction number 300 was the second aircraft to fly.

Almost a month after the last flight of the X-35A, the X-35C took off for its first flight on 16 December 2000. The US Navy version demonstrator took off at 09.23 hours local time from the Palmdale facilities. The pilot during this flight was Joe Sweeney, a Lockheed Martin test pilot and also a former US Navy pilot. He flew the X-35C straight to Edwards AFB in a twenty-seven-minute flight. The X-35C has more control surfaces and a reinforced structure to ensure the capacity for carrier landings, which have a higher impact on the structure of the plane. It did not take long before the first Navy pilot, Lt-Cdr Brian Goszkowicz, took off in the X-35C. It was the X-35C's fourth flight on 22 December 2000. On 23 January 2001 the eighteenth flight of the X-35C, a tanker qualification flight test, was initiated with a KC-10; it was also the first flight of USAF pilot Paul 'TP' Smith in the X-35C. As the X-35C would play a major part in the flight-test programme at Patuxent River, it was very important that the cross-continental flight could be done

The X-35C had a bigger wing to provide the greater control required for the carrier version trials. *Copyright Lockheed Martin*

The X-35C had three transfer flights, its first flight from Palmdale to Edwards AFB, from there to Fort Worth and finally to NAS Patuxent River. *Copyright Lockheed Martin*

The flashes on the tail unit actually represent the forward fuselage contours when seen from above. This would become really appropriate a couple of years later when the F-35 was named Lightning II. *Copyright Lockheed Martin*

The bigger flaps are fully deployed. Precise control of the plane shortly before a carrier landing can mean the difference between life and death. Engine power plays an important part in that control. *Copyright Lockheed Martin*

It was originally this aircraft that would assume responsibility for the STOVL tests but this was rearranged late in the production phase to assist commonality. *Copyright Lockheed Martin*

without too many stops. The tanker qualification test flights were completed successfully on 25 January 2001 with a couple of hook ups with a KC-10. Lockheed pilot Tom Morgenfeld was the fourth pilot to fly the X-35C on its nineteenth and twentieth flights.

USMC Major Art Tomassetti became the fifth pilot to fly the X-35C on 30 January 2001. He flew twice that day to gain experience for the planned transfer flight to Patuxent River. The X-35C became the second Lockheed JSF demonstrator to fly at supersonic speed on 31 January 2001 with Joe Sweeney at the controls. As the British were not only team members but also level-one partners in the JSF programme they also received the opportunity to fly the X-35C. Justin Paines was the first on 2 February followed by Simon Hargreaves on 7 February. On 9 February 2001 the X-35C was flown from Edwards AFB to the Lockheed Fort Worth division, where the F-16 production line was based, so that Lockheed employees could have close look at the new fighter. On 10 February 2001 the X-35C completed a cross-continental flight, a first for any X-plane. The X-35C was flown to NAS Patuxent River. The first leg was flown by Joe Sweeney and the second leg by Art Tomassetti. On each leg the X-35C was refuelled in the air five times to assure sufficient fuel in case of an emergency so that the aircraft could be diverted to a nearby airfield if required. The VX-23 Squadron was ready to help the Lockheed Martin team with the Navy test profile.

On the fiftieth flight of the X-35C the hundredth Field Carrier Landing Practice (FCLP) was performed. The X-35C's flight-test programme totalled seventy-three flights and the aircraft performed 250 FCLPs. The majority of the FCLPs, 152 to be exact, were flown in the last twenty-three flights, an average of 6.6 per flight. Beside the FCLPs there were two other important elements that had to be tested. One was a situation that is called a bolter, which is when an aircraft tail hook fails to catch any of the wires across the landing deck of an aircraft carrier. It is vital that an aircraft has enough power to take off again for another try before reaching the end of the landing area or the ship, because if it doesn't it is a very costly affair. A bolter can have different causes beside human error. It can also be caused by the wind, ship movement or hook simply bouncing over the wire. The second situation that needed to be accounted for was wave-offs, or in other words landings in progress that can not go ahead for any reason. An aircraft that lands on an aircraft carrier has a steeper sink rate than an air force fighter landing on a normal airfield. This was proven as well with the different X-35 versions. The X-35C had a sink rate of 11 ft per second, which means that the aircraft needs a heavier landing structure. The X-35A had a sink rate of 2 ft per second. It is therefore important to know the last moment that an aircraft can be waved off so that the it can still recover from its descent and return for another try when the reason for the wave off may have been solved or will hopefully not occur again.

On 8 March 2001 the X-35C was flown a total of six times, which was the highest rate of any day. The X-35C had already achieved five flights a day a couple of times. US Navy test pilot Greg Fenton had the honour of flying the X-35C aircraft on its last flight on 10 March 2001. It was the fifth flight of the X-35C that day and unlike the X-35A it was not flown back to Palmdale but stayed at NAS Patuxent River. The VX-23 Squadron continued to maintain the aircraft. The aircraft was donated to the US Navy Patuxent Museum.

The first prototype seen here undergoing structural ground testing. This aircraft can now be seen in the Patuxent River US Navy Museum.
Copyright Lockheed Martin

X-35C Flight Tests

Flight no.	Date	Pilot	Flight duration (hours)	Company or force
1	16 Dec 2000	Joe Sweeney	0.5	Lockheed
2	19 Dec 2000	Joe Sweeney	0.7	Lockheed
3	19 Dec 2000	Joe Sweeney	0.7	Lockheed
4	22 Dec 2000	Brian Goszkowicz	0.7	US Navy
5	22 Dec 2000	Joe Sweeney	0.6	Lockheed
6	03 Jan 2001	Joe Sweeney	0.8	Lockheed
7	03 Jan 2001	Joe Sweeney	0.9	Lockheed
8	03 Jan 2001	Brian Goszkowicz	0.4	US Navy
9	04 Jan 2001	Brian Goszkowicz	0.8	US Navy
10	04 Jan 2001	Brian Goszkowicz	0.4	US Navy
11	04 Jan 2001	Brian Goszkowicz	0.5	US Navy
12	04 Jan 2001	Joe Sweeney	0.9	Lockheed
13	04 Jan 2001	Joe Sweeney	0.3	Lockheed

Some things will never change and one is the smoke that comes of the tyres just after a conventional landing. *Copyright Lockheed Martin*

From this coastal scenery you can deduct that the X-35C was based at NAS Patuxent River. *Copyright Lockheed Martin*

Advances made for the JSF programme were to eventually find their way back to the F/A-22 Raptor, as commonality would reduce cost. *Copyright Lockheed Martin*

14	05 Jan 2001	Brian Goszkowicz	0.5	US Navy
15	11 Jan 2001	Brian Goszkowicz	0.9	US Navy
16	19 Jan 2001	Joe Sweeney	0.9	Lockheed
17	19 Jan 2001	Joe Sweeney	1.1	Lockheed
18	23 Jan 2001	Paul Smith	1.0	USAF
19	23 Jan 2001	Tom Morgenfeld	1.1	Lockheed
20	23 Jan 2001	Tom Morgenfeld	1.0	Lockheed
21	25 Jan 2001	Paul Smith	1.6	USAF
22	25 Jan 2001	Paul Smith	1.2	USAF
23	25 Jan 2001	Joe Sweeney	1.0	Lockheed
24	25 Jan 2001	Joe Sweeney	0.5	Lockheed
25	29 Jan 2001	Joe Sweeney	0.7	Lockheed
26	29 Jan 2001	Joe Sweeney	1.1	Lockheed
27	30 Jan 2001	Art Tomassetti	1.0	US Marines
28	30 Jan 2001	Art Tomassetti	0.5	US Marines
29	30 Jan 2001	Joe Sweeney	0.4	Lockheed
30	30 Jan 2001	Joe Sweeney	1.0	Lockheed
31	31 Jan 2001	Joe Sweeney	0.6	Lockheed
32	31 Jan 2001	Joe Sweeney	0.5	Lockheed
33	01 Feb 2001	Art Tomassetti	3.1	US Marines
34	02 Feb 2001	Justin Paines	1.5	UK RAF
35	03 Feb 2001	Tom Morgenfeld	0.3	Lockheed
36	05 Feb 2001	Joe Sweeney	0.7	Lockheed

37	07 Feb 2001	Art Tomassetti	2.0	US Marines
38	07 Feb 2001	Simon Hargreaves	0.8	BAE Systems
39	09 Feb 2001	Joe Sweeney	2.9	Lockheed
40	10 Feb 2001	Art Tomassetti	3.0	US Marines
41	13 Feb 2001	Art Tomassetti	0.7	US Marines
42	17 Feb 2001	Joe Sweeney	0.2	Lockheed
43	17 Feb 2001	Joe Sweeney	0.2	Lockheed
44	18 Feb 2001	Greg Fenton	0.4	US Navy
45	20 Feb 2001	Greg Fenton	0.9	US Navy
46	20 Feb 2001	Greg Fenton	0.4	US Navy
47	23 Feb 2001	Greg Fenton	0.2	US Navy
48	28 Feb 2001	Joe Sweeney	0.6	Lockheed
49	28 Feb 2001	Joe Sweeney	0.2	Lockheed
50	01 Mar 2001	Greg Fenton	0.5	US Navy
51	01 Mar 2001	Greg Fenton	0.9	US Navy
52	01 Mar 2001	Greg Fenton	0.5	US Navy
53	01 Mar 2001	Tom Morgenfeld	0.8	Lockheed
54	01 Mar 2001	Tom Morgenfeld	0.2	Lockheed
55	02 Mar 2001	Joe Sweeney	0.4	Lockheed
56	03 Mar 2001	Joe Sweeney	0.6	Lockheed
57	07 Mar 2001	Joe Sweeney	0.6	Lockheed
58	07 Mar 2001	Joe Sweeney	0.8	Lockheed
59	07 Mar 2001	Joe Sweeney	0.6	Lockheed
60	08 Mar 2001	Joe Sweeney	0.9	Lockheed
61	08 Mar 2001	Joe Sweeney	0.7	Lockheed
62	08 Mar 2001	Joe Sweeney	0.6	Lockheed
63	08 Mar 2001	Greg Fenton	0.6	US Navy
64	08 Mar 2001	Greg Fenton	0.5	US Navy
65	08 Mar 2001	Greg Fenton	0.5	US Navy
66	09 Mar 2001	Greg Fenton	0.7	US Navy
67	09 Mar 2001	Greg Fenton	0.6	US Navy
68	09 Mar 2001	Greg Fenton	0.6	US Navy
69	10 Mar 2001	Tom Morgenfeld	0.7	Lockheed
70	10 Mar 2001	Tom Morgenfeld	0.7	Lockheed
71	10 Mar 2001	Tom Morgenfeld	0.6	Lockheed
72	10 Mar 2001	Greg Fenton	0.7	US Navy
73	10 Mar 2001	Greg Fenton	0.6	US Navy

UK Government test pilot Justin Paines
on the Lockheed Martin X-35

Justin Paines was the UK government's evaluation pilot for the X-35 as was Paul Stone for the Boeing X-32. Justin Paines joined the RAF in 1988 and after pilot training he was selected to fly the Harrier. He graduated from the USAF Test Pilot School in 1995 as a Distinguished Graduate. After that he was based at Boscombe Down as the VAAC Harrier test pilot until 1999. The VAAC Harrier Programme (discussed elsewhere) was in support of the JSF program and it was only natural that he was selected for participation in the JSF program.

As with Paul Stone, Justin Paines describes himself as being at the right place at the right time, as both of them were selected from the available Harrier test pilots at the time. Justin Paines joined the Lockheed Martin team in January 1999 and became fully involved in the JSF programme by April 1999. Prior to this he had been closely involved in simulator work for both the Boeing and Lockheed Martin JSF teams. Justin Paines described the experience of joining the Lockheed Martin team as a privilege and the only negative thing he could find about the evaluation period was that it came to an end. To maintain proficiency Justin Paines and his colleagues flew F-16 and T-38 aircraft and shortly prior to flying the X-35B, in the latter part of the programme, he flew in the Harrier as well. He did not participate in the avionics flying test bed programme. The high fidelity simulator came very close to the real thing and it flew with exactly the same software that was in the actual aircraft.

Squadron Leader Justin Paines was the last of six pilots to fly the X-35A. His first and last flights were both on 18 November 2000. He accumulated 1.6 flying hours during the two missions. The X-35C carrier version was the next to be evaluated and this was one of the versions considered for the UK requirement. Prior to its transfer from Edwards AFB to NAS Patuxent River, Justin Paines flew the X-35C for the first and only time on the 2 February 2001. The flight lasted approximately one and half hours.

The next phase in the X-35 flight demonstration was to be more intense and Justin Paines role as a pilot in the programme became more active. During the flight evaluation of the X-35B STOVL version, the experience of the Harrier pilots put them in the driving seat. Justin

The word 'Legacy' could make the F-18 seem really older than it is. However it will need replacement soon and Lockheed offer the X-35C. Will European F-18 operators such as Spain, Switzerland and Finland follow the steps of fellow F-18 operators in Australia and Canada? *Copyright Lockheed Martin*

Paines became the third pilot to fly the X-35B on 30 June 2001. He flew the X-35B eight times, equalling a little more then four hours of flight time. Considering that Simon Hargreaves had flown twenty times and Justin Paines eight (both of them English) the English part of the team flew the majority of the X-35B flight test programme. All in all Justin Paines accumulated more then seven hours of flight time in the three X-35 versions. He also had the distinction of more time in the hover than either of the other X-35 STOVL pilots and was nick-named the 'King of Hover' by Maj Art Tommassetti.

Justin Paines described the flying characteristics as follows: 'The flying characteristics were exceptional. Very straight forward to fly, you feel in tune with the aircraft. It seems to deliver just the manoeuvre you ask for, just the amount of g, pitch or bank without you having to really work at it. It's also quite insensitive to pilot technique – so you can adapt a range of techniques and the aircraft still seems to do what you want. It's almost telepathic! In STOVL mode the X-35 was a handful because of small uncommanded changes in engine thrust and because it was a Harrier-like flight control system with manual control of thrust and thrust vector. The workload during high gain tasks in the X-35B was about the same or a little lower when compared to the Harrier, since the X-35B was more stable then the Harrier. The F-35 will have much very different handling qualities as a new flight control system for the STOVL regime has been selected (for more information on that see the part on the VAAC Harrier elsewhere) which will reduce pilot workload during the STOVL flight.

The US Navy has a tradition of more colourful jets then the USAF. *Lockheed Martin* **seemed to appreciate this. This F-16 is one of the exemptions to the rule.** *Copyright Lockheed Martin*

CHAPTER 6

TECHNOLOGY TEST BEDS FOR THE JSF PROGRAMME

From the early conception of the JAST programme office it was decided that first of all the technology had be matured before the actual strike fighter could be produced. The first step was to be able to recognise which technologies were promising and would bring tangible advantages to future pilots so that they would be able to fulfil their mission and perhaps more important get back home to fight another day.

The technology maturation programmes had to bring either survivability, lethality or supportability at an affordable price. The technology maturation programmes were divided among the following groups:

- Structures and materials

- Flight systems

- Manufacturing and production

- Mission systems

- Supportability

- Propulsion

The main technology demonstration was of course the propulsion, where from the start Boeing, Lockheed, McDonnell Douglas and Northrop Grumman all competed with a different propulsion proposal (more on the subject in Chapter 12). Some of these technology demonstration programmes are described below.

The F-16 equipped with the Diverterless Supersonic Inlet, the programme at the time was top secret but was released because of the JSF programme. *Copyright Lockheed Martin*

X-31 Quasi-tailless

Some of the technology for the JAST and later JSF programme was tested in separate X-programmes. During the summer of 1994 the JAST Flight Control Integrated Product Team had a meeting with the X-31 team to proceed with talks about a partly JAST-funded X-31 test programme. The programme was eventually called the quasi-tailless X-31 experiment or investigation. The goal of this programme was to evaluate whether or not thrust

The X-31 seen here in flight was used to evaluate for the JAST office the virtual tailless configuration. In the end the technology was deemed to involve greater risk than would the possible advantages. *US Navy*

vectoring control could replace the vertical tail control unit, not only for stealth purposes but also to make the aircraft more manoeuvrable. For the JAST office it was important to find out if even high-gain tasks could be executed without increasing the pilot workload compared with aircraft with conventional tail units. Gain is a term used in the aviation world to describe workload during a certain task. Examples of high-gain tasks are landing (especially on an aircraft carrier), aerial refuelling, gun tracking, ground attack profile and STOVL operations. Not all of these tasks could be evaluated but from the outset carrier landing and ground attack profile, including gun tracking, would be sufficient. The X-31 built by Rockwell International (now Boeing) and MBB from Germany was the first international X-programme. (MBB later merged with Daimler-Benz Aerospace, which was again one of the founding companies of EADS.). The X-31 was ideal as it was equipped with thrust vectoring capability from the outset and had just completed its original Enhanced Fighter Manoeuvrability (EFM) programme.

As the X-31 still had its vertical tail and new ground was to be explored it was decided to use the rudder control surfaces to cancel the stabilising effect of the vertical tail. The three thrust vectoring pads by the engine exhaust were used for yaw control and to stabilise the aircraft. For the JAST programme office there were two kind of flight regimes that were of interest and they were added to the programme in return for partial funding. The first flight regime was the highly critical carrier landing approach. This was imperative to JAST as the eventual winner would replace the US Navy's F/A-18 Hornets and controllability and responsiveness during this flight regime is an important Navy requirement. The second flight regime was a ground attack profile (strike profile). For the first flight regime (carrier landing approach) one of Edwards AFB's runways was temporarily equipped with a Fresnel lens landing system, as in use on the US Navy aircraft carriers. One problem, however, was that the landing gear of the X-31 was not strong enough to perform the actual landings and for this reason the aircraft were waived off at an altitude of 100 ft. Pilots during this programme were Rockwell test pilot Fred Knox (later Boeing's lead test pilot of the X-32A), USMC Major Christopher J. Loria and Mr Karl-Heinz Lang.

The major finding of the programme was that a tailless aircraft equipped with thrust vectoring would be feasible if it was designed without the vertical tail from the outset it would probably outweigh the negative side effects of system complexity. As a follow on to this project both NASA and the JSF programme office decided that the technology was promising enough to proceed with a real tailless flying demonstrator.

X-36

One separate programme that was produced for that purpose was the McDonnell Douglas/NASA X-36. The X-36 was an unmanned remote-controlled model of a proposed low-observable fighter. The X-36 was equipped with the Williams F112 turbofan engine. It was built on a 28 per cent scale to reduce cost. All controls were to be performed through thrust-vectoring nozzles and aerodynamic surfaces – the model was a vertical tailless aircraft design. The X-36 was unveiled on 19 March 1996 and had been treated as a black programme previously. The technology although promising had a greater risk than could be afforded at this stage and the maturation of this technology was thought to be too long and expensive, and for this reason it was no longer pursued by the JAST programme office as a requirement. The first X-36 was delivered to NASA Dryden Flight Research Center (DFRC) on 2 July 1996. As a result of this programme, McDonnell Douglas was more confident about including a tailless design in its bid for the CDP. McDonnell Douglas hoped to proceed with the development of its tailless technology by using the F-15 S/MTD (STOL/ Manoeuvre Technology Demonstrator) aircraft and even after McDonnell Douglas lost the selection for the CDP the company said that it would pursue the technology for the F-15 for future export customers.

The X-36 had its first flight on 17 May 1997 and was flown for the last time on 24 September 1997. The X-36 was designed and built by McDonnell Douglas and two were produced. The technology was so promising that McDonnell Douglas went on to fund its demonstrator called the Bird of Prey in its Phantom division. The main advantage was stealth and therefore during the CDP Boeing was evaluating this technology for its PWSC. McDonnell Douglas was by then absorbed by Boeing and the former McDonnell Douglas employees were in favour. As a result of Lockheed Martin's perceived stealth advantage they originally wanted to go ahead with the new technology but Boeing programme manager Statkus overrode that decision. Boeing proceeded with the development of its PWSC with the so-called four-poster tail similar to the tail unit used on the F-22 Raptor. A four-poster tail has two horizontal and two vertical stabilisers. Aircraft equipped with this besides the F-22A Raptor are the Northrop Grumman F-14 Tomcat, McDonnell Douglas F-15 Eagle and F-18 Hornet.

Diverterless Supersonic Inlet

Another technology that was not so obvious was the new inlet design of the X-35. When designing an inlet one has to take into account that engine reflection or visibility to radar has to be reduced; this has been facilitated by fly by wire and the unstable design of aircraft as the engine can be placed more aft. Other design issues are minimal drag induction and low weight and the inlet should also enable the engine to operate in all circumstances, giving the engine an all-round performance. The most difficult part of the latter point is that the inlet should slow the airflow at supersonic speeds so that the engine does not ingest air at supersonic speeds. Means of achieving this were compressing the air and having air bleeders to allow excess air to be redirected out of the inlet. The development of the technology was initiated in a private study by Lockheed in the early 1990s. In 1994 the JAST programme office recognised the benefits and initiated a trade study, the results of which showed a weight reduction and possible production cost reduction as well compared with contemporary inlets.

The Computational Fluid Dynamics (CFD) predictions now had to be tested for real to see if they were correct. A block 30 F-16ES was adapted with a Diverterless Supersonic Inlet

(DSI). The aircraft had the tail number AF83-1120 and was normally based with the 416th FLTS at Edwards AFB. The aircraft was equipped with a bump at the upper surface of the inlet; this was facilitated by the fact that straight above in the F-16 is a fuel tank. The bump reduced the height from the inner bottom side of the inlet and the upper inside of the inlet to 3.3 inches (82.5 mm). The bump is called a diverter, effectively making the term DSI incorrect, but in the name 'diverterless' refers to mechanical systems and the deletion of the splitter plate. The F-16 equipped with DSI made its first flight on 11 December 1996. Eleven more flights were conducted and during the total of twelve flights in nine days the total flight envelope of the F-16 was covered. No engine stalls occurred during these flights and at subsonic speed excess power was slightly better. The new inlet was tested up to speeds of Mach 2 on the F-16 without any engine problems. Joe Sweeney was the Lockheed Martin project pilot for the DSI testing; he was later involved in test-flying the X-35C.

Early in the CALF programme, when Lockheed Martin was making the Large Scale Powered Model, the X-32 design used the inlet design of the F-22 Raptor, including the splitter plate, as the DSI had not been proven yet. The new inlet was, however, tested from early 1996 on all wind-tunnel models. In August 1997 Lockheed awarded Alliant Tech Systems a contract for the diverterless inlet ducts for the two CDAs. The contract was valued at US $6.2 million. The new DSI technology was patented by Lockheed Martin in 1998. The two Lockheed Martin Concept Demonstrators, the X-35A/B and the X-35C were both equipped with DSI. This technology however was also to be also found on the fourth prototype of the Chinese-Pakistani JF-17 Thunder. The JF-17 was due to enter service with the Pakistan Air Force before the end of March 2007 so it beat the JSF in bringing this new technology into operational service.

E-brakes

Electrical systems were on the march to replace older systems all over the aircraft. Electrical systems were found to be more economical to maintain. Hydraulic systems in particular are maintenance sensitive, therefore BF Goodrich, Lockheed Martin and Boeing joined forces with the 416th Flight Test Squadron to develop and test electrical brakes for next-generation fighter aircraft. The Cooperative Research and Development Agreement (CRDA) between the Air Force Research Laboratory (AFRL) and BF Goodrich was signed in mid 1997.

With typical brake systems the hydraulic system engages the carbon pads onto the wheel. The hydraulic system activates whenever the pilot hit the brakes and also when the landing gear is being retracted as rotating wheels could damage the aircraft internally. The new system was installed in an F-16 (S/N 87-352) from 1 October 1998 to 20 November 1998. Further alterations during this period to the F-16 were the replacement of the existing brake control and anti-skid computers with a digital brake-control computer, which allowed for better communication with both the pilot and the maintenance staff. Before flight tests could be undertaken the new electrical system underwent thorough ground tests from 24 November 1998 to 30 January 1999. After this the electrical brake system was modified from 1 February 1999 to 19 March 1999. This modification required new ground-testing that was initiated on 19 March 1999 and completed on 7 April 1999. A total of sixty-one ground-test runs had been performed, equalling forty ground-test hours. An important part of the ground-testing was differential braking, or in other words braking asymmetrically so that the pilot can use the brake system to steer the aircraft. Applying brakes on the left landing gear would send the aircraft to the left. During the ground tests the speeds were increased in increments up to take-off and landing speeds. The ground tests were very thorough so that the risks during flight were minimal. Finally in December 1998 the F-16 equipped with the electrical brakes took to the air for the first time. A total of two flights were executed for this test programme, totalling 0.4 hours. This technology was, however, not used in any of the X-planes (CDAs) as risk reduction during that phase was paramount. However, this did not prevent problems as the Boeing X-32A suffered a brake malfunction on 24 October 2004. Boeing, however, was the first manned aircraft producer to commit to electric brakes when the company announced that customers (airlines) could choose between BF Goodrich and Messier-Bugatti electric brakes for the Boeing 7E7. Northrop Grumman had earlier committed to electric brakes for its Global Hawk unmanned surveillance aircraft. BF Goodrich hoped that the operational advantages of the system would be clear to potential Boeing 7E7 customers. As Lockheed Martin had opted for old-fashioned hydraulic pressure brakes the F-35 would not be equipped with electric brakes as it would require a redesign. It would be expensive to retrofit an aircraft fitted with hydraulic brakes with electric brakes according to BF Goodrich officials.

Integrated Helmet Audio Visual System (IHAVS)

This project was initiated to integrate different emerging products into one environment and test the resulting synergy. For this programme a TAV-8B was utilised and the tests were performed at the Naval Air Warfare Center Weapons Division (NAWCWD), China Lake Naval Air Station (NAS). McDonnell Douglas was the integrating contractor. As the project was a JAST (JSF) funded programme the test pilots were drawn from all active US services with the exception of the Army and the Air National Guard (ANG), which are not involved in the JAST programme. The pilots were USAF Major Donald Chapman (an F-16 pilot with 3200 flight hours to his name), USMC Major Jim Derdall (an AV-8B pilot with 1800 flight hours to his name), and the US Navy LCDR Brian Corey (an F/A-18 pilot with 2000 flight hours to his name). Chapman had absolved the USAF test pilot school while Derdall and Corey had absolved the USN test pilot school. It was planned that each of the pilots would fly about eight flights under the IHAVS programme. The eight flights were planned as follows:

• The first flight for each pilot was aimed at system familiarisation.

• During the second flight each pilot would drop a Mk 16 practice bomb with the aid of the Head Up Display (HUD).

• During the third flight each pilot would drop a Mk 16 practice bomb with the aid of the IHAVS.

• During the fourth flight each pilot would, with the help of the conventional instrumentation, ie HUD, perform a tactical ingress and simulate the release of ballistic weapons and the launch of the Maverick missiles against pre-planned targets and targets of opportunity.

The TAV-8B Harrier during the IHAVS programme. *US Navy via Gary Verver*

The Harrier is getting to a respectable age but before it can go into retirement it will be used to demonstrate some new technologies for the JSF programme, as with this example in the Integrated Helmet Audio Visual System (IHAVS) programme. *US Navy*

- During the fifth, sixth and seventh flights each pilot would, with the help of the IHAVS, perform a tactical ingress and simulate the release of ballistic weapons and the launch of the Maverick missiles against pre-planned targets and targets of opportunity.
- The eighth flight for each pilot was a comparison of HUD/RWR (Radar Warning Receiver) and IHAVS systems regarding threat warning, recognition and management.

The second and fourth flights were used to establish references with which to compare the results achieved in the third, fifth, sixth, seventh and to a limited extent also the eighth flight.

The IHAVS programme fell under jurisdiction of the flight systems Integrated Product Team (IPT) or rather a sub IPT called cockpit and aircrew systems. The aims of the programme were to:

- Reduce workload
- Increase situational awareness
- Use Helmet Mounted Display (HMD) for navigation and mission tasks
- Evaluate HMD weapon delivery potential (weapons evaluated were High speed Anti Radiation Missile –HARM – block 6, Joint Direct Attack Munition –JDAM – and the Joint Stand Off Weapon – JSOW)
- Display and evaluate sensor imagery on HMD
- Compare HUD vs Helmet Mounted Display (HMD) performance
- Evaluate 3-D audio threat management
- Demonstrate utility of voice interface technology developed by Smiths Aerospace
- Investigate HMD and 3-D audio designation point cueing
- Integrate the technologies into one human systems interface

The programme started in February 1995 and was supported by the following organisations: USAF Armstrong Laboratory supplying a 3-D audio system with Active Noise Reduction (ANR); GEC-Marconi supplying a Viper II binocular HMD; Lockheed Martin Aeronautics (formerly Loral) supplying NITE *(NITE* = Navigation IR Targeting Equipment) Hawk Self Cooled Forward Looking Infra *Red (FLIR)* Targeting Pods and Smiths Industries supplying the Interactive Voice Module (IVM). Smiths Industries was thought to be at the forefront in developing this technology as it was aimed from the outset for the Eurofighter Typhoon, which was also in the initial flight-test phase at the time. The integration of the IVM was easier because it had been tested in another AV-8B Harrier prior to the IHAVS programme. All these components were integrated into the TAV-8B by McDonnell Douglas. Other internal changes that were introduced for this programme were a Miniature Airborne GPS Receiver (MAGR); a mini Tactical Air Navigation (TACAN); the ASN-139 Inertial Navigation System (INS); the ALR-67 Radar Warning Receiver; the Enhanced Stores Management Set (ESMS); the night attack display computer and the XN-6 mission computer. External changes were weapon stores. Furthermore the aircraft was qualified for the captive carriage of the IR/Laser Maverick missile.

The GEC-Marconi Viper II has a binocular fully overlapping 40° Field Of View (FOV). It adds 1.54 kg to a standard US flying helmet but could be fitted on helmets from all other UK and US services. The Viper II was capable of presenting video images from for example FLIR to the pilot with flight and weapon delivery information superimposed. A magnetic head tracker was used to track the position of the pilot's head.

The aim of 3-D audio technology was to alert the pilot of any threats. The noise or auditory symbology that the system produced would be directed to the pilot from the exact direction where the threat was situated. The pilot therefore has improved situational awareness. A strike aircraft flying over enemy territory is most likely to encounter more than one threat at a time. The aim for the IHAVS programme was that the pilot could recognise four threats and that the 3-D audio system would prioritise the threats according to the amount of exposure to the different threats. There would be four levels of danger, meaning that a total of sixteen auditory symbols would have to be used (four threats and each at four danger levels makes sixteen auditory symbols). The sixteen auditory symbols had to be easily recognised to make the task simpler for the pilot. The auditory symbols, if possible, would have to be intuitive for the pilot to ease the workload. The danger level of a target can change over time. If the danger level changes (meaning also a change of auditory symbol) it should still be clear to the pilot that the signal is regarding the same previously indicated threat but at a different danger level.

Another problem, or rather something that had to be avoided, was that the auditory symbols should not be mixed up with auditory signals from other cockpit systems. The auditory symbols had to fulfil stringent requirements for identification and localisation purposes.

The requirements for identification are:

1   Each auditory symbol is individually identifiable when presented alone.
2   Each auditory symbol remains individually identifiable when presented together with other auditory symbols.
3   Multi-state auditory symbols indicate changes in a state without losing the perception of identity.

The requirements for localisation are:

1   Each auditory symbol is individually localisable when presented alone.
2   Each auditory symbol remains individually localisable when presented together with other auditory symbols.

In a previous programme called Auditory Representation of Threat Environments (ARTE) the Georgia Tech Research Institute had developed a set of auditory symbols that was deemed usable for the IHAVS project. The pilots, however, preferred another idea based on the auditory warning system of the RWR systems. The RWS auditory symbols were intuitive to the pilots and would not require them to learn a new set as would be necessary for the ARTE system. Both the RWR-based system and the ARTE-based auditory system were tested in a laboratory and in the Harrier.

The NITE Hawk targeting pod had been developed by Loral since March 1978. It was originally developed for the F/A-18 in the US Navy as this aircraft required a night/day strike capability. The NITE Hawk reached operational service in February 1985, although the first units had been supplied to the US Navy in 1983. The designation of the NITE Hawk was AN/AAS-38. Between the service introduction and the start of the IHAVS programme the NITE Hawk targeting pod was improved upon twice with modifications. The last modification entered service by the end of 1994 as the AN/AAS-38B.

The Harrier TAV-8B used for this programme was BuNo 163191. The first flight with the fully modified TAV-8B was achieved on 29 September 1995. The programme evaluated the combined systems during a total of twenty-five test flights, of which the last one occurred on 13 June 1996. The results were divided over the different technologies and the only one that was considered advanced enough was the ANR system. The conclusions and recommendations of the tests are listed below.

The conclusions for the HMD were that:

- Off-boresight HMD symbology had the greatest advantage.
- Off-boresight capability provided more attack options.
- Better threat situational awareness was provided using HMD symbology.
- Manoeuvre potential could be quickly assessed using HMD.
- 'Jitter' and 'latency' degraded HMD.
- The helmet was too heavy and would move on the pilot's head during manoeuvring.

The recommendations were as follows:

- The 'jitter' and 'latency' of the HMD must be improved so that it is similar to that of a HUD.
- The symbology required more study and in-flight evaluations.
- HMD-capable helmets with the same weight as present day helmets should be developed.
- Symbology should not be lost during manoeuvring.
- A simple and reliable boresight capability was required.

The conclusions for the IVM were that:

- It provided a simple/intuitive means of managing information and sensors.
- Command words were easily learned compared with mastering a complex Hands On throttle And Stick (HOTAS) mechanism.
- The recognition rate was not reliable enough.
- IVM lacked adequate feedback for the pilot of activated status.
- IVM mis-IDs were far worse than no IVM ID.

The recommendations were:

- Develop a simple, robust, and reliable IVM system with a larger vocabulary, able to recognise words under different stress, breathing and g conditions that requires minimal pilot training.
- The IVM must be as reliable as present-day HOTAS switchology.

It was concluded that the NITE Hawk targeting pod:

- Provided the capability to identify targets and employ weapons off-boresight.
- Validated system integration.
- Did not have state of the art targeting pod capabilities.

The recommendation was to provide it with a state of the art targeting pod. The conclusions for the 3-D audio system were:

- 3-D auditory cues with visual cues increased a pilot's situational awareness – laboratory studies were validated.

The first western operational STOVL fighter with its future replacement. This Harrier was also used for the IHAVS programme in 1996. *US Navy*

- Threat cueing, spread communication and waypoint directional cueing were demonstrated successfully.
- True 3-D is required to include elevation/azimuth/range to be provided by systems utilising audio.
- The systems allowed localisation of only two threats by pilots.

The recommendations were:

- To develop systems capable of supporting a 3-D audio (azimuth, elevation and range).
- To continue to develop and evaluate the 3-D audio system to improve multiple localisation.

The conclusions for the ANR were that:

- Unwanted background noise was eliminated.
- Radio and Intra-cockpit communications were more effective.
- The threat tones were clear and precise.

The recommendation was that the ANR was ready for incorporation.

The overall conclusions of the IHAVS were that it offered increased situational awareness/decreased workload:

- The HMD system provided on/off-boresight symbology and flight/attitude awareness.
- The IVM provided the simple capability to manage information /multiple sensors.
- The NITE Hawk targeting pod provided off-boresight identification and targeting capability.
- The 3-D audio system with ANR supplemented visual cues.

The overall recommendation was to continue to support the development and flight-testing of the involved technologies. The IHAVS technologies provided increased situational awareness and reduced workload. IHAVS further enhanced air–to-ground mission effectiveness and therefore was considered the basis for the next-generation Man Machine Interface (MMI) for tactical strike fighters of the near future.

The results of the IHAVS programme were fed to the Joint Helmet Mounted Cueing System (JHMCS) programme office as a future upgrade of the JHMCS was expected to be fitted in the future JSF. The Harrier used for the IHAVS programme was also used for chase flights at Edwards AFB during the CDP of the Lockheed Martin X-35 and the Boeing X-32

JSF Paintless Aircraft Program (JPAP)

An aircraft is painted every four years. The painting of any aircraft takes about twenty-four hours and has many side effects, especially for the environment. According to Boeing up to 90 per cent of all hazardous materials associated with aircraft are in relation to painting, stripping and repainting operations. During the process of painting or stripping the paint of an aircraft no other work, such as maintenance, can be performed. Another associated disadvantage is that a fighter plane can gain up to 800 pounds of paint from repeated repainting. This can influence the performance of any fighter and was enough reason for the JSF programme office to look into new technologies being developed. The JSF office released an RfP in May 1995, and on 30 June 1995 a contract was awarded to Boeing to evaluate the new technology.

The technology was based on appliqués: thin polymer films backed by pressure-sensitive adhesive. Boeing, in cooperation with 3M, initiated testing of the appliqués on a T-33 test aircraft, increasing the size of the appliqués and flight envelope. The T-33 was used for this programme from September 1995 to August 1996. The T-33 aircraft was fairly small compared with current fighter aircraft and a supersonic aircraft would have to endure heavier strain; it was therefore decided to use an F-18A. The appliqués were installed on the external fuel tank so that they could be tested in the supersonic flight regime. These flight tests were initiated on 25 April 1996. Other areas of the aircraft were covered with appliqués and a total of thirty-four flights (51.9 hours) were performed from May 1996 to November 1996. The appliqués were tested up to Mach 1.63 and showed no sign of peeling. To test the effect of damaged appliqués some of them were pre-peeled: these either broke off or wore away back to the sealed edge during flight.

A major worry that had to be addressed was corrosion in the air and highly corrosive salt water and for this reason Boeing received a contract extension in June 1997 to study maritime corrosion issues. By August 1997 a McDonnell Douglas F-18B with more than 90 per cent of the surface skin covered with appliqués based at the Naval Air Warfare Center Aircraft Division (NAWCAD) Patuxent River undertook 268 flights (equalling 399 flight hours). During this test period the F-18B had two detachments to aircraft carriers (CVN-65 USS *Enterprise* and CVN-67 the USS *Kennedy*) to expose it to the shipboard environment. The aircraft had a total of sixty-two catapult launches and sixty-two traps (successful aircraft carrier landings) and flew more than 3.5 hours supersonic and more than 1.5 hours in the rain. The test programme was completed on 31 August 1998 and improved supportability was considered demonstrated. During the Next Generation Paintless Aircraft test programme a fourth and a fifth generation appliqué was tested as well.

3M not only worked with Boeing but with Lockheed as well. The cooperation with Lockheed was not under the umbrella of the JPAP programme funded by the JSF JPO. The Lockheed test programme was funded by the National Institute of Standards. Lockheed tested the new appliqués on three separate F-16s, an S-3 Viking (from April 1997 for a five-week period) and a USAF C-130E Hercules. One of the F-16s was covered only on some parts of the tail surfaces. The second F-16's entire upper surfaces were covered and a third F-16 was used to test an external fuel tank covered in appliqués. Tests continued well into 2000 when an F-16 was tested with approximately 1300 square feet of its surfaces covered with appliqués. The Lockheed JSF CDAs, however, were painted in early June to reduce risks (the Boeing CDA also received the normal topcoat). During 1999 both manufacturers planned to propose the appliqués for their respective PWSCs. An intelligent laser system was developed to project adhesive-film appliqués to the exterior of the F-35. The system was expected to undergo testing before the A-1 prototype was ready. According to Rob Weis, Vice President Business Development, at Farnborough 2006 some parts of the aircraft would be covered in appliqués while other parts would have special paint applied. The exact parts were not identified for obvious reasons.

Low Observable Axi-symmetrical Nozzle (LOAN)

The USAF and the Navy wanted (on an affordable basis) the most advanced technology on their aircraft and therefore thrust vectoring technology was further developed. The technology was developed for the JSF programme office under the JSF Broad Area Announcement (BAA) 94-2 programme. The thrust vectoring nozzle on the F-22 Raptor's

F119 engine was considered too heavy. Pratt & Whitney therefore tested a newly developed nozzle on an F-16C equipped with a Pratt & Whitney F100-PW-200. The LOAN was lighter in weight, more appropriate for a lightweight fighter (JSF was and is considered lightweight although it much heavier than the F-16) and it was a low observable nozzle, meaning that it reduces the Infra Red (IR) and Radar Cross Section (RCS) signature as opposed to a conventional nozzle. The programme was also known under the name F-16 Ejector Nozzle Integration programme. The improvements to the nozzle are geometrical shaping for stealth purposes, an advanced cooling system (which has a side effect of more than doubling the technical life of the nozzle divergent flaps) and special coatings on internal and external structures. Ground-testing was performed in early November 1996. The F-16 was equipped with the nozzle within two days as a part of a rapid prototyping programme. Besides the F-16 the LOAN was also ground-tested on the Pratt & Whitney Joint Technology Demonstration Engine (JTDE) FX650 for the JSF programme. Lockheed had indicated that it would use this kind of technology for its PWSC, but did not, however, specify if it was the technology developed by Pratt & Whitney or by General Electric.

VISTA or Test-flying the Flight Control System (FCS)

Risk reduction was an integral part of the JAST and later the JSF programme. It was not considered enough to have tested the FCS in the simulator by Lockheed Martin. For this reason it was decided to test-fly the X-35's FCS in the VISTA F-16. VISTA stands for Variable In-flight Simulator Test Aircraft. The VISTA F-16 is a highly modified F-16D two-seater from block 30 with a Digital Flight Control System (DFCS). The serial number of the VISTA F-16D is 86-0048. Among the modifications that it underwent are that it has block 40 avionics. This F-16D flew after its VISTA modifications for the first time as the VISTA F-16 on 9 April 1992.

The VISTA F-16 has been used in support of other programmes such as the ATF and F-117. The test-flying took place at the Calspan Corporation in Buffalo, New York. For the X-35 CDP programme the VISTA F-16D received two upgrades. The upgrades were:

The VISTA F-16 is one of the most versatile technology demonstration aircraft. It was used for software development of the X-35, for HMD testing and for Virtual HUD testing. All very important features for the final JSF product. *USAF*

- The installation of a prototype Sargent-Fletcher Aerial Refuelling Tank/System (ART/S).
- A new computer to increase the capacity of the computational capacity.

Before the new systems could be flight-tested the F-16 had to be calibrated to match the dynamic response characteristics of the X-35. The calibration flights started on 29 March 1998 and lasted until 9 June 1998. During the first flight, the VISTA NF-16D was flown by John Ball and Jeff Peer, from the Calspan company. Jeff Peer had also helped Saab with the flight control laws for the Gripen 8 years before. The first flight went through all the predetermined test points, comprising commands in all flight axes (yaw, pitch and roll) during up and away flight and during one landing in power-approach mode. In total, ten calibration flights (equalling 11.5 hours) took place. The second part of the tests, the actual flight–testing, was initiated on 12 June 1998. In the second part of testing a total of thirteen test-flights were performed by four pilots, of which two were from Lockheed Martin and two from the government. The last flight was on 19 June 1998. One of the four pilots was Lt-Col Paul Smith, the USAF chief JSF pilot, the same man who would later play a major part in test-flying the JSF X-35 demonstrators. The FCS performed satisfactorily for formation flying, air-to-air tracking, Field Carrier Landing Practice approaches and conventional landings. There were, however, five areas where improvement would be justified. The five areas were:

1 The flight path change was not responsive enough to throttle input during approaches.

2 The cockpit lateral acceleration was too high during roll inputs.

3 The nominal lateral stick gradient was bordering on being too light. The heavier lateral stick gradient was preferred.

4 The pitch dropback preference was task-dependent. The higher dropback was preferred for formation tasks and the baseline dropback was preferred for air-to-air tracking.

5 The speed control, especially the ability to decelerate to control closure, was unsatisfactory for formation tasks.

Increasing Survivability Not Only During Peacetime

Spatial disorientation is a killer and all kinds of technologies were tried to prevent it from happening. For helicopters and Harriers it was evident that a large number of the accidents occurred during the hover phase of flight with special disorientation as a major factor. Visual indications on Head Down Displays (HDD), HUDs and finally on HMDs did not significantly reduce the accident rate. Other means were therefore tried.

One programme initiated by the Naval Aerospace Medical Research Laboratory (NAMRL) and the NASA Johnson Space Center would become of interest to the JSF programme office. The programme was funded initially by the Office of Naval Research (ONR). This specific programme was the Tactile Situation Awareness System (TSAS) and related to the touch senses of the pilot. This system was the first one to use the pilot's sense of touch and the already saturated visual senses. It would, however, mean another piece of equipment the pilot would be required to wear. The TSAS included as an interface with the pilot a Tactor Locator System (TLS), which was a torso harness equipped with twenty electro-mechanical tactors. Tactors are vibrating instruments located in such manner that the pilot can sense impulses through the skin. Until now, an unused method of communicating information to the pilot. The TLS was to be worn under the pilot's flight suit to make it effective. The tactors were placed in four columns with 90 degrees' interval between each column. To demonstrate the viability of the TSAS a T-34C aircraft was selected and one USN pilot, Navy Capt. James C. Baker, a flight surgeon and a test pilot. The TSAS programme in this phase was to demonstrate two things:

1 That a significant amount of orientation and awareness information can be intuitively provided continuously by the under-utilised sense of touch.

2 With the TSAS display a pilot, with no visual cues, can effectively maintain control of the aircraft in normal and acrobatic flight conditions.

The TSAS was provided with information from on-board sensors and therefore did not require any major system integration. The most difficult part would be to hook up the pilot and make it safe during the ejection phase as it would require an automatic quick-release. The rear cockpit of the T-34 was shrouded so that the test pilot would receive no cues from the outside world and flight instrumentation from the back cockpit was also removed. The security pilot in the front cockpit would fly the aircraft to a safe point from where the USN test pilot, Capt. James C. Baker, would take the controls and perform different manoeuvres without visual cues, relying on the TSAS for attitude cues. The first flight of the modified T-34C occurred from NAS Patuxent River with Capt. James C. Baker at the controls on 11 October 1995. It was the first flight of seven to be completed by 19 October 1995. Capt. James C. Baker demonstrated straight and level flight for five minutes, climbing and descending turns, loops, ailerons rolls, unusual attitude recovery and ground-controlled approaches. During the test programme two different TLS models were used – one for fine control of the aircraft and one for acrobatic manoeuvres. In the model for fine control only three tactors in each column was used and for the acrobatic five tactors in each column. From flight evaluation it was clear that three tactors in each column was more intuitive than the system with five tactors. The three-tactor column system, however, had a pitch and roll range of +/– 40 degrees as opposed to the five-tactor column with a pitch and roll range of +/– 180 degrees. As a result only the five tactors per column system could be used for acrobatic manoeuvres, leading to the conclusion that the TSAS should be developed for a certain flight regime – the best option would be a high-gain flight regime.

The second phase of the flight-test programme was held at Fort Rucker. It did not include the T-34 this time but an UH-60 helicopter. Three US Army test pilots were selected to evaluate the TSAS. This part of the flight demonstration was aimed at demonstrating:

• That a significant amount of orientation and awareness information can be intuitively provided continuously by the under-utilised sense of touch.

• The use of the TSAS display to show that a pilot, with no visual cues, can effectively maintain control of a helicopter in the complex rotary wing environment.

The UH-60 was modified with the TSAS, however it was impossible to cover the canopy so this time the pilot was blindfolded. In addition to the roll and pitch indications given by the tactors in the TLS, airspeed error tactile indications were given by tactors located on the arms and heading error indications were provided by tactors located on the legs. The first test flight by the UH-60 modified with the TSAS occurred on 11 December 1995. This part of the flight-test programme included nine flight tests and was completed on 20 December 1995. The test pilot equipped with TSAS was seated in the right-hand seat without access to visual indicators. During the nine test flights the pilots flew straight and level, standard rate turns, unusual attitude recovery and ground-controlled approaches. One major result from this evaluation was that heading error signals were out-saturated by the pitch and roll indicators. A way to solve this problem was to stay with the heading error signal until the pilot had achieved straight and level flight according to the TSAS indicators. The results of the programme were interesting enough to gain the attention of the JSF programme office.

This time the flight regime (especially), the hover phase and the transition from hover to forward flight were being evaluated. The JSF programme wanted to see if the TSAS:

- Could reduce pilot workload and enhance situation awareness during hover and transition to forward flight.

- Equipped pilot could effectively hover and transition to forward flight in a vertical lift aircraft with degraded outside visual cues.

- Could be integrated into military flight garments.

At the time that the integration work was initiated there were four companies identified that could produce high-quality tactors that would fulfil the state of the art requirements. The four companies were:

- Audiological Engineering producing a vibro-mechanical tactor designated Tactaid.

- Engineering Acoustics Inc. producing a vibro-mechanical electromagnetic tactor designated AT-96.

- Unitech Research producing a direct electrical tactor designated Audiotact.

- Carleton Technologies Inc. producing a pneumatic vibro-mechanical tactor designated model 2856-A0.

The tactor from Audiological was not considered suitable for primary flight information and was therefore eliminated from the list. Because of its size and weight and the low intensity of its tactile sensation the vibro-mechanical electromagnetic tactor made by Engineering Acoustics Inc. was considered unsuitable as well. Engineering Acoustics Inc. took the recommendations to heart and worked on a different tactor that was, however, too late for the integration but was considered suitable for future flight-testing. The Audiotact tactor was considered an emerging technology. It was not ready for evaluation at the time but due to its superior size, weight and tactile sensation intensity it was recommended to evaluate it at a future point. Carleton Technologies Inc. was selected for the flight demonstration funded by the JSF programme office.

To demonstrate the integration with military flight garments the pneumatic vibro-tactile tactors were utilised during the demonstration phase with an F-22 cooling vest. The tactors were integrated in the F-22 cooling vest, which remained lightweight. The most important advantage of the cooling vest was that it was connected to the cooling ambient air, which meant that the vest inflated slightly and thereby pressed the tactors to the pilot's torso increasing contact. The information for the pneumatic vibro-tactile tactors was provided by Commercial Off The Shelf (COTS) GPS/INS besides data from on-board systems. The GPS/INS was a C-MIGITS-II GPS/INS supplied by Boeing North American. Information from the GPS/INS and other on-board systems were fed into the TSAS NP-1 computer, which translated it into electronic signals that were sent to the vibro-tactile tactors. During the tests there was feedback from the tactors to the computer to note if they functioned properly and this information was presented to the test operator on a graphical user interface.

The UH-60 was selected as the test platform because of requirements such as cost, safety (it is dual control), previous experience, testing the TSAS in an as harsh as possible environment and aircraft availability. Dual control was required to seat a safety pilot who would also function as an instructor pilot to the pilot equipped with TSAS. A helicopter has

A pilot at work in the cockpit simulator. He is working the display system by touch, a new concept that will ease his workload but may cause screen deterioration problems and increase maintenance cost, the future will tell. *Team JSF*

A view into the F-35 cockpit simulator. There are no press buttons around the display screen. The display system shows clearly the different portals (windows) in different sizes adaptable by the pilot by touching the glass and voice activation. *Team JSF*

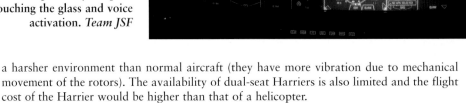

a harsher environment than normal aircraft (they have more vibration due to mechanical movement of the rotors). The availability of dual-seat Harriers is also limited and the flight cost of the Harrier would be higher than that of a helicopter.

Feedback from the evaluation pilots was very positive. However, one problem of the system that had to be solved was that the pilot could become too reliant on the TSAS. For this reason redundancy was built into the tests for the JSF programme office. There were eight columns integrated in the F-22 cooling vest. Therefore when the helicopter drifted in a certain direction the column with two tactors would give a tactile sensation to the pilot. The two tactors would supply the required redundancy. The speed of the helicopter drifting would be indicated by the number of pulses per second. The drifting speed ranges were selected as being from 0.3 m to 0.7 m per second, 0.7 m to 2 m per second, and higher than 2 m per second. During the slowest drift speed one pulse per second would be given to the pilot as indication, for the second four pulses per second and for the last possibility ten pulses per second so that it would be easily recognised.

The evaluation funded by the JSF programme office took place at two different locations, Fort Rucker, Alabama, and NAS Pensacola, Florida. Prior to the flight-test programme, however, the system was test-flown in the simulator. The first flight in the simulator was on 2 September 1997 followed by fifteen more simulator flights, of which the last three occurred on 11 September 1997. For this evaluation programme a UH-60 was used again and after modification it was first flown on 9 September 1997. The first two flights were used for a systems check-out and therefore could be done prior to completion of the simulator tests. Eight more flights followed, of which flight three to five were so-called familiarisation flights as three of the four pilots had no previous experience with TSAS in flight. After the familiarisation flights the test programme was transferred from Fort Rucker to NAS Pensacola and the flight evaluation was concluded on 19 September 1997. An important finding of the programme was that during the simulated instrument meteorological conditions all pilots reported reduced workloads, while the tactors' signal was considered strong enough for the helicopter environment, intuitive and not annoying. One important conclusion could be made and that was that pilots in hover or transition flight could pay more attention to other displays, which meant increased situation awareness.

From AGCAS to ACAS

To increase safety and reduce peacetime losses the endurance of systems (or Mean Time Between Failure – MTBF) was increased and the monitoring of systems was increased. Safety for the pilot was improved compared with previous-generation aircraft. There was, however, still room for improvement to help the pilot. Combat aircraft were lost during exercises. The pilot could as a result of high-g manoeuvres lose consciousness and during low-level/altitude flying exercises this could result in the pilot crashing and dying. This loss of consciousness is called GLOC or G-induced Loss Of Consciousness, a known reason for losing highly experienced and expensively trained pilots. Besides the fuel system Intertechnique also supplies the EROS anti-GLOC oxygen system, which enhances the pilot's endurance against GLOC. This actively helps the pilot to breathe during high g manoeuvres.

Another scenario with a similar end is the high-speed, low-altitude flight exercise, which is typical for a fighter mission. Pilot mishaps during these missions often have a lethal ending. These accidents are classified as Controlled Flight Into Terrain (CFIT). Budgetary reasons had kept the Automatic Ground Collision Avoidance System (AGCAS) system off the funded list, when in September 1995 AFTI programme managers met up with FMV and Saab people. For both parties the reason for cooperation was to reduce costs – both the US and Sweden had the technology available to develop the AGCAS. An obstacle to cooperation was that on the export market the F-16 was competing with the Gripen; this problem was, however, overcome. The programme was initiated in the autumn of 1996. The purpose of the programme was to improve the results from previous ground collision avoidance research carried out from 1985 to 1988 and 1989 to 1991.

Saab worked together with Lockheed Martin Tactical Aircraft Systems (LMTAS) to develop a system that could prevent 95 per cent of these accidents from happening. The development was paid for by the USAF and the FMV. The programme was led by the US Air Force Research Laboratory (AFRL) with the assistance of the FMV at Edwards AFB. The Swedes called the programme *Du kan inte flyga lagre* (you can't fly any lower). The USAF had in the ten-year period leading up to the programme (1987 to 1996) lost ninety-eight aircraft to CFIT.

By the end of 1997 the AFTI F16 team initiated a research into nuisance warnings. Nuisance warnings are when the AGCAS gives warnings about things with no immediate danger. The pilot might want to switch the system off during low-level flying missions and as a result the system would be useless. Criteria for nuisance warnings were set, from which the AGCAS designers could work.

The system developed was test-flown in the AFTI (Advanced Fighter Technology Integration) F-16 and was called an Automatic Ground Collision Avoidance System (Auto GCAS). The AFTI F-16 was in fact the sixth of eight Full Scale Development (FSD) F-16s (construction number 75-0750) to be converted. The AFTI has been updated many times since its first flight on 10 July 1982 piloted by Alex Wolfe. The nuisance testing was done on the AFTI 75-0750 until the beginning of November 1997 when the AFTI F-16 75-0750 was taken to Lockheed Martin for the installation of electro-hydrostatic localised actuators in support of the JSF programme. As a result the AFTI F-16 was replaced by an F-16DS/N 83-1176, production block 50, two-seater in the joint test programme.

The original AFTI F-16 was retired after its last flight on 9 January 2001. The AFTI F-16 is due to be put on display in the USAF museum in Dayton Ohio. In the middle of the programme the AFTI F-16 was replaced by an F-16D S/N 83-1176, production block 50. The 83-1176 was equipped with the standard flight controls, avionics, radar altimeter, Global Positioning System (GPS), Inertial Navigation System (INS) and Terrain Reference Navigation (TRN) system from production aircraft. Hardware changes included an Upgraded Data Transfer Unit (UDTU) in which a data cartridge would be inserted before flight with a terrain database. Other changes were mainly software-based and included the flight control computer, up-front controls, HUD, voice message unit and data transfer equipment.

Auto GCAS helps the pilot avoid flying into the ground. However, the system should not be a nuisance and interfere with normal exercises when there is no immediate danger. This was the difficult element of the design of this system. The system was designed to put the plane level again and then do a 5-g pull up. To warn the pilot that the system was activated and was about to take action, a warning signal in his HUD would be shown; the pilot could therefore take corrective action or prepare for the manoeuvres that the system would force on him. The signal shown in the HUD is two chevrons or arrows on the outer edge of the HUD moving to the centre. The moment that those two chevrons make contact in the centre a flash on the HUD combined with the aural warning in the pilot's helmet informs him that the AGCAS will make a maximum AoA recovery. After the recovery the AGCAS will give the pilot the aural signal to inform him he is back in control. The computer uses different sources such as GPS, terrain database, altimeter radar and speed among others to calculate the time the plane would need to take corrective measures to avoid crashing. The minimum descent altitude is selected by the pilot before the start of a mission. The operational version should be something between 50 ft and 150 ft. Things to take into account for the AGCAS are AoA, angle of bank, speed, altitude and the terrain and other obstacles in the immediate surroundings (for the Gripen most of this information is already collected by the NINS installed for the new landing system). Flight tests from Edwards AFB were flown from 8 July 1998 to 5 November 1998 – a total of thirty flights equalling 38.3 hours were flown in that period. During those thirty flights more than 350 test manoeuvres were flown by Swedish and US pilots. The Swedish pilots that participated in the flight-testing were Bjorn

Johansson from the FMV and Saab Chief test pilot Ola Rignell. The US pilots were from Lockheed Martin and the 416th FTS. The system was near nuisance-free, but the nuisance warnings that still came up were mainly due to TRN system errors, GPS system coverage blanks and discrepancies in the INS. GPS coverage blanks happen mostly during heavy manoeuvring when the antenna on the plane loses contact with the GPS satellites.

In fact, during a conference called Technology versus Terrorism, James O'Bryon (the deputy assistant secretary, US DoD deputy director, operation test and evaluation) recalled being at Edwards AFB where the Auto GCAS was test flown. The Auto GCAS was functioning so well that they tried the ultimate test for the Auto GCAS – trying to crash the aircraft deliberately. They tried fourteen times and each time the system took over and saved the plane and the pilot. Even after the test programme in the US was finished it was said that the Auto GCAS was 95 per cent ready. After the finalisation of the joint project the 412th FTS got funding to further test and improve the system.

The programme was so successful that another one was initiated but this time with the cooperation of Boeing as well. The first phase, the conceptual study, finished in May 2001. Boeing and Saab had the responsibility to each design the system algorithms in the first phase of the programme according to the eleven requirements that had been set.

Mid-air collision is the third leading cause for aircraft loss within the military. This was reason enough to do something about it. There were eleven requirements that the Auto ACAS (Auto Air-to-air Collision Avoidance System) would have to fulfil.

1. The system shall prevent air collisions between all aircraft (military and civil) and Unmanned Air Vehicles (UAVs). This is mainly because UAVs and military aircraft were to operate next to each other in any future missions.

2. The system shall operate with both manned and unmanned air vehicles. In a manned vehicle, the system will not interfere with normal pilot control of the vehicle except to prevent aircraft loss (ie it should be nuisance free). In an unmanned vehicle, the system will not interfere with normal operator control of the vehicle except to prevent aircraft loss.

3. The system must provide, as a last resort, an emergency manoeuvre to prevent collision with all other air vehicles. For a manned military aircraft, the ACAS initiation time is between ½ and 1½ seconds' time-to-escape prior to a collision.

4. The system shall provide a predictable response to avoid a collision; for example, one similar to that of an aware pilot or UAV operator.

5. The system shall not cause a collision with the ground during execution of an escape manoeuvre. The ACAS should therefore be able to communicate with or be connected with the AGCAS.

6. The escape manoeuvre shall only be long enough to avoid the collision and control of the aircraft must be released to the pilot immediately following clearance of the threat aircraft.

7. The system shall protect against unforeseen events that cause collisions.

8. The system must provide safe vehicle operation. It will be fully verified, validated, and tested with redundant elements as required. It will make extensive use of distributed integrity monitoring to ensure fail-safe operation without the use of brute-force redundancy.

9. The system will force a UAV to execute a collision avoidance manoeuvre prior to a manned aircraft.

10 The system shall have redundant elements to provide the necessary protection against failures.

11 The Auto ACAS system shall be designed for modularity and portability to enhance implementation onto multiple aircraft and UAV types, including military, civilian and commercial aircraft.

The second phase, the system design and flight–testing, started in August 2001. The best parts of each algorithm were to be further developed in a generic algorithm. Lockheed Martin was responsible for system integration into the VISTA F-16. The integration work was initiated during the autumn of 2002. According to Magnus Olsson, the Saab test pilot, the ACAS was tested in the Gripen simulator in Linköping by Swedish and US test pilots. The system will still allow for formation flying, but the aircraft will have an invisible safety area around itself calculated by the computer and the size will depend on speed and direction. If, for example, two aircraft are approaching each other and both would touch the safety areas around the aircraft the Auto ACAS system would activate and initiate a high g-manoeuvre to prevent a collision. The system was supposed to be based on data linked information but it should not be limited to that – other information sources were radar, FLIR and Infra Red Search and Track (IRST). Test-flying planned for June/July 2003 in the US under the lead of the AFRL. The flight-test programme was in fact completed with only the slightest of delays as the last flight of the ACAS programme occurred on 22 August 2003. During the flight-test programme a total of forty-three flight tests were flown, amounting to seventy-three flight hours.

The two described systems developed jointly were now being further developed separately by each partner for their own aircraft. The first US aircraft that was to be equipped with the systems was the F-35. The AGCAS system was to be evaluated for the first time on the A-3 prototype, which was the third CTOL prototype. The third CTOL prototype was due to fly in the second quarter of 2008 following the delay in 2004 but this was rescheduled. The F-35 will probably be either the first or the second operational aircraft to be equipped with this system depending on who is faster, the Swedish or the Americans. The ACAS has not been scheduled because the system was not mature enough in 2001 when the flight-testing schedule and the system requirements for block 1 to 3 were made. Block 4 could, however, have the ACAS system included if this is seen as a priority by the partners.

The AFRL initiated requests for further development of the AGCAS/ACAS in November 2006. The Automated Collision Avoidance/Fighter Risk Reduction Programme should provide AFRL with matured, modular designs for Automatic Ground Collision Avoidance System (AGCAS), Automatic Air Collision Avoidance System (ACAS) and integrated AGCAS/ACAS. Negotiations with Lockheed Martin had been completed by April 2007 and was followed by contract award on the 2 May 2007. The value of the contract was $34,475,885 cost plus fixed-fee.

In the US there was one organisation that was content to admit that both of the above systems would possibly save lives but would not remove the cause of the problem (spatial disorientation) and that was the AFRL at Wright Patterson AFB. The AFRL stated that the GCAS and ACAS take control from the pilot. A solution that keeps the pilot in control would be more desirable. This is easier said than done but research has been done to see if new technology can provide the answer.

Spatial disorientation is nothing new and all kinds of measures and technologies have been tried to reduce accidents mostly by training. According to the AFRL spatial disorientation costs the USAF on average $140 million annually. Furthermore, during Fiscal Year (FY) 1991–2000 slightly more than 20 per cent of the class A mishaps were due to spatial disorientation and they are equivalent to slightly less than 20 per cent of the fatalities. This was enough reason to do something about it. One area of research was a pathway in the sky presentation that could help the pilot in his spatial orientation. There are three types of spatial disorientation.

- Unrecognised: The pilot is not aware of his or her disorientation, and controls the aircraft completely in accord with and in response to a false orientational perception.
- Recognised: The pilot experiences a difference between what he feels the aircraft is doing and what the flight instruments tell him the aircraft is doing.
- Incapacitated: The pilot experiences a situation where he becomes incapacitated and is unable to react it.

The research is going to utilise the following technologies: visual attitude display symbology, 3-D localised audio and tactile stimulation. The 3-D technology and HMD technologies will find themselves in the F-35 anyway but for different reasons. It would make it easier for integration of this new system under development. The system called the Spatial Orientation Retention Device (SORD) was first to be evaluated in the fixed-based simulator, then in motion-based simulation and if the results grant it, also in flight. The AFRL believes that the SORD has a chance of succeeding because it is made up of different multi-sensory systems that should increase the pilot's situational awareness prior and during moments that spatial disorientation can occur.

VAAC Harrier

A Harrier technology demonstrator based at Boscombe Down in the UK was used to test an advanced Flight Control System (FCS). The Harrier under operation by the UK's DERA or later by QinetiQ is the second T2 prototype, XW175. The first T2 prototype crashed early in its career so it can be said without exaggeration that it is the oldest two-seat Harrier flying. VAAC stands for Vector thrust Aircraft Advanced flight Control and that was the purpose of the aircraft for many years before it was utilised for the JSF programme. The aircraft had been upgraded to T4 standard and after that the back cockpit was upgraded to a full authority Fly By Wire (FBW) cockpit with the front cockpit retaining conventional

Shipborne Rolling Vertical Landing has been proven on the VAAC Harrier with success on the French aircraft carrier *Charles de Gaulle*. Even after service entry of the F-35B it remains to be seen if the VAAC Harrier can be suitably replaced as it is really unique and most importantly it is a dual seater. *Crown Copyright Qinetiq*

The VAAC Harrier achieved the first automated landing, a major milestone in the development of a system to decrease the workload of the pilot during carrier landings. *Crown Copyright Qinetiq*

controls for safety purposes. The aft cockpit control inceptors, the throttle and stick, are completely disconnected from the conventional FCS. Instead, all inputs are routed through the Flight Control Computer (FCC). The safety pilot was helped by an on-board monitoring system, which is a software-based system that evaluates the FBW system being flown by the evaluation pilot in the back seat. The Independent Monitor (IM), as the on-board monitoring system is known, will disconnect the back-seat cockpit if a dangerous situation occurs and give full control to the front-seat security pilot. This VAAC Harrier is the only STOVL research aircraft with such a capability. It is unique and therefore ideally suited for new control technologies for any future supersonic STOVL fighter.

The Harrier, with its ingenious technology, was getting rather old. The technology dated from the 1960s. Since then FBW aircraft had become the standard and there were three reasons to look at improvements as the aircraft presented the

The Vector thrust Aircraft Advanced flight Control (VAAC) Harrier seen here approaching HMS *Invincible* for an automatic landing. *Crown Copyright Qinetiq*

pilot with a high workload during the V/STOL flight regime. The high workload during the STOVL flight phase could result in cognitive failures, which in turn could lead to the loss of the aircraft and more importantly the pilot.

According to Squadron Leader Justin Paines, RAF pilot, and James W. Denham, from the US Naval Air Warfare Center Aircraft Division. (NAWCAD) there were four reasons to improve the mechanical FCS of the Harrier:

1. The accident rate for the Harrier in the V/STOL regime is much higher than for the take-off and landing regime for any other conventional aircraft in the UK inventory (source: RAF Inspectorate of Flight Safety Database). The USMC has a higher accident rate with its Harriers as well.

2. The training burden is substantial. New pilots spend eight months converting to the Harrier at the RAF Operational Conversion Units (OCU). This compares with a four and a half-month course for the Sepecat Jaguar, an aircraft that had a similar operational role in the UK.

3. The high workload associated with recovering the Harrier to a vertical landing on board a ship results in more restrictive weather minima in which recovery can be performed safely, when compared, for example, with helicopter operations.

4. The Harrier is a demanding aircraft to fly; only those pilots who have performed well through training can then be sent to this aircraft with the confidence that they will successfully complete their training. The Harrier, therefore, tends to absorb a disproportionate number of good-quality trainee pilots, which constitutes a significant manning constraint for service planning.

As can be seen from the above the cost of training a Harrier pilot is higher because the training period is longer. As a result of the higher workload during the STOVL flight regime more cognitive failures occur, resulting in a higher accident rate, which is also expensive to the service. The higher workload restricted operations during certain weather types; operational restrictions are in wartime of course a danger. The best pilots were required for the Harrier units meaning that the other units did not get the right mix of people, having a possible effect on the quality and balance of the other units.

Basically, the handling qualities were to be improved; if the handling qualities were easier the training would be open to more pilots. The risk of cognitive error should be reduced or if possible removed entirely. This would reduce the accident rate to match conventional aircraft and the safety rate of those is ever increasing. Furthermore, the aircraft should have carefree handling, meaning that the aircraft cannot depart from controlled flight.

The actual work on a new control system was initiated in 1990. The aircraft was upgraded and it was not until 1994 that the VAAC Harrier was ready for a test flight. The system that had been developed was called Unified control. Although the development was not financed under the JAST programme office the system was evaluated by pilots from the UK and the US. The new Unified control was acclaimed by the UK pilots but criticised by the pilots from the US.

As soon as the flight-test evaluation was completed DERA continued with phase two of the programme by the end of 1994. The VAAC Harrier aircraft was returned again to the hangar for preparation and modification. In 1996 the VAAC Harrier emerged from the hangar again for a test flight.

The DERA programme pilot from February 1996 was Flt Lt Justin Paines (at the time he joined) and he was responsible for the programme. He prepared the flight programme for the other JSF pilots from the Boeing and Lockheed teams. The three flight control modes evaluated were called Unified, Change mode and Fusion. The three systems used different ways of controlling the Harrier during high-gain tasks. The new control modes and inceptors were meant to replace the current operational Harriers system, which includes a nozzle control lever that is located beside the throttle. If either were activated mistakenly it would result almost certainly in a disastrous loss of the plane and sometimes even the loss of the pilot. The three control units (throttle, control stick and nozzle control lever) are all called inceptors. The throttle and the nozzle control lever are both termed Left Hand Inceptor (LHI) and the control stick the Right Hand Inceptor (RHI). One of the RHIs used came from the Experimental Aircraft Program (EAP) technology demonstrator, which was used to develop technology for the Eurofighter Typhoon. The test flights that were initiated in 1996 culminated in a flight evaluation by a group of international pilots. The nine pilots were from different services, of which four pilots had no Harrier experience. Ship experience was not relevant as all tests performed would be land based. The pilots were from the following services:

- Three pilots from the USMC.
- Two pilots from the USAF.
- Two pilots from the RAF.
- One pilot from the USN.
- One pilot from the RN.

The evaluation was initiated in December 1998 and was completed in February 1999. During the evaluation the nine pilots accumulated sixty-five sorties. To be as objective as possible the pilots flew the different control modes (that is Fusion, Unified and Change mode) in different following order. The result of this evaluation was that both the Fusion and Unified control modes showed promise. The Change mode would, however, not be pursued further.

Lockheed intended to use a sidestick control similar to the one used on the F-22 Raptor and F-16 Fighting Falcon. It was, however, questionable if such a system was suitable for STOVL operations. Lockheed Martin, aware of the VAAC Harrier's capabilities, contracted DERA in 1998 to evaluate a sidestick. For this reason a sidestick RHI was installed in the rear cockpit. The throttle and the FBW controls were altered as well. The first flight with the RHI as a sidestick was flown on 24 August 1998 with Justin Paines and British Aerospace's Simon Hargreaves at the controls. The VAAC flight-test programme lasted thirty-six flights (a little more than twenty flight hours) and demonstrated satisfactorily that sidestick control was possible during STOVL missions. As the programme was funded by Lockheed Martin it was only natural that Lockheed sent its own pilots to participate in the evaluation. The Lockheed Martin pilots that participated in the programme were Tom Morgenfeld and Joe Sweeney. Furthermore, two USMC pilots that participated in this evaluation were Major Art Tomassetti and Major Jeff Karnes, who would fly the X-35 and the X-32 respectively. From 2002 the VAAC Harrier has flown exclusively with sidestick to facilitate workload comparisons with the actual end product.

As already stated both the Fusion and Unified control modes required further development. The further development was called the Follow-on Research Program (FRP). The funding came together in late 1999 and came from the Italian MoD Joint Strike Fighter Concept Demonstration Phase (CDP) contribution. As foreign pilots' participation in the CDP was limited the opportunity was taken to include two Italian pilots in the evaluation.

The JSF vehicle control Integrated Product Team (IPT) wanted not only to develop further the control modes but also to evaluate them in more realistic conditions, ie at sea. The problem was that during the EMD the first chance to evaluate these control modes at sea was in the 2007–2008 timeframe if there were no delays. It was clear that for the purpose of risk reduction further testing would be requires.

In 2000 the flight-test programme was picked up again where it had been left in 1999 in support of the JSF programme. Six pilots, including two Italians, were again put together for evaluation of the improvements on the two remaining flight control modes. The test programme was divided into two parts: a land-based portion followed by a ship-based portion.

Pilot	Service	Primary platform	STOVL experience	Shipboard experience	Primary mode
A	RAF	Harrier	Extensive	Minimal	Unified
B	RAF	Harrier	Extensive	None	Fusion
C[†]	RN	Harrier	Extensive	Extensive	Unified
D	USN	F-18	None	Extensive	Fusion
E	Italian AF	Tornado	None	None	Unified
F[†]	Italian Navy	Harrier	Extensive	Extensive	Fusion

[†] These pilots only participated in the land-based evaluation as they had extensive shipboard STOVL experience and the aim was to gain feedback from pilots with no or little experience with shipboard handling. The other reason was the limited time available. Pilot A was QinetiQ pilot Justin Paines.

During October 2000 the land-based trials were initiated with the goal of making the pilots proficient with the control mode prior to giving them the task formally to evaluate the control mode. During the land-based evaluation the six pilots amassed fifty-six flights. The shipboard flight tests were performed in December 2000 on board the Royal Navy aircraft carrier HMS *Invincible*. Squadron Leader Justin Paines, one of the RAF test pilots, had a busy programme as in the meantime he participated in the JSF CDP flight demonstrations. He flew two missions in the X-35A CDA in the US in the middle of November 2000. The trials were planned to take ten days; this meant the team had to average nine vertical recoveries per day to allow every pilot to complete all the planned test points in both primary and secondary control modes. This was quite aggressive as testing on board a ship is highly influenced by the weather and in December the weather is not at its best. As a risk-reduction measure during the shipboard trials it was decided that the Short Take Off (STO) would be performed with the normal Harrier controls by the safety pilot. When ready for the actual evaluation of the control modes the aircraft was handed over to the evaluation pilot. The four pilots accumulated fifty-four sorties during the shipboard evaluation. After conclusion of shipboard trials development of Fusion proceeded at such a pace that in June 2001 four pilots had the chance to evaluate an improved version of the Fusion mode called Enhanced Fusion mode. Of the four pilots three were Harrier pilots and one was an F-18 pilot. Each pilot flew four times to evaluate the improvements.

According to Justin Paines the consensus of the government's opinion weighed in favour of Enhanced Fusion by a narrow margin and this mode-type is recommended for implementation in advanced STOVL platforms. However, the choice of which mode to implement may come down to trade studies regarding pilot/vehicle interface limitations or inceptor availability, meaning that Unified still might be the control mode integrated in the yet to be selected PWSC.

When in October 2001 the Lockheed Martin team won the contract to build the F-35 QinetiQ was not awarded a contract despite all its work because Lockheed Martin wanted to use an in-house developed control mode. After a lot of pressure from the JSF programme office, Lockheed dropped its own control mode and selected QinetiQ to provide the control system. On 6 August 2002 Lockheed Martin selected the Unified control mode for the STOVL JSF. The reason for this choice was that there was no need for a thumbwheel and it turned out that the government's preference for the Enhanced Fusion mode stemmed from a fear that Unified was too radical to be adopted. In essence the Unified control mode was the best option available.

On 1 June 2001 QinetiQ also announced that it had used the VAAC Harrier to prove that an automated recovery was possible. During a programme called autoland, the ultimate test, the aircraft was flown to a point some 30 miles from the Boscombe Down test site. From that point the test pilot required from the guidance system a recovery trajectory that also took into account obstructions like local air space restrictions. The aircraft should find a moving spot back at the airbase, which was a simulated ship. The aircraft guidance system should descend and decelerate the aircraft until it performed a controlled hover alongside the moving spot that simulated the ship. The system worked on a relative GPS system. In other words the moving spot (simulated ship) location (GPS measurement), direction and speed were transmitted by data link to the aircraft. The aircraft's guidance system calculated a trajectory using its own GPS-measured location to the ship's data linked GPS location, the ship's data linked direction and speed, and the aircraft's speed. The pilots monitored the guidance system to the recovery area and did not need to interfere with the systems; it was so-called hands-free operation. The demonstration ended successfully when the aircraft hovered alongside the simulated ship. This was the first step in the development of a Joint Precision Automatic Landing System (JPALS) for a STOVL aircraft. The plan was to develop the system further to allow the aircraft actually to make an automatic landing without any pilot input. At this point it was not sure if the test would be land-based or ship-based. It was planned for the VAAC Harrier to be used again by the Integrated Test Force in 2004 for more STOVL control law flight-testing in connection with the sidestick control unit planned for introduction in the production types. The sidestick received excellent marks during high-gain tasks from both pilots and landing signal officers when the FCLPs were performed during the CDP with the X-35 demonstrator aircraft. Also the recovery test that was performed in the first half of 2001 for the autoland programme was further developed QinetiQ announced at Farnborough 2004 on 29 July. The Harrier performed a few manual approaches and landings on board HMS *Invincible* to evaluate the QinetiQ GPS systems on the Harrier as a risk-reduction effort at sea in preparation for the final test that was expected in 2005. The guidance system should work through all the steps and after each step the pilot should press a button to give the system the go-ahead to the next phase. The pilots that were involved in Unified Control risk reduction flights in December 2004 were Lt Schenk USMC, Lt Cdr Hayde RN, Mr. Tomlinson BAE Systems, Lt Col Cassidy USAF, Mr Knowles LM, Lt Col Sizoo and USAF, Lt Col Karnes USMC who was also involved in the flight testing the Boeing X-32.

From 9 to 18 May 2005 the VAAC Harrier was deployed to HMS *Invincible* for trials with an automatic landing system developed by QinetiQ under the autoland programme described above. The JPALS was funded by the US JSF programme office and the UK MoD Joint Combat Aircraft Integrated Project Team. During the period aboard HMS *Invincible* the Harrier made about thirty flights, during which over a hundred landings aboard HMS *Invincible* were executed culminating with the automatic landing performed by test pilot Justin Paines. The aim of the programme was to reduce pilot workload during landing so less pilot training would be required with the Harrier, and in the words of Justin Paines to make the task of bringing the aircraft back to the ship as trivial as possible. The technology demonstrated should open the way for easier ship-based UAV recovery.

Unified control is ready for first flight of the F-35B planned for May 2008. Unified Control however, may have some modifications to reduce the workload of the pilots even more and these were evaluated in February 2007. The Qinetiq and JSF programme office were studying some 'sub-modes' that could be added to the basic concept of Unified Control, including Translational Rate Command for the hover, where cockpit inceptors control a rate instead of an acceleration, and height rate control versus height acceleration control. The pilots involved in this testing were Lt Col Sizoo from the USAF, along with Mr Wilson from BAE Systems, Mr Tomlinson from BAE Systems, Lt Schenk from the USMC, Sqn Ldr Hackett from the RAF and Lt Sewell from USN.

Land-based Rolling Vertical Landings (RVL) are a routine with Harrier units. A requirement for the JSF STOVL version to be able to perform a land based RVL has always existed. This capability was now evaluated for shipboard operations. As a result of the F-35B's greater useable wing lift at low speeds, it is possible to either land with increased payloads or to reduce the stress loads on the propulsion system. Reduced stress loads lead to extended propulsion system life. Ship-borne RVL capability would add operational flexibility to ship-based units. The MOD has stated: 'Consideration of the aerodynamic performance of JSF, together with the available deck area of CVF design, has shown that significant benefits could be realised by extending the principles of land-based RVL to ship-borne operations and the UK is keen to exploit this opportunity.'

The UK was cooperating with the French on their new aircraft carrier design, Future Carrier Vessels (CVF) and in the spirit of that cooperation the evaluation of the RVL capability was performed on the French aircraft carrier *Charles de Gaulle*. One of the reasons for selecting the *Charles de Gaulle* was that the CVF will have a similar deck size.

Qinetiq deployed the VAAC Harrier to the French naval air base at Hyeres on 14 June 2007. The ship RVL trials were held on 19 and 20 June 2007. During those two days six evalution flights were flown and eighteen ship Rolling Vertical Landings were performed. Those flights were flown by Lt Chris Gotke as the safety pilot and the evaluation pilots were Justin Paines from Qinetiq, Sqn Ldr Hackett from the RAF and Lt Bachmann from the USMC. After the trials on 20 June the VAAC Harrier returned to Hyeres. The following day it returned to the UK.

Joint Precision Approach and Landing System (JPALS)

The SDD contract was modified on 24 February 2004. Originally the JSF was to be equipped with the Automatic Carrier Landing System (ACLS). This system was to be removed and replaced by the Joint Precision Approach and Landing System (JPALS). The modification has a value of $52.447.827 and contractual work should be completed by April 2012. Originally the ACLS was stated in the JORD as a "I like capability", meaning that it was not essential technology. JPALS on the other hand is a relative new system that requires no extra equipment on the aircraft. The only requirement is that a communications radio and/or data link is modified to function for the network requirement of the JPALS. On aircraft carriers however, the replacement of the ACLS will save more then 600 cubic feet and 9000 pounds. Furthermore the JPALS can replace the Instrument Landing System (ILS) at air force bases, that is, when current aircraft receive this system or are replaced. Development dates back to a requirement statement in 1992. The seriousness of the requirement gained momentum after a military transport aircraft landing accident in Bosnia in 1996. ARINC's Satellite Navigation & Air Traffic Control and Landing Systems (SATNAV & ATCALS) division received a contract to develop a system for the US Navy so that a tactical aircraft could land 'hands off' on a moving aircraft carrier. This required unprecedented precision as the allowable landing area on an aircraft carrier is only 20 ft (6.1 meters) wide and 130 ft long. The tactical aircraft must also stay exactly on the center line, since other aircraft are parked just 20 feet (6.1 meters) off either wingtip. Another challenge, besides landing on a very short and very narrow runway, is that also happens to be rising, falling, rolling and yawing.

In January 2001, The VX-23 Salty Dogs flew fully automatic approaches in an F/A-18A, nose number 110. A major milestone was achieved when the same aircraft made the first complete automatic deck landing on the USS *Theodore Roosevelt* (CVN-71) April 23, 2001. This was repeated several times during the same and following day, accumulating ten auto-coupled landings. As the system relies on GPS and safety is a major issue the system was also tested at Holloman AFB. A different aircraft was used this time, a USAF C-12J, a military version of the successful Raytheon Aircraft's Beech 1900C Airliner. 276 approaches were flown in clear air and in jamming conditions during the months of July and August 2001. Crews of the C-12J stated that the JPALS worked perfectly under all circumstances and that it was hardly noticeable if jamming took place. At the time of testing, the US GPS constellation comprised of 24 satellites circling the globe almost twice a day. The important feature is that at anytime four of these satellites would send a signal to a receiver be they on a ground station or on an aircraft. A JPALS developed by Raytheon was also tested for compatibility with the civil aviation world on a Federal Express Boeing 727-200. This made 16 approaches and six fully automatic landings during August 2001.

The technology demonstrations, although highly succesfull and performed in a short period of time, were unfortunately not sufficient for integration into tactical aircraft. The

Here seen during trials preceding the first automatic landing. The aircraft is complete with the JPALS title on its fuselage. Salty Dog 110 over the USS *Theodore Roosevelt*. This demonstration proved it could be done shortly before it became a requirement for the F-35C. *US Navy*

anti-jam GPS antennas were too large at the time for the JPALS programme office. Anti-jam GPS antennas were 14 inches with full capability or 7 inches with a significantly reduced performance. A requirement existed for a miniature anti-jam GPS antenna with a reduced size of 4.5 inches.

Two of the competitors of the JPALS programme, Arinc and Raytheon, announced that they would bid together for the next phase. As a result of their history in the JPALS programme they were considered front runners.

Data Fusion Risk Reduction

After the F-35 had been chosen Lockheed Martin and its partners had to show that they could work within budget and minimise risk. For this purpose Lockheed Martin in cooperation with Northrop Grumman initiated a nine-month two-phased flight-test programme. The sensor suite of the F-35 was to be the most advanced and complex ever flown. Experience with the F-22 proved and continued to prove that data fusion was an underestimated problem. A requirement review for the data fusion risk-reduction programme was held in August 2002. During the first phase only the sensors would be tested; this phase was to last three months. For the second phase, which was due to start in November 2003 and last six months, the sensors would be connected to the fusion software developed by Lockheed Martin. Risk reduction was mostly aimed at avionics software fusion, which would be phase two.

The flight tests began on 8 August 2003 with a first flight lasting 1.6 hours in a BAC 1-11 owned by Northrop Grumman Electronic Systems. It was equipped with the Electro Optical Targeting Demonstration System (EOTDS) delivered by Lockheed Martin Missiles

Fire Control located in Orlando. The EOTDS was a modified system from the CDP with the capability of IRST acquisition and tracking of airborne targets. The BAC 1-11 used for these trials was the N162W. Risk-reduction flights were initiated from Patuxent River Naval Air Warfare Center (NAWC). The BAC 1-11 used was equipped with two Electro Optical (EO) sensors recorded the imagery for evaluation on the ground. A third EO sensor would be added later in the flight-test programme. Besides the cockpit crew the aircraft was equipped with places for thirteen operators. During the first two flights the EOTDS sensors were evaluated. The EOTDS used had some limitations:

- COTS turret movement restrictions.
  Field of View (FOV) +/- 70 degrees azimuth and +5 to -90 elevation.
  Azimuth maximum track rate approximately 25–30 degrees per minute.

Inertial transfer of alignment differences.

No laser ranging.

Shortly after this flight a fourth-generation Active Electronically Scanned Array (AESA) multi-radar built by Northrop Grumman Electronic Systems was installed and test-flown on the third flight on 4 September 2003 in the same BAC 1-11. The radar was a modified CDP radar capable of the required air-to-air functions. At about this time the priority was still sensor check-out tests. The EO-DAS had its first flight a few days later on 9 September 2003. The third EO camera was installed for its first flight, which occurred on 24 November 2003. It was the eighth flight in the risk-reduction programme. During all these flights until the twelfth flight a T-39 Saberliner was used as a target aircraft for the sensors. On the thirteenth flight, the first flight in the new year on the 30 January 2004, for the first time two targets were used instead of one and both targets were T-39 Saberliners. The T-39 Saberliners were provided by Northrop Grumman. For the following flight for the first time an F-18 was used as a target. The flight was used for sensor characterisation of the EOTDS; this would be repeated on the nineteenth flight but this time the sensors were tested against flares. From this moment the flight-test programme gained some speed. However, it was not until the twenty-fourth flight on 11 March 2004 that all the systems were used together for

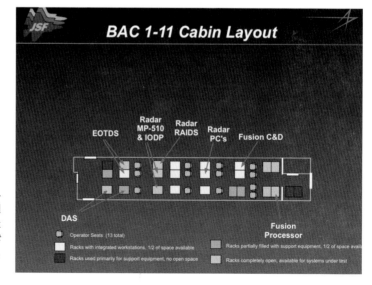

Layout of the Northrop-Grumman BAC 1-11 used for the data fusion risk reduction. *Copyright Lockheed Martin.*

the first time through the fusion avionics software. For this first full fusion flight a T-39 Saberliner was used as a target.

From flight twenty-nine the flight tests concerned fusion integration and all the systems were used from this flight onward during the remainder of the flight-test programme. Fusion integration was considered completed after flight thirty-four on 30 April 2004. Flight thirty-five was used as a final system check-out, which was successfully passed on 9 June 2004. After that flight different scenarios were test-flown and from this flight on only F-18s were used as targets. A total of fifty-three flights were flown by the BAC 1-11 aircraft culminating in a total of 110.3 hours and during the last five flights it had three F-18s flying simultaneously as targets during each flight. The T-39 Sabreliners that flew as targets during twenty-nine of those flights accumulated 67.2 hours plus one flight to test-fly the Advanced Range Data System (ARDS) pod. Each target aircraft had to have at least one functional ARDS pod for the test flights to be able to go ahead. The ARDS instrumentation and the F-18 target aircraft were provided by Patuxent River NAWC.

Environment Evaluation for STOVL Aircraft

This is not really a technology development programme but it was important as it provided a knowledge baseline to which future testing could be referred. The JSF programme office realised that the ground environment around a fighter taking off or landing vertically would have an effect that had to be studied. Both competitors had different approaches in their design. The JSF programme office wanted, however, to have a baseline to which it could compare the two designs and for this reason it decided to map important ground environment parameters so that it could compare them at a later stage with the X-32B and X-35B.

The ground environment is formed by temperature, pressure and acoustic levels. Acoustic levels are important because the STOVL JSF was supposed to operate from ships. The noise levels had to be acceptable. For example, eight-hour daily average noise exposure should not exceed 84 dBA and for every 4 dBA above this, exposure time should be cut in half according to the US Navy standards under which the USMC falls. The noise levels were measured far field, near field and in the cockpit. In the cockpit the noise level was measured with a microphone on the pilot's helmet and in the pilot's helmet under the protective earcup to record the noise level at the pilot's ear.

Temperature levels depend on the exhaust temperature. The exhaust will impinge from the tarmac to the sides and bounce up back to the aircraft – this phenomenon is called fountain flow. The place where the fountain flow meets the aircraft fuselage can reach higher temperatures and is therefore not suitable for appliqués, at least for the time being as existing appliqués would not be able to survive the temperatures that would be incurred. As the JSF programme office was evaluating appliqués for the replacement of the paint topcoat, this was highly relevant.

Pressure levels are shaped by the speed of the exhaust. One fear was that if the afterburner was required during the landing and or take-off that shipboard personnel could be blown off the carrier like confetti. Pressure in combination with heat could also damage the surface and that could have Foreign Object Damage as a side effect.

To create this baseline the JSF funded a flight-test programme with an AV-8B Harrier, BuNo 163854, which was assigned to the Naval Weapon Test Squadron at NAS China Lake. This particular AV-8B Harrier was equipped with a Rolls-Royce F402-RR-408 engine; this was important so that the exact propulsion system was specified to the baseline. The only modification to the aircraft was the application of temperature-sensitive tape.

Although the aircraft was assigned to NAS China Lake the tests took place at NAS Patuxent River. Testing started on 8 July 1997 and was completed on 11 July 1997. During this time a total of fifty-nine test points were accumulated, which equalled about one hour of recorded material that could be evaluated. The main objective was to measure the outwash velocity, temperature and acoustic noise at specific ground heights with regard to aircraft distance, heading and height Above Ground Level during hover and ground high power (no-go VTO) operations. Other objectives included evaluating the suitability of the test methods and procedures and of the candidate high-response transducers for future tests.

The tests were performed from a VTOL pad made of AM-2, which is an extruded aluminium planking with a non-skidding coating. It is used by the USMC for expeditionary airfields and VTOL pads. Temperatures of the VTOL pad material were measured during the no-go VTO.

Air Vehicle Prognostic and Health Management (AVPHM)

On 1 July 1997 the JSF programme office published a Broad Area Announcement 97-1 (BAA) requesting proposals for systems that could reliably predict system failures or malfunctions to prevent catastrophic failures. The JSF programme office was looking into three areas:

- Turbo jet engine rotor disk crack detection.
- Real time engine oil debris detection and analysis.
- Aircraft cables and connectors fault detection.

The first two technologies were supposed to be mature enough for demonstration in ground engine testing planned for fiscal year 1999. The third technology had one more year for development and realistic tests were required no later than fiscal year 2000. Three small contracts were awarded to small businesses at a total value of $2.8M. The three contracts were awarded to:

- Expertech Inc. for real-time oil debris detection and analysis.
- Foster Miller Inc. for on-line infra red oil condition monitoring.
- Management Sciences Inc. for cable and connector faults and failures.

Besides these three contracts four other contracts were provided to the main players in the CDP: Boeing for $8 million; Lockheed Martin for $8 million; Pratt & Whitney for $7 million; and General Electric for $5 million to perform Prognostic and Health Management (PHM) research in support of their CDP design and ultimately their PWSC proposal.

On 10 October 1997 Lockheed Martin announced that it had received a contract from the JSF programme office to demonstrate a proof of concept prototype of a PHM subsystem. The PHM subsystem will be used to store information about the health of the aircraft's systems and components. The PHM will also process the information and send the information to the maintenance crew by secure data link. The system should also be able to diagnose the problem and therefore tell the maintenance crew exactly which Line Replaceable Unit (LRU) or part should be repaired or replaced. This PHM subsystem is possible as a result of progress made in the sensor technology. The aim of the system is to reduce maintenance time and cost by minimising the need for preventive maintenance as the preventive maintenance could be carried out on the basis of measured wear and tear instead of any average approximate. The AVPHM system would have separate controllers under which the then different technology would fall. The separate Reasoners as they are called are:

- Propulsion Area Reasoner
- Avionics Area Reasoner electronics RF prognostics
- Structural Area Reasoner
- Other Area Reasoner (VMS, Subsystems, Signature)

The propulsion reasoner has a lot of subsystems; the most interesting exterior system is the Ingested Debris Monitoring System (IDMS). This monitors if any foreign objects are ingested by the engine, which can damage the engine. Other monitoring systems are:

- Oil Condition Monitor (OCM)
- Engine Distress Monitoring System (EDMS)
- Electrostatic Bearing Monitor (EBM)
- Electrostatic Oil Debris Monitor (EODM)
- Advanced Life Algorithms and Component Health Assessment (ALACHA)

On 27 March 1998 Lockheed Martin was awarded a modification to the earlier contract involving AVPHM and the Joint Distributed Information System (JDIS). The added value was US $6,138,388 and the research and development was to continue until February 2001. The JDIS is a data link-based system, which forwards the PHM's information to the maintenance crew so that spares can be ordered or even so that the order form is ready for sending. Spares should also be located by the system. The system can inform the unit commander when the aircraft will be available again for a mission, so it should help with mission planning as well. The JDIS should also be able to send the black box's information as well. This would all reduce down time and increase aircraft availability and therefore increase operational effect.

On 5 June 2000 Lockheed Martin announced that its prototype of the AVPHM and the

The C-17 T-1 in flight on 4 December 2003 for the JSF Propulsion Health Management programme. An unlikely aircraft for a fighter aircraft technology demonstrator. *NASA (Jim Ross)*

JDIS had proven itself during a simulation, which involved two aircraft flying together on a mission. In one aircraft a radar system failure was artificially induced. The time that the radar would remain functioning was predicted. The information was forwarded to the in-flight mission replanning software.

The replanning software calculated the options and then presented the options to the pilot of the simulated affected aircraft. The pilot selected the preferred option and shut down his radar. Through the JDIS he received radar information from the healthy aircraft and was able to complete the mission. Meanwhile, the PHM made a health report and using the JDIS sent it back to the home base. This means that a failure of an avionics system does not necessarily mean the end of a mission. The Autonomic Logistics System (ALS) was employed as well during the simulation. As soon as the ALS received the health report it started looking for the location of a replacement for the broken part and selecting which technician was properly trained to replace the broken item. The system continued to select a computer-based refresher course for the technician so he did not have to look up any information if required.

A NASA-sponsored technology maturation programme was used by Pratt & Whitney to test and mature the sensors for the PHM of the F135 engine. The flight-test programme was sponsored by NASA Dryden, Glen and Ames research centres. The programme achieved a milestone in 2001 and started using a C-17 (prototype T-1) for flight tests so that the functioning of the sensors could be tested in flight conditions. The C-17 T-1 belonged to the C-17 System Program Office (SPO) and for this reason NASA Dryden signed an agreement with the C-17 SPO to use the aircraft for the evaluation of Propulsion Control and Health Management (PCHM) technologies. The flight-test schedule was, however, mutually coordinated.

Four Pratt & Whitney F117 turbofan engines power the C-17 Globemaster. The F117 is a further development and derivative of the PW2000 engine used on the commercial Boeing 757. The C-17 T-1 was the first prototype and was therefore fully instrumented. The vehicle data acquisition system is capable of recording the parameters of the entire aircraft, including the four engines. The vehicle data acquisition system had reserve capacity to record data obtained from the additional sensors installed in engine #3, making the aircraft ideal for the purpose as minimum alterations would be required for the test flights.

For this programme, called the Propulsion Health Management (PHM) flight-test programme, only engine #3 was equipped beyond the so-called typical Bill Of Material (BOM) meaning that only this engine was used to evaluate the new sensors. The sensors tested on engine #3 were:

- EDMS
- High Frequency Vibration Sensor (HFVS)
- IDMS
- Stress Wave Analysis Sensor (SWAN)

Just like the IDMS, the EDMS measures the electrostatic charge of debris. The EDMS, however, measures this at the exhaust of the engine and for this reason was located in the upper actuator housing of the thrust reverser casing. During normal operation an engine will have metal parts in the exhaust as a result of erosion. However, an increase in metal parts indicates a problem.

The ability of the EDMS to recognise what the debris comprises could help diagnose the problem. The source could be ingested debris, erosion or possibly blade rub. The EDMS was installed on the C-17 T-1 during October 2001. The EDMS detected debris efficiently and perhaps more importantly it did not generate any false alarms.

A total of three HFVSs were installed on engine #3. Each one was fitted at a different location: one on the gear box, one on engine case flange B (forward) and the third on engine case flange P (aft). Each sensor tracked the high frequency response of the components being monitored.

The IDMS was installed on the C-17 T-1 during October 2001. It was removed in July 2002 as one of the sensors became unbonded. The IDMS sensor is a conductive metallic strip and if it had come loose entirely the results could have been catastrophic for engine #3. The C-17 is designed to be able to take off and land from unprepared strips; its engines ingest non-hazardous debris such as sand during the previously mentioned flight phases. It was important to establish if the IDMS could detect this kind of debris. The IDMS was designed not only to detect the debris, but also its size, quantity, velocity and to a lesser extent its composition. During the time that the sensors were installed any debris was properly detected and no false alarms were generated. The reason for the sensor becoming loose was under investigation.

It was announced on 7 December 2001 by Swantech, the company responsible for the SWAN sensor, that it had received a contract from Pratt & Whitney to deliver Swanview TM (sensor + accessories) for flight-testing on the C-17 T-1 operated jointly by NASA and the C-17 SPO. An important part of the evaluation was the capability to recognise false indications and reject them. However, the announcement was made rather late as the five SWAN sensors were installed on engine #3 during October 2001 according to NASA's Michael Venti, just like the EDMS and the IDMS. The SWAN sensors remained on the aircraft and as of March 2004 had generated no false alarms. Interestingly, NASA thought the SWAN technology to be in-between the Technology Readiness Level (TRL) 3 and 4. The lowest maturity or Technology Readiness Level is 1 while the highest Technology Readiness Level is 9. (for more info on TRL see Appendix 1)

The SWAN sensor measures structurally borne ultrasonic sound vibrations. If a break, friction, and/or shock occurs, it should be measured by the SWAN sensor. As the sensor is not mounted on the item being monitored, it has to be placed in a position that carries the mechanical sound path from the item monitored to the SWAN sensor. The five SWAN sensors are positioned on the engine gearbox and several flanges.

The fact that all the three sensors, EDMS, IDMS and SWAN, were installed and test-flown at the same time offered the opportunity to correlate measurements which were utilised.

An advanced PHM test system was expected to be flight-tested in 2005. By then the sensors would have more than hundreds hours of flight-testing, providing plenty of experience and time for the Pratt & Whitney engineers to mature the sensors and algorithms required.

For this programme more sensors were due to be test-flown but were too late to be included in the F135 development from the outset. The C-17 T-1 would continue test-flying new technologies and it would not be limited to the new sensor technologies described above but also other sensor technologies' algorithms and the software fusion of the measured data would be test-flown. The new technologies could, however, be integrated during engine upgrades. Operational requirements however had negative impact on aircraft availability for testing purposes.

The PHM technology proved to be an integral part of the ALS. The aim of the ALS was to reduce the cost of ownership. The ALS is a system that should provide the commander clear information about the status of the aircraft, the need for spare parts, the need for spares in the near future and the whereabouts of the spares, making it possible for the commander to increase Sortie Generation Rates (SGR).

Next Generation Transparency

A programme that was not originally initiated by the JAST or JSF office was the Next Generation Transparency (NGT) programme. This was initiated on 8 January 1997 by the Air Force Research Laboratory (AFRL) by issuing a Programme Research and Development Agreement (PRDA). It had the objective to prove the ability of the Injection Moulded Frameless Transparency Technology could meet the requirement of current and future missions but at reduced cost and maintenance. The requirements that the frameless canopy would have to fulfil are:

- Advanced abrasion resistant coatings
- Mission compatible coatings
- 500 Kt 4lb bird impact protection
- Emergency egress through the canopy
- Rapid transparency change out
- Combat hazard protection

Proposals were due by 7 March 1997. Boeing was awarded two contracts worth a total of $10.3M. The programme started with a Boeing presentation of their Integrated Product and Process Development (IPPD) on 10 September 1997. During a presentation by Robert E. McCarty from the AFRL on 1 October 1998, the JSF office agreed with the fact that because the Lockheed Martin F-22 Raptor canopy has been chosen initially as the technology demonstration platform, it would ensure that the new technology could be easily integrated as soon as the technology has been proven. This ensured that the technology would be ready for JSF production. For comparison, if the NGT produced a frameless F-16 canopy it would undergo nine production steps, while the original F-16 canopy would take 30 process steps and would have more than a 20% scrap rate after final optical tests. The ability to vary thickness would save weight and cost for material required for the Boeing JSF PWSC. The weight reduction was expected to be around 100lb. Other advantages expected were Life Cycle Cost reduction of bigger then 50% and part count reduction of 90%.

Explosive severance for egress through the canopy was tested on three full scale YF-22 canopies. The three demonstrations were successful and the Boeing JSF office considered the progress for this part of the project acceptable. It was demonstrated by October 2000 that the deep optical element parts exceeded the F-16 and F-22 specifications for optical distortion. After this, the design of full-scale demonstration of the NGT canopy was reviewed and shortly after approved. On 21 February 2001 it was decided on a cost and time constraints basis, that the Full Scale Development Article mould would be from P-20 tool steel. For the EMD phase of the programme the mould material could be changed to stainless steel. This decision was however to be made later. Several prototypes had been built, one for optical demonstration and another for structural demonstration. Optical surface demonstration took place in 2002. No agreement came fast for the Raptor programme, so to continue with the development, a mould for the T-38 windshield was produced. First flight of the T-38 injection moulded windshield was planned for October 2004. The NGT programme was progressing but in the mean time Pilkington Aerospace was given responsibility for the canopy using a relatively old production technique as it was used on the F-18C/D and the Saab Gripen, although in different shape.

CHAPTER 7

SYSTEM DEVELOPMENT AND DEMONSTRATION

This part of the development was formerly called the Engineering and Manufacturing Development (EMD) phase. The name of this phase was, however, changed as it had been tainted as a result of the EMD phase in the F-22 ATF programme.

Both teams had met the criteria or exceeded them but the Lockheed Martin design marginally exceeded it each time; the risk was considered lower and the future growth capability was considered larger. Immediately after the announcement of the winner of the JSF programme, the press inquired about the designation the aircraft would receive in service. The question probably took them by surprise and the answer given was the F-35. (Later on it was, however, denied that the designation was accidental.) The new F-35 designation stuck, further fuelling black project rumours, as the designations F-19 (F-19 was once allocated by the press to the F-117) and F-21 were still not in use but at least the heritage from the X-35 would be clear.

At the time of the signing of the System Development and Demonstration contract the first Low Rate Initial Production (LRIP) was planned as follows:

	Production run	F-35A CTOL	F-35B STOVL	F-35C CV	Total
LRIP lot I	Spring 2006 – Early 2009	6	4	0	10
LRIP lot II	Early 2007 – End 2009	14	8	0	22
LRIP lot III	Early 2008 – End 2010	20	20 + 5*	9	54
LRIP lot IV	Early 2009 – End 2011	30	32 + 9*	20	91
LRIP lot V	Early 2010 – End 2012	44	32 + 12*	32	120
LRIP lot VI	Early 2012 – End 2013	72	36 + 12*	48	168
Total		186	132 + 38*	109	465

*At the time of the contract being signed it was not decided yet which version the UK would choose and the choice was therefore not ranked under a particular type. The STOVL version was, however, the *raison d'être* of the British-American cooperation.

The announcement made by Ed Aldridge (the then Under Secretary of Defense for Acquisition, Technology and Logistics) on 26 October 2001 that Lockheed Martin had won paved the way to initiate the 126-month long System Development and Demonstration (SDD). The SDD officially started on 1 November 2001, which was a milestone called Authority To Proceed (ATP).

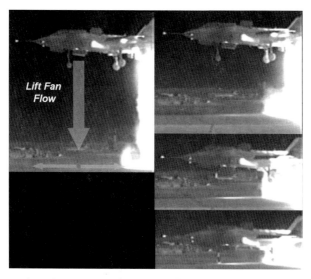

The infra-red images show how the cold air flow of the lift fan prevents the hot air from entering the main inlets which would kill the engine. This image shows the X-35B at different stages during the vertical landing. The Hot Gas Ingestion problem resolved by the forward downward thrust. *Team JSF*

A major question that was to be answered before the winner was announced was if the DoD should proceed with the winner takes all policy or whether it should force the winner to give the losing company a major part of the work to guarantee future competition. So when Lockheed Martin was announced as the winner the political discussion broke out as to whether Boeing should receive some of the work. Since the McDonnell Douglas team had lost and was dissolved, Northrop Grumman and BAE Systems had decided to team with Lockheed Martin, in return for a work-share of course; their respective work-shares were 18 per cent and 12 per cent. Lockheed Martin had discussions with Boeing but in January 2002 stated that its own work-share was actually very small, as a lot of work had to be given to foreign partners. Lockheed Martin would not be able to give Boeing a substantial work-share on the JSF. This was amplified by the end of 2003, when some of the partner countries started complaining about the work-share they were receiving, even though those same countries had previously agreed to work on the best value basis contracting. Lockheed had to sacrifice even that principle to keep everybody happy.

The main reason that Lockheed Martin won was the growth capacity of the lift fan technology. There were three important comparison factors used. They were thrust, airflow and exhaust velocity during STOVL operations. The direct lift engine (F119-611) at Intermediate Rated Thrust (IRT) – meaning any mid-level thrust setting less than military thrust but greater than idle – with the auxiliary air door open for increased airflow to the inlet, taken as the basis for comparison provided 100 per cent thrust. Compared with this the Shaft Driven Lift Fan (SDLF) system provided the same engine with 160 per cent thrust. This additional thrust translated into extra lifting capability that exceeded the extra weight incurred by the SDLF system by a factor of three.

Again, as the basis for comparison the direct lift engine provided 100 per cent exhaust airflow. The SDLF system-equipped engine provided 260 per cent exhaust airflow. The majority of this airflow was provided by the lift fan, which kept the temperature very close to ambient. This augmented airflow was also the source for the extra thrust. In fact the close to ambient airflow allowed for ground operations to take place within the same area as was possible with the AV-8B Harrier in service – a major plus.

The third factor, exhaust velocity, was again more favourable for the SDLF as compared with the direct lift system the exhaust velocity is 40 per cent lower. As the exhaust flow is divided over the four posts the velocity required is lower. The fact that the engine can be decoupled from the SDLF allows the engine to be optimised for up and away performance and no alterations to the engine are needed that would have a performance-reducing effect.

The production of the twenty-two prototypes would take place at the Lockheed Martin Fort Worth facility where in the future the F-35 will replace the F-16 production line. Fourteen of the prototypes were planned to be flying prototypes and the flight-test programme will encompass 10,000 flight hours. Seven prototypes were planned to be ground-test examples and the remaining prototype is for RCS testing (a pole model). Of the seven ground test prototypes for each version (CTOL, STOVL and CV) one would be structural and one would be a fatigue test bed, making six, and the remaining ground test aircraft would be used for specific tests required for the CV version, a so-called drop-test prototype. As the name suggests the aircraft will be dropped from different heights to test the landing gear and the structure as the aircraft will receive similar treatment during harsh landings in operational service.

According to the contract the first flight of the first CTOL prototype was planned for October 2005, forty-eight months after the ATP milestone. Lockheed Martin hoped to fly the first CTOL prototype two months before the contractual date. The first two prototypes are both CTOL prototypes and will be used for handling quality flight-testing. The following three CTOL flying prototypes were due to fly in 2006 and 2007. The five CTOL aircraft are responsible for about 42 per cent of the total flight-testing. One of the prototypes is due to be used for survivability tests in live fire exercises, similar to those that used to test the first Raptor prototype (4001). The aircraft will be filled with fuel and then go through simulated fighter manoeuvres then shot at and the damage will be evaluated and some structural or material changes might be introduced. The first STOVL aircraft would perform its first press up in early 2006 according to the contract. The STOVL version prototypes would be transferred as soon as possible to Patuxent River just like the CV prototypes. The first sea trials were planned for mid-2007 on a USN helicopter carrier, followed by tests in early 2008 on a Royal Navy aircraft carrier because of the Royal Navy's requirement of a ski-jump capability similar to that of the Harrier. The first F-35C prototype was planned for the fourth quarter of 2006, with all aircraft flying before 2008. Initial Operational Capability was planned by 2010 for the STOVL version for the USMC.

The STOVL and CV fighter prototypes would be based at NAS Patuxent River for the majority of the test programme and the main squadron to support the flight-testing with chase and target aircraft at this base would be the Naval Air Test and Evaluation Squadron

The final production design was decided on 27 June 2002. One can spot the slight difference when comparing the final design of the F-35 on the left with the X-35 in flight on the right. *Copyright Lockheed Martin*

(NATES) VX-23. The VX-23 had already supported the JSF programme during the CDP when both the Boeing X-32B and the Lockheed X-35C visited NAS Patuxent River. The NATES VX-20, also based there, will be responsible for supplying other support aircraft. Among the other support aircraft to be used are tanker aircraft such as the KC-130. Other support aircraft include the Grumman E-2C Hawkeye and the Lockheed S-3B Viking.

The design of the F-35 PWSC was still changing when the contract was signed. In fact, the outer lines of the aircraft were still changing according to the results Lockheed Martin received from wind-tunnel model testing. For production it was, however, necessary to put a datum up, after which the design could not be changed any more. This date was 27 June 2002. As a result of the positive experience during the CDP it was decided that the STOVL version could be made more common to the other versions by increasing the weapon bay size of the F-35B to the size of the two other versions. This would increase weight as heavier actuators and heavier structural bulkheads would be required. The changes from the CDA aircraft have been minimal. The changes include:

- Extending the forward fuselage by five inches better to accommodate avionics and sensors, and moving the horizontal tail rearward by two inches to maintain stability and control with the newly extended forward fuselage.

- Slightly adjusting the positioning of the vertical tails to improve aerodynamic performance.

- Raising by about one inch the top surface of the aircraft along the centreline, thus increasing the fuel capacity by 300 lb and extending the range.

- Adding slightly more twist to the wing camber (the curvature of the wing surface) on the CV variant to improve both handling qualities and transonic performance.

The basic configuration arrangement would be maintained as with the flight controls, propulsion integration and Integrated Flight Propulsion Control (IFPC), which would increase the maturity of the design.

The maturation of the systems has increased markedly since the Air System Requirement Review (ASRR) at the end of 2002. On 18 December 2002 BAE Systems announced that it had initiated the assembly of the first aluminium parts of the empennage and aft fuselage. The delivery of the empennage and aft fuselage was planned for October 2004.

The flight-test programme was planned from the outset to start in October 2005. However, preparation had already started from the ATP. The three variants were to be tested mainly at the Air Force Flight Test Center (AFFTC) and the Naval Air Warfare Center Aircraft Division (NAWCAD). A total of fourteen flight-test aircraft were required and according to the flight-test concept of January 2003 it was planned for the fourteen aircraft to fly about 5734 flights, equalling 10,185 flight hours. It was estimated that each prototype would be able fly on average twelve flights per month. This is pretty aggressive considering that the first F-22 Raptor (4001) prototype took about a year to amass that amount of flights. It was estimated that about 35 per cent of the flights would require air-to-air refuelling. The F-35B and the F-35C will have the bulk of flight-testing performed at the NAWCAD Patuxent River. It was, however, decided that the high AoA and air start testing would be performed with AFFTC at Edwards AFB as the lakebeds are there and as was proven with the X-32A on 24 October 2000 they offer the security of landing options in case of emergencies.

Below is the flight-test concept planned for the AFFTC part of the flight-testing. Note that the aircraft B-3, C-2 and C-3 are not scheduled to visit Edwards AFB for flight-testing. The testing for the B-1, B-2, B-4, C-1, C-4 and C5 noted are only the flights planned at the AFFTC. The remainder and majority of the flights will take place from the Patuxent River facilities.

Test task\Aircraft	USAF CTOL					USMC/RN/RAF			US Navy CV		
	A-1	A-2	A-3	A-4	A-5	B-1	B-2	B-4	C-1	C-4	C-5
Aerodynamics	366	186	0	0	0	81	0	0	176	0	0
Structural integrity	64	203	0	0	0	0	0	0	0	0	0
Shipboard suitability	0	0	0	0	0	0	0	0	0	0	0
Propulsion	43	81	0	0	0	19	0	0	0	0	0
VMS	146	0	4	0	0	0	0	0	0	0	0
Utility systems	22	0	6	3	0	0	0	0	0	0	0
Mission systems	6	0	365	245	193	0	0	0	0	0	0
Armament	0	135	6	0	0	0	0	0	0	0	0
Survivability	0	11	67	55	26	0	37	37	0	7	11
EEE	0	0	7	0	0	0	0	0	0	0	0
RM&S	0	0	20	0	0	0	0	0	0	0	0
Total flights	647	617	474	304	219	100	37	37	176	7	11
Total flight hours	1218	1026	956	625	454	191	71	71	334	13	21
Total flight months	54	51	39	25	18	8	3	3	15	1	1

The Preliminary Design Review (PDR) showed that the F-35 was 2 per cent overweight. Lockheed Martin expected to have the problem solved by June 2003. The weight problem was discovered early in the programme and therefore it was easier to do something about it. In previous programmes the weight problem was generally discovered at a later stage and therefore more difficult to resolve. Lockheed Martin was still on track for the first flight according to the JSF programme office if it could resolve the weight problems. The JPD General Jack Hudson wanted the weight issue resolved before declaring the PDR as finished and clearing the road for the critical design phase for Lockheed Martin and its subcontractors. The Critical Design Review (CDR) was originally planned for April 2004. However, this seemed unlikely to be met.

One of the most visible changes made to the STOVL version before the PDR was the inlet doors for the lift fan. On the X-35B the doors to the lift fan open sideways and were two small doors. The new door (rear-hinged from the lift fan) will open during short take-offs to 35 degrees, which minimises the drag caused. During vertical hover the door will open to 65 degrees. The reason for this small change is that the fatigue effects on the fan are reduced and therefore less maintenance is needed on the lift fan. The rear-hinged door basically takes over the function of an inlet; on the Yak-38 Forger and the Yak-141 Freestyle the inlets for the lift engine are also rear hinged. Another side effect is that during transition from normal flight to vertical flight the door will function as an airbrake.

An option that was under consideration to speed up the design process was using partner nation companies to prolong the design time. The idea was to have either GKN Engage or Boeing Hawker de Havilland in Australia take over the design work after the working day finished in the US. The work would then be transferred to Fokker in the Netherlands from which it would again come to Lockheed Martin in the US. This would give the design team an advantage as the problems and all other work would be worked on twenty-four hours a day instead of the usual eight hours. Something similar was pioneered by GKN Aerospace with its Australian subsidiary GKN Engage in Melbourne.

As a result of weight problems surrounding the programme it was decided to delay and therefore also prolong the SDD. The extra year was to be spent on weight-reduction efforts. The funding of the longer SDD would come from reducing numbers in the early LRIP. This would as well as the delay of a year have another delaying effect on the IO, with the estimate of the IOC now being 2013 instead of 2011. On 10 November 2003 the manufacturing of the first parts of the first F-35 prototype structure was initiated. Three structural items were under production from this day on: the radar bulkhead, upper fuselage station bulkhead for the aft fuselage at the rear of the wing section and the canopy shelf.

The empty weight of the F-35 estimated by the US government, in December 2002, was as follows:

F-35A CTOL	27,395 lb
F-35B STOVL	30,697 lb
F-35C CV	30,618 lb

Interestingly the basic aircraft was heavier than the 24,000-lb weight limit given originally by DARPA, although the limit only concerned the CDA. If one would were to use the rule of the thumb then this increase in weight would also mean an increase in cost.

After Operation Iraqi Freedom (OIF) the value of the A-10 Thunderbolt was proven once more in the Close Air Support (CAS) role. The USAF had now reason to ponder over its CAS capability options. A replacement aircraft other than the JSF was not an option as a result of the budget restraints, although the USAF was pondering the STOVL option for the CAS role.

The SDD contract was modified on 24 February 2004. Originally the JSF was to be equipped with the Automatic Carrier Landing System (ACLS). This system was to be removed and replaced by the Joint Precision Approach and Landing System (JPALS). The modification had a value of $52,447,827 and contractual work should be completed by April 2012.

The weight problem was, however, not easily solved so a dedicated team of engineers was assembled to combat it – the team was aptly called the STOVL Weight Attack Team (SWAT). A total reduction of 2700 lb had been achieved by 14 September 2004. Individually, some of the changes made had small weight impact but added together they made a large difference. For example, the starter/generator capacity was reduced from 160 kW to 140 kW and the decrease in weight that went with the capacity reduction was 16lb – this change would rather reduce the future required capability for the Directed Energy Weapon (DEW). The baseline battery had a weight of 55.8 lb whereas the newly opted Li-Ion battery would incur a weight of only 30 lb. The changes were not only for the STOVL version; they would also be introduced in the other versions to increase commonality. The weight reductions that were introduced, however, had to be checked against costs, survivability and supportability. If it would have a negative impact on any of these the change would not have been authorised. The SWAT also looked into reducing drag to increase performance. Ironically one of the changes that was made early in the SDD had to be undone – the weapon bay size had to be reduced again. Commonality suffered with this decision but the weight reduction was significant enough to warrant it. The USMC and Royal Navy were not too happy with this decision as it means that they can no longer carry internally, in other words stealthily, weaponry over 450 kg. On the other hand Lockheed Martin stated that there was no weight requirement for the F-35, only performance requirements. The F-35A and the F-35C meet their performance requirements. Lockheed Martin will, however, ensure that STOVL F-35B will meet its requirements by the time it enters service. This statement, however correct, does neglect the fact that weight has a major influence on performance parameters, most importantly on the fuel usage. The heavier the plane the more fuel it will require to get to the target and combat radius is one of the Key Performance Parameters (KPP). The hunt for weight reduction was such a big issue that Lockheed Martin paid its staff bonuses for every idea that would shave off some weight, however small. As a result the ideas came streaming in and some of them did pay off, both for the employees and the F-35.

Besides these changes some improvements related to propulsion optimisation were specifically made to the STOVL version. The auxiliary dorsal inlet for the main engine was improved; it was made wider than design 240-3. The design change was approved by the SWAT on 14 September 2004. Roll-post modulation was improved, which would increase the ability to take off and land with even more uneven loads than previously was thought. As a result of these improvements the flat deck Short Take-Off (STO) distance was reduced by approximately 100 ft. Vertical Landing Bring Back (VLBB) was increased by approximately 600 lbm.

If the weight could not be reduced enough then another option was to increase the thrust. That was the idea the US Senate also came up with on 5 August 2004 and it ordered a study into increasing the thrust of the lift fan. The study had a value of $15 million.

Northrop Grumman started assembly of the centre fuselage at its facility in Palmdale. The weight issue was still not solved by June 2004 and a rescheduling of the programme was inevitable – it was delayed by a year. This gave system developers that were on time and on schedule more leeway that they might not need. A delay in assembly was caused by the late delivery of both the left- and right-hand side inlet lips. The left-hand inlet lip was expected on 24 September and the right-hand was due to follow on 4 October 2004. These revised dates were not made either and were again rescheduled for respectively 6 and 24 October 2004.

On Monday 12 July 2004 the assembly of the forward fuselage was initiated at Lockheed Martin Fort Worth facility when one bulkhead was loaded into an assembly tool. About a month later on 23 August 2004 the assembly of the wings was initiated at the same location. This time it was the front spar produced by Thayer, the first of ten spars, which was loaded into an assembly tool together with an aluminium bulkhead produced by Progressive. The forward fuselage structure was completed on 13 October 2004 at the Lockheed Fort Worth facilities three months' after initiating the assembly.

On 21 September 2004 one of the first steps towards LRIP was undertaken by the JPO. The JPO requested an estimate of the liability for elimination of long lead materials, production engineering support and tooling for the LRIP. Lockheed Martin was expected to submit its estimate on 23 November 2004.

Early in November 2004 the Pentagon gave Lockheed Martin the green light to proceed with a lighter STOVL version. The newly designed STOVL shed 2100 kg from the baseline STOVL. Acting Acquisition Chief Michael Wynne signed the papers during the last week of October 2004. The new plan will reduce the weight of the first prototype but will have as a side effect a delay in the test programme – the first flight of the first STOVL prototype is now expected in late 2007. For the first CTOL prototype A-1, the first 'power on' was planned for 7 September 2005. This milestone called 'first power' relates to the electrical systems and not the engine power. The first flight engine was due by the year's end. The rescheduling of the programme meant some other changes. The most notable was that the number of flying prototypes, or production representative test aircraft as Lockheed Martin liked to call them, was increased by one aircraft and the SDD phase was prolonged. The fact that the first aircraft would be structurally different would mean that there would still be fourteen prototypes flying that are structurally identical to the production aircraft. The CDR for the redesigned CTOL aircraft was scheduled for February 2006. The carrier version was the most affected as its first flight was delayed from 2007 until 2009. The IOC of the carrier version was expected only to have a year's delay. This rescheduling also had an effect on the planned initial procurement. To even out the cost of prolonged SDD the initial procurement had to be reduced. As the STOVL version was the source of the problems it was also the aircraft that was scrapped from the initial procurement. Long lead procurement was expected to be awarded by March 2006. The procurement plans looked as follows:

	Production run	F-35A CTOL	F-35B STOVL	F-35C CV	Total
LRIP lot I	Spring 2006 – Early 2009	5	0	0	5
LRIP lot II	Early 2007 – End 2009	8	10	0	14
LRIP lot III	Early 2008 – End 2010				
LRIP lot IV	Early 2009 – End 2011				
LRIP lot V	Early 2010 – End 2012				
LRIP lot VI	Early 2012 – End 2013				
Total		13	10	0	19

For some unclear reason the JSF programme office did not clear the remaining LRIP numbers for public release. It was unclear if the UK and Italy would be successful in their bid to get production lines in their respective countries. At any rate, if the previous schedule is anything to go by then the UK would acquire five STOVL aircraft in LRIP lot III, similar to the US Navy ordering its first F-35C aircraft. Other details available are that for LRIP lot III the total US Navy order would be thirty-two aircraft, not differentiating between the two versions. Lot IV would be thirty-six aircraft and lot V strangely enough a slight decline to thirty-three aircraft.

The main reason for the extra development aircraft was that major construction of the first prototype was already under way. If all that work was to be cancelled then the first flight would be delayed even more. The first development aircraft was if not structurally then physically identical and could therefore be used for at least the aerodynamic testing. Structural testing, however, would not be relevant to the remainder of the development aircraft.

Northrop Grumman was keeping to schedule as the first centre fuselage was completed on 22 April 2005 in time to be handed over to Lockheed Martin during a ceremony on the day after. The centre fuselage was soon after sent to Lockheed Fort Worth for final assembly and due to arrive on 5 May. In fact, it arrived two days earlier. Lockheed wasted no time and the forward and centre fuselage were mated on 4 May 2005. The mating was predetermined to take 183 hours of touch labour, but the actual time it took was fifty-eight hours, giving hope that the design and production were on the right track. During production it was expected that some time would be shaved off with experience and again newer methods. Boeing, for example, announced, when it initiated production of the hundreth wingset for the F-22, that it had reduced required man-hours for the production of a wingset by 45,000. So much time saving could of course not be gained on this process but even a small reduction would have major cost effects on the entire production run for the JSF.

The wing was mated to the fuselage structure on 16 May. The aft fuselage was expected to be handed over during a ceremony on 17 May 2005 and then be shipped to Lockheed Martin's Fort Worth plant. Early in May the first work on the centre fuselage for the B-1 at Northrop Grumman was initiated – it was the first prototype to have the results of the SWAT team design changes integrated. The aft fuselage actually arrived on 31 May 2005 and was readied for final assembly on 2 June as it was lowered by crane behind the centre fuselage and on 9 June the aft fuselage was finally mated to the centre fuselage. System installation in the forward fuselage commenced on 17 June. The structure of the aircraft was complete except for the vertical and horizontal tails. The work continued on a busy schedule

A good shot of the rivets! Note the huge nose landing gear door which caused a slight roll after take off on the first flight. It was replaced by two landing gear doors on subsequent aircraft.. *Copyright Lockheed Martin*

as on 22 June the installation of electrical and hydraulic systems in the wing was initiated. The first power-on milestone is the moment when these systems will be checked and used for the first time and was planned for 7 September.

On 15 July 2005 BAE Systems announced that it had completed the vertical tails and that they should soon be followed by the horizontal tails; the left vertical tail had been delivered one week prior to the announcement. On 29 July 2005 it was announced that the horizontal tails were close to completion – the last of any structural parts. The horizontal tails were delivered but were not immediately installed. The first power on was achieved on schedule. Lockheed said it proved that the programme was on schedule since the rescheduling. After

The F-35 after its paint job. All the partner nations' flags are represented and on the tail the JSF logo. Note that the landing gear doors are missing. *Copyright Lockheed Martin*

Engine tests on the aircraft were performed up to full afterburner which had power in excess of 40,000lb. *Copyright Lockheed Martin*

completing the electrical, hydraulic and fuel systems in the wing the carbon-fibre composite one-piece wing skin was installed. Furthermore, the main and nose landing gear were installed.

After all the work from the SWAT the production of the first STOVL F-35 commenced. At Northrop Grumman the assembly of the first centre fuselage was initiated on 6 September 2005. BF-1 would be the second aircraft to fly but the first after the weight design alterations. The BF-1 was to be followed five weeks later by the BG-1, a ground-test prototype, and that would be followed by the BF-2 five weeks after that. The centre fuselage was planned to be ready for delivery by November 2006. A day after this milestone another milestone was achieved and that was the first time that the power was switched on. This target was on time, giving Lockheed Martin some reprieve from the pressure.

The nose landing gear was installed on to the first pre-production aircraft, as Lockheed Martin called its test aircraft. Later during the same month on 28 November the vertical tails were installed, followed by the horizontal tails on 7 December 2005. This milestone marked the last major component assembly for the first pre-production aircraft. The engine would be delivered by the end of December and was expected to be installed in early 2006. By the year's end Northrop Grumman had three centre fuselages in production, a clear signal that the programme was ramping up to speed.

The first flight engine arrived on 30 December 2005 on schedule. On 8 January 2006 the F-35 A-1 was lifted out of its assembly fixture and was moved to its new position where it would stand on its landing gear and jack stands. The engine was being prepared for installation, which was planned before the end of January 2006. The edges for the wings

Low speed taxiing was initiated early December. This meant that most of the issues around the subsystems had been resolved and the aircraft would soon be flying. *Copyright Lockheed Martin*

and tails produced by Lockheed Martin Aeronautics in Palmdale were delivered to Lockheed Martin Fort Worth. Without those edges the F-35 would not attain its stealth requirements. Test fit of the engine occurred on 20 January 2006.

On 2 February 2006 BAE Systems announced that it had initiated production of the first aft fuselage of the first STOVL aircraft. Four of the twenty-three development aircraft are under construction with another four to be added during 2006. Meanwhile, the A-1 development aircraft was planned to leave the factory hall shortly. The first flight-test engine was installed on 13 February 2006. Six days later followed the transfer of the A-1 to the flight line to initiate preparations for the first flight. The first tests that would be carried out were at the fuel facilities where the fuel system, including the tanks, would be thoroughly tested. Structural testing and vibration tests were to follow. In the late spring engine ground tests would prepare the way for the first flight.

Perhaps more important was the CDR that was held from 13 to 17 February 2006. The CDR results would be evaluated for another two weeks and from then on the aircraft would be more or less defined and would not alter in any major fashion, allowing for more detailed capability briefings to partner nations and other future customers. The CDR was just one review of many. The Defense Acquisition Board (DAB) would also review the programme to see if the long lead items for the first LRIP lot could be ordered. If the DAB acknowledged that the programme was on track then the long lead contract could be awarded as early as April 2006.

On 12 March 2006 the fuel system check-out was completed. A common problem during these kinds of tests is fuel leaks but none were noted during the entire fuel system check-out since it started on 19 February 2006. Leaks, although a common problem, could have caused unwanted delays. In fact, Lockheed Martin stated that it was quite remarkable and a first in a fighter that no leaks were found. During these fuel tests the aircraft is first fuelled up. The aircraft has three wheels, each of them located on top of a hydraulic lift, which allows the testers to change the position of the aircraft. The testers can simulate different positions that the aircraft will most likely go through during flight. The system check-out took less than a third of the time to complete than in other recent developmental aircraft programmes according to Lockheed. The aircraft was also weighted during these tests, which allowed for a comparison between the calculated (predicted) weight and the real weight of the AA-1.

CTOL AA-1	Total calculated	Total actual	Variance	Variance (%)
Airframe	9260.9 lb	9333.6 lb	72.7 lb	0.78
Systems	4282.4 lb	4162.6 lb	−119.8 lb	−2.80
Grand total	13,543.2 lb	13,496.1 lb	−47.1 lb	−0.35

Interestingly, in September 2006 in a briefing by Brigadier General Charles R. Davis, the Joint Program Director, it was announced that since the SWAT's formation in October 2004 the air vehicle weight growth of the STOVL was calculated at 363 lb.

The aircraft was immediately transferred to the structural tests facility to continue the ground tests required prior to first flight. As a part of the structural tests the F-35 was loaded with inert JDAMs and AMRAAMs on 24 March 2006. Control surfaces were activated and moved, including the weapon bay doors, as they would be during flight to measure the forces on the body of the aircraft. Eight different F-35 fuel- and weapons-load configurations were tested during the structural coupling testing. Structural testing was completed ahead of schedule on 2 April 2006, five days early. The programme was highly

General Moseley announced the name Lightning II at the inauguration. Representatives from all countries were there for the occasion. *Copyright Lockheed Martin*

paced and therefore ground vibration testing was initiated on 11 April 2006.

The F-35 still did not have a name but this was to change at the inauguration. The partners had been asked for suggestions for different names and the list of names included Spitfire II, Cyclone, Reaper, Piasa, Black Mamba and Lightning II. The USAF as the biggest customer had the right to make the final choice from these names. The name was announced by the Commander in Chief of the USAF General Moseley during the inauguration on 7 July 2006. The name was the Lightning II and it was selected because it had been used before for both an American and a British fighter. The American fighter had seen combat and was the first fighter ever developed by Lockheed. As the F-35 is thought to be the last manned fighter to be built it was rather fitting. The English Electric Lightning was the first British-built operational Mach 2 fighter. As the UK was a big partner the name was thought to be fitting as both fighters were one of the best at their time if not the best. General Moseley made reference to these fighters. However, there was one other fighter that carried the name Lightning II, albeit briefly. That fighter was the YF-22 and the name stuck until the roll-out ceremony of the F-22, when the name Raptor was announced. The naming had as a side effect a small change in the F-35 logo as well. The contrails in the logo changed into a lightning silhouette and the name Lightning II was added, replacing the abbreviation JSF. Lockheed Martin Chief Test Pilot Jon Beesley gave his thoughts about the name and said that it was very appropriate as the F-35 was the first electric fighter, so if any plane had the right to be called Lightning, then it should definitely be the F-35.

On 3 and 4 October 2006 Jon Beesley rehearsed the first flight of the F-35. For the first in-flight rehearsal he flew in an F-16. He was followed by two F-16s and one F-18. One of the F-16s was flying safety chase profile and the other was flying photo chase. The F-18 was the second photo chase. On the second day the same rehearsal was repeated but this time around Jon Beesley flew in the F-18, an aircraft in which he had no hands-on experience to make the rehearsal more realistic.

On Thursday 7 December 2006 one of the final steps before the first flight was taken. The AA-1 initiated its taxi tests. The first taxi tests were at low speed and would be followed by medium-speed and high-speed taxi tests. The low-speed taxi tests were initiated by Jon Beesley after systems checks had been carried out. After moving the throttle forward the F-35 taxied out of the hangar and up to the runway, testing the nosewheel steering and the brakes. Low-speed taxi testing is up to speeds of 30 knots (~ 35 mph). Lockheed Martin expected that the first flight would be very close as the aircraft had received flight certification but now it depended on the weather. In fact, the Friday before taxi testing was initiated it had snowed in Fort Worth. Medium-speed taxi testing was initiated on 11 December 2006. Medium taxi tests are up to a speed of 65 knots (~ 75 mph). High-speed taxi tests will be up to a speed of 80 knots (~ 92 mph). On 12 December 2006 the final taxi runs were completed by Jon Beesley. On the same day two F-16Bs (92-0455 and 92-0456) from the 416th FLTS were flown from Edwards AFB to Fort Worth Joint Reserve Base in preparation for the first flight.

It was now time to evaluate the data and prepare the aircraft for its first flight. It took a few days but on 15 December 2006 all the circumstances for the flight were right. Jon Beesley took off in the AA-1 from Fort Worth Joint Reserve Base (JRB) at 12.44 pm Central Standard Time (CST), that is, 7.44 pm UK time. The F-35 flew to 15,000 ft and at that altitude performed certain manoeuvres to check the aircraft handling and the operation of the engine and subsystems. Jon Beesley landed the F-35 Lightning II for the first time thirty-five minutes after take-off, at 1.19 pm CST. He said the aircraft handled better than the Raptor. The flight went according to plan but was cut short although Lockheed had hoped to perform a very extensive first flight. A sensor discrepency (air data probe) was slightly off and for this reason it was decided to return the aircraft. Lockheed Martin had hoped to cycle the landing gear during the first flight, however this was not done. Jon Beesley said that they flew what every other first prototype does during the first flight:take-off, flight handling manoeuvres and a landing. The F-35, being the first aircraft to fly from the outset with Electro Hydrostatic Actuators (EHA), performed as expected and the EHA performed flawlessly. Three aircraft were flying a chase mission, two F-16's (one of the Edwards F-16Bs and Lockheed Martin's own F-16D (90-0848)) and an F/A-18B. The F-16s were flown by Jeff Knowles from Lockheed Martin and Lt Col Dave Sizoo from the US Air Force and the F/A-18B (161723/SD-324) of the VX-23 Salty Dogs by Major Fred Schenk, US Navy. After the problem had been solved the weather prevented the aircraft from flying again. According to Jon Beesley some more taxi testing was performed on 4 January.

In the week following the first flight, on 19 December, Northrop Grumman completed the centre fuselage of the BF-1. Delivery to Lockheed Martin Fort Worth was planned for 8 January 2007. The final assembly was initiated shortly after. As the original date set for the delivery was November 2006 a slight delay can be noticed. The size of the delay was, however, small compared with previous programmes. On 19 December the assembly of the first carrier-version centre fuselage was initiated; it was the twelfth centre fuselage in production.

The second flight was early in the new year on 8 January 2007 and everything that was not fitted into the first flight was now performed. Approximately ten minutes into the sixty-two-minute flight Jon Beesley retracted the landing gear. He then continued to climb from 15,000 ft to 20,000 ft where he checked the handling qualities at Mach 0.6 (~ 450 mph) and Mach 0.7 (~ 530 mph). The handling tests included rolls, turns, AoA changes and engine throttle changes. After the flight Jon Beesley stated that 'The flight underscores that the Lightning II flies just as our engineers predicted. This was the first time that we have retracted the landing gear and the aircraft handling qualities were outstanding. I continue to be impressed by this marvellous airplane's performance and handling characteristics'.

Flight	Date	Pilot
3	10 January 2007	Jon Beesley
4	23 January 2007	Jon Beesley
5	24 January 2007	Jon Beesley
6	29 January 2007	Jon Beesley
7	30 January 2007	Jon Beesley

All flights were flown by Jon Beesley. During the first seven flights he was allowed to perform only half stick rolls. A half stick roll means that the pilot moves the stick laterally to ½ of its deflection.   This results in a lower roll rate – due to shaping of the input gradient it is 35 to 40 per cent of the full roll stick command. After these flights the AA-1 was grounded for a software upgrade that involved the HMD. It·was planned that the aircraft would fly again by March 2007. For January it had fulfilled the expected average of six flights per month which was pretty aggressive compared to the initial flight test phase of the F-22 EMD. Flight testing was resumed on 5 March with the Flight Test Upgrade 1 (FTU-1) software. During the flight, handling qualities with the gear down were evaluated and the landing was cycled. The eighth flight was cut short because the chase aircraft had a technical problem, however it was the first flight during which Jon Beesley could perform full stick rolls. The ninth flight, on 13 March, was also the last flight of that month. The weather proved to be the main problem according to Jon Beesley as it needed to be benign when flying a first prototype early on in the test programme. The process of mating the first F-35B forward fuselage to the centre fuselage was completed on 26 January.

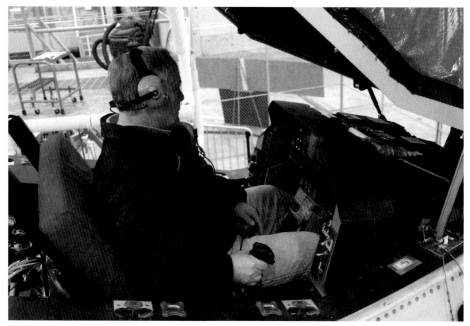

Jon Beesley in the cockpit of AA-1 during ground tests. At this time only half the panoramic display has been installed and note that the ejection seat has been replaced by something more comfortable. *Copyright Lockheed Martin*

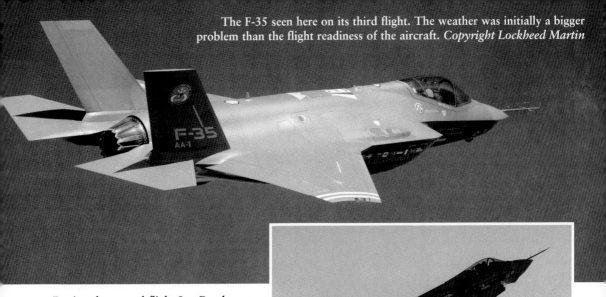

The F-35 seen here on its third flight. The weather was initially a bigger problem than the flight readiness of the aircraft. *Copyright Lockheed Martin*

During the second flight Jon Beesley was able to cycle the landing gear. This had not occurred during the first flight, something that stung Lockheed's pride because every press report made an issue of it. *Copyright Lockheed Martin*

Flight	Date	Pilot
10	4 April 2007	Jon Beesley
11	5 April 2007	Jon Beesley
12	11 April 2007	Jeff Knowles
13	12 April 2007	Jon Beesley
14	17 April 2007	Jon Beesley
15	26 April 2007	Jeff Knowles
16	26 April 2007	Jeff Knowles
17	27 April 2007	Jeff Knowles
18	2 May 2007	Jeff Knowles
19	3 May 2007	Jeff Knowles

During the 19th flight an electrical problem occurred. For 30 milliseconds the aircraft's electricity was cut off and the aircraft's computers reconfigured. Previously the AA-1 had only been flying up to 30,000ft. The problem occurred at a height of 38,000ft and was connected with one of the EHAs. Jon Beesley was happy that the problem was found out then and not when there were six planes on the flight line which would have delayed the flight test programme a lot more. When comparing the fighters that flew the chase missions, Jon Beesley noted that the F-18 has the biggest difficulty in keeping up with F-35.

Northrop Grumman was getting production of the centre fuselage up to speed, the third centre fuselage was delivered on 7 May 2007. It was the second STOVL centre fuselage and was for the first ground-test aircraft. Delivery was well ahead of schedule by about two and half months. The FTU-2 software was installed after flight 19. FTU-2 software was to allow for in-flight refuelling which would give the option of prolonging flights. For comparison the X-35A had its first aerial refuelling flight on its 10th flight.

For the first time in flight the afterburner was engaged. 'The F-35 started really burning and turning.' Jon Beesley said that he was pleasantly surprised with engine thrust being somewhat better then he had expected. *Copyright Lockheed Martin*

The F-16 and the F-35 flying in formation during the fourth flight. According to Jon Beesley the F-18 has more trouble keeping up with the F-35. *Copyright Lockheed Martin*

The seventh flight was the last where there was a roll-rate restriction. Gear down profiles were also still being evaluated. *Copyright Lockheed Martin*

CHAPTER 8

COST MEASURES DURING EARLY DEVELOPMENT

Weight has proved to be a major factor in increasing the cost of any fighter. For this reason it was clear from very early in the programme that a single-seat, single-engine aircraft would be the favoured option. One reason for heavier fighters was that all kinds of new sensors were needed and more systems were developed to make the aircraft more capable. All this technological progress came at the heavy cost of extra weight. A combat aircraft costs, by rule of the thumb, its weight in gold. JAST was therefore from the outset designed to use the smallest possible sensor suite and be dependent on external information sources such as E-8 Joint Stars, E-3 AWACS and other information-gathering sources. This idea was changed, however, as the industry was dependent on export and most of the export countries did not have the E-8 Joint Stars or E-3 AWACS or any similar aircraft in their inventory. The JSF office touted the programme as the first one where cost would be the driving factor but it had indeed forgotten about the Saab Gripen, which in fact became lighter and cheaper (to buy and to maintain) than its predecessor the Saab Viggen but more capable. The JSF would not become lighter than its predecessors and would therefore be more expensive to buy. On

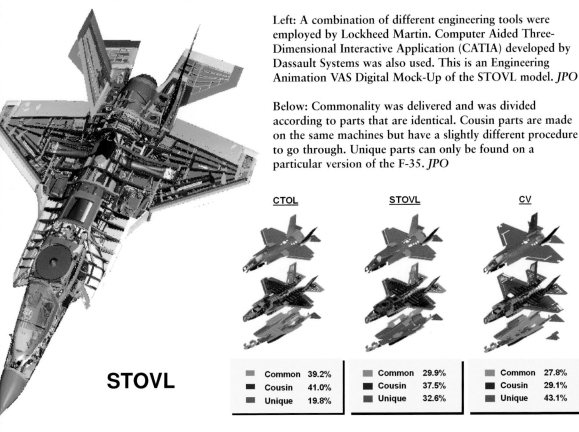

Left: A combination of different engineering tools were employed by Lockheed Martin. Computer Aided Three-Dimensional Interactive Application (CATIA) developed by Dassault Systems was also used. This is an Engineering Animation VAS Digital Mock-Up of the STOVL model. *JPO*

Below: Commonality was delivered and was divided according to parts that are identical. Cousin parts are made on the same machines but have a slightly different procedure to go through. Unique parts can only be found on a particular version of the F-35. *JPO*

STOVL

CTOL

STOVL

CV

Common	39.2%
Cousin	41.0%
Unique	19.8%

Common	29.9%
Cousin	37.5%
Unique	32.6%

Common	27.8%
Cousin	29.1%
Unique	43.1%

the other hand the JSF would be more capable in its stealth features than its predecessors and have internal weapon carriage providing better stealth signature and improved survivability.

Some cost-saving measures were taken to reduce the development cost and risk. The first risk reduction and most important one was the rule that the winning designs would have to build a Large Scaled Powered Model (LSPM) to prevent the repetition of a prototype incapable of lifting its own weight. Other measures taken by Lockheed were to use products used on previous fighter programmes. For example, the main landing gear on the X-35 was derived from the A-6E (one of the aircraft that was to be replaced eventually by the EA-18G Growler) and the nose landing gear from the McDonnell Douglas F-15 Eagle; the Environmental Cooling System (ECS) comes from the F-18E/F; the Auxiliary Power System (APS) comes from the Lockheed Martin F-22 Raptor; the engine-driven hydraulic pumps come from the YF-23; the airframe-mounted accessory drive comes from the B-2; the ejection seat comes from the McDonnell Douglas/BAE Systems AV-8B Harrier; two large colour displays were taken from the Lockheed C-130J Hercules; the engine is a further development of the Lockheed Martin F-22 Raptor's F-119 and many subsystems and controls come from the Lockheed Martin F-16 Fighting Falcon.

Boeing used the canopy of the AV-8B Harrier II, which gave the test pilots a similar view to what they were used to.

Another cost-saving measure was that it was decided from the early stages that the JSF would have a single cockpit. There would be no expensive trainer. This decision was made on the basis that avionics were one of the major costs in the development of new aircraft. Lockheed Martin played with the idea of placing the instructor in a ground station from where he would be able to see what the pilot student was up to in near realtime and if required could take over control. Experience with the Raptor data link would prove vital and the data link in the F-35 would be even better than that in the F-22.

On 24 January 1995 an RfP was initiated to reduce the development costs of a new fighter. The JAST Simulation Assessment and Validation Environment (SAVE) programme as it was called had the aim of reducing the Life Cycle Costs (LCC) with the help of virtual manufacturing.

The SAVE programme was split into two phases. Phase I was to last fifteen months and the demonstration should validate the core virtual manufacturing capabilities and point out where enhancements and refinements were possible. Phase II would last thirty-six months and pursue the enhancements and refinements recognised in phase I and possibly expand on them. Six proposals were received in response to the RfP. On 24 April 1995 a contract was awarded to Lockheed for the fifty-one-month programme with a value of $6,427,593. The programme was under the management of the AFRL materials and manufacturing directorate at Wright Patterson. The success of the programme or rather the applicability of the new technology developed to existing programmes was demonstrated by Lockheed throughout. Lockheed was at the time involved in the EMD phase of the F-22 and had carried out a presentation to the F-22 System Program Director (SPD) Colonel Michael C. Mushala who was so impressed with the work achieved he send a memorandum to Rear Admiral Craig Steidle, at that time Joint Program director (JPD), to ask for continued support of the SAVE programme.

In December 1996 Lockheed Martin used the SAVE-developed virtual modelling and simulation to assess the manufacturability and cost in connection with the F-16 horizontal stabiliser. This was a proof of concept demonstration, which freed the path to continue development of the SAVE. During the SAVE programme Lockheed had selected the CATIA system developed by Dassault and other programmes that were available to improve on the system, using the system that it had developed and was further developing to reduce the cost of its own PWSC.

The second demonstration was in August 1998 and concerned the redesign of the F-22 gun port, where the system proved that the different design systems with different manufacturing modelling and simulation tools provided meaningful feedback about cost and manufacturing.

A third demonstration of the system developed under the SAVE programme was completed in September 1999 and concerned the weapon door bay assembly of the F-22 Raptor. The engineers were experiencing a mismatch problem while mating the forward and the centre fuselage pieces. Here the system provided highly required tolerance and tooling feedback and helped the F-22 engineers. It was estimated that if applied and further developed it could reduce the LCC of the JSF by up to 3 per cent.

Modelling and simulation was to take up such an important part in the development that according to former JSF Lockheed Martin programme manager Frank Cappuccio it was important that both the manufacturer and the customer had to recognise what could be achieved with modelling and simulation. In fact, when Lockheed Martin made its offer it had already taken into account the savings that could be made by modelling and simulation. The customer should embrace Simulation Based Acquisition (SBA). During the first years of the SDD an oft heard complaint from Lockheed Martin and the JSF programme office was that the GAO did not take into account all the modelling and simulation work that had been done to reduce risk.

At the time when the selection for the SDD phase was announced it was made clear that in many ways Boeing was the equal of Lockheed but in key areas such as the airframe and propulsion Lockheed was superior. Boeing's bid was considered equal to Lockheed in the area of cost and affordability. Prior to the announcement it was expected that Boeing would be better as the company advertised that it had cut the production cost of the X-32B compared with the X-32A by 30 per cent.

Commonality was seen as an instrument to reduce cost. The question that has to be asked is how do you calculate commonality. Methods include counting common parts, individual component systems (engines, wings, ejection seat, avionics etc) and finally parts that can be manufactured with common tooling. For the JSF programme a combination of the three methods was selected. The commonality between the three JSF versions was expected to be between 70 per cent and 90 per cent. During the early CDP Boeing aimed at a higher than 90 per cent commonality with its PWSC but this proved too costly and the company had to reduce commonality to remain within the cost frame. Cost savings with a commonality of 70–90 per cent were estimated, projected at 25 per cent. To maintain commonality all the requirements set by one of the services were evaluated for their operational value, and after that they were evaluated for cost as well. The cost evaluation was performed by the industry.

The Joint Initial Requirement Document I (JIRD I) that was signed in 1995 was to set out a list of requirements against a certain cost goal. The cost was the major deciding factor for if a certain requirement was to be included the cost assessment industry was asked for a quotation for a particular technology. Cooperation with the industry was therefore required from the outset.

The exact points taken into account in the JIRD I were:

1 Affordability
2 Radar Cross Section
3 Speed
4 Manoeuvrability
5 Payload
6 Sortie Generation Rates (SGR)
7 Logistic 'footprint'
8 Commonality
9 Range

The JIRD I was also known as the Cost/Operational Performance Trades (COPT) I. It was an ever changing process and therefore called a living COPT until the JORD was signed by 2000. Even the signing of the JORD would not mean that the programme would progress to the next stage. An analysis of alternatives was to take place between the JORD and Milestone I. In between JIRD I and JORD was, however, a long time. Although it was a continuously changing process, it was needed at some point to pin down the more detailed requirements so in 1997 JIRD II was signed. Beside the main affordability requirement, new requirements were: shipboard compatibility, manpower, target acquisition, accuracy, identify target, IR signature, pass/receive timely info (data link), RCS verses ECM, RCS verses supportability and basing flexibility/carrier suitability. In 1998 the JIRD III was signed and in that again other requirements were defined. The requirements defined in JIRD III were: manpower, R&M, supportable LO, engine *R&I*, adverse weather/night, multi-role capability, mission planning, mission flexibility, accurate navigation, countermeasures, interoperability and system redundancy. The last step before the JORD was the JIRD IV signed in 1999. In this document the requirements were for low visual signature, hardening, *BDA*, weapons carriage versatility, low acoustic signature and maintainability.

Early in the CDP, a cost study team planned that the EMD phase would take eighty-four months and would incorporate 5000 flight-test hours. It was, however, noted that recent experience, which went back to the General Dynamics F-16 and the McDonnell Douglas F-15, had shown that these fighter developments had required 5000 flight-test hours each. But both the F-16 and the F-15 had only one version. The JSF had more versions, so for this reason the initial cost estimate had to be adjusted to a more realistic level. The eighty-four-month period was also thought to be too short for the software development. The rationale was accepted and eventually the EMD, later SDD, was prolonged to include 126 months and incorporate between 12,000 and 14,000 flight-test hours.

During the CDP Lockheed Martin managed to get into trouble. The trouble was of the financial kind. At the beginning of the CDP it was made clear to both contenders (Boeing and Lockheed Martin) that cost was a major issue. In fact, so much so that the two contenders were not allowed to use their own private funds. This was even put in the contract for the CDP. A breach was considered so important that it could even mean disqualification. The trouble came to light in January 1999 and was explained as partly a book-keeping error, a more expensive than expected lift fan and additional technologies introduced in the programme. Boeing, however, followed quite soon after that with the news that it was over budget as well, mostly as a result of the redesign of its PWSC and the connected wind-tunnel testing. Boeing thought, however, that it could compensate with funds previously marked for the assembly of the two CDAs as the assembly so far was below target.

Luckily for Lockheed Martin the international partners of the JSF programme put pressure on the US to let the company continue to ensure that the partner air forces would receive the best option. It was, however, a tough call for JPD USAF Brigadier General Leslie Kenne and Deputy Director USMC Major General Michael Hough and both Boeing and Lockheed Martin received a good scare. The programme was, however, on schedule and a reorganisation was thought be sufficient to solve the problem. At a special meeting on 9 April 1999 it was explained that a restructuring would be required and the companies would have to supply proposals on how it would affect the remaining part of the CDP. No extra funds would become available from the JSF programme office and proposals were due by the end of April 1999. Both Boeing and Lockheed Martin sent in proposals that basically affected the work in connection with the PWSC. The work deleted to save funds was related to fine tuning, modelling and simulation work. Both Boeing and Lockheed had reduced the number of upgrades required for their PWSCs by one. The JSF programme office accepted the proposals. Another way that Lockheed tried to cut costs was by changing the fact that from the outset Lockheed had planned to change the CTOL demonstrator into the CV demonstrator, which would require adapting the wing. Now the plan was to make the second prototype the dedicated CV demonstrator and let the CTOL demonstrator go through the conversion, saving time and money.

To reduce risk there were eight types of technologies identified that were vital for the JSF programme and needed separate development. One of these was the previously mentioned engine technology. The technology maturation was evaluated according to a system used in the industry, called the Technology Readiness Levels (TRL). The TRL were adapted to the aviation industry and formulated the following levels:

1 Basic principles observed and reported.
2 Technology concept and/or application formulated.
3 Analytical and experimental critical function and/or characteristic proof of concept.
4 Component and/or breadboard validation in laboratory environment.
5 Component and/or breadboard validation in a relevant environment.
6 System/subsystem model or prototype demonstration in a relevant environment.
7 System prototype demonstration in an operational environment.
8 Actual system completed and flight qualified through test and demonstration.
9 Actual system flight proved through successful mission operations.

During the CDP the GAO had a close look at the risk and cost element of the JSF programme and in its report advised delaying the programme. According to the GAO the technologies involved would not be at a sufficiently high TRL. TRL 7 was according to the GAO the minimum required standard to proceed to the EMD phase as the SDD phase was called at that time. Any lower would be too high a risk and would have a probability of increasing cost during the next phase. The GAO could not openly state which technology was in which TRL as that was considered sensitive information so the technology programmes were marked as technology 1 to 8. The argument of whether a technology had reached a high enough TRL remained a point of friction between the GAO and the JSF programme office contractors well into the SDD phase.

Cost predictions of the JSF units in US dollars in millions:

Year	CTOL	STOVL	CV
FY 1994	28	35	38
FY 1997	28	35	38
FY 2002	40	45–50	50

The above price predictions were, however, quite optimistic as we can see by the weight/price evolution that was already commented on by former Lockheed Martin CEO Norman Augustine. However, the new technology had to have as a side effect lower LCC. The increasing cost spiral of military aircraft and their systems was also known as the death spiral. The added systems and their increased weight caused aircraft to be heavier, more complex and more expensive, and as a consequence fewer were acquired to replace the previous-generation fighters. This in turn made development more expensive per aircraft. The spiral was said to end with every service in the US (USAF, US Navy and USMC) having to share the same aircraft.

It is, however, important to bear in mind that the original price was quoted in 1994 dollars under the assumption that the UK and the US combined would buy 3000 aircraft. With the TFX programme, only 489 F-111s (TFX) were procured, with the result of increasing the cost to about five times the original price. A more recent example is the F-22, which had its original order for 750 aircraft reduced in several stages – the original price was set at $50 million. With every reduction the price of the F-22 increased.

Year	Manufacturer	Type	Empty weight	Price (million US dollars)
1950	North American	F-86 Sabre	6276 kg/13,836 lb	0.22
1958	Lockheed	F-104 Starfighter	6760 kg/14,903 lb	1.4
1962	McDonnell Douglas	F-4 Phantom II	13,757 kg/30,328 lb	2.2
1968	General Dynamics	F-111	21,398 kg/47,175 lb	5.9
1978	McDonnell Douglas	F-15A Eagle	12,973 kg/28,000 lb	20
1990	McDonnell Douglas	F-15E Strike Eagle	14,379 kg/31,700 lb	40
1990	Lockheed Martin	F-16C/D Fighting Falcon	8663 kg/19,100 lb	25
1990	McDonnell Douglas	F-18C/D Hornet	10,455 kg/23,050 lb	30
2000	Eurofighter	Typhoon	9750 kg/21,495 lb	?50
2000	Dassault	Rafale		?50
2000	Boeing	F-18E/F	13,880 kg/30,600 lb	?60
2000	Gripen International	Gripen	6622 kg/14,599 lb	?30
>2005	Lockheed Martin	F-22 Raptor	+13,608 kg/30,000 lb	?120*
>2008	Lockheed Martin	F-35		?40*

* These figures are an estimate for these prospective fighters at the time that they become available.

Considering the generally accepted rule of the thumb that a fighter aircraft costs its weight in gold, it is difficult to say why the price for the CALF was calculated around US $30 million with an empty weight of 24,000 lb. That would make the CALF heavier than the Eurofighter Typhoon, marginally heavier than the F/A-18C/D and around 25 per cent heavier than the F-16 Fighting Falcon. The cost of the fighter would therefore, according to the table above, which also includes inflation and other effects, be more likely to be above US $50 million if not US $60 million.

An interesting comparison is the empty weight of the fighters that the F-35 is due to replace:

Aircraft	Empty weight	F-35	Empty weight	Change
F-16A/B	14,567 lb	CTOL	27,395 lb	88% increase
F-16C/D*	19,100 lb	CTOL	27,395 lb	43% increase
F-16C/D**	18,335 lb	CTOL	27,395 lb	49% increase
F/A-18A	23,050 lb	CTOL	27,395 lb	19% increase
F-18C	23,050 lb	CV/STOVL	30,618 lb/30,697 lb	<33% / >33% increase
AV-8B	13,968 lb†	STOVL	30,697 lb	119% increase
A-10	21,541 lb	CTOL/STOVL	27,395 lb/30,697 lb	27% / 42% increase
AMX	14,771 lb	CTOL	27,395 lb	85% increase
Tornado	30,620 lb	CTOL	27,395 lb	11% decrease
F-111	46,172 lb†	CTOL/CV	27,395 lb/30,618 lb	41% / 34% decrease

* With General Electric F110 engine.

** With Pratt & Whitney F100 engine.

† Operating empty weight (including fuel that remains in tanks).

As can be seen the increase in weight is quite large compared with the older fighters with the exception of the Panavia Tornado and the General Dynamics F-111. However, there is an explanation for the big weight increase. Many sensors that previously needed to be carried on stores were now integrated in the aircraft. Furthermore the F-35 had a much longer range (with the exception of the F-111) requiring air-to-air refuelling less often for its missions. The aircraft was able to carry its weapons internally, which ultimately requires a bigger airframe but reduces the stealth signature and makes the aircraft more survivable.

Another matter for concern was the cost of the development of the avionics. For example, the avionics of the McDonnell Douglas F-4 Phantom II accounted for 12 per cent of the fly-away cost. The McDonnell Douglas F/A-18 Hornet avionics already accounted for 30 per cent of the fly away cost. The development costs of the avionics of the Lockheed/Boeing F-22 Raptor were also one of the main reasons of the cost increases incurred during the prolonged development programme. The trend of the ever-increasing costs had to be beaten here as well. The JAST office hoped to learn from the F-22 programme as it had the most modern and integrated avionics suite. The Raptor programme was followed by avionics software stability problems. Risk reduction had been attempted with a Boeing 757-200 Flying Test Bed (FTB). Already during the CDP both Boeing and Lockheed flew with similar planes to emulate the function of the FTB and commit to risk reduction. But companies had the advantage of fresh experience with the F-22.

Production numbers of course would influence the price as well. For example, the F-86 used in Korea had a production run of 6000, the F-4 Phantom II a production run of 5200 and the F-16 Fighting Falcon a production run of over 4000. For this reason the JSF was planned to replace just under 3000 planes in the US forces. Exports were expected to run up to 3000 aircraft, although that is an optimistic figure as defence budgets were decreasing all over the world and have been since the Second World War, which was another reason for decreasing numbers of aircraft purchased. However, the export was no longer limited to sixteen NATO countries and some other allies.

The USMC was committed to the STOVL version of the programme, so much so that it wanted to replace not only its Harriers but also its F-18 Hornets to become an all-STOVL fleet. Budget constraints made for a lot of speculation and it was rumoured that the USMC would have to settle for the CV F-35C. This would be quite a bitter pill for the USMC, as most of the research was committed to the lift technology and the commonality between the designs. The decision by the UK to choose the STOVL version secured the STOVL F-35B from cancellation and meant shared cost for the UK and USMC. It meant as well that the politicians could not cancel the STOVL version as the UK had committed itself as well and therefore no cost saving on this could be achieved.

	1996	1997	1999	2005
USAF	2036	·1763	1763	1500
USMC	642	609	609	420
USN	300	480	480	260
Royal Navy	60	60	150	150

The thought of having the winner taking it all was generally accepted until shortly prior to the winner being announced. A study was requested to evaluate the cost of second Final Assembly and Check Out (FACO) facility. The cost of the second FACO facility was, however, found to be too expensive and the aim of the programme was to save the tax payer's money. For this reason the FACO originally planned to be run by Boeing was soon buried, not to re-emerge until the foreign partners started to lobby for this facility. Italy was the most eager, followed by the UK.

In December 2004 it was slowly accepted by the USAF leadership that the total number of JSFs that the service requested was probably not attainable and that a reduction would be unavoidable. The Quadrennial Defense Review (QDR) was thought to bring more clarity. The fact that the USAF was interested in the STOVL version did not help as it was a more expensive version of the CTOL model. The number of STOVL aircraft, however, depended also on the shape of the reorganisation of the US Army as the STOVL version would be mainly bought for Close Air Support (CAS) missions. The first time numbers were mentioned was by the Air Combat Command (ACC) to the GAO in December 2004 and it stated that the STOVL fleet would amount to 250 aircraft in the USAF inventory and the CTOL version would probably amount to 1300, meaning a reduction of 213 aircraft.

By October 2005 a change in the USAF took place. The change concerned personnel but had an effect on the USAF requirement of the STOVL version. USAF Chief of Staff General John P. Jumper retired and was replaced by General T. Michael Moseley on 2 September 2005. Moseley had a different view of the requirements of the USAF and said that for financial reasons the USAF could not afford to buy the STOVL versions as it wanted to retain a minimum number of F-35 aircraft. This could not be achieved if the USAF bought the STOVL version according to Moseley.

The logistic footprint of an aircraft is in the case of deployments a major cost factor. The budgets were getting smaller so if the support cost could be reduced this would consequently free those aircraft for other tasks, meaning that more could be done with less. At the time when the Lockheed C-141B Starlifter transport aircraft were still around, 14.6 C-141B were required to sustain twenty-four F-16s for thirty days while maintaining wartime operation sortie rate. For the F-15 this was 17.3 C-141B aircraft. As can be seen, to deploy a squadron involves a huge logistic footprint, which brings operational costs. When the Starlifter was replaced by the C-17 Globemaster III a twenty-four F-16 squadron required thirteen C-17s (for the initial thirty days). For the F-35 the number of transport aircraft was set in the Key Performance Parameters (KPP). For a twenty-four F-35 squadron the requirement was fewer than eight C-17 Globemaster III aircraft. The size of the logistic footprint depended on the supportability, maintainability and reliability of the F-35. Two phrases that would become very important were the Mean Time Between Failures (MTBF) and Mean Time To Repair (MTTR). The higher the MTBF, the less personnel was required for a squadron to maintain the aircraft. The shorter the MTTR, the more the aircraft was available for operations and, again, fewer maintenance staff would be required.

The Autonomic Logistics Information System, (ALIS) as it was also called, was switched on for the first time on 30 April 2007. It would, for the time being, support the AA-1 aircraft and the aircraft on the production line. The plan is that all aircraft that are going to be built will be followed here and this system will allow Lockheed Martin to take Performance Based Logistics (PBL) to new levels. PBL was initiated because of experience with the F-117 Nighthawk and other older aircraft. The USAF was paying enormous amounts for spare parts to keep their aircraft flying. This they wanted to change and for this reason started giving industry incentives to reduce the cost of maintenance. The definition of PBL is the alternative logistics support solutions that transfer traditional DoD inventory, supply chain and technical support functions to the supplier for a guaranteed level of performance at the same or reduced cost. PBL proved to be a sounding success for the DoD and was made a requirement across all new procurement programmes, the JSF program was not an exception. The UK had demanded to have autonomous disposal on their F-35s. According to General Davis this was not a problem, however there is probably a cost connected to that and would have to be carried by the UK. A seperate performance-based agreement was signed between the JSF Programme Office and the USAF for the first LRIP 1 aircraft in early September 2005. The agreement was signed by US Navy RADM Steven Enewold on behalf of the Joint Programme Office and Major General Jack J. Catton JR Air Combat Command (ACC) Director of requirements on behalf of the USAF. This agreement would only be for a limited period, however, it would form the basis for the follow-on performance based agreements. On the basis of the results of this performance based agreement estimates for full rate production was to be made.

Five criteria were important according to the agreement

> Operational Availability (1)
> Operational Reliability (2)
> Cost per Unit Usage (3)
> Logistics Footprint (4)
> Logistics Response Time.(5)

(1) Operational availability is calculated on the F-35 aircraft being mission capable, that is for the mission planned and available for use. For each mission it was therefore foreseen that mission essential subsystems lists and mission essential function lists were drafted. In that way the ALIS could continuously determine the status of each aircraft. The ALIS was to keep track if an aircraft was Full Mission Capable, in other words be able to fly every mission, or be Mission Capable.

(2) Operational Reliability is measured by mission effectiveness. It should provide an insight about the aircraft and its systems during mission execution. Mission effectiveness is measured by the amount of primary tasks and secondary tasks that are completed successfully. Mission effectiveness scores would be performed as follows:

100% mission effectiveness means that during the missions all the primary tasks are accomplished.

70% mission effectiveness means that during the missions more then 50% of the primary tasks and some secondary tasks are accomplished.

50% mission effectiveness means that during the missions more then 50% of the primary tasks and none of the secondary tasks are accomplished.

20% mission effectiveness means that during the missions less then 50% of the primary tasks and at least 70% of the secondary tasks are accomplished.

0% mission effectiveness means that during the missions less then 50% of the primary tasks and less then 70% of the secondary tasks are accomplished.

(3) Cost of operating will be innitially high but probably lower then at any time with previous generation fighters. The cost of usage depends on the amount of staff required to maintain the aircraft. The amount of spares required to operate the aircraft in a safe manner.

(4) Logistics footprint will be measured against the CTOL KPP set in the JORD. The logistic footprint KPP is measured in C-17 loads per 24 Primary Assigned Aircraft (PAA). After the LRIP 1 it was planned to measure the change against each previous period. Because of the simple reason that the LRIP 1 has only 2 aircraft this might be extended to the first two LRIP because the period of performance for this performance-based agreement was foreseen from the first LRIP 1 aircraft delivery to the last LRIP 1 aircraft delivery.

(5) This is the time required to get the aircraft or systems in flight-ready shape for the required mission. This would not include cannibalisations. Cannibalisation will only be allowed as 'last resort' solution and should be documented in the ALIS and Sustainement Performance Management System (SPMS) with justification and information on what part or system was cannibalised.

Lockheed Martin would be given Performance Based Logistic contracts on the basis of this document and its performance would also be measured by this document. But each time the experience grew the performance had to go up and accordingly the incentive would be given.

The USA and the partner nations had given its estimated procurement plans for over the next 20 years of the programme in the Production, Sustainment and Follow on Development (PSFD) Memorandum of Understanding (MoU). The estimated procurement totals were without specification as to which version was to be procured.

The decision that for the first LRIP only two CTOL aircraft would be funded instead of the five planned were described by General Charles R. Davis as highly disruptive. The first obvious side effect was that the two aircraft would be more expensive. Reducing the budget would also have a disruptive effect on the flight test programme. As General Davis stated, he did not know yet what the price would be but he was sure that the future would tell. Furthermore he shed a light on how he saw the immediate future procurement. Long lead items for six CTOL and six STOVL versions were planned for LRIP 2. However this does not necessarily mean that they would all be procured in LRIP 2, as could be seen by the LRIP 1. For LRIP 3 General Davis envisioned a small increase to eight CTOL and eight STOVL aircraft. LRIP 4 would see the first carrier version being ordered, however no figures for LRIP 4 were given at this point. It was clear that the above given US rates for the first three years would not be met, which would have consequences on the cost for the US and for partner nations.

Fiscal Year	2007	2008	2009	2010	2011	2012	2013	2014	2015	2016	2017
USAF Amount	5	16	47	56	64	103	135	157	160	160	160
Partner Amount	0	0	3	7	14	39	43	86	92	95	93
Fiscal Year	2018	2019	2020	2021	2022	2023	2024	2025	2026	2027	Total
USA Amount	160	160	160	160	153	148	118	110	110	101	2443 77%
Partner Amount	79	52	44	40	24	13	6	0	0	0	730 23%

CHAPTER 9

WIND-TUNNEL TESTS

Modelling and simulation were where major cost savings were expected. In fact, the JSF programme office expected savings of up to 50 per cent on aircraft development costs. Wind-tunnel testing, however, would still be required as a final proof of concept validation after Computer Fluid Dynamics (CFD) and other computer simulations. Wind-tunnel tests were therefore an integral part of the modelling and simulation. Wind tunnels are not a new means in aircraft development but they are a relatively cheap way to evaluate design and measure certain aerodynamic effects. There are different kinds of tests to be performed and from the outset of the ASTOVL programme wind tunnels have been extensively used to evaluate several designs and concepts. For the ASTOVL the most important part to overcome was the Hot Gas Ingestion and other ground effects that were to be expected during the transition from conventional flight to hover. After the Lockheed team had won the CDP it was clear that the PWSC had to be refined and, again, as cost was a major influence it was better to evaluate design changes in the wind tunnels. Lockheed Martin and its partners, however, had identified their preferred wind-tunnel facilities for the EMD phase as Lockheed announced on 14 February 2001. The wind tunnels to be used were located in the US (AEDC and Veridian engineering, Bihrle Applied Research, NASA Langley, Ames and Glen), the UK (BAE Systems, Aircraft Research Association) and the Netherlands (DNW). According to Lockheed all the facilities had confirmed the schedules of the tests and were fully committed.

Tests at the Veridian Facilities

The Veridian transonic wind tunnel in Buffalo, New York, was used for stability and control testing during the spring of 2003. A ⅛sth scale model was used and aerodynamic characteristics up to speeds of Mach 1.3 were evaluated and the results measured validated design improvements. On 9 June 2003 it was announced that General Dynamics had bought Veridian, including the wind-tunnel facilities, and the acquisition was completed on 11 August 2003. Further tests due at the wind tunnel would proceed as planned and the take over would have no influence on the schedule.

On 2 November 2004 a transonic wind tunnel was utilised for tests in relation to the STOVL and CTOL aircraft. The tests in the transonic wind tunnel were due for completion by the end of November. All transonic wind-tunnel testing regarding the STOVL and carrier version were completed on 12 September 2005. The tests confirmed the transonic and supersonic performance regarding lateral stability for both variants.

Tests at the DNW Facilities

The wind tunnel used in the Netherlands was part of Duitse Nederlandse Windtunnels (DNW) or German–Dutch Windtunnels. Several models have been tested in the Netherlands and perhaps one of the most remarkable models tested there was a one designed to test the acoustics when the weapon bays are open in the High Speed Tunnel and in the Slow Speed Tunnel. These tests were performed in March 2000, still within the CDP phase. The results of similar

A STOVL model is used here to provide details of near ground effects. The Dutch wanted meaningful work that would increase their knowledge on this and could be used for future projects. *DNW/Lockheed Martin*

tests on the F-22 had proved that forecasts made from the data accumulated in the wind tunnel were in agreement with the actual flight data accumulated later in the programme and are therefore considered extremely useful. The model used was of ⅟₁₅th scale of the 230-5 REV C configuration, although it had clipped wings. In the right-hand weapon bay a total of twenty-three pressure transducers were located for acoustics measurements, of which seven were on the weapons and the remaining sixteen on different locations within the weapon bay. The left-hand weapon bay was closed. As the wind tunnel itself is not without noise, acoustics were also measured on the wind tunnel wall and the nose of the aircraft model.

A 12 per cent scale model of the STOVL version was also tested in one of DNW's wind tunnels on contract by BAE Systems. The model was tested over the entire flight envelope for the STOVL versions, and also with tailwinds.

SJ-02   -00057

Another STOVL model evaluated in one of the DNW wind tunnels. Note that the 3-bearing Swivel Nozzle is not fully extended downwards. This model shows an interesting point, in that the nose landing gear door is representative only for the AA-1 prototype. *DNW/Lockheed Martin*

Tests at the AEDC Facilities

The Arnold Engineering Development Center (AEDC) also had its wind tunnel occupied by models from Lockheed and Boeing during the CDP. One was a ⅕ scale Lockheed model.

The AEDC 4T facility was used for testing store separation. The wind-tunnel test section size is 4 ft by 4 ft by 12.5 ft and the T in the name stands for transonic. The main advantage of this facility is that it can be used for altitudes below sea level to 96,000 ft above sea level. The weapon stores separation tests performed here with the STOVL model weapon bay were concluded by 14 March 2005. Stores that were tested first of all were the AIM-120C AMRAAM, the GBU-12 Paveway II and GBU-32 JDAM. The AMRAAM was tested in autopilot mode and without autopilot. One store that was also evaluated but not really an offensive store was the C-13 external fuel tank.

Another wind tunnel was used by September 2005 for the F-35. It was the 16-ft transonic tunnel and it would be used to collect data about the inlet performance, pressure loads and stability and control testing.

It was not only the engines that were tested at the Arnold Engineering Development Centre (AEDC), here a 1/12 model of the F-35 is seen in the 16 foot transonic wind-tunnel of the AEDC. *Copyright AEDC*

Multiple models were tested in wind tunnels to tweak the performance and improve the ultimate design. This is a scale model of the F-35 at the AEDC. *Copyright AEDC*

The 16-ft transonic propulsion wind tunnel was used to evaluate the aerodynamic loads on the wings, the overall aircraft and the horizontal tails. The model used had reconfigurable outer mould lines, making it possible to use it for both the CTOL and STOVL testing. The model used was of 12 per cent scale. Pressure tabs were put on the entire fuselage's wings and tail surfaces so that the loads could be measured. The tests for the CTOL and STOVL were completed by July 2006. The tests will only have to be repeated for the carrier version, and were planned to be performed by the end of 2006.

Tests at BAE Systems Facilities

Other tests included ground environment testing for the STOVL version in which BAE Systems had an experience advantage over its partners. In fact certain facilities owned by BAE Systems are unique in the world and together with the in-house knowledge and experience it was only logical that BAE Systems facilities were used. Problems unique to STOVL aircraft according to Andy Russell, BAE Systems Thermo-Acoustic Facility Lead include:

1 Ground Erosion (GEr)

Occurs when the hot exhaust gases cause the landing surface to degrade, resulting in damage to the landing surface and Foreign Object Damage (FOD), danger to the aircraft and crew.

Measured in the Advanced Gas Facility (AGF) at BAE Systems Warton.

operations the following people come within very close range of the aircraft: arming crew, taxi director, topside petty officer, jet blast deflector operator and aircraft final checkers. For the STOVL version the fear of having people blown around like confetti was a real one. This was therefore carefully measured already in the TAF, with safe areas and danger zones clearly identified as a result. Noise, being a major problem for carrier operations, was measured and evaluated as well. The Jet Blast Deflector (JBD) on aircraft carriers used for take off does not only deflect the thurst of the engine but also noise and heat.

A 7 per cent scale model was used for HGI risk-reduction tests. Different nozzles were tested on the model as a part of the risk-reduction effort in connection with HGI. The shape of the exhaust plume could affect HGI and the shape of the exhaust plume is affected by the nozzle. The tests at Warton were completed on 29 September 2004. The data collected would be used for the F135 full-scale plume testing scheduled for October 2004 but this was delayed as a result of engine availability.

A 7.5% scale model was used at BAE Systems to evaluate the position of the roll post. This effort was done on request by Lockheed Martin so that recommendations could be made to apply potential improvements to the F-35B STOVL variant to reduce lift loss in hover and transition phase of flight. The scale model was equipped with six positions for the roll post exhaust to be evaluated including the baseline position. Of the six positions, in the end only five positions, including the baseline positions, were evaluated during the wind tunnel tests. These evaluations were conducted at Warton in the 4 m and 5.5 m low speed wind tunnels. The evaluations on the 7.5% model were done in close cooperation with Lockheed Martin as they were performing tests on a 12% scale model.

Tests at the NASA Facilities

At NASA Langley spin wind-tunnel tests were completed on 26 November 2003. The purpose of the test was to determine the required size of the spin recovery parachute and the length of the cable from the aircraft called the riser. The tests were performed in the 20-ft vertical spin wind tunnel located at Hampton, VA. The 20-ft vertical spin wind tunnel is considered the best facility available for the evaluation of spin characteristics.

The VMS or the Vertical Motion Simulator at NASA Ames was used during the first quarter of 2004 for three weeks. Although the VMS is not a wind tunnel it is an excellent tool for simulation and therefore for maturation and risk reduction. According to NASA the VMS has an unequalled range of motion, up to 60 ft vertically and 40 ft horizontally, and vertical acceleration of nearly 3/4 g. Furthermore, the facilities' interchangable CAB can be modified to represent any cockpit, so for these tests the cockpit was reconfigured for that of the F-35. The facility had already been used for the JSF programme during the CDP by both Lockheed Martin and Boeing. Lockheed Martin chose this simulator so that it could evaluate the control laws for all three versions of the F-35.

By the end of 2005 Lockheed returned to NASA Ames for a four-week period, mainly to evaluate the STOVL version. The British MoD evaluated the shipboard rolling vertical landing procedure in part to evaluate if it had selected the right F-35 version. (It was not too late to change.) The shipboard vertical landing procedure includes touchdown dispersion and ramp clearance. Other things that were evaluated regarded flight control laws of the CTOL version with regards to high-gain precision tasks.

CHAPTER 10

SUPPLIERS OF THE F-35

Snader/Litton Amecon	Electronic Counter Measures Equipment (ECME)
Lockheed Martin	Electro Optical Targeting System (EOTS)
Northrop Grumman	Distributed Aperture Infra Red Sensor (DAIRS) thermal imaging system
Magellan Aerospace (Canada)	Twenty-four structural wing parts
Vision Systems International	Helmet Mounted Display (HMD)
Hamble Structures (UK)	Integrated canopy frame assembly
Cheltenham (UK)	Electrical power management
Martin-Baker (UK)	Crew Escape system
Michigan, Maryland and Florida	Weapons control and data electronics
New Jersey, Indiana, Washington (US) and Wolverhampton (UK)	Actuation systems and components included in the engine structure and other parts of the aircraft
Marconi Selenia (Italy)	Back-up radio
Honeywell (US)	Air Data System (ADS), Inertial Navigation System (INS), radar altimeter and Tactical Navigation Unit (TNU)
Vought (US)	Wing skins
Moog	Wing-tip fold actuation (for CV only)

These above and below views of the aircraft show where the skin-embedded antennas developed by Ball Aerospace are located. *Copyright Ball Aerospace*

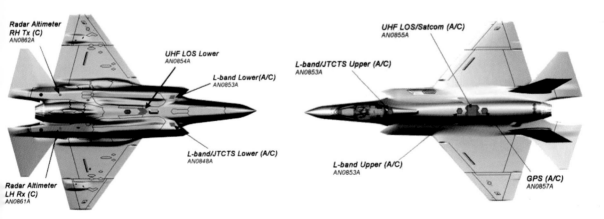

Smiths	Electrical Power System (EPS), RIOs
Goodrich Actuation (formerly TRW/Lucas)	Weapons Bay Door Drive
L-3 communications (US)	Panoramic Cockpit Display
L-3 communications (US)	Crash Survivable Memory Unit
Parker	Fuel system
Goodrich	Landing Gear System
Honeywell	Power & Thermal Management System
Hamilton Sundstrand	Electrical Power System
BAE Systems (UK)	Active Inceptor System
BAE Systems CS	VMC
Moog/Curtiss Wright	LEFDS
Moog/Parker	Electro-Hydrostatic Actuation System
Kaiser Aerospace	Main projection display
Honeywell Normal-Air Garrett	Life support system
Texas Instruments	Integrated Core Processor (ICP)
Ball Aerospace (US)	JSF antenna suite
Raytheon (US)	Anti Jam GPS sensor
Harris Corporation	Intra Flight Data Link (IFDL)
Stork SP Aerospace (NL)	Arresting gear

The origin of suppliers was very diversified and was not limited to the US and the JSF partner countries. In fact, during the SDD phase from 26 October 2001 to 31 December 2003 subcontracts were supplied to France, Germany, India, Israel, Poland, Russia, Spain and Switzerland. The GAO would not specify the companies and parts being produced in those countries. A lot of talk went into the 'buy American' act introduced by President Bush but in effect it did not affect the partner nations as they were considered on the same level as domestic industries as they had signed reciprocal procurement agreements. Another point that had to be taken into account by the DoD was that if it made an acquisition it should not be against the public interest to buy American. From the non-partner countries only India, Poland and Russia did not sign reciprocal procurement agreements. Fifteen years earlier it would have been unthinkable and probably laughable to award a company in Russia a subcontract for the most modern American strike aircraft.

Ball Aerospace received a contract from Lockheed Martin to develop the JSF antenna suite on 21 November 2002. Ball Aerospace had already worked with Lockheed on the F-22 Raptor on the L-band antenna. The antenna suite will include one S-band, two UHF, two radar altimeters and three L-band antennas per aircraft. The antennas for these systems have to be stealthy; in other words they should be within the surface of the aircraft so that they do not disrupt the RCS at any stage. The two UHF antennas are placed one on top of the centre fuselage (AN0855A – UHF LOS/SATCOM) and one on the bottom side of the fuselage (AN0854A UHF LOS Lower). These antennas should enable the pilot to communicate with everybody even though they might be out of line of sight. Communication is two-way so tactical information can be transferred to the pilot and the pilot give information, for example, about required maintenance.

On 20 July 1999 Lockheed and AlliedSignal entered a cooperative agreement to demonstrate two-way satellite communication on an F-16. AlliedSignal would provide the Commercial Off The Shelf (COTS) AIRSAT 1. The COTS AIRSAT 1 is cheaper than a military version and another advantage is that there was no need for another antenna as the AIRSAT 1 could be hooked up with the TACAN (Tactical Air Navigation) antenna. The technology was proved on an F-16D flown by Lockheed test pilots Steve Barter and Troy Pennington on 27 August 1999. The communication was possible as AIRSAT 1 produced by AlliedSignal was connected with commercially available Iridium satellites. The technology had been tested up to Mach 1.6 and the only problem encountered was a disruption in communication when the F-16 was inverted as the aircraft was only equipped with an antenna on top of the fuselage. The JSF F-35 will be equipped on both sides (top and bottom) of the airframe with an antenna so this problem should not occur. The demonstration was, however, using a commercial satellite and research into vulnerability to jamming proceeded. The F-35 will be the first aircraft equipped from the outset with the capability to communicate via satellite.

The two-radar altimeter antennas are located on the aft bottom side of the fuselage beside the engine bay. The two-radar altimeters antennas have the following designations: AN0861A (LH Rx) and AN0862A (RH Tx). The Low Probability of Intercept (LPI) radar altimeter itself is developed by Honeywell. The GPS antenna situated on the top centre fuselage had the registration AN0857A. Under each inlet an L-band antenna is located – one L-band/Joint Tactical Combat Training System (JTCTS) Lower or AN0848A and one L-band Lower or AN0853A. On the top of the fuselage there are two AN0853A upper units of which one is a JTCTS unit.

On 23 September 2003, Raytheon Space and Airborne Systems announced that it had been selected by Northrop Grumman for the SDD phase to develop and deliver the anti-jam GPS sensor. Northrop Grumman has the responsibility of mission system integration of the anti-jam GPS sensor for the SDD phase. The Digital Anti-jam Receiver (DAR) has to provide unprecedented precision in order to provide unchallenged precision strike capability for the F-35. This next-generation system is to combine a twenty-four-channel GPS receiver and an adaptive beam-steering anti-jam electronics in a single LRU but still be compatible with GAS-1 antenna electronics. The DAR is also calculated to be used for more functions such as the JPALS for which Lockheed Martin received a contract on 24 February 2004. The antenna is developed and supplied as described above by Ball Aerospace.

From 1 October 2004 a full-scale pole model built by Advanced Technologies Inc. of Newport News, Virginia, was used to test the L-band antennas installed in the model. The model weighs 8500 pounds and was produced in forty-four weeks. The full-scale model is equipped with interchangeable wing and tail components so that it can perform testing for all three versions. The tests took place at the AFRL in Rome, New York. Early test results were promising as the requirements were either met or exceeded. The model was also used for testing the CNI's systems satellite communications, GPS and UHF/VHF communication apertures. Another system to be tested was the EW system; these tests were due to start in 2005.

The tests performed at the AFRL with the full-scale model will reduce the amount of required avionics flight-testing. The full-scale model is situated on a pole on a mountain with an unobstructed view to give the evaluators the enormous amounts of information required. The pole facilitates almost any view of the plane. The advantage of using the AFRL facility in Newport is that the position of the plane is exactly measured to the antennas. The height of the mountain plus the pole means that a lot of data can be collected that normally would have to be collected during test flights. Eight minutes of these tests equal two hours' of flight-testing for collecting data and the data acquired is more precise due. On 20 March 2005 the model was inverted on the pedestal with the landing gear extended and even had external stores. From the initial tests the measurements of the radar altimeter aperture were evaluated and these showed that there was enough margin available even with the external stores and therefore no modifications would be required.

Hamilton Sundstrand

Hamilton Sundstrand delivered two FADECs (Full Authority Digital Engine Control) for the F135 engine aimed for integration in the Vehicle System Processing/Flight Control System integration lab facility. These two FADECs are the first two that are representative of Initial Flight Release (IFR) hardware.

Hamilton Sundstrand also received the responsibility for the Electric Power System (*EPS*). The EPS has completed its CDR. The EPS for the F-35 has to generate the same amount of electricity as the consumption of fifty homes. This CDR was followed by the CDR of the EPS software that was held on 10 and 11 December 2003. The CDR software includes 24,000 lines of codes and equals 24 per cent of the total software for subsystems being developed for the Vehicle Management Computer (VMC).

Honeywell

Honeywell is the supplier for many modern fighter aircraft and therefore it is only natural that the company was chosen as a supplier for the F-35. On 13 June 2003 Honeywell announced that it was selected by Lockheed Martin to provide key avionics hardware for the F-35. Honeywell supplied the INS/GPS, Tactical Navigation Unit (TNU), low observable Air Data System (*ADS*) and low probability of intercept radar altimeters for all three versions of the F-35. The Ring Laser Gyro (RLG) based INS is planned to be the smallest INS ever produced for military aircraft by Honeywell. The INS should give data throughout the envelope and for all mission requirements. It will provide precise positioning heading and stabilisation information for both targeting and navigation functions.

Honeywell will provide three TNUs per F-35 for all three versions. The TNU is equipped with inertial sensors to measure acceleration and gyro data. The inertial sensors feature Honeywell's Micro Electro Mechanical System (MEMS). The advantages of MEMS are reductions made in cost, size, weight, volume and power. For example, the navigator unit used in the F-15 in 2003 was 1000 cubic inches and the F-16 navigator unit at the same time was 480 cubic inches. The TNU for the JSF will be a 3 cubic inches MEMS-equipped system of equivalent or improved performance. In case of technical failure or battle damage of the primary navigation system the TNU would provide some kind of back up.

Besides the above-mentioned systems developed and provided by Honeywell, the company is also contracted for the On Board Oxygen Generating System (OBOGS). This system provides, as the name suggests, the oxygen for the pilot during missions.

L-3 Communications announced on 26 May 2004 that it had been selected by Lockheed Martin to design and manufacture a Crash Survivable Memory Unit (CSMU). L-3 Communications has major experience with flight data recorders and CSMUs as their products have found their way into the Saab JAS 39 Gripen and Lockheed Martin F-22 Raptor to name a couple. SDD for the CSMU was be completed in 2005. Although the aircraft is designed to be more survivable, its internal Prognostic Health Management systems should detect failures before they become catastrophic, and the aircraft should have more safety systems built in like the AGCAS and ACAS. Safety comes first as pilot training and aircraft increase in cost all the time.

This BAC One Eleven was used for intensive testing by Northrop Grumman. Here it is seen during trials in the CDP phase as the avionics flying test-bed. *Copyright Lockheed Martin*

Northrop Grumman

Northrop Grumman, a major partner in the programme, received responsibility for the Communication Navigation & Identification (CNI) system. More than 120 information-exchange requirements had to be fulfilled. This means that either 120 black boxes could be built and installed in the aircraft, creating a huge and heavy aircraft, or the different systems could be integrated to reduce weight. Weight equals cost so it is obvious that the latter approach was chosen. The software and hardware for the CNI for the first flight were handed over to Lockheed Martin in the autumn of 2004. On 28 October 2004 Lockheed Martin announced that it had installed the CNI into its Mission Systems Integration Lab (MSIL) at its Fort Worth facilities. CNI is an important part of the total avionics system. The main parts that were evaluated were UHF and VHF communication, radar altimeter, intercom, integrated caution and warning, and identification-friend-or-foe capabilities. TACAN was also part of the CNI system. TACAN is not a silent system and is easy to detect but it is widely used by the US and its NATO allies. In fact, there are many more systems that will be involved to meet the many information-exchange requirements. Furthermore, an important part of the CNI involves 3-D audio, voice recognition and voice messaging. It was during a conference briefing in September 2006 that Joint Program Director General Davis indicated that sixty-seven information exchange requirements were critical and did not meet the requirements of the KPP; this was the only one indicated as not meeting the requirements.

In April 2007 one of the critical points was exposed as to the main reason for the KPP not being met. It was that the US Navy was changing its communication satellite system and the requirements were for the new system. This was also under development by Lockheed Martin. It was on schedule but lagging behind the JSF programme. The US Navy's UHF Follow-On constellation is the current system in use but will be replaced by the US Navy's Mobile User Objective System (MUOS). The MUOS is under development but will not be ready for integration for block three. The US Navy however does not want to invest money in integration of the old system when it will be shortly switching to a new system. It was therefore decided that the MUOS integration would be delayed to block 4 so as not to further delay the CNI system. Block 4 development is planned to begin in 2010.

Communication	Navigation	Identification
Link 16	INS	IFF
Multi-function Advanced Data Link (MADL)	GPS	IFF interrogate
UHF	Radar Altimeter	
VHF	ILS	
SATCOM	TACAN	
SATURN	ICLS	
Survivable Radio Communication	JPALS	
SINCGARS	MLS	
Have Quick		
Joint Tactical Radio System (JTRS)		

Smiths Aerospace

Smiths Aerospace had different daughter companies that received at different times different contracts for the F-35. On Thursday 27 February 2003 Humble Structures received a contract from Lockheed Martin to produce and deliver canopy frames for the F-35. The first delivery was planned for early 2004. Humble Structures was making canopy frames for the Hawk, T45 Goshawk and the Harrier I. The canopy of the F-35 was forward-hinged as opposed to the X-35 demonstrator aircraft, which had a side-hinged canopy.

Texas Instruments

Texas Instruments Defense Systems was to win the contract to develop the Integrated Core Processor (ICP) on 3 June 1997. The ICP is the central computer system for the JSF. The ICP is the main source for computing power and provides digital processing power for al on-board sensors, display systems, communications, navigation, electronic warfare, guidance and control. The fact that the Texas Instruments Defense Systems and Electronics group was for sale to Raytheon would not alter the agreement. Originally the Common Integrated Processor (CIP) was expected to fill the function. However, it was considered outdated at the time and by the time the JSF would become operational this might also be the case for the ICP. The ICP is expected to be test-flown in the Cooperative Avionics Test Bed (CATB) BAC-one-eleven. Texas Instruments was taken over by Raytheon in mid-July 1997. The original CDP contract for Lockheed Martin was amended on 27 March 1998 when the JSF office had recognised that it would be beneficial to reduce the risk of the ICP technology. The value of the contract was US $28,744,813 and the work on the ICP technology demonstration was intended to be completed in June 2000.

Flight-testing for the ICP was initiated on 12 September 2005. The first tests concerned electromagnetic interference.

Vought Aircraft

Vought Aircraft Industries Incorporated was selected by Lockheed Martin to deliver the lower-wing skins for the twenty-two SDD aircraft on 26 August 2002. The value of the contract was $7 million. Vought was also awarded a contract by Lockheed Martin to provide technical support in the development of the integrated full-scale airframe test programme. Vought has an extensive background as it used to build Navy aircraft such as the Vought A-7 Corsair II and the A-8 Crusader. Shortly before, in July 2002, Vought had

The Advanced Fighter Technology Integration (AFTI) F-16 was used for the power by wire programme. Here it can be seen with the X-35 pole model. The pole model in the back ground was used for mission systems integration and risk reduction testing. *Copyright DoD*

been awarded a contract by Lockheed Martin for the F-22 Raptor programme to deliver the horizontal stabiliser. Almost two years later Vought delivered the first lower-wing skins on 16 August 2004 to Lockheed Martin, just to the start of the wing assembly structure at Lockheed Martin.

Power By Wire

New technologies that were being developed in the early 1990s were too late for installation in the F-22 if they required major structural changes and if those they were not mature enough. The AFRL initiated the More Electric Aircraft (MEA) programme under which multiple technologies would be developed. One programme supported jointly by NASA, USAF and the Navy was the Electronically Powered Actuation Design (EPAD) validation programme. This programme was split into three parts as three new technologies would be validated. The introduction of the new technologies was performed according to the risk connected with the new technologies. The three technologies were all new actuator designs:

1 The smart actuator
2 The Electro Hydrostatic Actuator (EHA)
3 The Electro Mechanical Actuator (EMA)

For this programme Martin Marietta Control Systems (later Lockheed Martin) was the main contractor, with HR Textron receiving responsibility for the smart actuator. The smart actuator was still dependent on the central hydraulic system but was locally controlled instead of being controlled by the central Flight Control Computer (FCC), rendering a huge amount of the wire bundle connecting the FCC obsolete and therefore reducing the weight substantially. Prior to flight tests the smart actuator was tested on the ground on a retired

Affordable, High-Performance Baseline for F-35

AFTI/F-16 Demonstration Validates
More-Electric Aircraft Technologies   ***Common Components***   **F-35 Subsystems Suite**
Identical to J/IST

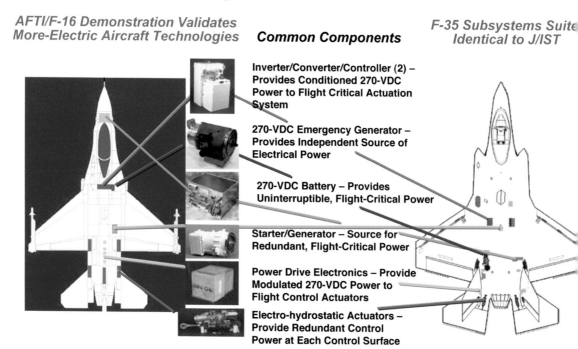

Inverter/Converter/Controller (2) –
Provides Conditioned 270-VDC
Power to Flight Critical Actuation
System

270-VDC Emergency Generator –
Provides Independent Source of
Electrical Power

270-VDC Battery – Provides
Uninterruptible, Flight-Critical Power

Starter/Generator – Source for
Redundant, Flight-Critical Power

Power Drive Electronics – Provide
Modulated 270-VDC Power to
Flight Control Actuators

Electro-hydrostatic Actuators –
Provide Redundant Control
Power at Each Control Surface

The technology transfer of the MEA (More Electric Aircraft) programme into the JSF
programme as it was planned by the Air Force Research Laboratory (AFRL).
Copyright AFRL

F-18 airframe, called the iron bird, for risk reduction. The smart actuator was tested for the
first time in flight on 24 May 1993 on the two-seat F-18B Systems Research Aircraft (SRA).
More than twenty-five flight hours had been generated during which no failures occurred.
The flight programme with the smart actuator was completed on 9 February 1994.

The EPAD validation programme was not only aimed at validating the EHA but also to
ensure that electrically powered actuators would not be a limiting factor in more electric
aircraft. Prior to testing the EHA in flight it was installed in the iron bird. After ground
testing had been completed the EHA was installed in the left wing aileron. Besides the actual
EHA other changes that were made to the aircraft were two independent interface boxes,
one Power Control and Monitoring Electronics (PCME) unit, one Power Conversion Unit
(PCU) and a pilot control panel located in the cockpit. The F-18B SRA with new systems
installed was test-flown for the first time on 16 January 1995 on flight number 564. During
the first five flights three failures were reported, on the first, third (flight 584 on 4 November
1996) and fourth flights (flight 585 on 12 November). From the fifth flight (flight 586 on
16 January 1997) onwards the system functioned without failure. A total of thirty-three test
flights equalling 28.5 hours were flown. During the EPAD validation programme it was
discovered that EHA performed equally well compared with production hydraulic actuators

and the electric actuator concept was considered proven.

In the mean time the development of the EHA had continued and it was reduced in size from 15.9 kg to 7.3 kg by September 1996 but its power had increased. The problem with the EHA was that there were still hydraulic fluids involved although no longer in a central system throughout the aircraft, meaning that a considerable reduction in weight and complexity would be achieved. The EHA was a Line Replaceable Unit (LRU) requiring less maintenance and fault location was easier. Both the EHA and the EMA were the responsibility of Lockheed Martin under the EPAD programme and are both considered as Power By Wire (PBW) actuators. The EHA was under subcontract to Dowty Aerospace and the EMA to MPC Products Corporation. So after the first generation of Fly By Wire (FBW) aircraft, the next generation would not only be Fly By Wire but also Power By Wire.

The EPAD validation programme continued with the next step, which was ground- and flight-testing of the EMA. EMA had some advantages over EHA as it was smaller, lighter and mainly less complex. The weight and size reductions were possible because there were no hydraulic fluids required in the EMA as opposed to the EHA. Maintenance requirements would therefore be lower and application would not only be limited to aviation. In fact, application of the EMA was not long in the waiting as it was introduced for the X-38 space experimental crew-return vehicle. The EMA was test-flown in the NASA F-18B SRA twenty-two times accumulating twenty-five hours and fourteen minutes.

Meanwhile the JAST programme office had sprung into existence and had looked around for new technology and was interested by the work performed at NASA Dryden Flight Research Center (DFRC). In a study performed by DFRC for the JAST programme office it was mentioned that the engine was the main logistics driver for the F-18A/B/C/D. The second to the sixth item were all hydraulic servos from the aircraft's controlling surfaces. These five items together were a bigger logistics driver than the engine alone. Furthermore, the Mean Time Between Failures (MTBF) of the servos did not meet the design specification and the MTBF fell short by factors ranging from two (Leading Edge Flap servo) to ten (stabiliser servo). This was enough reason to try and mature a new revolutionary technology.

Logistics driver F-18 in US Navy Service

F-18 Hornet	Design MTBF	Actual MTBF
Stabilisor servo	3224 hours	323 hours
TEF servo	3224 hours	428 hours
Rudder servo	4500 hours	1091 hours
Aileron servo	4273 hours	1239 hours
LEF servo	4518 hours	2000 hours

The new risk-reduction programme that would use the technology under development in the EPAD validation programme was the JAST Integrated Subsystems Technology or later JSF Integrated Subsystems Technology (J/IST) programme. Boeing, Lockheed and McDonnell Douglas identified the need to demonstrate two things prior to the decision if any of the J/IST technology could be integrated into their final designs. The two demonstrations were:

1 Starting the F119 engine using the integrated subsystem suite during the integrated engine and integrated subsystem ground demonstration.

2 Flying an F-16 with all the primary flight control surfaces powered electrically.

Under the J/IST the new system was further developed and tested and would eventually be test-flown on the AFTI F-16. The programme was initiated on 7 April 1995 by the JAST programme office by issuing BAA-95-3. Three interrelated contracts were awarded to three companies on 22 September 1995. Lockheed received one of the three J/IST contracts issued by the JAST programme office for an electric power generation/distribution system and electric actuation flight demonstrations with a contract value of US $48 million. The other two contracts went to McDonnell Douglas for the Thermal/Energy Management Module (T/EMM) and electric power and actuation ground demonstration and the other contract to Boeing for vehicle level cost/benefit analysis. The contract for McDonnell Douglas had a value of US $65 million.

The programme was led by the USAF research laboratory at Wright-Patterson AFB. Test-flying was to be initiated from the Lockheed Martin Fort Worth facilities in Texas followed by an early transfer to Edwards AFB where the main part of the flight-test programme would take place. According to Lockheed Martin the system is revolutionary as the hydraulic systems for actuation of control surfaces will be replaced by an electrical actuation system. The system has two major advantages: it is lighter than the hydraulic system and it requires less maintenance. Part of the Lockheed J/IST team were companies that supplied the following systems:

- T/EMM (Honeywell) – an integrated turbomachine providing auxiliary and emergency electrical power and environmental conditioning.

- Fan-duct heat exchanger (P&W) – development of both inconel and titanium heat exchangers to mount inside the F119 engine fan duct and provide the heat sink for the T/EMM system.

- Engine-mounted switched reluctance starter/generator (Hamilton Sundstrand) – electrical power-generation system providing dual, electrically isolated, 270 Volts Direct Current (V DC) aircraft power. (It also operates as a motor, when electrically driven by T/EMM, to start the F119 engine.)

- Electro hydrostatic actuation system – Parker Aerospace subcontractor and developer.

EHAs had been flight-tested on the NASA F-18B Systems Research Aircraft (SRA) under the Electronically Powered Actuation Design (EPAD) validation programme and were chosen as they presented the lowest risk compared with the EMA. The EMA was test-flown in 1998 under the EPAD validation programme but it was too late to be introduced in the J/IST programme although it is not clear if it was considered mature enough technology for the EMD (later renamed SDD) phase. The main objective of the J/IST programme flight demonstration was risk reduction so that the J/IST electrical power systems and electrical control surface actuation systems were considered to be mature enough for the technology to be integrated in the JSF EMD phase.

The CDR for the J/IST was successfully completed on 29 and 30 April 1997. Shortly after, the government go-ahead was given for the flight-demonstration programme, to include more than sixty test flights from 1999. Pre test-flight ground tests were initiated with the aircraft weighed prior to the modification after all the fuel had been removed. The next step was Ground Vibration Tests (GVT). This was also done prior to the modification to gain a database of baseline control surface structural vibration. The tests were performed with the aircraft standing on its own landing gear. The tests were not performed with the gear up and the aircraft suspended. After these tests the modifications took place. From May 1997 through to mid-2000 the AFTI F-16 was modified. The dual tandem EHAs were installed on the five primary flight control surfaces, that is, on the flaperons, horizontal tails and rudder replacing the Integrated Servo Actuators (ISAs). Each dual tandem EHA is equipped with a dedicated dual channel Power Drive Electronics (PDE) unit and a common triple redundant Control Electronics (CE) unit. The CE unit ensures overall control of the EHA, redundancy management and built-in tests.

The leading edge flaps, speedbrakes and landing gear retained their original hydraulic systems. A 10-kW AC generator has been added to power these systems. The AFTI F-16 was also equipped with a new power-generation and distribution system required by the new actuators to provide 270 V DC power. Other changes to the aircraft were recording and transmitting systems to record and transmit the performance of the new actuation and power generation and distribution systems during test flights. The team demonstrated in August 2000 on the ground the functionality of the system and with that also predicted cost reductions. All eight operating modes of the integrated subsystem were demonstrated, including:

- Self-starting
- Ground-maintenance electrical power
- Electrical start of the F119
- Avionics and cockpit cooling
- Emergency electrical power from a stored-energy source
- Transition from stored energy to air-breathing mode
- Cool-down motoring of the F119
- Electrical power transition from the engine-mounted starter/generator
- To power the T/EMM internal starter/generator

The acquisition cost should go down by minimally 3 per cent as opposed to the older systems used – a 10 per cent reduction in Life Cycle Cost compared with legacy fighters such as the F-16 and the F15.

Lockheed test pilot Steve Barter flew the first flight of the J/IST system in the AFTI F-16 (c/n 75-0750) on 24 October 2000 from the Fort Worth facilities. The first flight lasted seventy minutes and was twenty months overdue. The delays were mostly software related and therefore Lockheed was confident that as a result of the lessons learned this would not be repeated during the EMD phase. Because of the delay the number of flights was reduced and, furthermore, the entire flight evaluation would now take place at Fort Worth instead of Edwards AFB. This programme was considered such a major improvement, as the hydraulic and mechanical systems had all been removed, that it was awarded the Flight International's Aerospace Industry Engineering, maintenance, and modifications award in 2000. The removal of the hydraulic and mechanical systems will give a 5.5 per cent decrease in the gross take-off weight. Other side effects are that the vulnerable areas in the aircraft are being reduced minimally by 10 per cent. An area that was not discussed so often but quite important for operational use, was the fact that a 20 per cent reduction in Aerospace Ground Equipment (AGE) would be one of the consequences. AGE includes systems like electric generators, hydrazine servicing carts, air conditioners, high-pressure air carts, and hydraulic-fluid 'mules'. To deploy this AGE for a squadron of twenty-four F-16s would require sixteen C-141 Starlifters. So a 20 per cent reduction would translate as thirteen C-141 Starlifter missions, meaning that the logistic footprint would be smaller.

On 9 November 2000 during the third flight, which lasted forty minutes, Steve Barter flew the aircraft at supersonic speed and stated afterwards that the J/IST-equipped AFTI reacted identically to the production F-16. Only four more flights were performed in the AFTI aircraft under the J/IST programme. The last flight for the J/IST programme was on 29 November 2000. The AFTI F-16 S/N 75-0750 took off on 9 January 2001 from Fort

Worth, flying to its final resting place Wright-Patterson AFB, where it would be stored at the Air Force Museum located there.

This shortened test programme only proved that it was possible to integrate the technology and that it had certain weight advantages over the hydraulic systems. This was, however, calculated before testing but other features that required more prolonged testing such as reliability maintainability and supportability were also required for system LCC tests were performed on a different aircraft.

Before the all-electric F-16 was flown in 2000 for the JSF programme the technology had been flying a couple of years already on the Electric Starlifter, or ESTAR. For this test programme the second development C-141 aircraft was used (construction number 61-2776).

This aircraft was equipped with EHAs on the ailerons powered by electric motors instead of the centralised hydraulic system in place before. The EHAs and the electric motors to power them were first test-flown on this C-141A on 25 April 1996. The first part of the test programme was to ensure that the EHAs did not alter the responsiveness of the aircraft. The second part of the test programme was to evaluate the reliability, maintainability and supportability of the system. This was done by performing normal missions for the Air Mobility Command. The aircraft amassed more than 1000 flight hours flying to diverse destination such as Brazil, Korea and Germany. After the programme was completed on 29 July 1998, there was no requirement or test programme for this aircraft. Transferring it to NASA was considered but this did not happen, probably on the grounds that NASA did not have the funds to keep this aircraft in its inventory, and the aircraft was transferred to the AMARC on 7 August 1998 as no suitable museum was found for this particular aircraft either.

On 6 November 2001 Parker Aerospace announced that it would in cooperation with *Moog* be responsible for the primary control actuators and that for the first time in history a production aircraft would be equipped with EHA technology. Both the STOVL and the CTOL version would receive six units (two for the flaperons, two for the rudders and two for the horizontal tails) and the CV would receive eight units (two more units for the ailerons as the CV has an extended wing). The first EHA for F-35 development testing was completed by August 2003.

On 6 August 2002 Moog awarded Curtiss Wright a contract for the Lead Edge Flap Actuation System (LEFAS). Moog is responsible for the Lead Edge Flap Drive System (LEFDS). Curtiss Wright is supplying the LEFDS for the F-22 Raptor.

Hamilton Sundstrand was involved in the J/IST programme, for which it had to built an Electrical Power Generation System. This was cost effective as it could be further developed for use for the operational requirements of the JSF. The power requirements remained the same – 270 V DC.

Honeywell was involved in the T/EMM part of the programme. It was only natural that Honeywell was selected for the SDD phase. Honeywell achieved an important weight reduction for the F-35 programme as it integrated several systems into one. The milestone was described by Roger Wolfe, Vice President and General Manager of Airframe Systems, Honeywell Engines, Systems & Services as follows: By integrating the auxiliary power, emergency power, environmental control and electric power generation into a single system, Honeywell helped designers reduce the fighter's length by about 10 inches (250 cm) and weight by about 1000 pounds. Besides these reductions the integrated system also offers better reliability and lower LCC than separate systems. The integrated system was called the Power & Thermal Management System (PTMS). On 18 July 2004 it was announced at the Farnborough show by Honeywell that the company had initiated development testing of the PMTS. The PMTS provides for the following missions:

- Maintenance power and cooling for the aircraft on the ground, eliminating the need for ground carts. This makes it possible for the aircraft to operate from austere airfields, which is done on a regular basis with some new NATO partners.
- Starting power for the main engine.
- Total cooling for the aircraft throughout the entire flight envelope.
- Emergency electrical power generation should the main systems fail.

The Integrated Power Package (IPP), a subsystem of the PTMS, needed to be tested in combination with the F135 engine and was delivered to the Pratt & Whitney facilities in West Palm Beach on 19 March 2005. Tests on the IPP, connected to the Pratt & Whitney FX640 test engine, were due to start by 8 April 2005. The PTMS should start up the engine as part of the engine tests. Lockheed Martin announced on 29 April that the first engine start with the aid of the IPP had been successful. The IPP is a small gas-turbine engine 'turbomachine' that provides power to the engine-mounted starter/generator. The IPP fulfils the functions of the auxiliary power system, emergency power system, and environmental control in previous-generation aircraft. The IPP was run for the first time in AA-1 on 7 September 2006. The IPP was the first system to be switched on. This test is important as the IPP has to show that it can provide the aircraft with electrical power and cooling. The IPP is started by the pilot from the cockpit and requires no external equipment. The IPP would then in the next phase of testing start the engine. The IPP had started for a total of twenty times without requiring software updates. Prior to the first flight, the IPP had logged 62 successful self starts and 32 main engine starts. The first flight went without a hitch and so the 63rd self start was logged and the 33rd main engine start were logged when Jon Beesley powered the aircraft up for the first flight on 15 December, 2006.

Active Inceptor System

BAE Systems was already involved during the CDP of the JSF programme with the Active Inceptor *System* (AIS). BAE Systems held the first discussions around inclusion of its AIS in the JSF during 1996. The following year it was selected not only by fellow team member Lockheed but also by Boeing. The AIS is responsible for putting through the switch command from the throttle and the stick to the flight control system. The AIS comprises the throttle, stick and the inceptor control electronics. The Boeing plane had a 'normal' layout with a centrally located stick while the Lockheed candidate had a sidestick. During the CDP the AIS proved itself and reliability and mission goals were achieved. On 12 April 2002 BAE Systems was awarded a contract for the further development of the AIS for the SDD phase. The AIS comprises throttle controls and sidestick in the F-35's cockpit. Qualification testing of the first set, one throttle and sidestick, was completed in Essex, UK, on 16 December 2004 and six days later the first set for the A-1 prototype was shipped to Lockheed Martin.

Arresting Gear

Dutch company SP Aerospace received a contract to design and develop the arresting gear for the F-35 in late 2003. SP Aerospace had shortly before demonstrated its capabilities by test-flying a Titanium Metal Matrix Composite (TiMMC) on a landing gear unit of a Dutch F-16. A larger than 40 per cent weight reduction was achieved when the lower drag brace made from ultra high-strength steel parts had been replaced by a unit made from TiMMC. According to SP Aerospace further advantages of the TiMMC are better resistance to corrosion and fatigue. After extensive ground-testing the TiMMC lower drag base was installed on the F-16B 'orange jumper'. Ground-testing then followed on the F-16B, which included integration (does the landing retract correctly?), taxi and brake tests. The F-16B 'orange jumper' from the Dutch test and evaluation unit based at Leeuwarden AFB equipped with the TiMMC lower drag brace flew on 23 June 2003 for the first time. During this flight six landings were performed, from soft landings with low vertical speed to gradually very hard landings with a high vertical speed. The standard version of the F-16 drag brace weighs 7.7 kg. Stork SP Aerospace managed to achieve more than a 45% weight saving for the Ti-MMC version expecting to get the weight even further down as conservative methods were used during development of the prototype. Although the cost of the TiMMC was relatively high at this point it was expected to change with production volumes. SP Aerospace hoped that the technology would be used for aviation landing gears. The cost of developing the arresting gear was estimated at 2 million Euros but SP Aerospace had financial problems and did not have the financial means to commit this amount and therefore the company was taken over by Stork Aerospace. SP Aerospace received the contract to develop the arresting gear for the CTOL version. The contract for the carrier version arresting hooks went to Kongsberg Defence.

EO/IR System

One of the lessons learnt from the Gulf war in 1991 was that precision strike capability required Electro Optical (EO) pods with IR sensors. During the Gulf war British Panavia Tornados were complemented by Buccaneers. The Buccaneers were able to carry the targeting pods, so that precision strikes were made possible. The JSF was a strike platform from the outset and precision strikes were paramount for the future. For this reason as early as the BAA 94-2 a contract was given to Martin Marietta to develop an Affordable Modular EO/IR Sensor Subsystem. Also, it had to be introduced from the outset if possible and at an affordable price. Martin Marietta had worked on an IRST (Infra Red Search and Track) system for the ATF YF-22A programme together with General Dynamics before the ATF's requirement for the IRST system was scrapped shortly before the actual fly-off to cut costs.

On 16 January 2002 Lockheed Martin announced that it had recently received a subcontract from BAE Systems for an Electro Optical Targeting System (EOTS). The EOTS is a derivative of the Sniper XR pod in use on the F-16 and F-15. The EOTS is an integral part of the Electro Optical Sensor System (EOSS) which also includes the Electro Optical Distributed Aperture System (EO-DAS) and is being developed by Northrop Grumman. The EOTS was basically a further development of the Sniper Pod in a different package and without the TV capability. For the SDD phase Lockheed Martin was to supply 10 EOTS systems and 12 window assemblies.

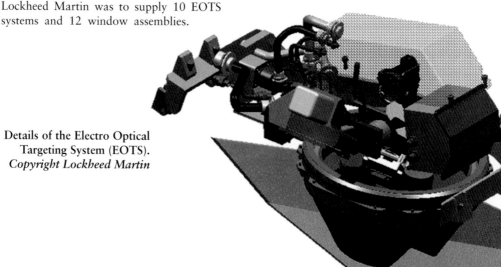

Details of the Electro Optical
Targeting System (EOTS).
Copyright Lockheed Martin

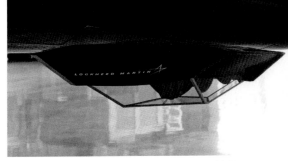

The weight has to be reduced for the JSF F-35's EOTS as the Sniper XR pod is 397 lb (181 kg). The weight target for the F-35's EOTS is 200 lb including the window assembly. BAE Systems received a contract from Lockheed Martin to supply the laser system, an integral part of the EOTS, on 19 September 2003. The new laser will be developed at the Edinburgh Avionics Sensor Systems Division. The laser was intended to provide precision range measurement and a laser-guided weapon designation capability. The EOTS was to be placed under the nose of the aircraft. The EOTS has a special saphire-shaped

The Electro Optical Targeting System (EOTS) Sapphire window close up. The window is designed so that the EOTS has an off-sight capability and should not be limited in any way. *Copyright Lockheed Martin*

window, faceted to allow it to work under all kinds of angles and also have minimum impact on the stealth signature of the aircraft, only four inches of the EOTS protruding at all times. The design of the window was taken from the ATF YF-22 programme. The EOTS is similar in size to an original 17-inch computer monitor (ie not a flat screen one) and is located between the radar bulkhead and the cockpit bulkhead. The dimensions of the EOTS are length 32.1 inches, width 19.4 inches and height 27.5 inches. It also weighs less than 194 lb. The EOTS provides the following capabilities:

- Air-to-Air targeting FLIR
- Air-to-Ground targeting FLIR
- Battle damage assessment confirmation
- Wide area IRST
- Laser designation
- Laser spot tracker for cooperative engagements
- Digital zoom for greater detail
- Geo-coordinate generation for joint series weapons

The Sabreliner has places for two pilots and two flight test engineers. The risk involved with this programme is reduced to a minimum because the EOTS is based upon the Sniper pod also produced by Lockheed Martin. *Copyright Lockheed Martin*

Because the EOTS is integrated in the aircraft the JSF will not have to carry any targeting pods. Ease of maintenance was kept in mind as well. If the maintenance crew wants to access the EOTS he lowers the panel and the system comes down with the panel, which is forward-hinged, providing easy access to the Line Replaceable Units (LRU) as he can stand up as he inspects or changes the LRUs because of the space that has become available between the radar and cockpit bulkheads in the forward fuselage. The CDR of the system's interface was completed by February 2004 followed by the hardware CDR in November 2004. As parts of the EOTS are evaluated in the EO-DAS flight-testing, actual flight-testing of the complete EOTS was planned for rather late in the programme. In fact, it was planned to put the first EOTS through its paces in the Boeing 737-300 CATBird. Installation in the CATBird was planned for June 2006, allowing for flight-testing to

The fact that the Sabreliner was used was because the CATBird was delayed. The test programme on the Sabreliner was pretty intense. *Copyright Lockheed Martin*

commence soon after. The first EOTS for the Mission Systems Integration Laboratory (MSIL) was planned for delivery by August 2007.

Flight of the CATbird was severely delayed. The flight test was prepared on a different aircraft. Preparations were started when the EOTS was initiated on a different aircraft. The aircraft selected was a T-39 Sabreliner, serial number 306-75, registration N11LX, from Lockheed Martin's own inventory. Design activity for the modification of the aircraft was started in February 2007. Integration activity began during the last week in April 2007. On 17 May 2007 the first Safety of Flight sortie was flown. During this flight the EOTS was switched off. The EOTS Sabreliner flight test programme was divided into three phases. The first was planned to run from May to August 2007 and involved maturing the FLIR and tracker algorithms against targets of opportunity as well as collecting IRST data. It was planned to last about 80 flight hours. The second phase has a planned 63 flight hours to mature the laser designator, laser spot tracker and FLIR against tactical targets to verify truth data and continues the IRST maturation. The third and final phase involves 43 flight hours with the F-35 Ownship Kinematics Model (F-35 Navigation System data) and completes the maturating of the FLIR and IRST against tactical targets. At the conclusion of the Sabreliner flight test programme, the system will be ready for integration into the CATB to fly with the entire JSF mission systems suite where it will be fully matured in a fused architecture.

The first phase started of five days later, on 22 May the first flight of the Sabreliner with the EOTS switched on. 'This first flight is a significant step toward ensuring the technical maturity of this infrared targeting system prior to final-stage integration on the CATB (Cooperative Avionics Test Bed) aircraft,' said Rich Hinkle, programme director, Joint Strike Fighter EOTS at Lockheed Martin Missiles and Fire Control. By 14 June 2007 the T-39 Sabreliner had flown eight flights with the EOTS switched on, accumulating about 13 hours.

Northrop Grumman as a major partner received responsibility for the EO Distributed Aperture System (DAS), also known as the EO Distributed Aperture Infra Red Sensor (DAIRS). Both the EOTS and the EO-DAS are part of the Electro Optical Sensor System (EOSS). The DAS should give the JSF 360° spherical threat warning. This will increase situational awareness, making it possible for the pilot to evade high-risk areas and have a greater chance of survival. Northrop Grumman was scheduled to build 74 sensors during the SDD.

14 are assets retained at Northrop Grumman to support software and hardware development and qualification testing

12 are assets to be delivered to Lockheed Martin to be used in their test facilities – the Mission System Integration Laboratory and the CATBird flying test bed.

36 are delivered to Lockheed Martin for installation on SDD aircraft.

9 are delivered as flight ready spares

3 are delivered as non-flight ready spares.

Planned DAS milestones were for the DAS system to be tested for the first time on a roof by May 2004. This would be followed by a first flight in a test bed by August 2005, then a first flight in a JSF prototype in the first quarter (February was the target) of 2007.

On 10 June 2003 it was announced that TNO-FEL from the Netherlands was selected by Northrop Grumman to supply the signal-conditioning algorithms for the EO-DAS system. The signal conditioning algorithms will increase clarity of the infrared image before it is transmitted to the pilot's HMD. A few days later on 15 June 2003 CMC Electronics Cincinnati received a contract from Northrop Grumman to provide the mega-pixel Infrared Detector Assemblies (IDA). The EO-DAS will be equipped with six IDAs. Furthermore, the

EOTS will also be equipped with an IDA, maintaining commonality and therefore reducing cost as the amount of spares required is reduced. The complete EO-DAS had received the AN/AAQ-37 designation by February 2004. The designation from the electronic equipment identification system, which originates from the US Army and Navy (AN), basically means that the AN/AAQ-37 is designed for a manned aircraft (A) and works on invisible light radiation (A) and has a special purpose (Q).

Another step initiated during 2004 was testing the sensors in dynamic fighter conditions in a pod under an F-16 at Edwards AFB. The pod used was a Sargent Fletcher new travel pod. The pod was modified to carry the early risk-reduction DAS sensors with appropriate apertures, ventilation and power. The F-16, with the tail number 86-0359, equipped with an Early Risk Reduction (ERR) sensor pod was from the 445th Flight Test Squadron (FTS). On its first flight on 17 June 2004, with the ERR sensor pod, the aircraft was piloted by Major Chris Hamilton. Other F-16s that were used for this evaluation programme were the AFFTC 83-1118 and 83-1119. The flight-test programme was designed to ease the work with DAS-related algorithms. The ERR pod recorded all the raw infrared digital data so that the contractor Northrop Grumman could analyse the results within forty-eight hours of each test mission. The DAS will enable pilots to have spherical vision from the cockpit, even on the darkest night. The F-35 pilots will have a special helmet that feeds them uninterrupted and seamless infrared video from the sensors. If a pilot looks down, the sensors will enable him essentially to 'see' right through the plane according to Tim Cacanindin, JSF ITF mission systems lead. This feature is expected to be especially helpful during STOVL operations. The ERR pod was equipped with only three of the six sensors that are to be integrated in the DAS system. The sensors in the ERR sensor pod are the same ones that will be integrated in the F-35 and were designed to indicate battle damage and detect live missile fire, which means both Surface-to-Air Missiles (SAMs) and Air-to-Air Missiles. Together with the EW system it was to provide the precision direction finding capability. For the STOVL version it should also provide a tool to help the pilot land the aircraft vertically with its capability to look through the floor. The pod was modified with new recorders and as a result a re-weighing was required for flight-test clearance. Flight-test clearance with the new recorders was issued on 9 February 2005.

An F-16 seen here during its first flight for the risk reduction effort of the Electro Optical Distributed Aperture System. At the controls is Chris Hamilton. *Copyright AFFTC*

There was another milestone for the Northrop Grumman team on 11 November 2005. The company BAC 1-11 was used to flight-test three of the EO-DAS sensors. The three sensors were employed simultaneously, providing a wide Field Of View (FOV) seamless image. The first complete EO-DAS system will be delivered in April 2006 to Lockheed Martin for tests in the JSF MSIL. The EO-DAS will be tested there with other mission avionics systems. The flight tests with the F-16 and the ERR pod were completed according Northrop Grumman officials by December 2005. Testing of the EO-DAS on the BAC 1-11 was expected to continue through the Block 2 software release in August 2008.

Landing Gear

BF Goodrich was involved in the JAST programme before it was selected by Lockheed for the SDD phase. In fact, McDonnell Douglas in May 1996 had selected BF Goodrich to supply the main and nose landing gear for its CDP aircraft proposal. Unfortunately for BF Goodrich McDonnell Douglas's design did not survive the CDDR phase. BF Goodrich was chosen as the supplier for the main landing gear. The main landing gear is a straightforward design yet highly space efficient for stowage. The main landing gear chosen was, however, equipped with hydraulic brakes as the technology of the electronic brakes was judged as not mature enough. Nevertheless, BF Goodrich hoped that this would change as the electric brake technology was, according to Paul Snyder, Vice President of BF Goodrich Wheels and Brakes, had matured enough by July 2004. As well as the lower weight, which was a major issue in 2004 for Lockheed Martin, ease of installation and no worries about leakages would be the major advantages. Paul Snyder stated as well that the fidelity of the electric brakes was higher. A breakthrough might happen if a major customer such as Boeing or Airbus selected the electric brakes. Airbus had committed itself according to Paul Snyder for reliability tests on an Airbus A-320 planned for 2006. He acknowledged, however, that this could be delayed. Another option that was still to be decided was Boeing opting for electric brakes on its Boeing 7E7 (later designated 787), for which a decision was expected during August 2004. After some delay Boeing announced on 10 November 2004 that the customer airliner would be able to choose from either Messier-Bugatti (part of the Snecma group) or BF Goodrich electric brakes. This was a major milestone, eagerly anticipated by Paul Snyder. For the time being the main landing gear of the F-35 was equipped with hydraulic brakes and BF Goodrich has worked closely with Lockheed Martin to achieve the highest level of commonality for the three versions. The landing gear struts will have a health monitoring system to ensure proper servicing levels are maintained and to keep the cost down. The STOVL Weight Attack Team (SWAT) had removed 2700 lb by 14 September 2004 without modifying the landing gear system, although according to some officials it was desirable to lose another 3000 lb. On 21 March 2005 BF Goodrich delivered the nose landing gear to Lockheed Fort Worth in time for assembly of the A-1 prototype.

BF Goodrich bought a division of TRW/Lucas. The TRW/Lucas division was chosen as the supplier for the actuation system of the weapon bay doors by August 2002. The contract value was US $21 million for the SDD phase. After the SDD, however, the value could go up to $650 million. The actuators are hydraulically powered and of the rotary type. The aircraft has two bays per aircraft, two doors per bay and the weapon bay is 14.8 ft long. The weapon bay must be able to open at supersonic speed. The system was chosen for its speed and precision. The fact that the STOVL version received a smaller weapon bay meant that the systems could be less powerful and therefore smaller, saving weight on the STOVL F-35B.

Pilot Flight Equipment

The population range of people that should fit in the cockpit was broadened. This could be seen in the requirements set for the ejection seat. This was also of importance for the flight suit. The standards of the population range were derived from a study performed by the AFRL human effectiveness directorate and the Dutch TNO. These institutions developed a database of new population measurements called the Civilian American and European Surface Anthropometry Resource (CAESAR) and its novelty was that the measurements were of the whole body in 3-D scans. The population measurements were carried out in Canada, Italy, the Netherlands and the USA. The Netherlands was chosen because it has the tallest population in NATO and the opposite is true for Italy.

For the JSF life support working group the American portion of CAESAR was sampled, which totalled 1119 males and 1261 females. This group was reduced through selections based on weight and age among others. The age was set at twenty-one to fifty to take into account reservists that fly. Out of this group remained 646 males and 695 females, which were called the JSF CAESAR pilot size sample. This sample did not, of course, correspond with the sample for the Dutch and for the Italians.

A long way into the SDD phase Lockheed Martin awarded RFD Beaufort with a contract for the pilot flight equipment. RFD Beaufort was responsible for the Eurofighter pilot's garment and had upgraded it and this was, according to Lockheed Martin, the most cost-effective solution. RFD Beaufort had further developed the pilots' equipment and it was now called the Advanced Garment Integrated Life Support Ensemble or AGILE. AGILE includes a fully integrated flight jacket, featuring a flotation collar, survival kit, Chest Counter Pressure Bladder and the RFD Beaufort proprietary arm restraint solution.

Display System

Man Machine Interface (MMI) or Pilot Vehicle Interface (PVI), whichever term you want to use, has become a major science. Lockheed had paid attention to what was happening with its F-22 Raptor and had decided that for the design of the cockpit instrumentation the company needed to be extra prepared. It was not that Lockheed had not been prepared with other programmes, but now it was a different situation. This aircraft was not developed for only one service. The avionics had to be used by all services and every service had to be 100 per cent happy with the avionics to avoid a situation where one service would walk away, which had happened with the General Dynamics F-111. The Head Down Display would be one of major information providers for the pilot and a means to let the aircraft communicate with the pilot. The number of sensors and other integrated systems on the aircraft was unprecedented even compared with the F-22 Raptor. What all manufacturers of the European fourth-generation fighter aircraft had already encountered was the problem of information overload. The biggest problem for the pilot is that the display system presents the information to him in a two dimensional format, the pilot has to translate this information into three dimensional reality. For this reason the requirements for the displays in the aircraft were higher as they had to be more advanced but on the other hand more reliable and easier to maintain. In short, they should have lower Life Cycle Cost.

Kaiser Aerospace, a Rockwell Collins subsidiary, was selected in December 2001 to develop and produce the main projection display for the F-35 cockpit. Long before this contract was awarded Kaiser Electronics had been busy competing for this contract. In fact, on 16 March 1999 Kaiser Electronics signed an MoU to optimise the Multi Functional Display (MFD) system ahead of the EMD phase (later renamed the SDD phase). In 1999

AA-1 with a strange occupant strapped in. The FOD shield covers the display, this is done so that during the assembly process the display does not get damaged. *Copyright Lockheed Martin*

The AA-1 cockpit. This cockpit has the projection display from Kaiser Aerospace and Electronics. On which aircraft the L-3 displays will be installed for test is not clear. *Copyright Lockheed Martin.*

Kaiser Electronics provided Lockheed Martin with a fully functional 20 inches by 8 inches display system for evaluation in the Lockheed Martin JSF fighter evaluation centre. The new display would not be on the Active Matrix Liquid Crystal Display (AMLCD) based technology. It would involve projection technology bringing a host of advantages, one of them being that it was developed using COTS components. The commercial components are the graphic chips, network interface and LCOS. Another advantage is that a single 'optical engine' design can be used for different display formats. This technology has been put to operational use for the first time in the F-18E/F with a display size of 6 inches by 6 inches. The F-22 Raptor was the second aircraft to receive a projection display of the size 8 inches by 8 inches.

The MFD system should enormously improve the MMI. One novelty introduced is the touch-screen interface, which besides improving MMI should also reduce the pilot's workload. Although the introduction of touch screen is a technological advance, it was not seen as a risk as no back-up buttons were situated around the display screen. Besides the touch screen another way of controlling the MFD is by voice command. If both these relatively new methods, although both considered primary, should fail there is another back-up system built in on the HOTAS system. A cursor controller on the throttle; the Left Hand Inceptor (LHI), is used to 'click on' the active touch icons to change the display size or window. The MFD system has only three Line Replaceable Units (LRU), of which two are identical, making the number of spares required on the flight line smaller. The MFD system is naturally, like all fourth-generation or post fourth-generation fighters, night-vision compatible.

To increase redundancy the MFD system has been developed to operate without ECS (cooling) air for thirty minutes in a reduced display mode. This allows the pilot to return to base in peacetime or in war time closer to the battle-edge front to make survival and enemy capture evasion and search and rescue more likely to succeed.

By October 2002 Three-Five Systems was given a contract to deliver silicon chip microdisplays to drive the 51 cm x 20 cm rear projection display.

Before the projection MFD was test-flown in any prototype the technology was to be test-flown in 2005 in the Cooperative Avionics Test Bed (CATB) Boeing 737-300, also known as CATBird. The new CATbird will be used alongside the Northrop Grumman BAC-1-11 that has been fulfilling this role up to now. The Boeing 737-300 will be equipped with an aerodynamically neutral canard to emulate sensor positions on the wing and a special extended nose with a radome for the AN/APG-81. By January 2004 it had flown 28.7 hours

The cockpit of the F-35 complete with both displays installed – however, the two displays will form one unit. As the displays are controllable by touch there is no need for buttons around the display saving valuable space.
Copyright Lockheed Martin

of baseline testing.

On 16 November 2005 it was announced by L-3 Communications that its L-3 Display Systems division had received a contract to design, qualify and manufacture a high-resolution, high-brightness night vision-compatible 20 inches by 8 inches AMLCD. The Panoramic Cockpit Display (PCD) as it was now called would provide the pilot as well as the normal flight displays, sensor displays, communication, radio and navigation systems and identification systems. The PCD would give the pilot total situational awareness. L-3 also fulfilled another requirement for the PCD as it had put together an international supplier team from partner countries. Suppliers were Logic Sistemi Avionici of Milan, Italy; Aydin Yazilim ve Elektronik Sanayii A.S. of Turkey; and Philips Mobile Electronics of Heerlen, the Netherlands, among others. According to John Kent of Lockheed Martin the commercial industry had moved away from projection displays and the JSF had to follow this trend to keep the cost down. However, the early SDD aircraft will be equipped with the projection displays from Kaiser Aerospace. The AMLCD is brighter/clearer, weighs less and offers better performance. Commonality issues would have to be dealt with by the L-3 side as VSI was too far advanced to readapt to this new supplier. Similar to the projection display, the new display will in fact have no buttons around the display area. All the touch functions are on the screen. The touch-screen technology that was tried out in the YF-22 but considered not mature enough for the F-22 has matured sufficiently to now be integrated to help lower the pilot's workload. The PCD is divided into different windows, each called a portal. The upper inch of the display has icons for household functions, such as engine function, fuel and hydraulics. If required, the pilot can make it a full portal by a touch on the screen, voice command or cursor hook. The remainder of the display screen can be divided into twelve portals and the pilot can select the size of the portals to increase his situational awareness at any given time. If the pilot selects to use the maximum 12 portals he uses four main displays (larger sized portals) with eight subdisplays (smaller sized portals) below them. The pilot can select images from the radar, EO-DAS, EOTS, EW System or a mixture of all on the tactical display. The tactical display will display the information gained from all the sensors and will give the pilots options on how to deal with the threat. Out of fear that there might be information lost, it will be possible for the pilot to call up a dedicated screen for each system, for example for the EW System.

From HUD to HMD

In 1996 a joint venture was formed between EFW Inc., a subsidiary of Elbit Systems from Israel, and Rockwell Collins to pursue opportunities for the marketing and developing of Helmet Mounted Display (HMD) systems for fixed wing aircraft all over the world called VSI or Vision Systems International. Elbit's subsidiary had developed the Display And Sight Helmet (DASH) Helmet Mounted Sight (HMS). This evolved into the DASH HMD system, which is also in VSI's portfolio. The *raison d'être* for the joint venture was the Joint Helmet Mounted Cueing System (JHMCS) developed for the F-15, F-16 and F/A-18 and possibly for the F-22. The HMD had proven that its worthwhile in diminishing pilot's workload, as it was able to present data to the pilot in three dimensional format as opposed to the head down displays. It was clear at that point that the ultimate JSF would be equipped with a HMD system. What was unclear, however, was what the exact requirements were for the HMD system. In the Operational Requirements Document for the JHMCS it was stated that the JHMCS should retain excess throughput and growth capability beyond that necessary for cueing to allow the aircraft energy and positional state to be displayed. A further development of the JHMCS to enable commonality and to reduce costs seemed the most likely option.

At the Paris Air Show Le Bourget of 1997 it was announced that Lockheed Martin had selected Flight Visions to supply a Head Up Display (HUD) for the CDA. The system chosen was the newly developed Nighthawk weapon delivery system/HUD with a 30-degree FOV and 150-mm aperture. The contract was only for the two CDAs and was granted on a cost value basis. A total of seven HUDs would be delivered to Lockheed. Flight Visions most recent success included the Czech Aero Vodochody L-159 ALCA, the Swiss Pilatus PC-7 and PC-9 and the Polish PZL Turbo Orlik. Flight Visions thought that Marconi Avionics was its biggest competitor

The alternative Helmet Mounted Display (HMD) was a requirement for the UK. Cost and funding however killed the programme rather quickly. *Copyright BAe Systems.*

for the EMD and production phase. Marconi Avionics was eventually selected by Boeing by September 1998 for the CDP. But for the production phase or even the EMD phase the competition came from a completely different direction than was expected. Flight Visions commenced deliveries to Lockheed in October 1998.

VSI worked with both competitors, Boeing and Lockheed Martin, from early 1997/8. The requirements were changing but Lockheed Martin came to the conclusion by May 2000 that it wanted to go for a cockpit without HUD. The requirements normally set for a HUD were now set on the HMD. Boeing followed suit shortly after, pushed by the government also to develop a cockpit without HUD. Technology advances make it possible to track the pilot's head position – for this purpose two head-tracking devices are installed in the cockpit and therefore the system knows where the pilot is looking. Furthermore, the exact position of a regular HUD is also known so that the normal information found on the HUD, including gun-aiming device (normally integrated in the HUD), will be displayed on the HMD in the HUD region. The accuracy in the HUD region has to be for this very reason very tightly controlled. The accuracy of the HMD is to be unrivalled as it has to replace also the HUD gun-targeting system and for Navy pilots the landing information display. The JIRD II for this reason stated that mission management should require minimum pilot input and include a system to display flight/mission information with the ability precisely to target and employ off-bore sight weapons. This would mean, in other words, to ease pilot workload only Primary Flight Reference (PFR) should be displayed, plus the immediate mission-related (targeting) information. PFR, however, as stated earlier, can be service dependent and that was the major difficulty to overcome with the development of the display. Another hope and risk was that spatial disorientation could be reduced but only under careful examination of the requirements and careful design of symbology. The fact that the HUD and therefore the PFR would always be in front of the pilot's eyes no matter where he looked was expected to lower the chances of spatial disorientation. A major challenge that had to be taken into account as well, if spatial disorientation was to be prevented, was not only the attitude of the aircraft but also the pilot's head position in relation to the attitude of the aircraft.

A technology demonstration or a feasibility programme was required and a Lockheed Martin-led team set out to demonstrate that the technology required was available. This was, however, quite a step because HMD systems were just about becoming a regular sight in cockpits but they were not the standard yet. The requirement to have the HUD information including the PFR also displayed on the HMD was a big challenge. The virtual HUD programme was born and was to be evaluated on the VISTA F-16. BAE Systems participated as well and delivered a BAE Systems Viper IV HMD, a 40-degree Field Of View HMD installed on a slightly modified HGU-86/P helmet shell. The Viper IV was cleared for windblasts up to 550 Knots Indicated Air Speed (KIAS). This was important in case of emergency egress. Honeywell supplied the HUD electronics switching unit, the HMD camera electronics unit and the advanced metal tolerant head-tracking system. A secondary research that was performed during the tests was the evaluation of the Verbex 'Speech Commander', a speaker-dependent Voice Recognition System (VRS). For this reason the MBU-20/P oxygen mask was equipped with an electro voice M-169A/A1C microphone. The Viper IV HMD, including the MBU-20/P oxygen mask and the head-tracker receiver was about 1.5 pounds heavier than a standard USAF helmet. The survival vest, an SRU-21P, was equipped with two microphones, a microphone power supply and a Digital Audio Tape (DAT) recorder.

The flight-test programme took place from 17 May until 16 June 2000 and in total twenty-three flight tests were performed by pilots from the US Navy, USAF, Lockheed Martin, BAE Systems and Veridian Flight Research Group. The Joint Cockpit Office co-funded the programme, at least for the US government pilots involved. Two contractor pilots functioned as engineers to ensure that the system was functioning as advertised. Seven pilots functioned as evaluation pilots, of which three were from the US services. Three pilots had experience with HMD systems so they flew only once. The other four pilots without HMD experience each flew three times. Safety pilots were supplied by the Veridian Flight Research Group and included Jeff Peer, Randy Bailey, Tom Landers and Karl Hutchinson. Flight-testing was initiated from the Veridian Flight Research Group facility at Buffalo-Niagara International Airport. As the VISTA F-16 was a two-seater the evaluation pilot would sit in the front and the safety pilot in the back. For the first two flights the crew in the front and back seat were both from the Veridian Flight Research Group. The aim of these two flights was systems debugging, troubleshooting and calibration flight manoeuvres and they accumulated a total of 2.6 flight hours. Two more flights were flown by Lockheed Martin test pilots to complete the check-out and calibration phase totalling 2.4 flight hours. After the calibration phase four flights were flown by BAE Systems and Lockheed Martin

The Striker Helmet will be the basis for the alternate HMD for the JSF. The AHMD never made it further than the simulator mainly because the UK had to carry the financial burden on its own and it was deemed that the BAe Systems HMD had not progressed as far. *Copyright BAe Systems*

pilots in the front seat to complete the virtual HUD operation and functionality; these two pilots were not evaluation pilots and did not participate in the evaluation. During the eight flights so far 10.2 flight hours had been accumulated.

For the evaluation two different versions of the virtual HUD were to be evaluated, together with the normal HUD for comparison's sake. Of the virtual HUDs tested one version had off boresight capability and one did not. The symbology used was the same for the three systems evaluated: HUD, virtual HUD without off boresight capability (called fused) and virtual HUD with off boresight capability (called split). Fused offered the symbology only in the area where normally the HUD would be located but now the information would presented on the Viper IV HMD. If the pilot looked away from the Field of View of the normal HUD position the information would disappear from the Viper IV HMD visor.

Jon Beesley with HMD used during initial flight test of AA-1. The HMD was supposed to go through some more slight external changes and probably also on the inside. *Copyright Lockheed Martin*

The remainder of the flights were flown by the evaluation pilots from Lockheed Martin, the US Navy and the USAF. The first evaluation flight involved also the transfer from Buffalo-Niagara International Airport to Fort Worth Naval Air Station (NAS) joint reserve base from where the remainder of the flight evaluations were performed. This is also where the F-16 production line was based so excellent support facilities were available. In each evaluation flight four tasks had to be performed to evaluate the virtual HUD concept including its usability as the Primary Flight Reference (PFR) display. The four tasks were:

- A high-speed precision instrument control task (three times per flight if the weather allowed it)
- A low-speed precision instrument task with simulated instrument landing system approach (three times per flight if the weather allowed it)
- Unusual attitude recovery (three times per flight if the weather allowed it)
- Power approach and landing (two real ILS ((Instrument Landing System)) approaches if the weather allowed it)

Besides the above tasks two other tasks were performed to evaluate the VRS, one on the ground and one once airborne. Reactions from the pilots were normally good as to the potential of the technology but one thing that was clear was that the technology involved required more development prior to entry into service.

The monocular HMD did get some negative pilot remarks, which made it obvious that the HMD developed for the JSF should be a binocular one. One of the evaluation pilots was quoted as saying:

The other thing that bothers me, and is going to give me a headache after a period of time, is in the air now I'm noticing the monocularity of the display. I'm feeling heaviness in my left eye. It's obvious that I'm looking through one eye to do this task so I think my right eye is generally getting a little tired of being

The HMD as it was during its development in early 2004 without the mask. The HMD is going to replace the HUD for the first time in any production fighter. *VSI*

taxed a little bit.

The VRS system pleasantly surprised some of the pilots as they had expected worse. Again, the system was used for household tasks and not for mission-determining tasks. For this the technology was considered not reliable enough and in a full-out war it was questionable if one would get a second chance to do the job.

In a press statement at Farnborough 2000 BAE Systems announced that the Striker HMD system was the only system that had been tested to 600 knots' windblast and the nuclear, biological and chemical levels required by leading NATO air forces. Boeing performed its fourth full mission simulation for its PWSC with the BAE Systems Striker HMD as an integral part of its pilot vehicle interface. During the 100 missions flown by US and UK pilots the Striker HMD was seen as a major step in technology maturation by Stan Kasprzyk, Boeing JSF cockpit manager. Unlike the BAE Systems' Viper IV HMD used on board the Boeing 737 Avionics Flying Laboratory (AFL), the Striker HMD utilises an advanced optical tracker, which eliminates the need for the magnetic mapping of each cockpit, which applied to earlier HMDs. Furthermore, the Striker HMD does not use Light Emitting Diode (LED) or Cathode Ray Tube (CRT) display technology. It uses Liquid Crystal Displays (LCDs), also eliminating the need to route high voltages to the helmet.

The shell of the HMD changed design as can be noted from the previous picture. *VSI*

The JSF would be the first fighter since the introduction of the HUD to fly without one. The deletion of the HUD provides a cost and weight reduction. More importantly, it clears important space for other instruments within the instrument panel. The HMD system for the JSF has a binocular wide FOV with a twenty-four-hour mission capability, meaning also night vision capability and compatibility. The FOV is 30° by 50° partially overlapped binocular; this will feel slightly unusual to the pilot as it does not mimic the natural human eyesight (full overlap does mimic natural human eyesight). Binocular HMD will be better suited as both eyes will be employed. The disadvantages of a monocular HMD became more than apparent during the virtual HUD programme. The HMD is supposed to integrate with all pilot systems. The HMD was planned to be a relatively lightweight 4.25 lb with a balanced centre of gravity, ensuring safe ejections. 3-D audio would be integrated, giving cues to the pilot about the direction of a danger or from which side a certain pilot is communicating to him. To make this system work better the HMD system is also equipped with an Active Noise Reduction (ANR) system. The visor would protect the pilot against laser with the Joint Aircrew Laser Eye Protection (JALEP). Besides the helmet there is one LRU in the aircraft plus two head-tracking devices. To minimise cost and increase commonality the same graphics card as the one used for the display system is used for the HMD. VSI has also reduced the cost by using COTS components in digital electronic parts of the system. VSI signed an exclusive teaming agreement with the Lockheed Martin team in 2000, which was confirmed by a contract award for the SDD phase in January 2002. Boeing had selected BAE Systems as its preferred supplier for the HMD system for its PWSC.

On 27 February 2003 VSI awarded English company Helmet Integrated Systems Ltd a contract to develop a helmet for its HMD system. Helmet Integrated Systems Ltd is also responsible for the helmet used in the F-22 Raptor. On 27 August 2003 VSI received a contract from Lockheed Martin for the further development of the HMD system and delivery of units to be used in JSF development and integration laboratories, simulators and prototypes. Options for further units required for Operational Test & Evaluation and for new technology insertions are also included in the contract.

Development for this HMD system was initiated in 2003. Although it was based on technology for the Striker HMD system developed for the Eurofighter Typhoon, the HMD system for the JSF did not have any detachable image intensified Charge Coupled Device (CCD) camera devices. VSI has a different approach, because it believes that an ejectable system can be hazardous to the pilot and also have a negative influence on the quality of the image. The solution was basically to have the aircraft's EO-DAS hooked up with the HMD. The head tracker would inform the aircraft where the pilot was looking and the avionics would pick the segment of the EO-DAS imaging that had been collected representing where the pilot was looking and send that information back to the HMD to display. This would be continuously updated as the pilot moves his head all the time and should be presented in such a flowing fashion that the pilot will not notice that his screen is presented in short bursts.

The JHMCS is a clip-on system meaning that each pilot will have his own helmet but can actually share the cueing system that is clipped onto the helmet. As a result of the requirements this was not possible to maintain with the new HMD for the JSF. It was to be a totally integrated system and for each pilot a HMD system would have to be bought as every pilot has a different sized and shaped head.

On 18 February 2004 Lockheed Martin received a contract as a part of Foreign Military Sales (FMS) to conduct an alternative HMD integration study and design for the UK. The value of the contract was US $14,339,010 and it was expected to be completed by March 2005.

By April 2004 mock-ups have been used for demonstrations of the VSI HMD system, including in a Pitts S-2B aircraft (construction number 5325, registration N597TJ). Several combat manoeuvres were made and to make it more realistic the combat manoeuvres were made in conjunction with a Su-26 monoplane (registration N6211X). The pilots during these evaluation flights pulled up to 6 g. Tom Burbage said during a presentation on 4 October 2005 that at the suggestion to evaluate the weight and centre of gravity of the HMD in the centrifuge there were very few volunteers – the evaluation method in the Pitts S-2B was preferred by the pilots. The HMD was tested by F-35 ITF test pilots and according to them improvements had been made in comfort, stability and fit. In the week of 27 September 2004 the Pitts aircraft was used again but this time slippage and buffeting problems encountered during prior tests had been eliminated. HMD flight-testing in an F-16 was planned by the F-35 Integrated Test Force (ITF) for 2004.

On 8 September 2004 BAE Systems announced that it had been awarded a contract by Lockheed Martin for the development of an alternative HMD. The BAE Systems HMD is to be based on the Striker HMD designed for the Eurofighter Typhoon, which was in the final stages of its development. The head tracker would be based on that used for the Striker HMD. The capabilities of the new HMD would include the displaying of HUD symbology, video imagery from the F-35 sensors and compatibility with helmet-mounted night-vision cameras. The HMD is aimed at the UK forces and other Eurofighter countries equipped with the Striker HMD. For BAE Systems it was a return to the JSF programme for its HMD system as the company had been chosen previously by Boeing as its prime partner for the HMD system during the CDP, even though Boeing had been closely cooperating with VSI on the JHMCS.

On 1 November 2004 VSI initiated HMD centrifuge testing at the AFRL facilities at Brooks AFB. The HMD was tested together with the AVOX Systems oxygen mask and the tests were completed on 3 November 2004. Shortly after completing these tests the Technical Readiness Review (TRR) was held for the HMD on 9 November in preparation for the windblast testing due to be performed at Patuxent River. Windblast testing is important for three reasons:

1 The head and neck loads experienced by the pilot are examined.

2 Compatibility of the HMD with the ejection seat is evaluated.

3 The structural integrity of the helmet is tested.

Windblast testing is less expensive than the sled tests or wind-tunnel tests. They are, however, not sufficient to guarantee safety of flight. Windblast tests are good, however, for comparing results with HMD systems or normal helmets that have been certified for safety of flight.

A Martin-Baker Mk 16B seat with another head pad provided by Lockheed Martin was used for the windblast testing, which took place from 15 to 17 November 2004. Different size mannequin heads were used during the test trials so that they would be representative of the different head sizes of actual pilots – these tests were primarily for head and neck loads. The compatibility with the ejection seat tests were performed at Martin-Baker's test range in Northern Ireland. As the HMD system was going to replace the HUD, the F-35 had to be equipped from the outset with an HMD. The plan was revised slightly in 2005 and the revisions included the fact that for the first prototype A-1 the HMD would meet the first flight requirements but would be day-only qualified. The A-3 aircraft would receive the first day/night qualified HMD for its first flight, buying almost two years of extra time if not more as delays could still be incurred.

When Lockheed Martin F-35 programme manager Tom Burbage was asked during the Paris Air Show in 2005 if using the BAE Systems HMD would be an option he stated that the VSI HMD was a lot closer to fulfilling the F-35 requirements than the BAE Systems HMD. The BAE Systems HMD was therefore not considered an option at the time. The first things that were required for the safety of flight qualification were continued windblast testing and the ejection sled testing. According to a press release from Gentex dated 22 February 2005, the windblast tests had been completed to 660 KEAS (Knots Equivalent Air Speed, which is calibrated airspeed corrected for compressibility effects) with its MBU-20/P oxygen mask, which was an integrated and essential part of the VSI HMD system for the F-35 pilots. According to *Gentex* the windblast tests were executed at Dayton T. Brown's windblast facility in New York. The MBU-20/P oxygen mask was also used in connection with the JHMCS so the two companies were familiar with each other. The windblast testing for the HMD was accomplished above 600 knots on 7 June 2005. Windblast testing is important as these tests should prevent facial injuries when the pilot ejects. According to Tom Burbage, this was a major relief as it was one of the more difficult tests. However, Louis Taddeo remarked at the Paris Air Show 2005 that the upcoming ejection sled testing was more of a nerve-racking. According to Louis Taddeo the tests were due to start either during the Paris Air Show or shortly after. The high-speed ejection sled tests were completed on 24 August 2005. Holloman AFB is equipped with a high-speed test track and for these tests a JSF forebody equipped with an F-16 ejection seat was utilised. A large mannequin equipped with a mock-up VSI HMD was ejected at the equivalent speed of 600 knots airspeed. According to Louis Taddeo the test was a success as the HMD remained intact and protected the pilot's head. Furthermore, it was, according to the knowledge of VSI officials, the first HMD truly tested up to that speed and to fulfil that requirement. For comparison VSI's other HMD system, the JHMCS, had been tested in this manner up to 450 knots. It was, however, acknowledged that an ejection at the speed of 600 knots was an extreme.

It was only for a short while that the development of the alternative HMD continued as the British MoD also had financial problems and needed to make some choices. Most, if not all, the MoD's procurement programmes were over budget and it had to decide where to save money and as the alternative HMD for the JSF was only requested by the MoD it had to provide the funds. It was therefore the most obvious element to be sacrificed in 2005. As the funded study was expected to last only until March 2005 the funding for the following phases of development was not issued. The fact that funding was not released for the alternative HMD was good news for VSI as now its HMD system would equip all the F-35s.

VSI had received the responsibility to select the oxygen mask from Lockheed Martin. However, VSI was told to choose an existing COTS oxygen mask. The COTS oxygen masks available did not meet the requirements requested by the customer. The HMD was expected to be delivered in June 2006 in time for the planned first flight. The hardware is not the

Detail of the VSI HMD from the right side at Holloman AFB. *VSI*

Detail of the VSI HMD from the right front at Holloman AFB. *VSI*

A mannequin equipped with VSI HMD in the seat ready for the VSI's 600 KEAS Sled Test at Holloman AFB. *VSI.*

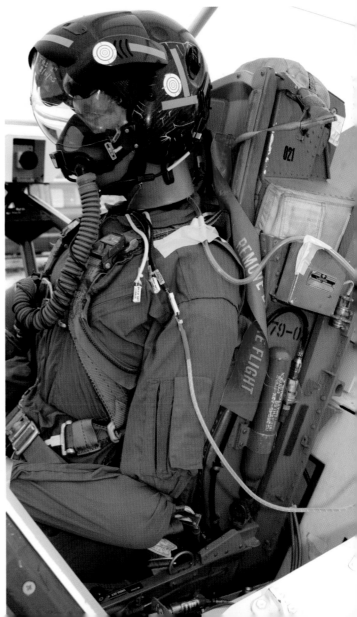

problem: the problem is the software. The software and the hardware for the first flight have been evaluated in the MSIL. The first power on for the HMD was in an unspecified F-35 laboratory. Dynamic symbology was projected onto the HMD visor utilising the Vehicle Management Computer (VMC) and the Display Management Computer (DMC). It is also planned to integrate both these systems in the F-35.

In December 2006 the HMD was not deemed flight ready and for this reason Jon Beesley flew the AA-1 aircraft without the HMD on its first flight. The aircraft was not equipped with a HUD, so flying was more work intensive. This was one of the reasons why it was decided that for the initial part only, Jon Beesley would fly. After seven flights the aircraft was grounded for a software upgrade which made it possible to fly with the HMD. After the software upgrade there were two verification flights in March 2007. On the 10th flight, April 4, 2007, Jon Beesley was at the controls with a functional VSI HMD which was only a pound heavier than the helmets in use with current fighters such as the F-16, F-15 and F-18. After 19 flights of the AA-1 Jon Beesley said that flying with the HMD had become natural really quickly. He mentioned that latency, or delay of the display image when moving the head was good, the VSI folks had done a really good job to get the latency down to a minimum. He stated that while testing the HMD, he had not been bumping up and down with his head as this is not the way how the HMD would be used by pilots in service. However prior to this flight Jon Beesley had urged for the HMD flight testing to commence. He stated to the engineers jokingly, 'you try to park your car while looking at your radio'. The HMD that was being flight tested would be however slightly different externally from the final version that would go into service. Furthermore the HMD had been tested in the F-35 up to 3.5g. The AA-1 would not be used until its full 9g capability was proven. The tests in the Pitt Special were only up to 6g. The HMD would be tested during the summer of 2007 in the UK in a BAE Systems Hawk.

CHAPTER 11

CREW ESCAPE SYSTEM

Ejection seats, normally standard equipment in military aircraft since the Second World War, were more important in STOVL aircraft as they were more prone to crashes, especially during the development stage. The only western operational VTOL aircraft, the Harrier, has a higher attrition rate as a result of high pilot workload during the transition phase from conventional flight to vertical flight. Even other projects concerning VTOL aircraft had encountered these problems and often with fatal results. For example, the Dassault Balzac crashed twice during development and killed its pilots on both occasions, although one death was due to the fact that the parachute did not open. The Bell-Boeing Osprey was also prone to accidents during its development and this was a major reason for delays in development and service entry. Another problem that was affecting cost was that the main US services used their own ejection seats, the USAF the ACES and the US Navy the NACES. For the new programme, to save money, both services would have to settle for the same seat.

The ejection system did not become a great issue during the CDDR although Lockheed did look at the Automatic Ejection System (AES) developed by Yakovlev as it provided a possible new safety system. In 1995 Lockheed invited several Yakovlev engineers. Yakovlev's jet VTOL aircraft family (Yak-36, Yak-38, Yak-141) is the only one in the world that is equipped with the AES. All the world's military combat aircraft have different types of crew escape systems. And in all of them only the pilot or any other crew member can initiate the ejection sequence. It is quite natural that the human brain appreciates the situation and takes the responsibility for the crucial decision – to eject. (This, of course, is in normal circumstances, not taking into account situations where GLOC is the reason for loss of control.) That was the way to survive an emergency for decades up to the appearance of VTOL-type aircraft. Unfortunately, the interval between vertical or short take-off and the end of transition, short as it is, presents a great threat to VTOL crew safety in the event of an engine or jet reaction controls failure. The only way to survive in these accidents is to eject.

In 1959 when the Yakovlev Design Bureau came to develop the experimental VTOL Yak-36 – a single-seater with two side-by-side jets with rotating nozzles – it was evident from the beginning that its scheme was very dangerous in the event of an engine failure. The mathematical modelling showed that it takes only 1.5 to 2 seconds for an aircraft to turn over in a roll. It was clear that the pilot would not have the time to appreciate the situation and eject. It was decided that some 'smart' system should perform this task. Thus the unfavourable, from an engine failure point of view, VTOL layout gave birth to the AES and a long-term programme of its development.

The British P1127 developing team didn't run into these problems because the future Harrier layout did not react as violently after engine failure and the team stuck to the old philosophy of manual ejection in all flight regimes. The Yakovlev VTOL family of aircraft was all equipped with the Lift Plus Lift Cruise (LPLC) propulsion. Besides Lockheed, the McDonnell Douglas team with its GCLF propulsion system and later the LPLC propulsion system would encounter the same problem. Boeing was the only contender pursuing a direct lift system similar to that of the Harrier. The Harrier was, however, difficult to control during conversion flight; it required more concentration and was trickier than conventional aircraft. This was one of the reasons that the peacetime rate of losses was higher compared with conventional aircraft.

Analysis of the Yak-36 emergency dynamics showed that AES should follow the VTOL attitude during the interval between vertical take-off and the end of the transition to conventional flight. In the event of the aircraft violently misbalancing it should eject the pilot in the safe envelope of the ejection seat.

Naturally, the VTOL ejection seat was required to have as wide an envelope as possible for safe ejection in terms of sink rate, pitch or roll angles. After exhaustive experimenting with AES logic schemes it was decided to use the aircraft pitch and roll angles and pitch and roll rates as the main criteria for the AES algorithm structure. All other aircraft and engine parameters were discarded as unacceptable for reliability, accuracy, interface or other reasons. The first Russian experimental jet VTOL Yak-36 entered its flight-testing phase with the escape 'complex' comprising the Yakovlev design ejection seat K-20 and AES. For the first time in aviation history the pilot's life was trusted to a 'black box'. Not all pilots liked it and this can be understood. This psychological problem would have to be considered as well if Lockheed Martin decided to use it.

The 'black box' that picked up vertical gyro and roll-rate and pitch-rate gyro signals and 'decided' whether or not to eject the pilot was a sort of nonsense to experienced test pilots. They demanded the installation of a switch to arm or disarm manually the AES. And with that compromise the AES was brought into experimental operation. But the psychological problem between the pilot and the AES wasn't finally solved in the Yak-36's short-term programme with only two flyable experimental prototypes and flight experience without major accidents.

The real psychological battle took place in the Yak-38 operational VTOL full-scale development programme. The Yak-38's combined power plant, comprising two lift-jets and a cruise-lift engine with two rotating nozzles, presented the same problems in the event of any engine failure in vertical or transition flight. So the Yak-38 inherited the AES principle from its predecessor. The AES was tested and certified by the beginning of Yak-38 series production. The 'complex' on the first fourteen Yak-38s consisted of Yakovlev's K-21 ejection seat and AES. All aircraft after the fifteenth were equipped with more effective 'Zvezda' design K-36VM ejection seats and the same AES. Apart from some minor details it kept to the principle of the experimental VTOL: the AES was switched on and off by the pilot and by cruise-lift engine rotating nozzles. The AES executed the ejection through the canopy transparency if the VTOL pitch and roll angles or pitch and roll rates exceeded the limitations coded in the electronic decision (solver) unit.

The AES lost the first round of psychological opposition between Yak-38 pilots and the 'black box'. Ironically, the first automatic ejection in a Yak-38 was a false one. On 4 March 1976 the military test pilot, Hero of the Soviet Union, Colonel V. Chomyakov was to perform the serial Yak-38 acceptance flight from Saratov plant airfield. In the transition phase, while rotating the cruise-lift engine nozzles, he was unexpectedly automatically ejected in level flight at the height of 70 m. He safely landed on the airfield not far from the take-off area and asked the aircraft service team, what may be literally translated as: 'What the hell is going on?'

Meanwhile, under autopilot control, the aircraft continued its climb in transition mode. There was a tumult in local anti-aircraft defence when a UFO that didn't respond to any communication signals appeared in the Russian sky. The higher authorities were informed and it was decided to shoot down the intruder. By that time the fuel was exhausted and the 'pilotless' Yak-38 landed nearly vertically in the snowy field. Its cabin was looted by two peasants but otherwise the aircraft was in a good state. It took nearly a month to define the reason for the AES malfunction. The electronic system defect was eliminated, the AES team was severely criticised, the pilot was rewarded and the grounded Yak-38 Forgers were put back into service.

The psychological climate for the AES was not favourable after this incident. Only after the dramatic automatic ejection of civil test pilot Isaev at the same Saratov facilities on 15 January 1977 did the clouds begin to disperse. This time the life of the pilot was saved by the AES after cruise-lift engine thrust loss in transition. The automatic ejection took place 0.2 seconds before the aircraft crashed in flames.

After that demonstrative accident, there occurred another one of a different kind. The experienced flight instructor A. Belokopytov lost his life while performing a short-leg Yak-38 ferry flight in the Crimea. He didn't switch on the AES. During the landing in transition flight he didn't notice that one of the two lift engines had failed to start and when the aircraft lost speed it violently dived, turned over in two seconds and crashed in flames. There was no attempt to eject.

After that fatal accident the military authorities issued an instruction that it was compulsory to switch on the AES in compliance with the Flight Manual. Whether the pilot switched on the AES or not was recorded by the flight recorder. More than 200 Yak-38s entered service with the Russian Navy. There were nineteen automatic ejections in different emergency situations in hover or transition flights, including two automatic dual ejections from two-seater Yak-38Us, and all of them were successful. The AES proved to be a reliable life-saver for VTOL pilots on vertical regimes. There were also more than a dozen successful manual ejections in conventional flight over sea and land. These figures show that not unlike the Harrier many accidents occurred during the transition flight regime.

Thus the Yak-38 escape 'complex' system, including the AES, the efficient K-36VM ejection seat and other components, achieved 100 per cent success with automatic and manual ejections. The psychological barrier was overcome and the pilots' opinions were changed. That is why, when the supersonic VTOL development programme was initiated at the Yakovlev Design Bureau there was no more hesitation in selecting the escape system arrangement: the second-generation electronic AES with improved parameters was developed and tested together with the K-36LV lightweight ejection seat. The Yak-141 escape complex was the most sophisticated system used to save a pilot's life. Its efficiency was demonstrated dramatically with the manually initiated ejection of Yakovlev test pilot V. Yakimov in a vertical landing over the air carrier deck during a test flight.

The events in this short account of AES development took nearly two decades. AES saved nineteen VTOL pilots in situations where manual ejection in the safe envelope was very problematic and very unlikely.

The Yak-141 was cancelled and the system was not further developed and the reasoning for this was that it was only of value for VTOL aircraft. Lockheed found the information interesting and Yakovlev's engineers were invited to advise Lockheed's engineers on this system. It would be immense value for the X-35B because if the lift fan malfunctioned during hover the pilot would not have the time to react and would be most likely killed. It remained to be seen if American pilots would accept this safety system, as a pilot wants to be in control. It also remained to be seen if it would be used at all in the Lockheed F-35, although it was studied for integration. A separate programme office took it upon itself to research a digital version of the AES. It was recognised that the system eliminated the danger of pilots' delayed reactions and the Advanced Technology Crew Systems (ATCS) programme office located at the Naval Air Warfare Center Aircraft Division (NAWCAD) at Patuxent River. The time that a pilot has to react during lift fan failure and eject is ~500 ms as the pitching moment is so forceful. This is not enough time as a pilot on average requires about two seconds after a catastrophic failure to assess the situation and eject according to the ejection seat manufacturers. The AES ejects the pilot when sensors indicate that preset thresholds for aircraft static and dynamic parameters such as pitch angle and pitch rate and roll angle and roll rate have been exceeded. The AES should only be activated in the flight region when all aerodynamic control surfaces begin to lose their control power and the aircraft is dependent on the propulsion control only. The AES will be dependent on the redundant Vehicle Management System (VMS) in conjunction with redundant aircraft sensors to make a decision to eject during such an event. As with any other system in the F-35 this system must also be able to perform a check on its own integrity, a so-called Built in Test system. As Yakovlev was the intellectual proprietor of the technology its representatives in the US, Russian American Science Inc., was the only company allowed to develop further the system and adapt it to the US requirements.

From February 1996 Martin-Baker became involved in talks with different Weapon System Contractors (WSC) in the JAST programme. At this time Martin-Baker was in talks with the three teams that remained during the CDDR. The three teams, Boeing, Lockheed Martin and McDonnell Douglas, had to answer a Request for Proposals (RfP) issued by the JAST office in March 1996 for two CDAs. With previous programmes, like the ATF programme, the ejection seat, like the engine, was funded separately and was delivered to the aircraft manufacturer as Government Furnished Equipment (GFE). This time the responsibility was given to the WSC and was considered Buyer Furnished Equipment (BFE). This measure was taken to lower the cost and increase compatibility with the cockpit environment. The competitors were Boeing (producer of the ACES II: Advanced Concept Ejection Seat II), the Russian company Zvezda with the K-36D seat represented by IBP in America and BF Goodrich's subsidiary UPCO and Martin-Baker with the NACES (Navy Advanced Common Ejection Seat) and Mk.16A. BF Goodrich in the mean time bought IBP to strengthen its market share in the diminishing ejection seat market.

Talks were initiated with all three teams and Lockheed Martin sent a Request for Information (RfI) to all competitors. The first response to Lockheed Martin by Martin-Baker was given in March 1996. Talks continued and Martin-Baker offered the NACES and Mk.16A. The NACES was used in the T-45 Goshawk, McDonnell Douglas F-18C/D and E/F, and the Grumman F-14D Tomcat. The Mk.16A was used in the Eurofighter and Dassault Rafale and had been in service since August 1996 in the Eurofighter. However in December 1996 as a cost measure Lockheed Martin chose Stencel SIIIS – AV-8B ejection seats – for its X-35 CDA. Lockheed used the Stencel SIIIS seat in connection with a Miniature Detonating Cord in the canopy glass. Martin-Baker was more successful with Boeing and a version of the Mk.16A was chosen. The NACES was a seat that would pass all the technical requirements but it was heavier. The reason for the development of the Mk.16 from the outset was the requirement to reduce weight and the weight reduction achieved was in excess of 30 per cent compared with the Mk.14 NACES (91.4 kg). The weight reduction was important for the STOVL version so the choice for the Mk.16 was relatively easy. The weight of the Mk.16A was less than 64 kg excluding oxygen and survival equipment. Low weight is not only important to reduce aircraft weight but also for the safety of the pilot during ejection as he endures high g-forces during the ejection. The lighter the seat the less pressure the seat will put on the pilot's back, and chances of injuries to the spine are reduced. Other seats such as the Zvezda K-36 weighed 100 kg, the K-36L 95 kg and the Mk.10 82 kg. The weight reduction had been achieved by reducing the structure weight. All seats previously made by Martin-Baker were made out of the seat and

The high speed test track was used with the forward fuselage mock up, the Mk.16 seat is seen here shortly before deploying the main chute. *Copyright BAe Systems*

the rocket structure – these two structures were then connected. When developing the Mk.16 for the Eurofighter it was decided that the rocket installation, the gun tubes, would be an integral part of the seat, thereby making the seat lighter as no connecting technology and fewer structures would be required.

McDonnell Douglas was eliminated for the CDP and therefore never came to a decision. The forward fuselage unit used for the sled testing was made by Advance Technologies Inc. Newport News, VA, in 1998. Martin-Baker conducted a sled test for the McDonnell Douglas X-32 at 260 knots on 23 September 1999. It used an X-32 CDA representative forward fuselage. The version tested and used in the X-32 CDA test aircraft was designated the Mk.16B. The Mk.16B seat had been tested up to 600 knots. All the tests were performed at Martin–Baker's Aircraft Langford lodge facility. Some changes to the seat compared with the Mk.16 were the addition of two canopy-breakers to help the seat go through the AV-8B canopy used on the X-32A CDA. The parachute used was the Irvin-GQ Ltd Type 5000 similar to that used in the Dassault Rafale, Eurofighter Typhoon (both equipped with Mk.16 ejection seats) and on the F-14 and F18 equipped with NACES.

For the PWSC both WSCs had again issued RfPs in two rounds and Martin-Baker came out as the best value supplier, taking into account technical excellence and cost evaluation.

Boeing announced its decision on 17 August 2000 just a month after the Farnborough Air Show. BF Goodrich was disappointed that its proposal for a lightweight westernised version of the Zvezda K-36 was not selected. It hoped, however, that there was a back door in the programme through the Joint Ejection Seat Program (JESP) created by the US Congress to ensure the existence of a US ejection seat manufacturer. The irony, however, was that both BF Goodrich and Martin-Baker were selected for the JESP. The aim of the JESP was to provide a better seat that was compatible with current and future fighters such as the F-22 Raptor, F-15 Eagle, F-16 Fighting Falcon, F-18E/F

A dummy being fired out of the cockpit during a zero speed/zero height test. *Copyright BAe Systems*

Super Hornet, T-38 Talon, T-45 Goshawk and of course the JSF. It was, however, not clear how this would affect the price of the Mk.16 that would be used initially in the development aircraft, because if, for whatever reason, the seat was not be successful with the JESP the development costs of the Mk.16 for the JSF would have to spread over a smaller amount of seats and would make this not a very cost effective part of the JSF programme. However, the JESP came to a quick demise when budget constraints ended the programme in mid-2002 when no funds were made available.

Martin–Baker's Mk.16 series was the best choice as it was already in service in the USAF Raytheon Texan II (JPATS) aircraft. The Mk.16A was used in the Eurofighter Typhoon, proving that the seat also performed well in the newest generation of high-performance fighters and it functioned flawlessly when the Spanish DA6 Eurofighter two-seat prototype crashed and the two crew members ejected safely on 21 November 2002. Work for the Boeing X-32 CDA could also be used for the F-35 as both had two vertical stabilisers instead of the Eurofighter Typhoon's single tail. The clearance required for the Eurofighter Typhoon was greater than with both Boeing's CDA or Lockheed F-35s as the tail was straight behind the cockpit and the tail was higher.

The Mk.16 ejection seat is equipped with sixteen cartridges that activate different devices. There are three types of cartridges. The first cartridges set the seat in motion, the second activates devices such as arm and leg restraints and the third type are time-delay cartridges. The previous generation of ejection seat, the Mk.10, has fourteen cartridges. Other differences are that the previous generation of seats was equipped with nitro-cellulose primary and secondary cartridges to set the seat in motion, whereas the Mk.16 ejection seat system is equipped with an improved primary cartridge based on the so-called 'choked' cartridge technology.

The ejection sequence has eight phases that have to happen in a very short period of time depending on height and the situation of the aircraft during the ejection sequence. The eight phases are:

1 Initiation of the ejection by the pilot
2 Canopy fragmented by the Miniture Detonating Cord (MDC) or the Transparancy Removal System (TRS)
3 Catapult phase
4 Rocket motor phase
5 Stabilisation of the seat
6 Seat/man separation
7 Deployment of the parachute
8 Parachute descent

In fact, if required, the Mk.16 ejection system was able to perform steps one to seven in two seconds.

For the SDD phase the seat designation chosen was the Mk.16E or for the US market it was called the US16E. The Mk.16E would be a common ejection seat for all three versions of the F-35. The ejection seat should meet previously unattained performance balance. Key improvements to be made are the suitability for a wider range of people, ie taller, smaller, wider, lighter and heavier. The so-called nude population weight range was set from 103 lb to 245 lb. For example, taller pilots would not have had the same comfort in previous ejection seats as the average pilot. In the F-35 it would be possible to adjust the ejection seat's position higher or lower over a range of 7.4 inches (18.5 cm). The adjustment is achieved by a 28 V DC actuator. Another adjustment that is possible is the 5.73-degree tilt, meaning that the seat is not at a fixed angle as in previous fighters. The tilt angle of the seat is set prior to the flight by the ground crew. In previous fighters the angle of the seat was in such a position that it would help the pilot counter the g-forces. For every pilot to have the same level of comfort even the throttle and stick are adjustable. As the HMD replaces the function of the HUD the position changes have to be relayed to the HMD to give the right display angle and information to the pilot. The HMD has two functional seat interfaces:

- Helmet Transfer Unit (HTU)
- Quick Disconnect Connector (QDC)

The HTU is mounted on the headpad. It generates a magnetic field, which is detected by the receiver on the HMD. The farther the HMD is displaced from the HTU, the higher proportionally the voltage output of the HTU. The headpad of the original Mk.16 seat was metallic and had to be replaced by a composite construction for the Mk.16E so that it would not influence the magnetic field generated by the HTU.

Besides the man machine integration issues mentioned above the legacy ejection seats in use with US services were compared. The ejection seat terrain clearance capability charts were amalgamated. From this chart the best performances were put together and these became the minimum requirements for the Mk.16E.

As the population range was larger than with previous ejection seats the parachute that was used in the original Mk.16 seat, the Irvin-GQ Ltd Type 5000, could not fulfil the requirements set and a replacement was needed. The requirements set for the new parachute were:

- Parachute-borne mass range of 144 lb to 337 lb.
- Maximum deceleration during parachute inflation of 25g across specified mass range.
- Vertical descent velocity of less than 24 ft/sec.
- Selectable/de-selectable drive and turn capability.
- The parachute that was selected by Martin-Baker was the Irvin-GQ Ltd Type 6000.
- The Mk.16E has the following sub-assemblies:
- A wide seat bucket within which is located the survival aids container, a backrest and Under Seat Rocket Motor (USRM). The 19.5-inch wide seat bucket is based on the one used for the NASA T-38N upgrade programme.
- A twin-tube catapult with integral penetrators. On the catapult structure is an energy-absorbing head pad, a drogue parachute container, the main parachute container, an inertial retraction device and a third-generation COTS triple redundant electronic sequencer.
- Side-mounted guide rails.
- Fully integrated life support and HMD equipment.

To give the third generation COTS triple redundant electronic sequencer an autonomic capability it is connected to thermal batteries mounted on the seat. In

The flying suit including the HMD on a female pilot. Since the JSF is offered internationally, consideration has been given to the differing body sizes of different nationalities. However, a limiting factor is the ability to fit in the ejection seat.
Copyright Lockheed Martin

other words the sequencer is independent of aircraft power supplies. The sequencer selects drogue, parachute and harness release times. The release times are dependent on the altitude and speed measurements of the sequencer. To reduce the effects of seat rotation on the speed sensor the sequencer had to be mounted near the centre of gravity, which is between the catapult tubes. The Mk.16E would become the first ejection seat in US service with HMD safety issues integrated from the outset.

A Preliminary Design Review (PDR) of the Mk.16E was held from 13 to 16 January. The PDR was considered a success by the participants. The participants included Martin-Baker's representatives, members of the Lockheed Martin Integrated Product Team and also suppliers of equipment for the ejection seat. The design baseline for the Mk.16E seat was now set.

A little more than a year later from 2 to 4 February 2004 the CDR of the Mk.16E was held. The CDR was attended by representatives of Lockheed Martin, BAE Systems and, of course, Martin-Baker.

For the SDD phase Martin-Baker was to provide fourteen ejection seats for the flying prototypes. The ejection seat underwent a design review in early 2004.

A replica of the forward fuselage of the F-35, intended for ejection-seat testing, was produced by Advanced Technologies Inc. The replica was transported to the Martin-Baker facilities in England where high-speed tests of up to 608 knots (700 mph) would be performed. However, not all the tests were to be performed in England; some of the tests were to take place at Martin-Baker's facilities in Northern Ireland. The rescheduling, due to the weight issue, also affected Martin-Baker. Instead of fourteen ejection seats the company now had to deliver fifteen.

Martin-Baker undertook several proof of concept ejection tests during 2005. On 20 September 2005 an ejection test was performed at Chalgrove airfield in Oxford using its company-owned Meteor T7 aircraft, registration WL419, at 165 knots. This test (and prior tests) evaluated design improvements and also proved the Transparency Removal System (TRS).

On the US16E seat, the Auto-eject Unit (AEU) that actually fires the seat is made by Martin-Baker. However, the signal comes from the Ejection Seat Firing Module (ESFM), which is provided by another company. Martin-Baker delivered the first flight-qualified seat for the first F-35 AA-1 in August 2006. There were still issues regarding safe seat departure through the canopy for the CTOL version in November 2006 but fortunately they were all resolved so that the first flight was not delayed beyond 2006. At the Le Bourget 2007 conference General Charles Davis mentioned that recently the first F-35B STOVL ejection seat was tested. The test was performed because the F-35B has a different canopy and the break up and separation of the canopy was thought to be an issue. The test went really well according to programme director General Davis.

The Meteor aircraft owned by Martin Baker that has been used for many ejection seat development programmes and now also for the most modern seat in the Martin Baker range.
Copyright BAe Systems.

CHAPTER 12

ENGINES FOR THE JSF

When DARPA awarded the contract for the second phase of the STOVL programme two different technologies were under development. One was the Gas Coupled Lift Fan (GCLF) propulsion system that was under development by McDonnell Douglas and its partner General Electric based on the F-120 engine. The other was the Shaft Driven Lift Fan (SDLF) under development by Lockheed and its partner Pratt & Whitney based on the F119 engine.

The SDLF design from Lockheed's Advanced Development Company (LADC or Skunk works) for the lift concept was met with some optimism as it seemed to tackle most of the problems. The idea for the SDLF design was updated by Skunk works engineer Paul Bevilaqua and his team and was patented in 1993.

Lockheed was using a large-scale aerodynamic and propulsion model without wings for tests at Pratt & Whitney's West Palm Beach facilities. The interesting thing about this model was that it was equipped with Pratt & Whitney F100-PW-220+ engine. The engine was equipped with a 2-D thrust-vectoring nozzle similar to that developed for the F-22 or the F-15 S/MTD, which also has variable area control. Other changes to the engine were that the engine was equipped with a PW-229 fan and a low-pressure turbine with a PW-220 core. After the tests were completed the model was returned to Lockheed Palmdale where wings and tails would be installed for testing at NASA's Outdoor Aerodynamic Research Facility

Both airframes developed by the two teams (Lockheed Martin with Pratt & Whitney and McDonnell Douglas with General Electric) would be tested in the Outdoor Aerodynamic Research Facility (OARF) at NASA's Ames. The main things to be tested were ground effects, Hot Gas Ingestion (HGI) and of course the lift parameters. The circulation of hot gases around the airframe is an important factor as an engine's continuous functioning is dependent on the re-ingestion of hot gases or rather dependant on H61 not occuring. The Large Scale Powered Model that Lockheed tested at NASA Ames showed one positive thing, which was that the lift fan exhaust blocked entirely the higher temperature exhausts from the roll posts and the main engine *thereby HGI*. The SDLF was tested in a scaled-down version (91 per cent) integrated in the LSPM for 200 hours during 1995 and 1996.

The McDonnell Douglas/British Aerospace ASTOVL team was committed to finding a solution with a propulsion system based on the GCLF. The GCLF propulsion system dictated a larger airframe as the ducting (from the main engine placed aft in the airframe forward to the lift fan just behind the cockpit) required more space. As the fuselage area already required space for the air intakes, internal weapon bay and other aircraft systems, this was a major disadvantage of the GCLF propulsion system. The GCLF propulsion system required ducting to the lift fan. This ducting would transport the heated gas, which meant that special heat resistant material was required for the ducting and also for the fuselage surrounding it.

The JAST programme office had a different approach to a normal programme. It was

first to develop the new technology that would be needed for the next-generation strike aircraft. When matured, that technology was to be introduced into the JAST technology demonstrator. On 22 December 1994 two engine manufacturers received a contract to develop technology that was thought to be vital for the next-generation strike aircraft. General Electric received a contract to develop low-cost nozzles for enhanced strike effectiveness and a turbocooler engine demonstration for flexible thermal management. Pratt & Whitney received a contract for maturing technologies and JAST propulsion system demos. As the Navy had agreed finally to accept a single-engine aircraft both engine manufacturers were told that engine reliability was a greater issue than ever before.

Lockheed was already working on models before an F119 engine was available that could fulfil the requirements for the wind-tunnel tests at NASA's AMES research centre. The model used was an 86 per cent scaled version similar to the X-35, but under the CALF programme the model was designated the X-32, which could at a later stage be the cause for some confusion. The model was equipped with a Pratt & Whitney F100-PW-220 engine and an Allison shaft-driven fan. Although the lift fan design was patented by Lockheed Martin, Allison Advanced Development Company (AADC) was responsible for developing and producing the lift fan. The lift fan is equipped with a telescoping 'D'-shaped hood or Telescoping Vectoring Nozzle (TEVEN), to deflect thrust backwards to provide forward momentum during transition. The lift fan's clutch was produced under subcontract by BF Goodrich.

Preventing HGI is important because it can cause loss of engine thrust or engine stability. Loss of thrust during vertical flight or landing can have very damaging effects on the aircraft, let alone the pilot. In the Harrier the hot air was pushed down under the wings, which increased the danger of HGI. The Boeing X-32 demonstrator, applying a similar approach to the Harrier, therefore had the air intake under the nose to eliminate or reduce HGI to an acceptable level. The X-35B demonstrator again had its roll prevention ducts under the wing. The hot gas coming out of them was considered not such a hazard because the temperature from the roll post ducts was not that high. Furthermore, the length of the ducts ensured that the HGI was brought down to acceptable levels. During phase two of the ASTOVL CALF programme the LSPM from Lockheed was tested with canards and with horizontal stabilisers aft of the wing. Both versions were tested on the LSPM and the advantage was deemed too small to incorporate the canards. Lockheed proceeded with a normal tail configuration as HGI was practically eliminated. Carrier approaches were, however, the main reason for choosing the tail-plane version.

The Conventional Take Off and Landing version engine layout. The space freed by the lift fan is used to extend the range by placing fuel tanks there. Other options besides the fuel tanks are under study. *Team JSF*

In February 1995 General Electric tested for the first time a GCLF propulsion system based on the YF120 engine, which was previously used in the Lockheed YF-22. General Electric introduced variable cycle technology in its YF120 design. Pratt & Whitney, however, during development of the ATF engine (later the F119 engine) decided against this technology because of weight and complexity penalties. It was Pratt & Whitney that had extensive experience with this type of technology as its J58 engine, which powered the legendary SR-71 Blackbird, was based on it. The advantage of variable cycle technology is that it allows the engine to operate as a turbofan at subsonic speeds, but at supersonic speed it allowed the engine to operate as a conventional turbojet, which increases fuel efficiency.

Compared with the successful GE F110 engine, the YF120 engine had 25 per cent fewer parts and 63 per cent fewer rotating parts, which should reduce maintenance requirements and costs.

An advantage is that during conventional flight the engine exhaust is pushed out through the main nozzle, which was planned to be an axisymmetric thrust-vectoring nozzle, giving increased manoeuvrability. A diverter valve located just behind the YF120 engine's turbine frame can redirect thrust to the two aft-placed rotating nozzles that are similar to those found on the Harrier and to the lift fan, which is located just behind the cockpit. The two rotating nozzles located at the rear will prevent the aircraft from rolling. To reduce cost further the lift fan uses parts from existing engines. The first stage fan of the F101 engine is used and two stages from the Low Pressure Turbine (LPT) of the F110 engine. By March 1995 Rolls-Royce completed its take-over of Allison Advanced Development Company (AADC).

The four contenders for the joint strike Weapon System Concept Demonstration (WSCD) programme were quickly reduced to three as Northrop Grumman joined the McDonnell Douglas design effort. The Pratt & Whitney F119 engine had been under development since May 1983 and had not flown in service. The other engine in contention was the YF120 developed by General Electric. General Electric was chosen as a partner by McDonnell Douglas but this company changed its mind during the second quarter of 1995 after joining forces with Northrop Grumman.

McDonnell Douglas changed its plans quite late in the programme, by switching engine partner-company. From General Electric's F120 engine McDonnell Douglas opted instead for the F119 from Pratt & Whitney. General Electric stopped developing the GCLF propulsion system, which required a lot of bleed air to power the lift fan, and instead McDonnell Douglas transferred to the lift plus lift cruise (LPLC) configuration. This is the same configuration that was being pursued by Yakovlev with its three designs, (Yak-36 Freehand experimental V/STOL, Yak-38 Forger and the Yak-141 Freestyle).

Although it was good news for Pratt & Whitney to have been chosen by all the contenders it meant a lot of developmental work as well because each of team had a different lift system for the STOVL version of the JSF. Studies that had already been started as early as 1994 by the three contenders for the JAST programme and the CALF programme under the directive of DARPA had helped, however. Lockheed was developing an SDLF, which it had been testing with models. McDonnell Douglas was looking into a lift engine and Boeing into an aircraft with swivelling nozzles as in the Harrier. All concepts had different technological challenges for the engine manufacturer. Three versions of one aircraft were to be built and at least two of them had different engine requirements. The STOVL model was supposed to be the most demanding design for the engine manufacturer. The CTOL and the CV did not need any special alterations for their engines. On 13 December 1995 Pratt & Whitney received a Cost Plus Fixed Fee (CPFF) contract with a ceiling amount of US $28,354,675 to study the engine design concepts for each WSC. This contract was expected to be completed by September 1996 and preliminary design engineering for the definition and development of all three proposed propulsion systems was required to enable a proper evaluation for the CDP phase.

The F119 engine design had to be optimised for single-engine use. In other words, it had to be made more powerful as the F119 was basically designed for a twin-engine aircraft. The fan had to be scaled up (size of scaling dependant on aircraft design) and an additional low-pressure turbine stage incorporated so that the engine would have a higher thrust than the baseline F119 destined for the F-22 Raptor. Improvements made for the JSF engine may well find their way into the Raptor at a later stage. The core of the F119 engine would remain the same, ie the compressor, combustor and High Pressure Turbine (HPT). A newly developed fan and Low Pressure Turbine (LPT) would be used for the JSF engines for all the WSC. Although it was studied, thrust vectoring was not made a requirement because of the cost. The USAF did not want the JSF to become competition for the F-22, the main task was the strike mission.

The designation of the McDonnell Douglas engine was JSF119-615. As McDonnell Douglas had opted for the LPLC system the separate lift engine was to be produced by a consortium of General Electric, Rolls-Royce and Allison. The lift engine received the designation GEA-FXL.

During wind-tunnel testing of the propulsion system for the McDonnell Douglas team it became clear that a redesign of the GEA-FXL exhaust was required to solve a hot gas ground environment problem. It was, however, refuted that melting asphalt was an issue as the temperature of the exhaust of the GEA-FXL was calculated to be several hundreds of degrees lower than that of the main cruise/lift engine. The GEA-FXL had a 1.2 m diameter and was less than 1.5 m high to fit in the centre fuselage behind the cockpit. The GEA-FXL was to be equipped with a vectoring exhaust nozzle for the transition flight regime from conventional flight to vertical flight and vice versa. The GEA-FXL was expected to provide a thrust-to-weight ratio of around 10:1. AADC were planning to use technology developed under the Integrated High Performance Turbine Engine Technology (IHPTET) programme, to be specific, based on technologies demonstrated in its XTC16 Advanced Turbine Engine Gas Generator (ATEGG). This technology was offered in an engine designated GMA800 for the A-X and MRF aircraft programmes. The technology from the XTC16 was considered ahead of technology available at either Pratt & Whitney or General Electric.

The exhaust of the lift fan the Baby Carriage Hood is in folded position. The exhaust has also a D-shape. *Copyright Lockheed Martin*

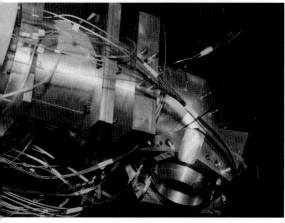

The three bearing swivel module for the X-35B in early design and test phase. As a result of development and testing during the CDP the production aircraft will see a different three-bearing swivel module system in the F-35B. *Copyright Lockheed Martin.*

After the announcement that the Boeing and Lockheed Martin designs had been chosen for further development Pratt & Whitney's work could be reduced to four engine models. Pratt & Whitney received the contract for the CDP in January 1997 for both the Boeing and the Lockheed version. The Boeing design was given the designation X-32 and the Lockheed Martin designs the X-35. For the X-32 the F119 engine development was designated SE614 and for the X-35 SE611.The X-32A CTOL engine had the full designation F119-SE614C (C for Conventional) and the X-32B STOVL engine received the designation F119-SE614S (S for STOVL). The F119 SE611 engine versions received the same treatment. For each WSC (Lockheed and Boeing) Pratt & Whitney received a contract to build two developmental engines, two qualification engines and two flight-test engines with the designations YF001 and YF002. YF001 was, according to the plans, to be used for the CTOL version and the YF002 for the STOVL version. According to the contract the First Engine To Test (FETT) milestones were to be achieved by April 1998.

Although the engines were supposed to be based on the F119 and the F120 engines new promising technology developed under the IHPTET programme was to find its way into them. General Electric *Alternate* Engine Team received a contract from the JSF programme office to develop further the YF120 core. The contract had a total value of US $96 million and was shared with partners Allison and Rolls-Royce. The designation that was given to the further development was the YF120-FX. The core development was to take four years until 2001. The core development programme was planned to be followed by a turbo fan development programme for which a contract was expected during 2001. New technologies expected to be integrated in the new engine included a new low-observable nozzle under development by General Electric. The new nozzle had been tested in 1996 using a pole-mounted F-16 model. Reduction in heat signature as radar signature was expected from the nozzle, increasing survivability.

On 20 February 1997 Pratt & Whitney received a modification to the original engine ground and flight demonstration programme. The modification had a value of US

Propulsion
STOVL Configuration 240-4.1

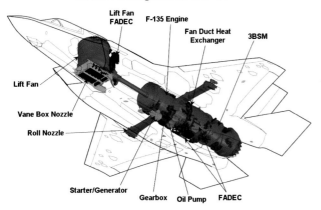

The STOVL version layout is a showcase of technological innovation to the highest degree. Not only is the propulsion system is an innovation but the JSF will introduce many other new technologies. *Team JSF*

$29,321,000 and work was expected to be completed by January 2001. The new contract provided for PWSC engine technology studies. The IHPTET programme was initiated in 1988 to increase the baseline capabilities of engines then under development such as the YF119 and YF120. The IHPTET programme results were, however, not only aimed at these engines but at all kinds of engines. For this reason almost every organisation with an interest in engine development was involved: NASA, ARPA, Army, Navy, Air Force, Allison Advanced Development Company, General Electric and Pratt & Whitney. The IHPTET was divided into three phases and each phase was expected to bring an improvement over the baseline engine technologies from 1988. The separate propulsion technology gained viability because, of the entire gross take-off weight of any aircraft, the propulsion system including the fuel would take up about 40 to 60 per cent. A small improvement would have a great effect on operational capabilities. When it became clear that the JSF was a serious development programme the newly developed propulsion technology was directly aimed to be introduced to the JSF, however older engines would profit from the new technologies where possible. For fighter/attack aircraft propulsion improvement the goals were set as follows:

	Thrust/weight ratio	Fuel burn	Completion scheduled
Phase I	+ 30%	-20%	1991
Phase II	+ 60%	-30%	1997
Phase III	+ 100%	-40%	2005

Several test engines were built to test different new technologies for the IHPTET programme. As the programme was not only aimed at military engines but also limited life or expandable engines and civil engines and the width of cooperation was across the US engine industry, there was a system of designations applied.

X	Experimental
T	Technology
C	Core
E	Engine
L	Limited life or expandable

Each team also had a different designation for clarity: Allison received designation 1; Teledyne received designation 2; Allied Signal received designation 3; General Electric received designation 4; Lycoming received designation 5; Pratt & Whitney received designation 6; General Electric/Allison received 7; Williams received designation 8 and General Electric/Allied Signal 9. Lycoming was, during the programme, bought by Allied Signal. The second digit would indicate the generation of demonstrator engine funded by the US Navy and USAF. The IHPTET phase I engines were engine generation 5, IHPTET phase II engines were automatically generation 6 and so on.

Production by Pratt & Whitney of the first JSF test engines started in March 1997. The machining of the titanium billet that eventually became the first-stage fan integrally bladed rotor was the first production item. For the Boeing propulsion system several components were tested during the first seven months of 1997. The Boeing nozzle test facility at Seattle was used to test the direct lift components produced by Rolls-Royce. The tests were performed on a scale model and mainly the transition from conventional to vertical flight and from vertical back to conventional flight were tested. The Preliminary Design Review of the Pratt & Whitney engines was completed by April 1997.

AADC tested the lift fan nozzle for the F119-SE614S at the NASA Lewis Research Center. The lift fan nozzle was tested in the powered lift rig and the tests started in April 1997 and lasted to mid-July 1997. The nozzle was tested under vectored angles from 15 degrees forward to 60 degrees backwards. To vector the thrust of the nozzle an inverted 'baby carriage' hood was used to deflect the thrust. The thrust area remained constant and was not affected by the hood. Previously Allison had performed Computational Fluid Dynamics (CFD) analysis and the results of the tests performed at the NASA Lewis Research Center were in line with the CFD analyses. At the same the PDR of the lift fan took place and was completed by May 1997. The PDR was conducted at AADC's facility in Indianapolis.

At AEDC a 13 per cent scale model of the Boeing X-32 was used to test the high-speed inlet/forebody compression system. The tests lasted three weeks. The tests were important to prove that the inlet could provide the engine sufficient air under all flight regimes.

The first F136 engine to reach the test milestone was an important step on the way to the full SDD contract awarded in August 2005. GE-RR had however not anticipated that it would be such a battle to retain the funding for their engine every year. *General Electric – Rolls-Royce*

Rolls-Royce and General Electric shape the Fighter Engine Team. Here is their STOVL engine undergoing test. Rolls-Royce and General Electric counted on the UK as being their first prime customer after the US. Furthermore it is hoped that others will follow. *General Electric*

General Electric, Rolls-Royce and its daughter company Allison came to an agreement during the summer of 1997 that a separate entity should be formed to develop, manufacture and sell the YF120-FX engine similar to the CFM company. The change would make Rolls-Royce and Allison equal partners with each holding 20 per cent and General Electric would hold the remaining 60 per cent. A CDR was initiated in August 1997 of all the four derivatives of the F119 engine and was completed by the end of September 1997, allowing production work to commence after the first compressor section was completed on 19 September 1997. Work on all four engines had commenced by October 1997. By 28 January 1998 Pratt & Whitney had completed the first core for the JSF engine straight from the F119 production line.

Lucas Aerospace received a contract from Allison to produce the shaft that was to drive the lift fan for the CDA by the end of November 1997. Lucas Aerospace was also responsible for the lift fan clutch.

The FETT for the X-35A CTOL engine (JSF119-611C) with the designation FX661 was achieved by Pratt & Whitney on 11 June 1998 at its own West Palm Beach facilities. Sea-level tests were to be conducted there and after finalising those tests the engine would be transferred to the AEDC. The FETT milestone was achieved for the Boeing X-32A CTOL engine (JSF119-614C) with the designation FX651on 21 June 1998. The milestones were two months' late but that was to be expected as the time scale set by the contract was very aggressive.

The lift fan was an entirely new type of propulsion. No other aircraft had been equipped with a lift fan. The CDR was indeed very important for the STOVL version and all the companies involved with propulsion were participating; it was a cooperation between Allison, Rolls-Royce, Pratt & Whitney and other participants were the members of the government programme office and of Lockheed. The CDR of the lift fan was therefore a major milestone. The LiftFanTM is a 50-inch diameter two-stage counter rotating fan with a performance of more than 20,000 lbf vertical thrust – the remainder of the vertical thrust is provided by the main engine and the two roll posts.

The F119-SE611S engine for the STOVL X-35B had replaced the axisymmetric thrust-vectoring nozzle replaced by the 3 Bearing Swivel Nozzle (3BSN) developed by Rolls-Royce, similar to the one on the Yak-141 Freestyle. To prevent it from rolling over during vertical take-off or landing, two auxiliary exhausts were to be used to balance the JSF. The auxiliary exhausts were called control or roll ducts and are produced by Rolls-Royce. The roll ducts are powered by fan air emission diverted from the engine through a duct/blocker arrangement. A disadvantage of these control ducts was that they reduce ease of engine removal and installation as they were built into the wing structure. This problem was solved, however, with a fast connector system and the roll post folds back into the wing. Engine removal time is far superior compared with the legacy aircraft (the Harrier in this case). The power of flow in the control ducts is, however, adaptable. This means that the flow on the left-hand side can be stronger than on the right-hand side. This makes it possible to take off and land with anti-symmetric loads. A major positive feature of the roll ducts is that the exhaust temperature is not so high. It is considerably lower than from the main engine, allowing for use of composites. There are no restrictions on the use of composites in the wing and fuselage part in the immediate vicinity of the roll ducts.

Beside the control ducts the major technological advance was the shaft driven fan in front of the engine. The Rolls-Royce contra-rotating lift fan compresses the air, which is then allowed to expand, creating thrust. As there is no combustion the lift fan is lighter than a specific lift engine, as used by the Yak-38 Forger and the Yak-141 Freestyle. Another major advantage is that the danger of hot air re-ingestion by the F119-SE611 engine has been almost eliminated. Thrust from the lift fan and engine will balance out – it can actually be

A STOVL engine under test. Note that the exhaust of the lift fan is being removed as well to prevent the test-bed being damaged. *Copyright Pratt & Whitney*

balanced to use it for pitch control. The one major disadvantage of this construction is that the lift fan takes up important fuselage space, which is used in the CTOL and CV for fuel tanks, giving those versions the edge over the STOVL version in range. This problem was not encountered with the STOVL engine F119-SE614S as it does not need a separate lift fan.

The lift fan for the first STOVL test engine (FX662) was delivered in October 1998. On 10 November 1998 The FETT milestone was achieved by the F119-611S and during the same month the F119-614S (designation FX652) followed suit. This means that four engines were undergoing tests in this highly aggressive test programme. Before the season holidays had commenced both STOVL engines had achieved some impressive milestones. The F119-

611S had seen its 3 bearing nozzle through the full 108 degrees of vectoring it was capable of. Meanwhile, Boeing's STOVL engine had achieved 90 degrees of vectoring, although it had fewer test hours accumulated than the Lockheed engine. By the end of 1998 all four engines had accumulated around 200 test hours. Testing of both Boeing and Lockheed Martin derivative engines had started at the AEDC. The turbine temperatures measured at this time were lower than expected

The F119-614S engine for the X-32B CDA had a direct lift system with similar nozzles to the Harrier. The two lift nozzles were located between the turbine exhaust case and the engine augmentor. The lift nozzles are located just behind the X-32B's centre of gravity and can move from 10 degrees forward of vertical (meaning thrust pushing the aircraft backwards) to 45 degrees aft vertical, giving the X-32B a shorter take-off capability to VTOL capability. The main nozzle is totally closed so that all thrust goes through these two nozzles during vertical operations. The HGI problem has been solved by a nozzle placed under the inlet, blowing cool air and preventing hot gas entering the inlet. Boeing applied the same DSI technology as Lockheed because the DSI programme was funded by the JSF programme. Assembly of the first flight-test engine for the X-32A was completed on 4 November 1999 and delivery to Boeing was planned before the year's end. Pratt & Whitney had completed over 600 test hours on the ground-test engines for the Boeing CDA. The STOVL engine for the Lockheed CDA exceeded vertical lift thrust requirements during tests on 28 January 2000. The Lockheed Skunk works received the first flight certified engine for its CTOL demonstrator in February 2000. The first flight-test engine was delivered to Boeing on 6 March 2000. Another milestone completed in the meantime by Pratt & Whitney and Rolls-Royce was that they completed Accelerated Mission Testing (AMT) for the STOVL X-32B demonstrator. Although the engine for the X-35 had completed testing in April and the engine for the X-32 in the first week of May 2000, both engines had to wait for flight clearance from the JSF programme office. JSF CTOL engines received flight clearance in the latter part of May 2000. The engines could now be installed and the prototypes prepared for their respective first flights.

Pratt & Whitney completed testing of a combustor destined for the Advanced Turbine Engine Gas Generator (ATEGG) by August 2000. The testing was part of the IHPTET programme phase III. The Impingement Film Floatwall (IFF) combustor developed by Pratt & Whitney demonstrated extremely high fuel/air ratios with a low temperature profile. The low temperature was important, as it would reduce demands on materials in the turbine. The new technology should be a template for the JSF engine technology. The first ATEGG core equipped with IFF combustor was planned to begin testing at the AEDC during November 2000.

On 6 April 2001 the Lockheed Martin propulsion team had completed the F119-611 AMT. The AMT equalled 132 missions, 249 Total Accumulated engine Cycles (TAC), 115.6 hours of STOVL system operation and 171 dynamic lift fan clutch engagements. This was in addition to the twenty-six lift fan clutch engagements with the ground-test engine in the X-35B prototype, which were done shortly before. To put this into perspective, the engine would never operate longer thaen ten minutes in the STOVL mode during an average operational mission.

When the X-35 was chosen to continue to the next stage it meant that Pratt & Whitney had only two engines left to develop further, the F119-SE611C and the F119-SE611S. The designation of the engine was changed to F135 as it had become a different engine from the F119 and it would fit with the ultimate designation of the JSF, F-35. The Pratt & Whitney F135-100 was the new designation for the CTOL version instead of the previously used designation F119-SE611C. The new Pratt & Whitney F135-400 designation was for the Carrier Version. The new Pratt & Whitney F135-600 designation was used for the STOVL

F-35B version instead of the previously used F119-SE611S. For the SDD phase a production of thirty-two engines was planned. The thirty-two engines were supposed to be production version compliant. Twenty of these engines were to be used for the SDD test-flight programme. For the F135-600 the aircraft would receive enlarged roll posts so that the production F-35B would have increased stability during hover flight and increased effectiveness of modulation of the asymmetric loads.

It had already been decided for a long time to keep a viable industry base and competition alive, and just like the F-16 the JSF would have alternative engines to give the customer the option and reduce the price. The General Electric engine received the designation F-136 as the Alternate Engine Program (AEP). Each version of the engine would receive the same different designations as the Pratt &Whitney F135, so for the CTOL version the designation would be F136-100, for the STOVL version F136-400. The competition between the General Electric and the Pratt &Whitney engines, although very tough, would require a high level of cooperation as the engines should be interchangeable at the flight line. This meant an aircraft originally equipped with a Pratt &Whitney engine could after a technical failure or planned maintenance receive a General Electric engine instead. For this reason on 6 June 2001, a JSF engine agreement was signed by Steve Finger (President military engines) on behalf of Pratt &Whitney, Russell Sparks (vice president and general manager military engines) on behalf of General Electric and Darleen Druyun (acquisition executive) on behalf of the USAF, and Paul Schneider (acquisition executive) on behalf of the Navy to ensure technical compatibility and interchangeability. Competition was seen as healthy, however some considered that Pratt & Whitney was in an advantageous position as General Electric would only offer its engine from lot 4. The Pratt & Whitney F135 was planned to have the first three Low Rate Initial Production (LRIP) batches secured while in LRIP batch 4 and 5 would be split between the F135 and the F136. From batch 6 the engines would have to compete with each other. This gave a cost advantage to Pratt & Whitney as the engine was also based on the F119 technology, which was entering production during the SDD stage of the F135. The F136 engine did not have a production engine on which the technology was based. The other side of the coin was, however, that General Electric's engine was not developed parallel to its competitor but in tandem and would have, according to the original schedule, forty more months to develop its engine and achieve similar milestones. This gave General Electric a precious technological advantage.

Some thought that the AEP increased the cost of the programme and that Pratt & Whitney had learned its lessons from the engine war anyway and would supply a technological mature engine design. They thought that the extra cost connected with the other engine was better spent on increasing the number of development engineers on the F135 project to reduce the risk at that end. This would, however, mean that General Electric would have only the F414 engine in military fighter aircraft (F-18E/F) after the F-18C/D had been replaced by the F-35.

The AEDC was planned to be used for both the F135 and the F136 engines. The AEDC needed to upgrade its facilities and the final check-out of the upgrades took place on 30 January 2004 in the propulsion test cell J-2. Other propulsion test facilities at the AEDC that would be used were the development test cells C-1 and SL-3.

When developing new carrier-suitable fighters the issue of pop stalls when the aircraft is on the launch catapult has to be considered. A pop stall is when the engine stops functioning as a result of HGI. The HGI was not due to engine exhaust entering the inlets, but the steam from the catapult in use on the aircraft carrier. The launch catapult during normal operation emits steam. Although improvements in the launch catapults have reduced the amount of steam, the problem has not been eliminated the entirely. HGI for engines is a problem especially so early in the flight process and with the aircraft having a single engine the risk is greater than with a twin-engined aircraft. A pop stall during a launch with a single-engine aircraft would mean the loss of the aircraft if not the pilot. In prior programmes such as the Boeing F-18E/F Super Hornet and the T-45 Goshawk the problems that occurred had to be solved during the test phase and most of the time the solutions were quite expensive because they had to be found late in the development programme. For this reason a risk-reduction programme was initiated by the JSF programme office to evaluate for the first time the pattern of steam during an aircraft launch from an aircraft carrier with the aid of the catapult. Engineers from Lockheed Martin, Pratt & Whitney, General Electric and NAVAIR cooperated in this one-of-a-kind test to reduce the risk for the F135/F136 engines. The test was performed prior to full-scale tests of the engines so that the results could be evaluated before the production engines were built.

The F-35 programme ran into trouble late in 2004 when it was recognised that the STOVL version was too heavy. As is described in Chapter 9 a lot of effort was made to maintain commonality, change the structure and save weight in other ways. More importantly, it was realised that it would be beneficial to have a greater margin of vertical thrust. On 9 Tuesday August 2005 Pratt & Whitney received a contract modification valued at $7,999,915 for the lift fan thrust improvement programme. This would be aimed at future growth versions of the STOVL version.

SDD of the F135

For the SDD phase Pratt & Whitney was to use twelve dedicated ground-test engines and twenty flight-test engines. Of the twelve dedicated ground-test engines three were CTOL engines, four STOVL engines and the remaining five engines were not specified. According to the contract the target date for the FETT SDD engine was 30 October 2003. System Requirement Reviews (SRR) was one of the first milestones passed by Pratt & Whitney in December 2001. Pratt & Whitney completed the Integrated Baseline Reviews (IBR) by March 2002. Pratt & Whitney finished the Preliminary Design Review (PDR) two months later in May 2002. Ametek Aerospace announced on 22 July 2002 that it had been selected by Hamilton Sundstrand to provide a suite of eight sensors for the F135 engine. The sensors are used to measure vibration, temperature, pressure, speed, speed oil level and engine light off.

Several configurations for the F135's combustor were tested at the AEDC propulsion development cell T-11 during April 2003 in preparation for forthcoming tests. The combustor tests had to be completed to a tight schedule before the CDR planned for May 2003. It was planned to be tested all the F135 test engines were at one point or another at the AEDC. Pratt & Whitney planned to test a modified lift fan clutch for the F135-600 in June 2003.

Testing was due to start on the Pratt & Whitney F135 engine in the third quarter of 2003, achieving FETT. This depended on the results of CDR. On 12 September 2003 assembly was completed of the first engine of a total of seven, of which three were CTOL versions and four were STOVL versions. The first STOVL test engine, FX641-1, was expected to achieve the FETT milestone by April 2004. The second STOVL test engine, FX642-1, was planned to follow suit in June 2004, the third test engine, FX643-1, by August 2004 and the fourth test engine, FX640, by October 2004. The General Electric F136 engine was planned to achieve FETT in mid-2004. The actual FETT for the F135 was achieved on 11 October 2003 with test engine FX631-1 representative of the F135-100 CTOL and F135-400 CV engines. Another milestone took place on 27 October 2003 and that was when the FX631 achieved military power, meaning full power without the use of the afterburner. On 8 November 2003 the same engine employed the afterburner for the first time. The afterburner has three zones of afterburner and this test only used one of the zones. The same engine achieved its first test with full power with full afterburner using all three zones by 2 February 2004. The second CTOL engine, FX633, initiated testing by mid-January 2004. The FX633 would be used for fan evaluations then Accelerated Mission Testing (AMT). The third CTOL engine, FX632, was scheduled to perform tests at the AEDC facilities. The FX632 was delivered on Thursday 22 April 2004 to the AEDC to start testing in the J-2 propulsion development cell. By 29 July 2004 the FX632 had completed about thirty-two hours' of engine operations in seven test periods.

Rolls-Royce had a good start to 2004 and achieved three milestones within the first two months. The first milestone achieved in February was that Rolls-Royce demonstrated the lift fan clutch technology life expectancy of 1500 engagements. For the CDP only 150 engagements were required; the operational requirement, however, was obviously higher. The second milestone concerned the 50-inch lift fan. Testing was planned shortly after the new test facility for testing the lift fan in Indianapolis, Indiana, had opened on 9 January 2004. The actual testing of the first SDD lift fan was initiated on 2 February 2004. The lift fan had undergone some modifications compared with the one used in the X-35B demonstrator. The third milestone related to the assembly and successful testing of the first 3 Bearing Swivel Module (3 BSM) and its shipment to Pratt & Whitney. The module is capable of changing the direction of the engine's thrust from horizontal to vertical in 2.5 seconds.

The lift fan nozzle had changed considerably compared with the one used in the X-35B. The lift fan nozzle was no longer equipped with the inverted 'baby carriage' hood but with a variable area vane box assembly similar to venetian blinds to change the nozzle vector angle and also to control the thrust area to increase thrust. The extended inverted baby carriage hood was a major mechanical moving part; its replacement is a part of the centre fuselage structure.

The Telescoping Vectoring Nozzle (TEVEN) or the inverted 'baby carriage' hood on the liftfan was a rather heavy item and a trade study was initiated to replace it with a completely redesigned nozzle. The new nozzle was expected to offer performance benefits besides the lower weight incurred. This new concept, the vane nozzle box concept, was evaluated on a 7.5% scale model by BAE Systems. They had to evaluate the STOVL Jet Effects compared to the TEVEN. The vane nozzle box concept went through several design reviews and was changed because of the results during these evaluations. After several design changes the Variable Area Vane Box Nozzle (VAVBN) was born. It was found so promising that if the Lockheed Martin PWSC was selected they would develop it further. Now in the SDD it was decided that a full scale version would undergo testing to prove that the small scale tests would also work as predicted. The full scale item was tested at one of the Aero Systems Engineering (ASE) facilities early in the SDD phase.

On 23 March 2004 Rolls-Royce announced that in conjunction with Spanish Industria de Turbo Propulsores (ITP) it had delivered the roll posts to Pratt & Whitney in time for the FETT milestone for the STOVL version, which was planned for April 2004. Rolls-Royce is a 47 per cent shareholder in ITP and gave ITP the responsibility for the roll posts. Subcontractors for the roll posts are Hamilton (hydraulic actuation system) and Perkin-Elmer (ducts and flex joints). On 7 April 2004 the first dynamic clutch engagements were performed at the newly opened facilities. It was only a week later on 14 April that the first clutch engagement at idle power was completed.

A day prior to that on 13 April 2004 Pratt & Whitney achieved another milestone and the FETT with FX641 was well ahead of schedule. The fact that weight issues can delay or threaten the JSF programme had no effect on the contract and Pratt & Whitney was totally focused on keeping its part of the programme on schedule for the first flight of the CTOL version by October 2005. Although Pratt & Whitney was confident that everything was running smoothly one setback could hold the company back and therefore there was no reason to slacken pace even though the company was two months ahead of schedule. One thing that could be measured was the noise level of the F135 so that it could be compared with the engine noise of the fighters that it was replacing. The noise level is important as hearing loss is the number one US DoD disability. The F135 engine noise level measured at 50 ft radius 135 degrees of the nose centreline was at military power 148 decibels and with afterburner 152 decibels. This does not constitute a major increase but as stated is important, especially on US Navy ship decks where people stand within the immediate vicinity of the aircraft when it takes off with afterburner on.

Milestones started to be achieved now in rapid succession as on 12 May one of the CTOL engines initiated testing at the AEDC. On 24 May 2004 Pratt & Whitney announced that the FX641 had demonstrated 39,700 pounds of thrust, which is required for the F-35B to be able to hover. At this stage the FX641 was under the contractual specified weight with more weight cuts planned. The planned weight cuts should get the weight between an estimated 3 per cent and 6 per cent below the contractual specified weight. However, on 7 June 2004 an erosion problem in the FX641 caused STOVL engine-testing to be halted until a cure was found. The problem was, however, not STOVL specific so the other engines would have to be modified as well. Early in August it was stated that the FX641 would soon join testing again.

On 19 July 2004 Pratt & Whitney released an overview of the entire engine test programme.

- Engine FX631-01 had accumulated 320 hours. This engine was to be tested for CTOL sea-level performance and operability, CTOL augmentor development, high/low rotor stress (NSMS) and fan performance mapping.

- Engine FX632-01 had accumulated 100 hours of test running. This engine was used for fan/HPC stress and operability, engine performance, augmentor performance, nozzle stress and HPT/LPT NSMS.

- Engine FX633-1 had accumulated 230 hours. During these 230 hours a total of 425 TACs were achieved. 245 of these were AMT TACs. The 245 AMT TACs were achieved during 56 AMT missions.

The only STOVL engine so far was the FX641-1 and that engine had accumulated fifty-one hours. Test objectives were STOVL sea-level performance and operability, STOVL augmentor development, low rotor stress (survey) and software logic development. The erosion problem found in engine FX641 was due to the size of the 'restrictor plate' that regulates the flow of cooling air in part of the engine; the plate's old 'undersized' design was not allowing enough cool air to reach the second-stage vanes of the turbine section. The other engines had already received the revised restrictor plate and the solution seemed to work and it was thought that the problem would have no further effects on cost or schedule. Another three STOVL engines were planned to join the test programme. The first flight-test engine was planned for production in early 2005.

The FX643 was delivered to the Pratt & Whitney test facilities in mid-August 2004 and the first test followed shortly after on 20 August 2004 according to schedule. Shortly after, Pratt & Whitney announced that the five ground-test engines had accumulated over 700 test hours. On 29 September 2004 Pratt & Whitney announced that all five F135 SDD test engines combined had completed 1000 test hours earlier during the month, showing an acceleration in the number of testing hours. The remaining engines, FX642 and FX640,

A STOVL engine in the test stand. The STOVL engine can be recognised by the lift fan inlet that can be seen above the inlet ducts of the main engine. The small squares in the exhaust gasses are called shock diamonds. *Copyright Pratt & Whitney*

One of the flight test engines is put through its paces in Fort Worth prior to the first flight of AA-1. *Copyright Lockheed Martin*

would initiate testing during October 2004, further increasing test capacity.

The first STOVL test engine, FX641, was expected to follow shortly and rejoin the programme. Pratt & Whitney said it was on target to reach the 2000-hour test mark by the end of the year. Another two STOVL engines were planned to join the two first STOVL test engines before the year was over, making a total of seven test engines.

On 29 September 2004 Pratt & Whitney announced that all the F135 SDD test engines had accumulated 1000 test hours. By the end of January 2005 another milestone was reached when a total of seven test engines had accumulated 2000 test hours. At the time four STOVL engines and three CTOL engines were being tested. Another three engines were planned to join these seven engines during 2005. F135 plume survey testing was to be performed on the FX643 shortly after Thanksgiving.

On 21 March 2005 Pratt & Whitney announced that it had accumulated 2500 test hours with the seven test engines. Although slightly delayed compared with the original plan, Pratt & Whitney was working towards Initial Flight Release (IFR). IFR was now planned for January 2006. The first flight-test engine would be delivered to Lockheed one month ahead of IFR and the first flight of the A-1 prototype was now set for August 2006. On 18 August 2005 Pratt & Whitney received a contract to fund the prolongation of the SDD phase required as a result of the Lockheed reschedule. The value of the contract was $968.6 million and should also cover the cost of aligning Pratt & Whitney with the Lockheed schedule. By August 2005 the engine had accumulated 3400 test hours. Production of the first flight-test engine was initiated on 23 August, on schedule for the delivery date.

Another important milestone for the first STOVL prototype was the delivery of one of the first structural elements of the STOVL B-1 aircraft. This structural element was part of the STOVL propulsion system but was planned not to be removed during the lifetime of the aircraft, which was calculated at 8000 flight hours or approximately thirty years. The propulsion element was the Variable Area Vane Box Nozzle (VAVBN). The VAVBN is capable of directing the 20,000 lb thrust of the lift fan through 54 degrees in two seconds. The torque, or the force in the turning moment, on the vanes is larger than the torque produced by a Cadillac car engine. This module replaces the so-called baby carriage hood that was used on the X-35B lift fan.

The AMT for the IFR was to be performed by the FX634 for the first flight of the A-1. FX634 was shipped from Middletown, Connecticut, on 15 September to arrive in West Palm Beach, Florida, where the test facilities are located and the AMT testing would take place.

It was announced by Pratt & Whitney on 30 November 2005 that an important milestone had been achieved when the ground test engines had amassed over 4000 test hours. This milestone gives an idea of the maturity of the technology applied in the engine. As Pratt & Whitney pointed out, the engine was a further development of the F119 and most of the newer technology had been tested already during the CDP phase in which the technology demonstration engines had already amassed 3500 test hours. On 5 December 2005 the first flight-test engine was finished during *a last bold ceremony*. The engine was completed on schedule. On 7 December another milestone was achieved in the Arnold Engineering Development Center when tests were initiated in test cell C-1. The tests in the Aeropropulsion Systems Test Facility signalled the transition from development to qualification testing. IFR is not possible without these tests. As John Kelly, one of the *ATA* project engineers on this programme, said 'Without this testing, flight-testing cannot begin'. *ATA* is the AEDC's support contractor, which in turn is a joint venture of Jacobs Sverdrup, Computer Science Corp. and General Physics. The first flight-test engine was delivered on 30 December 2005 to Lockheed Martin Fort Worth.

The cooperation between Rolls-Royce and Pratt & Whitney for the STOVL version was further secured beyond the SDD phase. This was assured by an MoU signed on 16 February 2006 for the remainder of the programme. This secured Rolls-Royce work for the life of the programme as the company would deliver the three STOVL components and spare parts of the STOVL version.

According to a press release from Pratt & Whitney on 24 April 2006 5000 test hours were accumulated by all the F135 test engines combined. The F135 was still considered to be on schedule for the first flight and to amplify this statement it was said that the company had recently completed the AMT. Flight clearance testing was expected to be completed before the June 2006. The first flight-test engine was put through its paces at the Naval Air Station Joint Reserve Base hush house facility in Fort Worth in preparation for engine runs in the aircraft starting on 31 May 2006. The tests that were performed related to test cell acoustics and vibration surveys. Also tested were snap accelerations from idle to military power, that is, maximum power without afterburner, and from idle to maximum afterburner. These tests qualified the hush house and allowed Pratt & Whitney to use the facility for engine testing during the SDD. Shortly after, on 10 June 2006, the second F135 flight-test engine was delivered to Lockheed, only to be followed by a third flight-test engine to support all activities leading up to and after the first flight.

The third flight-test engine was delivered by Pratt & Whitney to Lockheed Martin in support of the flight-test programme, making the tally of engines produced during the SDD twelve. It was announced by Pratt & Whitney on 24 August 2006 that the JSF programme office had cleared the F135 engine to initiate installed engine runs. At the time nine ground-test engines had accumulated 5700 hours.

Eight days after starting the IPP in AA-1 it was time to start up the engine as well. The first time that the engine was started in the first prototype was on 15 September 2006 for idle engine runs. The power of the engines was increased during each engine run and it was only three days later on the twelfth engine run that the engine was running on full afterburner, that is 40,000 lb of thrust.

The engine was certified for its first flight on 23 October 2006. The first flight was now planned for the end of November, early December. November went by and on 1 December 2006 Pratt & Whitney received a modification to the original development contract. The gearbox had to be redesigned. In fact, the current gearbox was the responsibility of Hamilton Sundstrand. Six days later the F-35 moved out of the hangar, for the first time powered by the F135 engine.

15 December 2006 was an important date for Pratt & Whitney and Lockheed Martin. It was the first time that their engine was put through an air test. As the engine performed as expected, Pratt & Whitney waited with impatience as to when they could announce a specific milestone for the engine. It was with great pride and also relief that they did not have to wait too long as on 24 January 2007, during the fifth flight, the afterburner was lit for the first time. The next milestone for the F135 engine came on Thursday 13 March when the F-35 piloted by Jon Beesley took off with afterburner. Bill Gostic, programme manager for the F135 engine at Pratt & Whitney, said that eleven ground-test engines had been produced and three flight-test engines, of which the first powered the AA-1 during its first flight. The eleven ground test engines were however taken apart three or four times and examined to see what could be improved or what required changing. So in fact the equivalent of 30 engines had been assembled. He estimated that that after 19 flights, about 21 flight hours, had been accumulated. Flight test hours would dramatically increase in the year 2009 when all versions would be flying. Ground testing was however a completely other story and he estimated that he was over halfway through the ground testing required.

AEP F136

To preserve competition General Electric was granted a contract to develop further one engine in November 1995. The choice of engine was between a further development of the F110 and F120 engines. The further development of one of these engines had to give similar or better performance than that of the F119 engine. On 11 March 1996 the cooperation on the GEA-FXL, between General Electric, AADC and Rolls-Royce, was extended to the main engine and any other future applications, but the engine was still to be decided. By the end of March 1996 it was recognised that of the two engines the YF120 was the most promising for further development for use in the JAST programme. After giving Lockheed and the Boeing and McDonnell Douglas team the option between several upgrades of either the F110 or the YF120 engines, the airframe producers said that they preferred the YF120 versions. The engine choice was therefore decided. The end of phase I of the Alternate Engine Program had been reached.

The YF120 had been developed for the YF-22 and YF-23 together with the YF119 and they had to fulfil similar size parameters. In the case for the further development of the YF120 the same condition applied. This was considered phase II of the development of the alternate engine. This contract ran to 2001.

The successful CDR of the JSF F120 engine core was followed by a contract awarded for the next phase in July 1999. The engine core received production number 652-001 and was due to be tested before the end of phase II.

Shortly after the announcement of the winner of the CDP phase General Electric received a contract for phase III of its pre-SDD effort on 13 November 2001 to test turbofan engines in both the STOVL and CTOL. The two engines due to be tested in 2004 under phase III were engines 625-002 and 625-003. The high-altitude facility was tested using 625-002 and it was expected that total testing would be for 400 hours. The second test engine due to be tested was 625-003, which was a 'near production' engine in STOVL configuration and it was planned to undergo 200 hours' of testing.

The General Electric team achieved the PDR milestone in July 2002. By October 2002 General Electric received clearance from the JSF programme office to begin assembly of the first turbofan for the F136 engine. This also cleared the way for General Electric to order long-lead products from its suppliers. This made an FETT in mid-2004 possible. The F136 engine was equipped with a Lamilloy High Pressure (HP) turbine nozzle, advanced turbine blades, a low observable exhaust, axi-symmetric nozzle, a vaneless contra-rotating Low Pressure (LP) turbine, single annular combustor, a tripass diffuser, corrosion-resistant bearings, advanced HP turbine blades with thermal coatings and a rugged blisk (bladed disk) HP compressor.

Rolls-Royce was also a partner with General Electric on its version of the engine. Rolls-Royce was therefore assured of production of all control ducts, lift fans, and the three bearing thrust vectoring nozzles, whichever engine was chosen. A full SDD contract was expected in 2005. If the programme keeps to its original schedule the F136 engine will receive its *Initial Service Release (ISR)* in 2011, making the engine available from the fourth LRIP.

Early in 2003 it became clear that there would be budget cuts for the JSF SDD phase. The main problem was that the JSF programme office did not want to delay the first flight, therefore it was imperative that both Lockheed Martin and Pratt & Whitney were both freed from any budget cuts. This left only the option of budget-cutting open towards the General Electric engine, the F136. The budget cuts would have a delaying effect of two years, postponing the into service date from 2011 to 2013. The F136 was planned to be available from the seventy-second LRIP aircraft, which meant that the F135 would be installed in the first seventy-one production aircraft. The biggest loser besides General Electric would be Rolls-Royce as it had a 40 per cent work-share in the F136 STOVL version, not including the common parts of the Pratt & Whitney engine in which Rolls-Royce has a stake. The UK was thought to be the launch customer of the F136 engine as a result of the higher stake held by Rolls-Royce but this would be unlikely if the engine would delay the into service date. An option would be to exchange the engines at a later stage, as they are supposed to be physically and functionally interchangeable. Extensive lobbying eventually prevented the cuts from materialising.

For the alternative F136 engine, Rolls-Royce had succeeded in acquiring an important part of engine parts production. Rolls-Royce attained responsibility for the engine fan, the LP combustor and the second and third stages of the LP turbine as well as the STOVL lift system. Rolls-Royce had in fact received 40 per cent responsibility for the engine and therefore in 2002 was keen on setting up a limited liability company with General Electric to develop and produce the F136 engine. The American DoD, however, did not see the point of this and therefore these plans were put on hold for the time being. In the test concept of the JSF for the SDD it was foreseen that the F136 integration flight-testing would commence during the eighty-fifth month of the SDD. In a presentation by General Jack Hudson (USAF and Joint Program Director) in October 2003, he indicated that the FETT for the F136 was planned for August 2004.

Phillips Aerospace of the Netherlands was awarded a contract for the alternative GE F136 engine by Rolls-Royce. Phillips Aerospace is to supply the fan cases for the GE F136 engine.

Rolls-Royce delivered the first fan module for the F136 engine to General Electric on 15 June 2004 on schedule for the FETT milestone now planned for July 2004. On 22 July 2004 the CTOL engine achieved FETT and this, according to Bob Griswold, President of the GE-Rolls-Royce Fighter Engine *Team LLC* was one day ahead of schedule. Assembly of a second test engine, a STOVL version, would continue in preparation for testing by 2005. In 2005 it was expected that General Electric would receive the go-ahead to proceed to the SDD phase from the JSF JPO.

On 3 November 2004 the General Electric/Rolls-Royce Fighter Engine Team (FET) received a contract to finance the period from pre-SDD phase III to SDD. The contract was for long-lead hardware procurement and risk reduction/transition effort. The value of the contract was US $122,155,880. The work was expected to be completed by July 2005, at which stage the SDD contract would be signed.

The F136 STOVL engine achieved its FETT milestone on 10 February 2005. A total of 300 test hours would be completed by the STOVL engine by May 2005. By March 2005 more than 110 test hours had been amassed with the first CTOL engine. General Electric had to deliver its final proposal by 30 April 2005 and hoped to receive a contract for fifteen test engines in the SDD phase. The ideal situation would be that the company could continue work without interruption on 1 August 2005. If that date was kept then the planned ISR milestone for 2012 would be achievable. On 9 May 2005 the AEP team announced that they had completed all conventional and STOVL engine testing required prior to SDD.

After a long wait, or at least longer than expected, on 19 August 2005 General Electric received a contract for seven ground-test engines and seven flight-test engines (six flight-test + one reserve engine). The value of the cost-plus-award-fee, cost-plus-fixed-fee contract is $2,466,258,499. Of the fourteen engines the first is planned to be switched on in mid-2008. General Electric will, however, use the pre-SDD engines for risk-reduction tests and these were initiated in 2006. The first flight of the F136 is scheduled for 2010 and the engine should be available to customers from 2012, which means from LRIP IV according to the current schedule.

The ink on the contract was not even dry, when in December 2005 it was discovered that the US Navy did not want to finance the alternative engine. The US Navy had made no provisions in its budget for the engine. During the following period there was a lot of political lobbying between the UK and the US. Rolls-Royce had hoped to secure a larger involvement through the engine and would lose out on the main engine business if the F136 was indeed cancelled. General Electric was of course lobbying from its side but also tried to show that it was on schedule and would initiate risk-reduction tests slightly ahead of schedule in 2006. To show its commitment the General Electric/Rolls-Royce team delivered engine 625-003/2 to the General Electric test facilities at Peebles in Ohio ahead of schedule on 22 December 2005. The lobbying did not have much effect on the US President as he did not allocate any funds for the General Electric/Rolls-Royce engine. The fight was not considered lost as General Electric had not been told to stop working. It was hoped that Congress would overturn this decision. Risk reduction engine tests commenced on 8 February 2006, a good milestone prior to the Asian Aerospace trade show held in Singapore. Congress listened to the prayers from General Electric, Rolls-Royce and the partner nation the UK.

The battle was won, the war however continued and the following year the same battle had to be fought although this time around it was less dramatic. General Charles R.Davis, the JSF programme director, stated that he had no problem with alternative engine. He had a problem with the fact that the funding would not be sufficient or be taken away from elsewhere in the programme.

	GE F136		P&W F135	
	CTOL/CV	STOVL	CTOL/CV	STOVL
Maximum thrust	40,800 lb		43,000 lbf / 191.3 kN	43,000 lbf / 191.3 kN
Short take-off thrust	N/A		N/A	38,100 lbf 169.5 kN
Hover thrust	N/A		N/A	39,400 lbf 175.3 kN
Main engine	N/A		N/A	15,700 lbf
Lift fan	N/A		N/A	20,000 lbf
Roll posts	N/A		N/A	3.700 lbf
Length	221 in/5.62 m		220 in/5.59 m	369 in /9.37 m
Inlet diameter:				
Main engine			46 in/1.17 m	46 in /1.17 m
Lift fan	N/A	50 in /1.27 m	N/A	50 in /1.27 m
Maximum diameter		51 in /1.30 m	51 in/1.30 m	51 in /1.30 m
Bypass ratio:				
Conventional			0.57	0.56
Powered lift	N/A		N/A	0.51
Overall pressure ratio:				
Conventional			28	28
Powered lift	N/A		N/A	29

One engine ready for testing. The technology in the F135 will be the most thoroughly and matured engines tested prior to introduction into service. *Copyright Pratt & Whitney*

CHAPTER 13

THE JSF BOEING 737-300 CATBIRD

As is usual with military aircraft development, all kinds of aircraft are used to test certain systems in the air prior to installation in the actual aircraft. The JSF programme was not going to be different in that sense. The Lockheed Martin team took the idea one step further. As a result of experience with the F-22, certain lessons were learned and pittfalls encountered around the avionics on that programme. Lockheed Martin wanted to avoid them if possible. All systems were to be flown on one aircraft, to test the software fusion and interoperability of all these systems. Lockheed went in search of an airframe suitable for the task. The requirements of the airframe were that it should not cost too much, so it should be readily available. The second requirement was that it should at be capable of being three hours on station for test purposess. The third requirement was for the selected airframe to fly at altitudes and speeds representative to that of the F-35 this of course within realist limits. The fourth requirement was that it should be capable of doing all the above while carrying the entire F-35 mission system suite

The aircraft selected for this mission was a Boeing 737-300, acquired by Lockheed Martin from Lufthansa. The aircraft was originally owned by the German airline with registration D-ABXH, c/n 23528, line number 1290. The aircraft had however been leased to Indonesian Airlines carrying registration PK-IAA. It was still in the Indonesian Airlines livery, only the titles had been removed from the fuselage and the Lufthansa registration applied. The aircraft flew for the first time in support of the JSF programme on 17 December 2003 from Mojave Spaceport, on the date of celebrations for the century of powered flight. The aircraft carrying registration N35LX was equipped with structural and system sensor by BAE Systems. The following day the Boeing 737 flew again for its baseline testing. It flew 9 January 2004 for the last time as part of the base line evaluation flight testing, the day after it disappeared into the hangar not to reappear for more than two and half years.

During that period the airliner was to undergo some dramatic changes. The Boeing 737-300 was equipped with an aerodynamically neutral canard to emulate sensor positions on the wing and a specially extended nose with a radome for the AN/APG-81 and the EOTS. The canard is placed just aft of the forward entry door on the former airliner. In fact the neutral canard, meaning it was to have minimal aerodynamic influence on flight characteristics of the aircraft, was not only to copy the shape but also the exact position of the sensors and the distance between the leading edge and the radar cone is close to the real thing, if not exactly the same. Most of the other sensors would be positioned on the fuselage in direct relation as to where they would find themselves in the F-35. Other changes to the exterior of airliner include a 42 ft long spine on the top of the aircraft, a 10 ft long canoe on the belly of the fuselage filled with Line Replaceable Units (LRU). Another change although insignificant to the result of the flight testing, was the change of the livery. Changes

This avionics test-bed is more advanced then any other previously built. It is configured in such a manner that even the wire harnesses emulate the real thing. *Copyright Lockheed Martin*

in the interior of the plane have been no less dramatic. 20 work stations for test engineers that will assess the performance of the F-35 mission system suite have been installed. Furthermore the aircraft has been filled with equipment racks that will record all the data collected during the test flights. Besides the 20 test engineers occupying the 20 work stations, the aircraft has seating for 8 observers. If the CATBird is used to its maximum, it will carry a crew of 33 people. All together the modifications were expected to have a slightly limiting effect on the maximum speed and altitude of the aircraft. The higher drag induced to the aircraft by the external modifications will reduce range, overall performance and endurance. The aircraft however was still able to fulfill the three hour on station requirement.

The Cooperative Avionics Test Bed (CATB) or CATBird was planned to fly again in July 2006. BAE Systems Electronics & Integrated Solutions were working hard to meet that milestone and had called it the 'CATBird Fly in July'. A critical milestone for that first flight after the modifications occurred on March 18, 2006 and that was the first power-on, meaning electrical power. Although work was done seven days a week and double shifts were worked to beat the fly in July milestone, it was not met. Just like the AA-1, the first flight of the Boeing 737-300 was also delayed. According to John Wall director of flight operations at BAE Systems for the sensor systems, the main reason for delay was the fact that 'The modifications to the CATB platform are among the most complex ever undertaken for a flying test bed. There are over 35.3 kilometers of wiring which have been integrated into the platform, all requiring various distances of separation between them for successful operation. This presented a significant systems engineering challenge, which was resolved by inserting plugs into some of the windows, providing additional space for wire routing.' The wiring harnesses again were made the same length as in the F-35 to copy the real situation on the real thing. Even the spacing of the wiring harnesses was adjusted to emulate the F-35. This, all because of the experience Lockheed Martin had gained previously with the F-22 testbed.

On 17 November 2006, almost three years after the baseline testing had been innitiated, the Boeing 737-300 performed its first taxiiing tests since its refurbishments. Several more

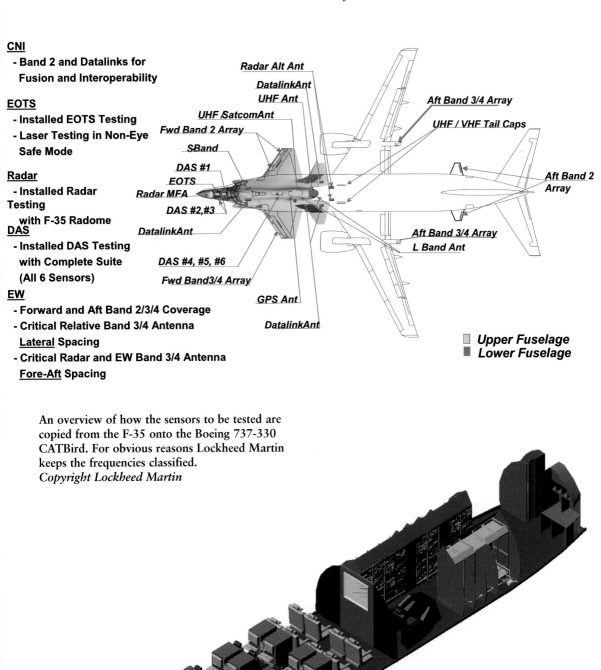

CNI
- Band 2 and Datalinks for Fusion and Interoperability

EOTS
- Installed EOTS Testing
- Laser Testing in Non-Eye Safe Mode

Radar
- Installed Radar Testing with F-35 Radome

DAS
- Installed DAS Testing with Complete Suite (All 6 Sensors)

EW
- Forward and Aft Band 2/3/4 Coverage
- Critical Relative Band 3/4 Antenna Lateral Spacing
- Critical Radar and EW Band 3/4 Antenna Fore-Aft Spacing

Radar Alt Ant
DatalinkAnt
UHF Ant
UHF SatcomAnt
Fwd Band 2 Array
SBand
DAS #1
EOTS
Radar MFA
DAS #2,#3
DatalinkAnt
DAS #4, #5, #6
Fwd Band3/4 Array
GPS Ant
DatalinkAnt

Aft Band 3/4 Array
UHF / VHF Tail Caps
Aft Band 2 Array
Aft Band 3/4 Array
L Band Ant

Upper Fuselage
Lower Fuselage

An overview of how the sensors to be tested are copied from the F-35 onto the Boeing 737-330 CATBird. For obvious reasons Lockheed Martin keeps the frequencies classified.
Copyright Lockheed Martin

The outward changes are obvious, however the inward changes are only shown to some of the lucky ones. This drawing however represents the final disposition of the interior of the CATBird.
Copyright Lockheed Martin

low speed taxi tests followed with some engine runs. The Boeing 737-300 flew for the first time after these modifications on 23 January 2007. It was the first flight to evaluate the new aerodynamics of the CATBird and the flight lasted two hours. Aerodynamics testing is expected to take about one month or 20 flights.

Specification CATBird	Prior modification	Post modification
Length	33,40m (109ft 7 in)	115ft 5 in
Wingspan	28,88m (94ft 9 in)	28,88m (94ft 9 in)
Height	11,13 m (36 ft 6 in)	11,13 m (36 ft 6 in)
Weight	31,895 kg (70,320 lb)	Not available
MTOW	57,606 kg (127,000lb)	57,606 kg (127,000lb)
Range	5278 km (2,850 nm)	5278 km (2,850 nm)
Ceiling	37,000 ft	33,000 ft
Max. speed	Vmo/Mmo = 340 KIAS / 0.82 Mach	Vmo/Mmo = 300 KIAS / 0.76 Mach

'Upon completion of the Performance and Flight Quality testing, we will populate the aircraft with the balance of Mission Systems racks and workstations and complete installation and testing of the equipment liquid cooling system.' Followed by 'Formal delivery of the aircraft to Lockheed Martin which is planned for August 2007.' According to John Wall. 'The majority of the mission systems equipment and sensors will be installed by Lockheed Martin in Fort Worth.' Among them will be an F-35 cockpit which will display sensor inputs just like in the real F-35. On March 2, 2007 the 24th flight, the CATBird was flown from Mojave to Fort Worth where the next phase of the modification was to be initiated immediately after the first flights had proven that the modified airframe was safe to fly over the entire flight envelope. The CATBird had accumulated over 70 flight hours during those 24 flights. Today's milestone initiates a phase of unprecedented integrated avionics test capability,' said Eric Branyan, Lockheed Martin Vice-president of F-35 Mission Systems. 'The rigorous testing performed on board the CATBird will ensure that mature functionality is delivered to the F-35 Lightning II.'

The first system to be tested on the CATbird was the Communication Navigation Identification (CNI) System. Integration and testing of that system was expected to be initiated by July 2007. Flight test was expected to start by October 2007. CNI testing was, during the F-22 test programme, considered problematic so for this reason it was planned to fly CNI tests first. After the CNI the following systems would be installed step by step in the following order given Electronic Warfare (EW), AESA Radar, Electro-Optical Targeting System (EOTS), Electro-Optical Distributed Aperture System (EO-DAS). Although the CATBird had been severely delayed General C.R. Davis said that he was still confident to get his money worth out of it. Lockheed Martin chief test pilot Jon Beesley was again confident the sensor fusion would be less of a problem because the people that were involved with the Lockheed Martin F-22 Raptor had transferred to the F-35 programme bringing along their knowledge and lessons learned. The first software block to be tested on the CATbird is block 0.5.

SURVIVABILITY OF THE F-35

Survivability of the F-16, F-18, A-10, AV-8 and Harrier GR.7 was in doubt in the future strike mission environment. Enhancement in the air defence systems made the above-mentioned fighters extremely vulnerable and they would not be able to strike at will. More Suppression of Enemy Air Defences (SEAD) support aircraft would be required for each strike mission. The other assets required would increase as well (tankers, transports) to sustain the operations. Without dedicated SEAD aircraft the current strike aircraft would not be able to disrupt enemy ground forces, with the risk of more losses on the ground. SEAD requirements, however, would divert assets away from the original strike mission. To make an aircraft more survivable there are different approaches. The approaches are:

- Electronic warfare
- Counter measures like flares
- Stealth
- Flight characteristics

From the above list, stealth is the technology that has, since the Gulf war, proved itself as highly effective in all kinds of scenarios. Stealth is not only achieved by shaping the aircraft but by use of materials and sensors in such a way that the enemy or opponent does not know that you are there. In fact there are seven observable signatures. Those are radar, infrared, electromagnetics, acoustics, engine smoke, contrails and visual signature. The 'easiest' to work on or to influence are the radar, infrared and electromagnetic signatures.

The first stealth fighter came out of a programme called *Have Blue*. This resulted from a DARPA request for a fighter aircraft with significantly reduced radar detectability dating from 1974. Originally Lockheed was not invited, as it had not produced a fighter aircraft since the F-104 Starfighter. However its experience on the SR-71 made Deputy Head of Lockheed Advanced Development Programmes (ADP) better known as the Skunk Works, Ben R. Rich, convinced that they had to offer something to the air force in this respect. The SR-71 known for its speed and sleek features was one of the first, if not the first Lockheed aircraft, where stealth features were applied. After formal approval had been given by the CIA, Lockheed was able to discuss the stealth features of the SR-71 with DARPA. Lockheed's work was based on the work of several scientists. The first one was Scottish physicist James Clerk Maxwell (1831-1879), his work was refined by German electromagnetic expert Arnold Johannes Sommerfeld (1868 –1951). A set of mathematical formulas predicted the manner in which a given geometric configuration would scatter or reflect electro-magnetic radiation. A paper by Russian physicist Pyotr Ufimtsev, in which he described a more simplified method that concentrated on electromagnetic currents at the edges of geometric shapes was also studied. The work of the first two gentleman was widely available to anyone in the world but surprisingly the Russians deemed the work of their Physicist Pyotr Ufimtsev of no tactical value and therefore made it available to the free world. It was Lockheed's retired mathematician Bill Schroeder and Skunk Works software engineer Denys Overholster who designed a computer program called Echo 1. It Was Bill Schroeder's idea to replace the curving features of a 'normal' fighter aircraft with two dimensional surfaces. To keep the reflections to a minimum it was realised that surfaces had to have the same general direction. If this three-dimensional shaped aircraft could still generate lift to fly, then the fly by wire flight control system would keep it in the air. With the help of Echo 1, Denys Overholster designed an aircraft model which was tested at a Skunk Works electromagnetics facility. It was at this point when pole-mounted signature model testing began that the project gained its name *Have Blue*. In April 1976 Lockheed was awarded a contract after winning the DARPA competition. The results of the tests were so significant that the programme became highly secret. The level of secrecy stopped it from existing to those not involved. It disappeared into the so-called black world to reappear on 10 November 1988 when the Pentagon finally acknowledged the existence of the F-117 and showed a hazy picture. The F-117 had been flying operationally for five years. Interestingly, Pyotr Ufimtsev was later (1995-2000) employed as Principal Engineer at the Northrop Grumman Corporation, Lockheed's partner in the CDP and SDD phase of the JSF programme.

The shaping of the F-117 and its success, also had its effect on the design of the F-22 Raptor. This aircraft retained the general idea of the F-117 with two dimensional sides. If one puts the F-22 Raptor upside down one can recognise a rough triangular shape, as with the F-117. The purpose of stealth is to make the aircraft invisible to the radar of enemy aircraft and ground defences. In the design of the Lockheed JSF model from the early stages similarities to the F-22 design could be noticed. The F-35 has however smoother curves then either the F-22 Raptor or the F-117 Nighthawk.

Stealth technology, besides a technical issue, is also a political issue. Stealth technology is closely guarded by the Americans as they have a technological advantage. The idea of freely transferring that technology to other nations received the usual reluctance. The transfer of this technology was, however, inevitable if the export customer wanted to maintain its own aircraft, which is common sense.

There were some options to choose from:

• Downgrade stealth for export customers
• Remove all sensitive technology for export customers
• Not exporting JSF (not a real option)
• Downgrade stealth standard across the board (not a real option)

The possible political ramifications were that nations might be angry to be sold second-rate equipment. In fact, instead of buying inferior products those foreign governments might decide to select a different aircraft, which would affect the cost of the American planes as the price for spare parts and upgrades would not be shared with as many customers. Politically, this would also mean losing influence. The US counted, however, on offering a better plane at a better price than the competition was able to do and that the foreign states would swallow their pride. The F-22 and the JSF were being advertised as the only fifth-generation fighters around.

Operational side effects would mainly occur during coalition efforts as commanders would have to be aware of the different capabilities of the aircraft and not every unit could be used for the same task. Stealth technology is supposed to increase survivability of the crew even in harm's way. (Bear in mind the example in Afghanistan where the Dutch,

Danish and Norwegian air forces formed one unit with F-16s but could also fly with American units in the same mission. If the export version of the JSF is downgraded or lacks the sensitive technology it would mean that non-US coalition aircraft would be running a higher risk during the same mission, or would have a higher probability of giving the position of the strike package away.) A US DoD report to the US Congress stated the following: 'Operation Allied Force highlighted a number of disparities between US capabilities and those of our allies, including precision strike, mobility and command, control and communications capabilities. The gaps in capabilities were real, and they had the effect of impeding our ability to operate at optimal effectiveness with our NATO allies.' NATO allies were credited for major contributions in total sorties and strikes but the limited interoperability constrained effectiveness. In fact, the JSF was advertised as being the answer to all the problems and able to bring commonality to all services, including to those of the partner nations.

Some of the countries, however, were so eager to join the JSF programme that they were not in the least bothered that they would be buying a downgraded version of the F-35 in the sense that they accepted that they would get an F-35 in line with the US National Disclosure Policy (NDP). In fact, Lockheed received a contract on 10 November 2003 with the aim of designing, developing and verifying a delta version (D version). The contract also stipulated testing a version of the JSF air system that was as common as possible with the US air system within the NDP. The value of the contract was $602,594,580 and the work connected with this contract modification was expected to be completed by April 2012 in time for the required deliveries.

The extent of stealth technology as such has enormously increased, as the most stealthy aircraft carry their weapons and fuel internally and not on the under-wing stores. In fact, the GAO questioned the sense of the Radar Cross Section (RCS) reduction investments made for the F/A-18E/F. For comparison the GAO used as examples designs such as the Lockheed F-117, Northrop Grumman B-2, Lockheed F-22 Raptor and the cancelled General Dynamics A-12 Avenger design and even the designs developed for the A/F-X programme. According to some experts weapons carried under the wings can undo most of the RCS reduction measures that have been implemented on any conventional fighter. The GAO expressed the opinion that the F/A-18C/D would have done the job of the F/A-18E/F just as well for a smaller investment. The F/A-18C/D would, however, have reached its development limits while the F-18E/F had plenty of growth capacity, which was probably not taken into account by the GAO. Furthermore, stealth required a lot of maintenance, and that maintenance requirement was already being approached by the F-22 CTF (Combined Test Force). In fact, maintenance was the reason why the Initial Operational Test & Evaluation (IOT&E) report of the F-22 concluded that its suitability was limited. Lockheed Martin and its partners were working on more maintainable stealth technology.

Early in the programme during the Concept Definition and Design Research (CDDR) phase the JAST office initiated several studies regarding structures and materials. The three study programmes were:

1 Advanced Lightweight Aircraft Fuselage Structure (ALAFS)

2 Affordable Fighter Aft-fuselage Structure Technology (AFAST)

3 Inlet Duct, Edges and Front Frame (IDEFF)

ALAFT was envisioned as a primarily composite, centre fuselage/inboard wing section, which was fabricated and assembled using advanced, low-cost manufacturing technologies. Specific goals were to reduce the cost of that section of the aircraft by 30 per cent and the weight by 20 per cent. This was to be achieved by weight reduction (as weight equals cost) and low manufacturing costs of the fuselage elements and was to be proved on the F-18E/F Super Hornet.

AFAST concentrated on issues specific to the aft fuselage region of a fighter – in particular, the high temperatures around the engine. Specific technical issues involved high temperature joints and seals, high temperature composites, and improved casting and welding technology, high temperature Radar Absorbent Structure (RAS), and improved durability and damage tolerance of high temperature components. This was of increased importance with the different lift systems installed as they would increase the areas where heat resistant materials were to be used in comparison with the conventional fighters.

On 4 April 1995, the JAST office initiated through a Broad Agency Announcement (BAA) 95-2, a programme for technology maturation in new stealth technology. It was called the IDEFF signature reduction programme. The aim of the programme was to develop new affordable technologies that would reduce the head-on RCS and therefore increase the chances of mission success and survival over hostile territory. The proposals were due by 19 May 1995 and the CPFF contract award was planned for 30 June 1995. The project was expected to run in two phases; the first one twenty-two months from the contract award were for concept definition and validation and planning the next demonstration phase. In the second phase the new technology was to be demonstrated.

Survivability of the JSF is going to be a major issue as most aircraft brought down during recent conflicts were fighter aircraft with a single engine, as planes that had two engines had a better chance of returning home even if they had sustained severe damage. A good example was when USAF Captain Kim Campbell managed to fly her A-10A (81-0987) back to a forward operation base in Kuwait after she was hit by anti-aircraft fire over Iraq on 7 April 2003. This example is particularly apt, as the JSF should ultimately replace the A-10A in its Close Air Support (CAS) mission. An aircraft's vulnerability is taken into account at the early design stage. A combat aircraft should be able to survive some battle damage. The A-10 is a prime example for survivability, even with high level of battle damage. Battle damage is classified in the following groups:

Battle damage forces the crew to eject over enemy forces. This means if the crew ejects safely they may be captured by enemy forces.

Battle damage allows crew to retain control until returning to friendly troops. This means that if the crew eject safely they are ready to fight another day.

The crew is able to return to base even though the aircraft has incurred battle damage.

Modelling and simulation tools were used from early in the SDD to reduce the vulnerability to battle damage by trying to cover damage-sensitive items in the aircraft by other systems. Each fuel tank wall is evaluated and accordingly the right quantity and kind of fire suppressant technology is applied. Some of the data is deducted from previous programmes, however the F-35 has some new systems that are expected to reduce the vulnerability of the aircraft to battle damage, such as the Electro Hydrostatic Actuator (EHA) technology which will reduce the vulnerable hydraulic system in the aircraft.

Most aircraft losses have been incurred by infrared guided missiles and therefore the USAF paid extra attention to the Low Observable technology used to reduce the infrared signature of the aircraft also required by the USMC, which wanted to use the JSF for CAS where Radar Absorbing Materials (RAM) were of little or no use. Some services (the US Navy and the RAF) wanted the JSF to function as 'a first day of war survivable plane', although for the USAF this was not a requirement as it had the F-22 at its disposal.

Lockheed was already looking at the RCS section and other measures to reduce signature during the CDP. It built a full-scale pole model that was transported to its Helendale measurement facility in California in early September 1999 where it would be assembled. The model was produced in the latter stages of the CDP so that the Signature Measurement Aircraft (SigMA) would resemble the final PWSC as much as possible. During February 2000 the tests were initiated with the X-35 pole model. The Supportable Low Observables (SLO) materials were tested both in perfect condition and after damage repair so that the effectiveness of repairs could be evaluated. Lockheed had an advantage of experience with stealth technology with the F-117 and the F/22A. The problem with stealth technology was that RAM was damaged by handling of access panels and doors. To increase supportability a requirement was set for zero restoration need for access panels and doors. This would decrease maintenance requirements and increase ease of deployment as the logistic footprint would be reduced.

For the SDD phase another full-scale pole model was funded for more profound testing. One of the twenty-two prototypes was to be the model so that the testing could be more accurate.

Electronic Warfare

Electronic Warfare (EW) systems are another means to increase survivability of any aircraft. For this reason Lockheed had already invested money during the CDP to evaluate the positioning of sensors. Lockheed built a full-scale mock-up and put it on a 12-m high tower. The mock-up was able to rotate and was part of a high fidelity sensor integration facility at its Fort Worth facility. A remote cockpit station connected to COTS processors and the imbedded sensors in the model enabled functionality tests to be performed and reduced the risk of software fusion.

The Electronic Counter Measures (ECM), a part of the EW system in current and previous generation fighter aircraft, functions by jamming the enemy's weapons radar system used to track and guide missiles aimed at the aircraft. For this reason ECM technology and techniques have been continually updated to remain effective. Stealth means that the regular weapon systems pose a smaller threat and therefore the EW System can and has to work in a more passive way. If an active system is used, then the stealth aircraft could give away its position. The EW system should provide information to the pilot where the threats are located and their range thus ensuring that the pilot can choose the optimum route through a complex air defence system. The EW system is also now a piece of the equipment that has to provide the pilot with situational awareness.

The EW system was so advanced that the F-35 was thought to be able to fulfil the function of an Electronic Attack aircraft. The Electronic Attack version of the JSF, also known as the EA-35, was in favour with the USMC, however the US Navy preferred the EA-18G or the Growler as a replacement for the EA-6 Prowler. The major disadvantage of the JSF was that it was for the time being developed only as a single-seater and the US Navy preferred a two–seater, making the EA-18G the hot favourite. Furthermore, the EA-18G was derived from the F-18F Super Hornet, which was already operational in mid-2002. BAE Systems, however, had come up with a design of the forward fuselage with a twin crew cockpit that had no effect on the fuel capacity of the CV version and would not have any adverse effects on the production methods. A two-seat STOVL version was deemed near impossible – it was for this reason that the USMC was interested in finding out what the capabilities would be of a single-seat EA-35 version.

Lockheed offered two solutions – a short-term and a long-term solution. The short-term solution was an F-35 equipped with ALQ-99 jamming pods and an EW suite. The ALQ-99 jamming pod was in use on the EA-6 Prowler. The long-term solution would have a more integrated capability without the requirement of a pod. The maturity of the F-18F made the decision in favour of the F-18G relatively easy, as the requirement of stealth in an Electronic Attack aircraft was questionable.

In the JSF programme it was BAE Systems located in Nashua, North America, that was responsible for the EW suite. Since the contract award in October 2001 BAE Systems had been occupied with developing a lightweight EW suite and had managed to reduce the weight by 60 lb per aircraft. The first flyable EW suite was delivered in August 2004 to Lockheed Martin. Test-flying was planned to start on the Cooperative Avionics Test Bed aircraft (CATB), also known as CATBird, in 2005. The first flight took place on a T-39 Saberliner on 18 July 2005 and lasted two hours. Two days later the second flight was performed and the third flight followed on 21 July 2005. Each of the flights lasted about two hours. As planned, the following week two more flights were executed according to schedule. The EW system that was test-flown was close to the production version of the EW suite for the F-35 fighter and according to BAE Systems officials still below the weight and cost requirements.

One of the prototypes was to be used for survivability tests due to be held at Wright Patterson AFB. If the programme progresses in a similar fashion to the Raptor then it would be logical to assume that it will be the A-1 prototype that undergoes these tests.

The BAe Systems test team in front of the Sabreliner used for Electronic Warfare System flight testing. *Copyright BAe Systems*

CHAPTER 15

THE WEAPON SYSTEMS

The JSF was, due to its stealth design from the outset, designed to be survivable in the first day of a war. It was argued that combat aircraft with weapon loads under the wings would in the future not be survivable. The JSF F-35 therefore has internal weapon bays. The many missions and aircraft it was supposed to replace also dictated a wide assortment of weapons. The missions that were to be fulfilled with the JSF included Close Air Support (CAS) – for the USMC the most important role – strike and attack missions, interdiction, Suppression of Enemy Air Defence (SEAD) and reconnaissance missions.

To spread the cost of development and integration of all the proposed weapons it was

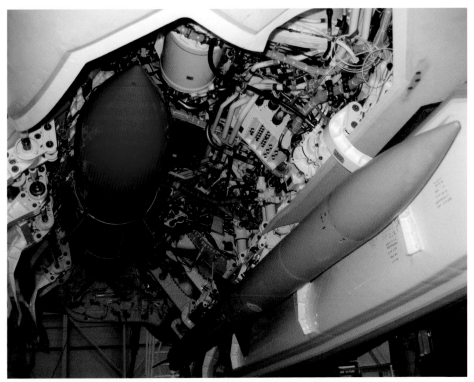

A close-up of the weapon bay. Note the JDAM and the AMRAAM loaded into the aircraft's weapon bay. This photo was taken during ground tests of AA-1.
Copyright Lockheed Martin

decided to divide the weapons into three blocks. Block 1 capability started development in 2003 and flight tests will run through to 2009. Block 1 capability would give the JSF basic war fighter capability with AIM-120 AMRAAM and JDAM integrated. Flight-testing of Block 1 was to be initiated forty-eight months after ATP and be completed ninety months after ATP. Block 2 would start development in mid-2004 and would enhance the air-to-air capability, make the JSF more air-to-ground weapons qualified and add CAS and SEAD capability. Flight-testing of Block 2 was to be initiated eighty-three months after ATP with flight-testing completed by the end of 2010. Development of the third block would be initiated in 2006 and was expected to be completed early in 2012.

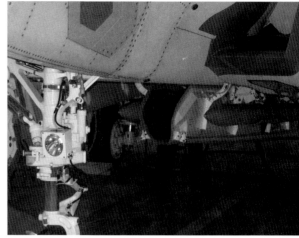

As the weapon bay opens the AMRAAM missile extends outwards automatically, as it is attached to the weapon bay lower door, thus positioning it in the aircraft's slipstream. *Copyright Lockheed Martin*

Block 3 would make the JSF fully compliant with the requirements set and integrated flight-testing would be initiated ninety-six months after ATP and be completed eighteen months later. The flight-testing of Block 1 was delayed as a result of the weight problems encountered during the PDR.

The aircraft therefore had to be from the outset big enough to have internal weapon bays; this requirement made the aircraft bigger and therefore also heavier. The maximum empty weight that was set by DARPA limited the size of the JSF, however. As a result of the limited space in the internal bays the F-35 was still equipped with under-wing pylons. The under-wing pylons were to be used when stealth was not so important or when air supremacy had been achieved and threats from ground-to-air weapons had diminished to ensure survivability. The F-35 would be equipped with a total of six under-wing weapon stations.

Aircraft	Payload
F-35A	18,000 lb + internal cannon
F-35B	15,000 lb no internal cannon
F-35C	18,000 lb no internal cannon

As a result of the weight problems encountered early in the SDD phase the weapon bays of the F-35B were reduced in size. However, this would cause an increase in testing to be done specifically for the STOVL version as there would be different doors and lighter mechanisms to open the doors. Extra flight-testing time would have to be allocated to test the new aerodynamic situation, although this could, up to a point, be carried out in wind tunnels.

F-35 weapon stations and their weight limits are shown in the table below.

Station	1	2	3	4	5	6	7	8	9	10	11
F-35A weight (lb)	300	2500	5000	2500	350	1000	350	2500	5000	2500	300
F-35B weight (lb)	300	1500	5000	1500	350	1000	350	1500	5000	1500	300
F-35C weight (lb)	300	2500	5000	2500	350	1000	350	2500	5000	2500	300

All stations with the exception of station 6, the external centre fuselage station, would be qualified for air-to-air weaponry. All stations with the exception of external stations 1 and 11 and internal stations 5 and 7 would be qualified for air-to-surface weaponry. Furthermore, besides the internal weapon bay size reduction of the F-35B, which caused the loads of station 4 and 8 to be reduced by 1000 lb, the centre under-wing station carriage capability was also reduced in a similar fashion. An important part for ship-based aircraft is the 'bring back load' capability. The F-18C/D, for example, had to dump some of its unused weapons in the sea prior to landing. This was one of the reasons why the F-14 Tomcat remained the weapon system of choice even when its replacement was in the arena. The F-14 Tomcat never needed to dump any weaponry because it had no problems with bringing its weapons back to the ship. The F-35B had a bring back load of 5000 lb, which meant that the internal stores could be brought back at all times, and a fully loaded F-35B could not land vertically.

Suspension and Release Equipment

Another relative novelty to be introduced on the F-35 was that the launch of weapons would be executed using non-pyro technology. In the previous generations small detonations were used to release weapons from their pylons. The pyro technology involved, however, required a lot of maintenance and therefore was a major financial burden on operations. Only the F-22 Raptor was equipped with this new technology in the shape of the LAU-142/A AMRAAM Vertical Ejection Launcher (AVEL), although the new technology was, however, test-flown on the Raptor from 1999 onwards. The new technology stemmed from a programme in 1986 when EDO demonstrated the possibility of launching weapons through a pneumatic charged energy source that required minimal maintenance. The programme sponsored by the USAF was called the Alternate Conformal Ejector Rack (ACER). The new system could be buried in the wing as it did not require the same amount of maintenance as the pyro technology-based weapon racks and release systems. The new technology was based on a pneumatic energy source.

The system was, however, not in service yet, as the technology was not deemed mature enough. However, the USAF was interested in the technology and wanted to see the capability further developed but it took until 19 April 1995 for a Request for Proposals to be released. The name of the new programme was Weapon Carriage Technology (WCT). EDO joined forces with Boeing as the programme required the system to be installed into an aircraft for ground-testing. The programme was to consist of three phases with an optional fourth phase. The phases were Phase I: Concept Development/Detail Design (nine months), Phase II: Fabrication (twelve months), Phase III: Ground Test (nine months), Phase IV: (optional) Aircraft Integration/Flight Test Support (sixteen months). The aim of the WCT programme was to develop a Suspension & Release Equipment (S&RE) technology not based on a non-pyrotechnic energy source that could be used on conventional weapon racks and internal weapon bays so that it could be used to support the JAST programme at a later stage. Otherwise, the S&RE should be compatible with air-to-air and air-to-ground weaponry.

Boeing announced on 22 April 1996 that it had received a contract from the USAF to ground-test an advanced concept of weapon carriage for the next-generation fighters such as the JSF. The value of the contract was US $2.5 million. EDO would be the prime subcontractor. These pneumatic systems take advantage of the elimination of pyrotechnic cartridges, cleaning and the logistics of the cartridges, thereby enhancing the LCC and overall system affordability according to EDO. In early January 2002 EDO was rewarded for all its efforts, receiving a contract valued at $24.8 million from Lockheed Martin to develop pneumatic weapon suspension and release equipment.

Weapon bay loading for fighter aircraft is quite a novelty for most services, except for the USAF and the Australian Air Force using their F-IIIs. In line with the programme, Northrop Grumman invited the services to evaluate and give input on the design of the weapon bays. To optimise the loading techniques, procedures and technologies teams from the USMC (drawn from VMFA (AW)-121), USAF, RAF, US Navy and the Royal Navy had been invited by Northrop Grumman for two terms, the first one from 7 to 15 November 2003 and the second from 28 November to 4 December 2003, to its facility in El Segundo, California. A similar exercise was performed from 23 March to 25 March 2004 with the representatives of the UK forces. During the exercise, weapons that were tried out for loading were the AIM-120 and AIM-132 air-to-air missiles and 1000-lb and 2000-lb versions of JDAM.

On 23 February 2004 Lockheed Martin received a contract to revise the weapon capability baseline for the JSF.

Joint Advanced Weapons Guidance/Weapons Integration Precision Target Demonstration

The JAST office, however, did not want to put all its eggs in one basket and looked into improving precision targeting as well. The JAST office released BAA 95-1 in late 1994 to start Joint Advanced Weapons Guidance/Weapons Integration Precision Target Demonstration (JAWG/WIPTD). Proposals were due by 13 January 1995. This was delayed to 3 February 1995 as the ASTOVL programme was merged with JAST and suddenly received a more international identity. The JAST office received a total of thirty-one offers and on 20 March 1995. Westinghouse Electric Corporation Electronic Systems Group was the one company that received a CPFF contract with a value of US $5,025,186 from the JAST office under BAA 95-1. Under this contract Westinghouse was to focus work on strike warfare targeting and target identification. The programme was expected to last until July 1997.

Small Diameter Bomb (SDB)

The problem with a single-engine strike fighter is that it is relatively small. The fuselage space had to be shared by the engine, fuel tanks, air intakes, aircraft systems and now also the internal weapon bays, which was quite a challenge. It was for this reason that the industry was requested to look into stealthy weapon systems so that either no weapon bays were required, making the aircraft lighter, or more weapons could be carried without affecting the Radar Cross Section (RCS).

The industry argued, however, that it would be cheaper to develop smaller weapon systems so that in the same weapon bay more weapons could be carried and multiple targets destroyed during the same mission. Development of the Small Diameter Bomb (SDB) was born. The SDB with a 250-lb warhead has the same effect as the 500-kg JDAM. On 29 June 2001 a Request for Proposals was issued by the SDB programme office based at Eglin AFB. Initial Operational Capability (IOC) was aimed to be achieved somewhere in fiscal year 2002/2007. By the autumn of 2001 two companies (Lockheed Martin and Boeing) were provided with contracts for the SDD, each worth US $47 million. Each team was to design and develop two versions, of which one version INS/GPS and the other version would have an additional terminal seeker Automatic Target Recognition (ATR).

A detail of the Small Diameter Bomb (SDB). It may eventually replace the JDAM (Joint Direct Attack Munitions). *Copyright Boeing*

The SDB seen below a test F-15. It has now reached front line F-15 Strike Eagle units. Flight tests on the F-22 started early in 2007, thus giving Lockheed Martin some experience before integration of the weapon. *Copyright Boeing*

Although the SDB programme was a USAF one from the outset, already early in the programme it was aimed for use on the JSF. As a result it was only logical to make it a joint service programme. Although the US Navy had not been participating in the programme its requirements had been reflected in the Operational Requirement Document (ORD) already issued by the USAF.

On 20 October 2003 McDonnell Douglas, a Boeing subsidiary, received a $188,300,000 cost-plus award-fee contract to proceed with the SDD of the SDB. Boeing had to further develop the GBU-39 and GBU-40 SDB. Boeing won the contract to further develop the SDB, but one DoD official, Darleen Druyun, was found guilty of corruption and she admitted in court that she had favoured Boeing over the other competitors in several procurements. The GAO was asked to look into the best way to proceed as a result of that admission, although in the mean time the programme proceeded as normal.

As the name of the SDB suggests, it has a small diameter of 18.75 cm and a length of 177.5 cm, with a weight of 250 lb. The warhead case is made from steel for penetration purposes. In fact, the SDB should be able to penetrate 6 ft of reinforced concrete or more than 3 ft of steel-reinforced concrete and the damage should be caused by 50 lb of high-explosives. The SDB has a stand-off range of 60 nautical miles, which should be increased somewhat if launched supersonically from any aircraft, but in particular from the F-22 as it has supercruise capability. The SDB will be guided to its fixed target by a Guidance Differential GPS/INS and is of course autonomous and has an all-weather capability.

The SDB was a strike weapon and it was therefore natural that the F-15E Strike Eagle

The SDB prior to impact. This was during a proving trial against hardened shelters. *Copyright Boeing*

Effective! This shows the effect a SDB can have. Bunkers and hardened shelters are no longer safe havens for aircraft or any other material. *Copyright Boeing*

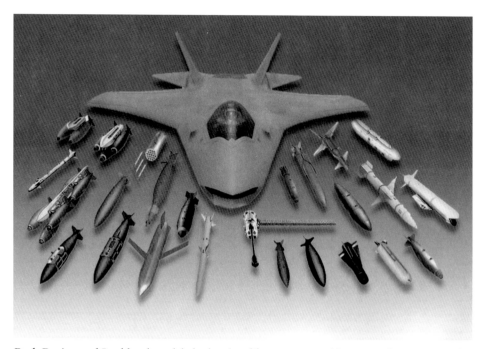

Both Boeing and Lockheed models had to be able to carry a wide range of weaponry. The Boeing Preferred Weapon System Concept is seen here with its planned armament. Note the BK-27 cannon originally selected by both contractors. Increasing cost however made a change inevitable. *Copyright DoD*

was chosen to perform the weapon qualification trials as it was also a Boeing aircraft. The first flight test with the SDB took place on 25 February 2003 below an F-15E. The F-15E became the test vehicle for the entire programme. Soon afterwards, on 13 July 2003, there followed a test flight with SDB Accuracy Support Infrastructure using wide area Differential GPS.

The SDB GBU-39 was launched for the third time from an F-15E Strike Eagle from the 46th Test Wing at Eglin AFB during the autumn of 2004. The first target actually to be hit was a barge situated in the Gulf of Mexico. The first flight against a barge was on 25 May 2004. An initial production order was due by April 2005, also depending on the GAO report on the right and wrong doings of Darleen Druyun during the selection process.

The GAO's findings were severe enough to make the next stage of the SDB development open to competition again. Lockheed Martin, however, realised that Boeing had the advantage of recent experience in developing the original weapon and Boeing realised that Lockheed Martin was entering the weapon market at high speed with an innovative design. For this reason they decided to cooperate on the next design phase and bid together to increase their chances.

For the JSF programme, now the F-35, the JDAM had been selected as the weapon of choice. The SDB complements and might even replace the JDAM quite soon, as on 28 April 2006 a contract modification was awarded to Lockheed Martin to integrate the SDB with the F-35A CTOL version, giving the SDB a bright future. The contract, however, also had some side effects and one of them was that the programme to integrate the Wind Corrected

Munitions Dispenser (WCMD) was eliminated from the F-35A CTOL version integration effort. Boeing or its subsidairy McDonnell Douglas received a contract on 15 December 2006 to deliver test assets for the SDB integration on the F-22A and the F-16 blocks 30, 40 and 50. The F-22A, because of its relevance of integration into weapon bays, is a small step in the direction of integration of the GBU-39 with the F-35.

LOCAAS

Another programme that was started in 1990 with the ATF in mind and transformed itself as a result of the changing requirements in the following decade was the LOCAAS. LOCAAS stands for Low Cost Autonomous Attack System and was developed initially as a free flight stand-off weapon for an intelligent stand-off loitering weapon system. With the capability to loiter for forty-five minutes it can penetrate enemy defences and as it is equipped with a two-way data link it can be used to attack time-sensitive targets, something that had proved to be of immense importance during Operation Enduring Freedom and Operation Iraqi Freedom (OIF). The LOCAAS has an internal database of targets and searches the ground, sending information via data link to the operator. If, or when, it finds a pre-programmed target, the LOCAAS will destroy it. If, however, the operator sees a better target of opportunity, he can redirect the LOCAAS through the secure data link to the target of opportunity. LOCAAS therefore also functions as a reconnaissance tool in the information war. If the pre-programmed target has not been found within the forty-five minutes and no other suitable target has been found, to prevent collateral damage the LOCAAS flips upside down and detonates, thereby ensuring that the direction of the blast is upwards and the only damage on the ground will be from falling debris. During August 2002 a $\frac{1}{5}$ scale model of the LOCAAS was tested at Arnold AFB to determine separation characteristics in connection with aircraft equipped with internal weapon bays. These tests were for multiple systems to share the cost; the results of these tests could be used by the F-22 and F-35 programmes and any future Unmanned Combat Air Vehicles (UCAV) programme. The model used was an F-111.

RATTLRS

The Office of Naval Research (ONR) was looking for Revolutionary Approach To Time-critical Long Range Strike (RATTLRS). The aim was to demonstrate a capability and it was not yet a weapon development programme. This, however, might soon change, if the demonstration was successful.

The ONR awarded the RATTLRS programme phase I contract to Lockheed Martin Corporation, McDonnell Douglas Corporation, Orbital Sciences Corporation and Raytheon Company on 1 March 2004. This was followed by the phase II contract, which was awarded to Lockheed Martin on 1 February 2005.

The RATTLRS had its design roots clearly traceable to the SR-71 and the D-21 drone. In fact, Frank Cappuccio told the media at Farnborough that the design of the inlet of the SR-71 could not be much improved, which is a great compliment to Kelly Johnson, the designer of the SR-71 and founder of the Skunk works.

The RATTLRS is a missile that can be launched from aircraft, surface ships or submarines and has the capability to fly at a speed of Mach 3. The RATTLRS will carry munitions internally and launch these weapons near the target. This means that the mothership does not need to penetrate tight air-defence systems. For the time being it is a

A graphic presentation of a RATTLRS being launched from an F-35.
Funds and capability requirement will see if this will become reality.
Copyright Lockheed Martin

demonstration programme but that is how the JSF programme was initiated as well. The programme is led by the ONR and supported by the USAF, NASA and DARPA. The RATTLRS is developed by Lockheed Martin with the propulsion system developed by Rolls-Royce Liberty (formerly Allison Advanced Development Company) works based on the technologies found in the YJ102R engine. The high-performance non-afterburning turbine offers high supersonic speed, extended range, high fuel efficiency, and the ability to trade speed for increased range. The Allison YJ102R developmental engine provides more than

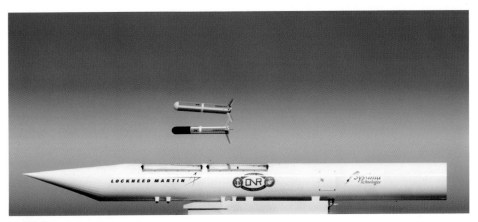

High-speed sled test was performed to test the ejection of the munitions of RATTLRS at supersonic speeds. The functionality was proven and the system was on the road to its first flight. *Copyright Lockheed Martin*

six times the specific thrust of the engines in the SR-71. As the RATTLRS will be expandable the simple and inexpensive design makes the engine extremely suitable for the purpose.

The first flight of the RATTLRS is planned for next year, while recently Lockheed Martin announced that on a high-speed sled track at Holloman AFB an innovative weapon dispense system had been tested. 'This round of testing evaluated innovative dispenser systems that overcome the complex dynamic flow associated with a supersonic weapon,' said Frank Webster, Lockheed Martin sled test lead. 'This includes an ejection device that closes up the airframe cavities to eliminate disruptive air flow and provide extra support to reduce significantly pitching and allow for more rapid stabilisation.' Prior to these tests, subsonic tests were performed on a sled test with four representative guided munition simulants also being dispensed successfully. As is mentioned above it is only a technology demonstation programme but that is how the JSF programme started out as well and RATTLRS could be carried under the wing of the F-35. The range combined with the RATTLRS speed would extend the effectiveness of the F-35.

Laser/Directed Energy Weapon

Laser, or its use in combat, is thought of as science fiction by most people, although laser is regularly used in combat in a relatively non-destructive form. Laser stands for Light Amplification by Stimulated Emission of Radiation and was invented in 1960. It has been used for three functions in the military: laser target ranging, laser acquisition systems, and laser-guided munitions. Lethal or destructive use of laser (laser as a weapon system) has been under development for quite some time. Some important breakthroughs have been made in recent years and 'Star Wars' is close by. Star Wars is on our doorstep, or at least it was another step closer when the AFRL and Lockheed Martin signed an agreement to research the possibility of equipping fighters such as the F-16, F-22 and the F-35 with a high-energy air-to-air laser in June 2002. There were three technology breakthroughs required and one had already been achieved when it was proved during the JSF flight demonstration programme of the X-35B, the clutch and the shaft that can power anything not just a lift fan. The second breakthrough was being developed under the More Electric

Aircraft (MEA) programme and was further developed under the High Power Aircraft (HiPAC) programme, both funded by the AFRL. The technology referred to was the Power & Thermal Management System. The electrical power was from the outset planned to be 160 kW. The weight problems of the STOVL meant a reduction to 140 kW, which was a small setback. The other breakthrough that was also addressed by the MEA and HiPAC programmes was cooling. A Directed Energy Weapon requires a lot of cooling as much heat is generated during a laser shot, which has to be dealt with.

Advanced Development Programmes of Lockheed Martin Aero looked into replacing the lift fan of the F-35B with a high-energy laser. The laser would be driven by the same shaft that powers the lift fan, meaning that 27,000 horse power would be available to power the high-energy laser. Volume wise there should be enough space to fit the laser system. The high-energy laser would enable the F-35B to destroy incoming missiles, either launched from the ground or in the air, and other soft targets on the ground. The location of the turret would be a deciding factor in what kind of target would be suitable. The size of the technology will ultimately influence the number of turrets that can be installed. The advantage of a laser over a bomb is that there is no explosion and no traces as to what has happened, and very low collateral damage, which is very important when the public revolts at any images of children and women in hospital. The other advantage is that as long as the laser has the energy and is sufficiently cooled, the pilot cannot run out of ammunition. Ammunition is normally the expensive part of warfare. Furthermore, it gives an aircraft persistence and the pilot becomes the limiting factor regarding endurance and persistence. Lockheed Martin looked at different partners for the programme among them its partner in the ABL, TRW, but settled with the laser from Raytheon. During development the laser would initially be installed into a pod and further into the test programme in a prototype F-35. Demonstration of the laser was expected to begin after 2010; at this time early production aircraft should be available for this task if the prototypes are too busy. The minimal effective range of the laser is expected to be around 6 miles and a laser burst will

A computer drawing depicting the F-35 destroying a Sukhoi fighter with a Directed Energy Weapon (DEW). As a result of three technology breakthroughs the JSF will probably be the first fighter ever to be equipped with a DEW. *Copyright AFRL*

take about four seconds. The system should cool down again for an approximately equal period and can then be used again. Lockheed Martin hoped that help for the funding would be forthcoming from either DARPA or the AFRL's directed energy directorate at Kirtland AFB.

For another programme a Boeing 747 has been prepared for testing as an Air Borne Laser (ABL) designated YAL-1A, which stands for prototYpe Attack Laser 1A. The programme should introduce laser as a defensive system against missiles. Lockheed Martin and TRW are responsible for the Laser Beam Control System (LBCS) developed for this programme. The problem with laser technology is that it needs a minimum power level of 25 kW to be effective as a weapon system; this amount of minimum power was only achieved by a chemical laser. Not every aircraft has the capacity to carry a chemical laser, which is why the Boeing 747 aircraft was chosen for the ABL programme. Raytheon was also developing solid-state lasers but these had never before achieved the minimum power level of 25 kW. The main advantage was that they did not need the chemical reaction required for chemical lasers. Raytheon had demonstrated a capability thus far for a solid-state laser of 2.65 kW. The solid-state laser was powered by electricity, and for this simple reason the shaft-driven propulsion was ideal. Raytheon and TRW achieved some success when they each received a contract on 6 December 2002 to participate in a demonstration of a 25-kW solid-state laser, which was seen as a stepping stone for developing a weapons grade laser. The programme was managed by the AFRL in Albuquerque, NM, and the contract included funding for two phases. The first phase was a fourteen-month period in which Raytheon had to demonstrate in a laboratory a laser of around 10 kW with a high-quality beam. The second phase should last ten months and ultimately demonstrate a 25-kW solid-state laser. There was also an option for a third phase but that depended on the success of the second phase. Raytheon had focused its research on three areas: diode pumped lasers, Ytterbium material for lasers and coherent change detection, a process of maximising high-quality beams. In all three areas Raytheon stated it had made progress. The Ytterbium material used reduced heat production by about 75 per cent compared with the more frequently used neodymium-based lasers. This was very important as cooling was one of the major problems for lasers to be carried by small aircraft. There are two tools for cooling, air and fluids. With the F-35, air would be the most available, especially with the doors and panels already in place in the aircraft's structure. In fact, for the cooling the Power & Thermal Management System (PTMS) was very important. It was calculated by AFRL that an energy output of 1.177 kW would result in a 100 kW laser and 1076 kW waste heat. Waste heat is a loss of energy and for this reason the AFRL was busy looking into a PTMS that would somehow use the wasted energy.

Another example suggesting that laser technology is not too far away into the future is the fact that a Northrop Grumman Tactical High Energy Laser (THEL) was tested at White Sands. It shot down a Katusha missile for the first time on 6 June 2000 under a US Army test programme. A total of twenty-eight Katusha missiles have been fired since and all have been shot down by the THEL. To see if the THEL would also be effective against smaller projectiles it was tested successfully against artillery and later also against mortar rounds. The THEL managed to shoot down three simultaneously fired mortar rounds. Although this was a ground-based system, the effectiveness of the system and its functionality were proved. Now it had to work as well in an aircraft. However, the size of the aircraft and the cooling of the laser system were important.

A simulation held at Kirtland AFB by the AFRL with the goal of developing tactics for fighters equipped with airborne laser weapons was held during the latter part of 2004. The aircraft used for this simulation was the F-16 and it was equipped with simulated laser cannon with an off-bore sight capability of ± 35 degrees. This was not the only study, as in late 2005 another study performed by the AFRL was called THELUS, which stood for Tactical High-Energy Laser Utility Study. During THELUS six pilots, all tactically rated, were assembled for the evaluation. The pilots were split up into two teams, a blue team (two pilots) and a red team (four pilots). Two scenarios were evaluated. In the first scenario both aircraft groups (red and blue) were equipped with similar capabilities and missiles. In the second scenario the blue team was equipped with a Directed Energy Weapon while the red team retained its conventional weapons. These studies were held for the developer and the military planners so that both would know where more funding was required to push this programme closer to reality. The fact that these studies followed so shortly one after the other only emphasised that the maturity of the technology was increasing and getting closer to the point where it could be put into service. The F-35 with its shaft-driven power source is the ideal tactical fighter to introduce a laser weapon.

Cannon

Although advances were made in the development of the Medium-Range Air-to-Air Missiles the gun was far from obsolete. It might not be used for the air-to-air combat role, but as a strafing weapon against ground targets it would remain a formidable weapon destined to be integrated in the JSF. Weight issues, however, prevented the natural choice of the current M61 20-mm cannon, which was also installed in the F-22 Raptor. The USAF favoured developing a new cannon. The USMC was not sure what effect the weight of the cannon would have on the performance of the STOVL version and preferred a gun-pod version similar to that in use on its Harrier. Another thing that had to be considered was that for the F-22 a door over the muzzle of the gun made the gun invisible to prying radars. Such a mechanism was, however, rather complex and it was not certain if it could be fitted in the smaller JSF. The Royal Navy more or less followed the USMC with its requirements, although any agreement had not been reached by the middle of 1997. The development of a new cannon was estimated to cost around US $60 million. A decision was expected by the time that the JIRD II would be signed.

Some of the requirements set for the JSF gun were:

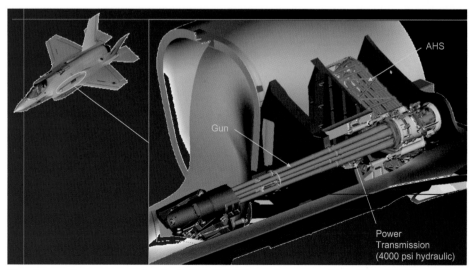

Gun integration was even for the F-35B STOVL version no problem if the USAF would request it for their STOVL machines. *GDATP.*

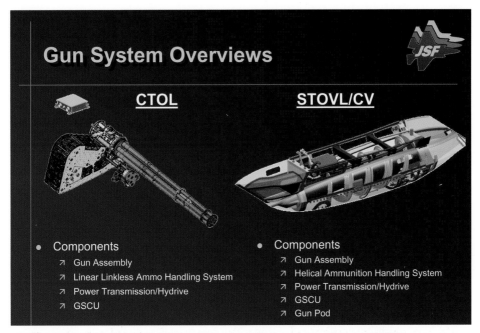

Comparison of the internal and the external podded cannon system. *GDATP.*

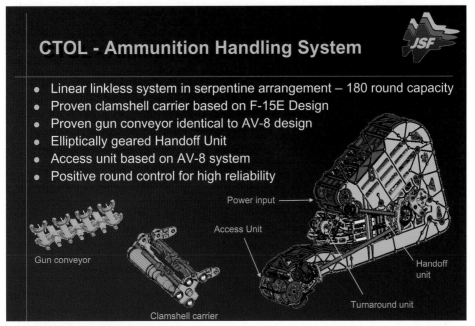

The Ammunition Handling System (AHS) for the CTOL version will be Linear Linkless System, unlike the gun-pod version. *GDATP.*

- A minimum slant range of less than 2700 m
- A maximum slant range between 4300 and 4600 m
- A maximum weight of 134 kg without ammunition
- A maximum weight of 238 kg with 150 rounds of ammunition

On 29 July 1998 Boeing announced that it had teamed up with Mauser-Werke Oberndorf of Germany and Primex Technologies Inc. to market a version of the Bordkanonen 27 (BK-27) for the JSF. If chosen, the production would be handled by Boeing. Primex Technologies would produce existing munitions under licence and develop High Explosive Dual-Purpose munitions (HEDP). The HEDP munition is able to sense if the target is either soft or hard and will automatically select between penetration or blast mode to increase effectiveness. Other aircraft equipped with the BK-27 include the Alpha Jet, Panavia Tornado, Saab Gripen and the Eurofighter Typhoon. Major competition was expected from the General Dynamics 25-mm GAU-12, which is, as previously mentioned, in clip-on format used on the AV-8B.

The BK-27 was based on the revolver principle – it was, in fact, the most compact light-power revolving gun. The clean weight of the BK-27 is 220 lb (100 kg) including the 37 lb (17 kg) barrel. It has a maximum firing rate of 1700 rounds per minute, however the weapon does have a variable rate of power down to as low as 1000 rounds per minute. The BK-27 is a high-energy gun that can operate in an automatic radar-guided mode to increase the hit probability and its muzzle velocity is 3360 ft/sec (1025 m/sec).

On 25 March 1999 an advanced 27-mm cannon derived from the Mauser-Werke BK-27 fired forty rounds in four ten-round bursts during a demonstration at the Arizona National Guard range in Florence. The demonstration was for government, military, and industry officials as Boeing hoped to sell it for use in the JSF, whichever candidate won the CDP. HEDP munitions were also demonstrated but in the 30-mm calibre. On 28 April 1999 Boeing announced that it would install a derivative of the BK-27 in its PWSC. According to Boeing the 27-mm cannon has greater lethality, improved supportability and lower costs than the current systems in use.

Costs, however, were on the increase and as Lockheed Martin provides contracts on a best value basis contractors are continuously evaluated. ATK, the BK-27 integrator, did not make the grade and therefore there was a another competition. General Dynamics, which had withdrawn from the earlier bid, had a history with Lockheed Martin dating back to 1953 and was asked to perform a study and come back with some options. The study took a month to six weeks. General Dynamics presented Lockheed Martin with the different options. The options were, according to Mr Tim Haddock from General Dynamics Armament and Technical Products (GDATP):

- The BK-27
- A GAU-12/U: five-barrel variant
- The GDP 425: a four-barrel cannon with a calibre of 25 mm again based on the GAU-12/U

Lockheed Martin announced on 25 September 2002 that it had selected General Dynamics Armament and Technical Products to supply a derivative of the GAU-12/U. The strange thing was that Boeing had declared that the Mauser BK-27 had lower costs than the current systems in use. The CTOL version would be the only version with an integrated cannon – both the carrier version and the STOVL version would be equipped with a pod version of the gun.

Cannon	Calibre	Projectile weight*	Muzzle velocity	Rate of fire RPS	Weight
BK-27	27 x 145B	260 grams (9.17 oz)	1025 m/s (3360 ft/s)	28	100 kg (220 lb)
GAU-12/U	25 x 137	180 grams (6.35 oz)	1100 m/s 3600 ft/s	13–70**	123 kg (270 lb)

*Weight of the calibre is given for conventional munitions not for the PELE munitions.

**For the GAU-12/U there are two rates of fire supplied. The first one indicates the speed in the [first?] 0.5 second. The second indicates the speed after spin-up has been attained. Spin-up is required by all rotary guns.

In contrast with the Mauser-Werke BK-27 the modified GAU-12/U 25-mm gun had five barrels, which made it heavier. On the other hand the spread of the barrels would lead theoretically to a higher hit probability as the projectiles were dispersed in a controlled manner in the path of the target. The F-35A would be the only version actually to have the derivative of the GAU-12/U 25-mm gun mounted internally. The CDP had provided Lockheed with sufficient confidence that the heavier gun could be accommodated; it was partially this change that caused the aircraft to be overweight. The F-35B and the F-35C would be able to carry the modified GAU-12/U 25-mm gun in a dedicated pod under the fuselage. It is a five-barrel Gatling gun version with a weight higher than the 220 pounds (123 kg) of the GAU-12 without the ammunition for the F-35A CTOL version, which is equipped with a conventional linear linkless feed system in a serpentine arrangement. The gun system for the F-35B STOVL and F35C CV version would weight 724 pounds (329 kg) without ammunition, and be equipped with a helical linear linkless feed system similar to the GPU-5/A. For both versions the requirement is a maximum of 4000 Shots Per Minute (SPM), although the current GAU-12/U 25-mm gun achieves 3300 SPM. The muzzle velocity depends on the kind of ammunition used: 3400 ft per second (1036 m/s) for Armour Piercing Incendiary (API) ammunition or 3560 ft per second (1085 m/s) for Target Practice (TP) and High Explosive Incendiary (HEI) ammunition. API and HEI ammunition are designed to start fire. The amount of ammunition carried should, according to the requirements, be 180 rounds for the F-35A CTOL version and 220 rounds for the gun-pod version. As can be seen in the above table the weight difference of the ammunition was 80 grams and the weight difference between the cannon was 23 kg. One hundred and eighty rounds of 25-mm calibre would have a total weight of 3444 grams whereas the 27-mm calibre ammunition would weight 4680 grams, making up for only 1236 grams. The BK-27 would still be lighter with ammunition.

The major change for the modified GAU-12/U 25-mm gun was that instead of the four barrels it would be equipped with five barrels. Other design changes involved the loading drive, the transfer unit, recoil spindles, remote safing, firing/safing cam assembly, rear cover, the muzzle clamp and the mid-barrel clamp. The last two were of course required because of the number of barrels that had changed. The GAU-12 was supported at the mid-barrel clamp while the five-barrel derivative would be supported at the muzzle. The Gun System Control Unit (GSCU) would be new and not only controlled gun functions but also operated doors in front of the muzzle. The requirement for the ammunition capacity for the CTOL version was exceeded by two, with a total of 182. The requirement for the STOVL and CV version was met exactly.

The ammunition carried would depend also on the USAF's satisfaction with a new kind of ammunition developed by Diehl from Germany. The new ammunition had been selected by the USAF for the F-16 Vulcan cannon. It had been developed to minimise the collateral damage of munitions and reduce the cost.

The solution is called PELE and stands for Penetrator with Enhanced Lateral Effect. The main difference between normal ammunition and PELE ammunition is that is the latter has neither fuse nor explosives.

Clear advantages of the PELE ammunition are:

- The chance that the ammunition might explode in the barrel of the gun while flying does not exist with the PELE ammunition.

- The air force does not need practice rounds. The air force can use the real thing, which means reduced cost.

- A stockpile of ammunition with explosives and fuses has the risk of exploding with fire and special security measures have to be in place. All this is not required with the PELE ammunition.

- If the ammunition is not suitable anymore (for example the calibre is no longer in the inventory) disposal is easier.

PELE has no explosives and no fuse but has the requirement for the same or better effect on target. The principle behind the munitions is based on kinetic energy. The outer skin of the ammunition is made of a high-density material capable of penetrating the target, such as steel and/or tungsten. The inner core of the ammunition round is lower-density material such as aluminium or plastic. On impact at the target the outer shell of high-density material has no problem penetrating the target, however, the inner core is dramatically slowed down on impact and a kinetic force drives the inner core forward. The inner core will move forward and pressure build-up in the ammunition shell will increase and reach gigabar values. The shell will disintegrate and the fragments that will be thrown forward will cause damage similar or more effective than previous-generation ammunitions. The PELE technology is a combination of High Explosive (HE) ammunition and the Armor Piercing High Explosive (APHE).

On 15 June 2003 it was announced that Terma A/S from Denmark had teamed up with GDATP. Terma is a recognised name for reconnaissance pods, for example the F-16 and Gripen are equipped with pods designed by the company. Terma would sign an agreement on 17 June 2003 with GDATP during the Paris Air Show Le Bourget. For the internally carried gun the CDR was completed on 13 January 2004. A development contract was awarded by GDATP to Terma for the pod on 2 April 2004. In the first quarter of 2004 GDATP was contacted by Lockheed and informed that weight problems would have to be solved and solutions had to be found across the board, including the gun pod. However, to retain commonality this would also affect the design of the internally carried gun for the CTOL version. One of the changes to the gun that was implemented was that a new four-barrel gun was used instead of the five-barrel gun. Another change under development was the titanium barrel clamps. Design of the four-barrel version was initiated in March 2004. All the design changes would have a cumulative effect of a 42-lb weight saving, although both the gun mechanism principles and basic installation geometry were retained. One of the other benefits that this change brought about was that for the five-barrelled gun a visible fairing was required on the top of the fuselage, which had negative effects on aerodynamic performance and stealth. With the four-barrel version this fairing on top of the fuselage could be reduced. PDR of the gun pod and the four-barrelled gun was held in November 2004. The CDR for the gun-pod version was expected by 1 February 2005. In the mean time risk-reduction tests were initiated with the five-barrelled gun in the last quarter of 2004.

A Terma-designed blast bottle was tested at the GDATP Burlington test site on 27 October 2004. The tests proved that the gun blast pressure was contained by the bottle and that as a result the remainder of the pod could be made of lighter material, which would be important during STOVL operations and for the Vertical Landing Bring Back (VLBB) load.

As the USAF was pondering how many of the STOVL version it was going to acquire, another question was whether the service's STOVL fighters would be better off with an internal gun instead of the gun *podits*. It was not certain that this would become a requirement as a cost study and analysis of how this would affect the performance of the STOVL version would be prerequisites before it could turn into a requirement. The two most obvious advantages of an internal gun would be the stealth features of the aircraft and a higher accuracy opposed to the gun-pod version. Furthermore, the gun-pod version needs to be calibrated with the aiming computer and takes up room where other weapons could be carried. The new gun underwent its 5000-round testing at the GDATP Ethan Allen firing range in Burlington, Vermont. After the gun concluded the test on 29 March 2006 with 5035 rounds fired it was torn down and inspected. As no major problems were found it was expected that follow-on testing with 10,000 rounds would follow within three weeks of the tear down and inspection. As the gun required a proper designation, it was designated GAU-22. By September a total of 11,836 test rounds had been fired with the longest burst being 181 rounds – the entire internal capacity of the GAU-22.

SRAAM

When the Advanced STOVL programme was initiated, or even later when the name of the programme was changed to CALF, the US Navy and the USAF each had different types of Sidewinder Short Range Air-to-Air Missiles (SRAAM) that could not be interchanged. The cost of developing new missiles was a burden on the defence budget and the US Navy and the USAF were forced to consider joint weapon development. It was mainly for this reason that the US Navy and the USAF initiated a joint programme with the Raytheon AIM-9X, the latest model of the Sidewinder family. Full-scale development began early in 1997 and to give it an edge over older Sidewinders it was to be equipped with thrust-vectoring control and off bore lock-on capability. The first live firing was made from an F-18C on 18 March 1999. The AIM-9X Sidewinder As was realised by Lockheed Martin and Raytheon with the F-22; the internal weapon bays made Lock On After Launch (LOAL) capability for the SRAAM an imperative. With the F-35 this LOAL capability would have to be achieved by the AIM-9X Sidewinder and other SRAAM missiles such as the ASRAAM in the English inventory or the *IRIS-T* that was in development for numerous air forces in Europe. The ASRAAM was from the outset a requirement for the UK as the IRIS-T was a requirement from the outset for both Norway and Italy. The ASRAAM was a weapon that was set for integration in the block 3 development programme. The AIM-9X was, however, selected only as a weapon for carriage on the under-wing pylon, making the LOAL capability a nice feature but not a requirement. The ASRAAM missile was, however, to be integrated in the weapon bays and not intended for the under-wing stations. The integration of these air-to-air missiles would involve more work than with the average fighter aircraft, the simple reason being that the weapons would be launched from an internal weapon bay. This would involve weapons being released from the weapon bay under high g manoeuvres or rolling movement. For example, for the rolling AIM-9 Sidewinder separation test programme on the F-22 seventeen missiles were launched and none of those launches had to be repeated. If launches should go wrong then more missiles would have to be used. It is not clear how much data from the F-22 Raptor tests can be used as the weapon bays have a completely different shape.

Barely had the Python 5's existence been released to the public and the Israeli Air Force

(IAF) was already looking to the future. For the F-35 the IAF wanted a smaller, lighter missile and this was thought to be the Python 6 missile.

Beyond Visual Range

If more than 30 per cent of air combat ends up in close-in combat then more than 60 per cent ends Beyond Visual Range (BVR). The reliability and effectiveness of the BVR weaponry had increased and was not going to diminish. In fact, from the outset when the Key Performance Parameters were set the AMRAAM missile was set to be carried internally on the JSF.

The dimensions of the Raytheon AIM-120/AMRAAM missile are:

Length:	365 cm
Max span:	63.5 cm
Body diameter:	17.8 cm
Launch weight:	156.8 kg/345 lb

The AMRAAM was the only air-to-air BVR missile in US service since the AIM-54 Phoenix had been retired. The AMRAAM has achieved a good reputation as a result of its service in action. On 27 December 1992 the AMRAAM achieved its first operational success. A couple of Lockheed Martin F-16D fighters were vectored in towards two Iraqi MiG-25 Foxbats. The MiG-25s entered a no-fly zone protected by an international force. An F-16D fired an AMRAAM missile at one of the MiG-25 Foxbats and achieved a confirmed kill. Not even a month later An F-16C achieved the second AMRAAM kill above the no-fly zone in Iraq. This time the victim of the AMRAAM was an Iraqi MiG-23 Flogger. As a result the AMRAAM immediately became more marketable. The AMRAAM was not always that successful. At some point above Iraq, there were six AMRAAMs fired at two MiG-25 Foxbats but all six missed. NATO forces in Yugoslavia had many reasons to be happy about the AMRAAM missile – many coalition fighters shot enemy fighters down with the AMRAAM, making its success and quality even more known. The first non-US air-to-air victory with an AMRAAM was by a Dutch F-16AM, which shot down a Serbian MiG-29 Fulcrum – it was the first air-to-air kill of the Royal Netherlands Air Force since the Second World War. The CDP, although aggressive, did not include any missile firing. Only Boeing opened its weapon bays for acoustic tests. The Lockheed Martin CDA did not have weapon bays. It was not clear which version of the AMRAAM would ultimately be integrated in the F-35 aircraft as development was still continuing on new versions of the AMRAAM missile. As part of the structural ground tests two AMRAAMS were loaded onto the A-1 on 25 March 2006. An interesting feature of the weapon system is that the pilot can mark aircraft on the display outside the AMRAAM's range. Once the target aircraft enters the missile's range the pilot can see it on his tactical display. The pilot will then launch the missile. On the display the missile is connected with its target by a line plus the number of seconds that the missile requires to get to the target. Once the target is destroyed the pilot gets confirmation through its EO-DAS and EOTS systems, which will have noticed the flare of the explosion.

Although obviously the weapon of choice for the services that had bought the AMRAAM for their current fighter aircraft, there were nations such as the UK that wanted to develop their own air-to-air BVR missile. The UK's Defence Procurement Agency selected the European-developed Meteor missile in December 2002 and did so on behalf of the European partner countries, Italy, Germany, Spain and Sweden. A test platform for the Meteor missile had to be chosen and the Eurofighter was favoured as most countries would have that aircraft in their inventory. It was, however, decided after careful evaluation early in 2003 that the Gripen was a more mature aircraft and therefore better suited for the initial tests. On 21 April 2004, Saab undertook the first trial fit of a geometrically representative Meteor missile using the Gripen's Multi Missile Launcher (MML). Meteor missile firings were planned for late 2005. One problem, however, was that the Meteor was slated as not able to fit in the internal weapon bay, meaning that the Meteor missiles would have to be carried on the under-wing pylons of the JSF, reducing much of its coveted stealth characteristics.

JDAM – Joint Direct Attack Munition

Lethality was a major cornerstone in the JAST programme. Experience from the Gulf war in 1991 and target engagement analysis showed a requirement for rapid targeting and engagement of mobile targets such as tanks, armoured vehicles, artillery and ships, and fixed tactical targets such as airfields, supply depots and communication centres. The most effective weapon against these targets was a variety of 1000-lb weapons according to analysis carried out for the JAST programme office, which is how the requirement for the JDAM came into existence.

The JDAM is not a weapon as such but a tail kit that is supposed to transform general-purpose bombs into high-accuracy, all-weather, autonomous munitions for both the USAF and US Navy. The advantage was that old general-purpose bombs were transformed into relatively modern weapons and with a relatively small investment. JDAM is guided after launch to its target by the INS/GPS, which will have downloaded target information from the host aircraft. Normally this is done prior to the mission but with data link coming of age other options were being studied.

JDAM was going to be the standard weapon on the JSF. JDAM was set in the KPP for the JSF and intended to be carried in the internal weapon bay. The requirement called for two internal 1000-lb JDAM units. JDAM was becoming the standard in the US forces during the development of the JSF programme. As the JDAM was in the requirements specification from the start during the CDP Boeing was committed to demonstrating its avionics software capability in connection with JDAM. Using its Avionics Flying Laboratory (AFL), Boeing 737-200, it had gathered data from on- and off-board systems, fused the information and then sent the targeting information securely via Joint Tactical Information Distribution System in Link 16 format to an F-15. The F-15 then attacked the target with a GPS-guided GBU-32 JDAM. After the strike the AFL on-board sensors provided target damage assessment. The target damage assessment was sent to the F-15 and to the ground station.

At a later stage in the CDP when Boeing was test flying its X-32A, instrumented AMRAAMs and JDAM were inside the weapon bays. Boeing had learned from the ATF project that aggressiveness during a fly-off could pay off. Furthermore, it was seen as a way to reduce risk in the future. A comment made by a Boeing official before the start of the flight-testing that test-firing weapons was on the programme suddenly seemed very plausible, but whatever the reason it never went that far. Lockheed Martin did not go as far as Boeing as there was no requirement for this.

There were several versions of the JDAM available and three versions were to be integrated during the initial block of the SDD phase. A fourth version would be integrated at a later stage. The three versions that were to be integrated during the SDD were the GBU-31 JDAM 2000-lb (MK-84 Warhead), GBU-31 JDAM 2000-lb (BLU-109 Warhead) and the GBU-32 JDAM 1000-lb (MK-83/BLU-110 Warhead). The fourth on the wishlist, but which did not fit in budget-wise, was the GBU-38 JDAM 500-lb (MK-82 Warhead).

As the ultimate strike weapon, at least from the outset, JDAM was tried out during the ground tests. Two inert JDAM were loaded onto the A-1 prototype on 25 March 2006. There was one JDAM in each weapon bay, together with an AMRAAM missile in each weapon bay. If a group of F-35s flew during a mission the F-35 Lightning II weapon system would allow the leader to assign targets not only to his own JDAM weaponry but also to his wingman and all this without voice communication but with the help of the datalink systems.

Advanced Interdiction Weapon System or the AGM-154 Joint Stand Off Weapon (JSOW)

Even though the F-35 had stealth features and would be able to evade radars, for some areas it was still considered better to have a stand-off weapon. The Raytheon (earlier Texas Instruments) AGM-154 JSOW was the natural choice as it was a recently developed weapon when the SDD of the JSF programme was initiated. The Raytheon AGM-154 JSOW was to be integrated both on the internal and external hardpoints. The JSOW existed in several versions and had been selected for integration during the SDD phase. The AGM-154 is a modular weapon and three versions exist.

The AGM-154A is the baseline version. A total of 145 BLU-97/B CEM (Combined Effects Munition) bomblets shape the warhead of the AGM-154A, which are released by a cluster bomb dispenser. The bomblets can defeat armour, have incendiary effects and have a fragmenting case so that they cause a lot of material damage. The AGM-154B was designed with six BLU-108/B *SFM* (Sensor Fuzed Munition) dispensers, each of which can release four 'Skeet' terminally guided anti-tank submunitions. The third version was developed for the US Navy only. It was equipped with a *BROACH* multi-stage penetrator warhead. The AGM-154C was furthermore equipped with an Imaging Infra Red (IIR) seeker and an Autonomous Target Acquisition system. The Autonomous Target Acquisition system compares the images of the imaging infrared seeker with a preset reference image to identify the target. The autonomous target acquisition system replaces a two-way data link, which was originally planned for this weapon.

The AGM-154 is a glide weapon with a range depending on its launch height and speed. The range of the AGM-154 is from 15 nautical miles (low-altitude launch) to 40 nautical miles (high-altitude launch). As can be deducted, AGM-154 depends on kinetic energy and no booster and for this reason is relatively cheap. The way that the AGM-154 achieves this range is with the aid of folded wings that unfold shortly after launch. The AGM-154 JSOW is guided to the target by a GPS/INS that works independently from launch, which means that it is a fire and forget weapon. For homing and navigation the AGM-154 employs the aforementioned GPS/INS but also uses IIR and a data link. The all-weather capability increases its flexibility.

HARM

The US Navy initiated an upgrade programme for its AGM-88 High-speed Anti Radiation Missile (HARM) by the end of 2002. A new rocket, a Variable Flow Ducted Rocket (VFDR) ramjet engine provided by Atlantic Research Corporation, should increase the missile's range from 80 miles to 100 miles and increase its speed from approximately Mach 2 to Mach 3.5. Furthermore, the HARM missile should be prepared for internal carriage. The fins of the HARM do not fold so like the AMRAAM it should be adapted in a similar way (AMRAAM fins were clipped for use in the F-22).

The weapon systems below were intended to be integrated on the F-35 during the SDD. Other weapons might be added according to the needs of the different operators. Obvious weapons that come to mind for integration that are missing on the list are the European-produced weapons such as the Meteor and IRIS-T. BAE Systems hoped it would receive the responsibility for the European weapon integration.

Internally and externally carried weapons

MK-82 500-lb LDGP

MK-82 BSU-33 500-lb LDGP

MK-82 BSU-49 Ballute 500-lb HDGP

MK-82 BSU-86/B 500-lb HDGP

MK-62 Quickstrike 500-lb LD mine

MK-20, CBU-99/100 Rockeye II Cluster Munition

GBU-12 Paveway II 500-lb LGB (MK-82 warhead)

CBU-78/B Gator

RN 540-lb LDGP (MK-116 tail)

RN 540-lb HDGP (MK-118 tail)

GBU-32 JDAM 1000-lb (MK-83/BLU-110 warhead)

GBU-32 JDAM PIP 1000-lb (MK-83/BLU-110 warhead)

MK-83 LDGP 1000-lb

MK-83 BSU-85/B Ballute 1000-lb HDGP

MK-63 Quickstrike 1000-lb LD mine

CBU-103/104/105 WCMD

CBU-87/89/97 Cluster Munition

RN 1000-lb LDGP (MK-114 tail)

RN 1000-lb HDGP (MK-117 tail)

GBU-31 JDAM 2000-lb (MK-84 warhead)

GBU-31 JDAM PIP 2000-lb (MK-84 warhead)

GBU-31 JDAM 2000-lb (BLU-109 warhead)

GBU-31 JDAM PIP 2000-lb (BLU-109 warhead)

AGM-154 JSOW Glide bomb

MK-84 LDGP 2000-lb

Compressed Carriage AMRAAM

AIM-120A/B AMRAAM

AIM-132 ASRAAM

Brimstone / Modernised Hellfire

GDATP GAU-22 25-mm (CTOL version internally only, CV and STOVL externally in a pod)

External weapons*

LAU-61/68 Rocket pod

LAU-10 Rocket pod

MXU-648648/CNU-88 baggage pod

AGM-65 Maverick

AIM-9X Sidewinder

AGM-88 HARM

AGM158 JASSM

AGM-84C/D Harpoon

AGM-84H SLAM(ER)

RN Stormshadow

SUU-20/SUU-5003 Practice Bomb and Rocket Dispenser

BDU-57/58/60 Laser Guided Training Round

Missionised gun pod

MK-83 BSU-50 Ballute 2000-lb HDGP

GBU-24A/B Paveway III 2000-lb LGB (BLU-109 Warhead)

GBU-24/B Paveway III 2000-lb LGB (MK-84 Warhead)

GBU-16 Paveway II 1000-lb LGB (MK-83 Warhead)

RN 1000-lb Paveway II LGB

GBU-10 Paveway II 2000-lb LGB (MK-84 Warhead)

480-gallon wing tank

600-gallon wing tank

* These stores are integrated exclusively on under-wing pylons during the SDD.

The KC-135 and the X-35A had several refuelling couplings over the Edwards area. It was one of main advantages over Boeing during the Concept Demonstration Phase. *Copyright Lockheed Martin*

CHAPTER 16

THE RANGE OF THE F-35

Range was important in the Key Performance Parameters. As was noted early in the programme by DARPA, the lift fan could easily be replaced by a fuel tank, increasing the volume load and making it the ideal replacement for the F-16. In theory this meant that as a result of increased fuel volume there would be a reduced requirement for tankers, which would make deployments less expensive and easier.

Boeing was aware of this fact and to have a chance in the competition had to offer at least a similar fuel volume as its competitors because it could not save on the engine as its aircraft would have the same engine as the Lockheed and McDonnell Douglas teams from the outset. It was this requirement that made Boeing opt for the delta wing as it had the highest capacity for fuel. McDonnell Douglas did not encounter this problem as in the early design stages the company was designing its aircraft around the Gas Coupled Lift Fan (GCLF) and at a later stage changed to the Lift Plus Lift Cruise (LPLC) design. Similar to the SDLF further developed by Lockheed, McDonnell Douglas could remove the lift fan for the GCLF concept and with the LPLC concept could remove the dedicated lift engine, also gaining the same volume for the fuel tank.

As McDonnell Douglas was the first to fall victim to the JSF programme, it was up to Boeing to compete with Lockheed with its slight disadvantage. However, if Boeing succeeded in equalling the fuel load of the CTOL version of the Lockheed design then the STOVL version automatically would have a bigger range than the Lockheed proposal. The interesting thing is that when the selection was announced on 26 October 2001, it was stated that both aircraft had fulfilled the design requirements and had passed with mark of 10 out of 10. This means that Boeing had matched or had come close to this goal.

One of the design changes that was implemented by Lockheed Martin to the PWSC during the SDD phase was the raising of the top surface of the aircraft along the centreline of the aircraft, thereby increasing the fuel capacity by 300 lb. The range increase compared with the fighters the F-35 was to replace was quite big. However, later-block F-16s equipped with the Conformal Fuel Tanks would have a similar range to the F-35. The penalty of having Conformal Fuel Tanks would be in manoeuvrability and a reduction in load capability.

Aircraft	KPP combat range	Internal fuel
F-35A CTOL	590 nm	18,498 lb
F-35B STOVL	450 nm	13,326 lb
F-35C CV	600 nm	19,624 lb

All the services, however, did not want to rely on internal fuel capacity so they required the

additional capability that was and is standard in the fighters that the F-35 was due to replace – aerial refuelling. Besides the advantage for the services it can also have advantages for test reasons as it can extend the time available during a test sortie. Strangely, on 28 April 2006, when a contract modification was signed so that the SDB could be integrated with the F-35A, the external fuel tanks qualification was eliminated from the SDD budget and programme for the foreseeable future, at least for the F-35A CTOL version. This might have been a calculated move to find funding from abroad for this requirement, even though the range had already increased and there were not many air forces that required such force projection as the USAF.

Fuel can also have another effect on the aircraft. It can prevent an aircraft from landing if it is too heavy, especially for carrier landings. This was the reason for the installation of a fuel dump system, mainly required for the US Navy. The fuel dumping system was tested on the AA-1 aircraft as the Critical Design Review of the carrier version was planned for June 2007. On the sixth flight of AA-1, when Jon Beesley opened the valve to dump, fuel still came out slow and in small amounts and continued along the wings towards the fuselage. The valve was replaced and foam was installed to give a different direction to the flow of fuel. On flight 18 the test was repeated and the valve opened, the flow almost immediate and it was found suitable for the carrier version. A piece of information given by Jon Beesley at the Le Bourget in Paris 2007 was that the AA-1 had a small problem with its fuel system and so far had not used its full fuel capacity of 18,498 lbs. The longest flight of the AA-1 was about 1.5 hours. He estimated that with the full fuel tank an easy two hours of flight could be achieved without air to air refuelling. On April 12 the first step towards air refuelling was made when Jon Beesley refuelled the AA-1 in flight for the first time.

Refuelling Commonality

Another cost factor was the different refuelling requirements of the services. The USAF was the only service from the four main services (USAF, USMC, US Navy and the Royal Navy) that required boom-technique refuelling. The reason the GAO was looking into this and seeing if it would be profitable to change the refuelling system of the USAF, was that in 2004 the USAF required refurbishment of its tanker fleet. The tanker aircraft in service with the USAF were the KC-10 (fifty-nine aircraft) and the KC-135 (534 aircraft). The KC-10s had

The USAF will be forced to change its flight refuelling tanker fleet to the drogue system favoured by the majority of the world's air forces. *Copyright Lockheed Martin*

a service life of twenty-two years and the KC-135s, even more impressively, had an average service life of forty-four years. The age of the tanker fleet made replacement a high-priority requirement. The question was if the USAF really needed to hold onto the boom technique or if it should adapt to the other services to increase commonality, not only with its fighter aircraft but also with its tankers. The GAO was asked to look into the matter and summed up the disadvantages of the different aerial refuelling systems for the US government.

The advantages of the boom aerial refuelling technique were:

- Less chance of damage to JSF low-observable features. This would also count for other stealthy aircraft.
- Weighed 4.1 lb less than drogue assembly.
- No modification of existing tankers for multi-point refuelling or purchase of additional boom to drogue adapters.
- As was shown with Boeing's CDA aircraft, with the prototypes that are equipped with pitots the risk of the pitot breaking does not exist.

A frontal view of the X-35A. The fuselage is bulkier than that of the F-16 for the simple reason that the weapon bays occupy a lot of space and the amount of extra internal fuel storage that has to provide the JSF with a longer range then its predecessor. *Copyright Lockheed Martin*

The slenderness of the F-16 when compared to the X-35 is obvious, but the X-35 is a more survivable and lethal aircraft, although the F-16 was revolutionary at its time. *Copyright Lockheed Martin*

The advantages of the drogue technique were:

- Permits refuelling by half the KC-135s and the British L1011 tankers (during coalition interventions).
- Permits multi-point refuelling on thirty-five US tankers, not to mention future tankers.
- Increased JSF commonality.
- Less time required to refuel a four-aircraft JSF flight, which means the aircraft can fly faster to the target as there is no requirement to loiter, thereby increasing range.
- Avoids $3.19 million developmental cost.
- Improved allied interoperability.
- Saves $180 million in JSF total cost.
- Could reduce the number of new tankers required.

Besides the financial advantages the JSF is designed to increase commonality with US allies and here, according to the GAO, there was an opportunity to increase that interoperability. A major problem was, however, that with the aircraft already in the inventory such as the

F-22 Raptor and the F-117 Nighthawk, the KC-10 would remain in service. The extra weight of the drogue system was not such a big problem for the CTOL version but weight was more of an issue with the STOVL version. As the JSF was already delayed by one year and more delays were likely to appear, it was unlikely that the KC-135 would require refurbishment before retiring as the new tanker would be entering service as well. The USAF would, however, require tanker aircraft capable of both methods of refuelling as it was planning to buy the STOVL version as well. The STOVL version is equipped with a probe for the drogue system. As a result of the lift fan inlet door and the auxiliary inlet for the main engine the required receptor for the boom aerial refuelling technology would be almost impossible to place as the fuel tank placed there in the CTOL was replaced by a lift fan. This meant that the USAF needed the probe and drogue system anyway. It was, however, clear that the longer the decision was delayed to change the boom refuelling system on the CTOL version, the more expensive it would become. From the tanker perspective the USAF still required the boom-equipped tankers for the big aircraft such as the Boeing B-52 Stratofortress, Boeing C-17 Globemaster, Northrop Grumman B-2, Rockwell B-1 Lancer (now Boeing) and the Lockheed Martin C-130 Hercules.

Another method of increasing range is with external fuel tanks. External fuel tanks are the norm when ferrying aircraft. The range could be extended and the tanks could be dropped prior to entering enemy air space, meaning that the aircraft could return on internal fuel and still be stealthy during the main part of the operation. This is important when tanker aircraft are in short supply and this was the case. From the outset the requirement existed for external fuel tanks for all three versions. The USAF, however, cancelled the integration of the external fuel tanks in a contract modification on 28 April 2006. With the increase of internal fuel (compared with the previous-generation fighter that the F-35 was replacing) the range was considered sufficient and not such a big issue. Integration of the external fuel tanks could always be done at a later stage and a future export customer might have the requirement and be willing to pay for it.

CHAPTER 17

COMPUTER SYSTEM OF THE F-35

During the Final Design Review (FDR) in 1998 for the CDA, the only major change that was made was the processor of the Vehicle Management Computer (VMC). The original processor selected in 1996 was replaced by a newer and more capable unit. As the speed of development of faster processors was driven by the private sector, the change of processor did not result in any major cost increase. In fact, it was expected to happen more often over the life of the JSF programme. Data fusion from systems such as EO-DAS, IRST and the flow of that information to the HMD, has to be smooth so that the pilot is not hindered by delayed imagery.

The VMC for the F-35 was developed by BAE Systems. This computer is designed to receive upgrades even during the development if more powerful processors become available as COTS equipment. The VMC is about the size of a shoebox and before being installed in a prototype it will be installed in the Vehicle Systems Integration Facility, which is a full-scale test rig for utility and flight control items. Three VMCs will find their way into the F-35 to give triple redundancy. The VMC has hardware and software for the Flight Control System (FCS), fuel hydraulic and electric systems. Two Motorola PowerPC chips form the foundation of the VMC and make it all possible.

An important part of the computer is of course the software. Without software the aircraft would not be able to perform its required tasks, let alone fly. For the software the development was split into different blocks. For the flight-testing to start software block 0.1 was developed. The role of block 0.1 was the basic function to get the aircraft flying. It would not include any mission systems software. This development block would support seven development aircraft. It would, however, only be for the early stages. The next block in the development is block 0.5. Software block 0.5 will include initial mission system architecture and sensor infrastructure. This will make it possible to initiate weapon testing but just like block 0.1 it will only be installed on the development aircraft. Development of block 0.1 was initiated immediately after the announcement by the end of October 2001 that Lockheed Martin had been selected. Block 0.1 was due to fly on the first prototype. It was, however, still challenging as the software also controlled the HMD, which would now present the pilot with Primary Flight References. This is totally new as the F-35 is the first aircraft where the HUD has been replaced by the HMD. In a briefing, JSF Programme Executive Officer General Brigadier Davis told that by August 2006, 2.04 million lines of code, equivalent to 83% of the planned total, had been developed for Block 1. For software Block 0.5 the amount was on 1.41 million lines of code equivalent to 64%.

The first block to be installed on operational aircraft will be block 1. Software block 1 aircraft will be fully flight-qualified with initial war fighting capability as it has a baseline air-to-air capability and air-to-ground capability. Block 1 will allow the services to start training their pilots and their maintenance personnel. Block 1 flight-testing is supposed to start early in 2009 in the CATBird and will last until well into the fourth quarter of 2010. The next step is block 2. Block 2 will allow the services to start supplying aircraft to operational units. The capability for Close Air Support (CAS) and interdiction roles will be added. This means that for these roles additional weapons will be qualified on the aircraft. Units will be able to start planning deployments with these aircraft. Flight-testing of block 2 will be initiated during the first quarter of 2010. Flight-testing will be initiated on the CATBird and when the testing of the block 2 is deemed mature enough it will, just like block 1, transfer to the prototypes. Block 2 will be the first block that will undergo Operational Test & Evaluation (OT&E). OT&E is supposed to be initiated as early as the fourth quarter of 2011.

Block 3 is the version that will allow the Initial Operational Capability (IOC). It further adds the Suppression of Enemy Air Defences (SEAD) role. As with block 2, this means that additional weapons will be qualified. Development of block 3 was initiated in 2005. Flight-testing is, however, not due until the third quarter of 2009 and that is if everything goes smoothly and according to plan with the previous software editions. Block 3 is expected to have around six million lines of software code, around six times as much as block 0.1. Flight tests of block 3 are planned to last around two years, followed by OT&E. OT&E is to last until the third quarter of 2013.

It is still to be determined what will be included in the next block. Service requirements from the US or partner nations will have an influence on what exactly will be developed in block 4. One thing is certain, block 4 will be one of the first blocks where integration from non-US weapons will be initiated. The question as to which weapons will be first depends on the number of countries interested in integrating these weapons onto the F-35. The USA is, however, already considering more weapons for integration, particularly those that would increase the persistence of the aircraft. Furthermore, in block 4 the SDD corrections and deferrals should be solved. A data link for the weapons is considered. Infrastructure-wise it is considered that the high temperature power electronics are integrated. For increased survivability adding band 2 and 5 RWR has been considered. Integration of a Tactical Aircraft Directional Infra Red Counter Measures (TADIRCM) pod is also under consideration.

Further blocks are also under consideration. In fact, blocks 4 to 7 have still to be defined but all of them are basically formed by technologies that are presently not mature enough but will be in the future. It is planned that the spiral development will continue to at least 2040, although many predict that strike missions in the future will be taken over by UCAVs (Unmanned Combat Air Vehicles).

CHAPTER 18

RADAR SYSTEM

A novelty of the new generation of fighters was that the radar would now be based on Active Electronically Scanned Array (AESA) technology. From the outset this was a new technology for the ATF, which had been introduced for the first time in F-15 Eagles based in Alaska. The next step was the F-18E/Fs, which were introduced into service with the US Navy shortly after. The F-22 Raptor followed suit with this technology in 2005. However, before these events the JAST programme office was interested in further developing and maturing AESA technology.

The AESA radar system had several advantages. The most important one was that it could be used for multiple tasks and the second was that it gave the radar a Low Probability of Intercept (LPI). The AESA was not only a radar and those further functions and capabilities had to be explored. The new functions and advantages would be:

- Data communication and data linking
- Jamming
- Jammer nulling through beam agility
- Directed energy weapon

On 9 August 1995 BAA 95-4 was issued for a Multifunction Integrated Radio Frequency Systems (MIRFS) by the JSF office in support of the JSF programme. Proposals were due by 29 September 1995. The contract was expected to be awarded by 10 November 1995. It was anticipated that the two Cost Plus Fixed Fee (CPFF) contracts would be awarded at a total value of $100 million and run from the contract award until July 1999. The idea was to develop AESA technology, not a specific radar. The F-22 was the first fighter to be equipped from the outset with an AESA. The technology for the F-22 was relatively new and therefore rather expensive. The aim of the JAST office was to achieve:

- Lower T/R module cost
- Lighter weight
- Reduced power/cooling requirements
- Wider bandwidth for air-to-ground radar plus some EW and CNI function besides the air-to-air radar

Contracts for this risk reduction were awarded on 12 February 1996 to Hughes Aircraft Company (later taken over by Raytheon) and Westinghouse (at a later stage taken over and integrated into the Northrop Grumman Electronic Sensor Division). The CPFF contract at a value of US $48,163,860 received by Westinghouse was for developmental studies and limited demonstration of the MIRFS. This programme was to be completed by June 2000. The other contract awarded to Hughes Aircraft Company had a value of US $54,618,018 for similar studies and was also planned for completion by June 2000. These two contractors were chosen out of three that had responded to the BAA 95-4. The programme was divided into three phases:

- Phase I concept definition (this was completed in FY 1996)
- Phase II integration and ground demonstration
- Phase III flight demonstration

Northrop Grumman division of the stages was as follows:

- Multifunction Array (MFA) Design Refinement: 10/96 - 10/98
- Prototype Transmit/Receive (T/R) Module Build: 12/96 - 07/98
- Production T/R Module Build, Deliverable MFA Build: 10/98 - 05/99
- System Integration and Test (Production MFA): 03/99 - 06/99
- Ground Demos (Production MFA): 07/99 - 09/99
- Flight Demos (Production MFA): 07/99 - 11/99
- Phenomenology Array Deliveries (2): 04/99

It would be up to the Weapon System Contractor to decide which system would provide the best technology advance for its PWSC. Lockheed soon linked up with Westinghouse and Boeing with its competitor Hughes Aircraft Company. The technology that was the responsibility of Westinghouse, which was at a later stage taken over by Northrop Grumman Electronic Systems Sector, was further developed from the F-22 Raptor radar, the AN/APG-77 that was developed and produced by Northrop Grumman and Raytheon. The main design factors were size and cost factors. Manufacturing commonality was desired not only with the AN/APG-77 but also with the AN/APG-68 to lower costs by sharing technology with the other programmes. The standard of the radar for the F-22 in 1991 is described by Robert Hendrix, Chief Engineer of Airborne Surveillance Systems at Northrop Grumman Electronics Systems as a third generation active aperture antenna.

Rooftop testing on the Northrop Grumman owned MFA prototype was initiated by October 1998 followed by flight testing on the BAC 1-11 two months later. The production MFA, which were government owned started rooftop testing in June 1999 and flight testing

A detail of the AN/APG-81 installed in Northrop Grumman's BAC 1-11 flying test bed. The first flight of the radar was seen as a major milestone in 2005. Software fusion for the radar had already been flight flown on another aircraft. *Copyright Northrop Grumman*

was started only one month after that. The Multi Function Array (MFA) was just like the AN-APG-77, classified as a fourth generation antenna. The performance MIRFS/MFA exceeded expectations during the rooftop and flight tests. During the flight tests that were flown in the BAC 1-11 several operational radar modes were evaluated, such as air-to-air, Synthetic Aperture Radar (SAR), Ground Moving Target Indication (GMTI) and active and passive electronic warfare.

The transmitter/receiver radar modules had been undergone ground tests to test system reliability but after 27,000 hours were simulated the tests were interrupted. The lifetime of the aircraft is calculated at only 8000 hours. The JPD General Mike Hough hoped that the radar antenna would not require any maintenance during the lifetime of the fighter, reducing the Life Cycle Cost. For previous radars the average Mean Time Between Failures (MTBF) is 200 to 300 hours, but the Blue Vixen radar used in the Sea Harrier FA2, for example, has only a MTBF of eighty hours. As the JSF was going to replace the Sea Harrier FA2 this was an important comparison; the salty sea air could be the cause of a higher corrosion and therefore the reliability problems. The AN/APG-77 was predicted to have MTBF higher than 450 hours. Another pointer to the quality of the MIRFS/MFA was that the US Navy tested the transmitter/receiver modules in its own labs at China Lake independently and during these environmental tests found no signs of degradation of performance and no failures occurred. Northrop Grumman believed that the logistic footprint of the radar would not only be reduced but overall support costs would be reduced by more then 50 per cent compared to the current (2002) mechanically scanned array radar systems.

The last radar developed for any US fighter was designated AN/APG-80 for the F-16E/F for the United Arab Emirates. The designation for the radar developed for the F-35 was therefore AN/APG-81. According to the US Army Navy (AN) electronic equipment identification system, the system was for a manned aircraft (A), the type of system was radar (P) and the main function was fire control (G). In other words the radar for the APG-81 was the eighty-first radar produced for integration into manned aircraft.

During the SDD, Northrop Grumman was to produce 14 radar systems. Of these systems five were to remain with Northrop Grumman to support software and hardware development and qualification testing. One radar for the Mission System Integration Laboratory (MSIL) at Lockheed Martin, Fort Worth and another one for the Boeing 737-300 Cooperative Avionics Test Bed, (CATB) or CATBird. Another six radars are due for delivery to Lockheed Martin for installation in the SDD aircraft. The last remaining radar is a spare.

Planned radar development milestones were:

- First radar rooftop test in August 2003
- First radar test bed flight in March 2005
- First F-35 JSF radar flight in February 2007 planned for prototype A-3

Besides the obvious functions of the radar the AESA can jam airborne threats. In fact, the jamming capacity is supposed to exceed those of the EA-6B Prowler as it was in service in 2003. A specialised EA-35 was not actively being considered after the EA-18G had been selected by the US Navy, but Northrop Grumman said that such a specialised version would be possible and would therefore be more capable.

On 18 August 2003 the Northrop Grumman BAC 1-11 was used for risk-reduction efforts for the data fusion. The Electro-Optical Targeting Demonstration System (EOTDS) developed by Lockheed was test-flown. An unspecified fourth-generation AESA multi-radar was added to the sensor suite in the aircraft.

On 27 May 2004 Northrop Grumman announced it had initiated rooftop testing, three quarters of a year behind schedule. The radar is supposed to be able to perform near-simultaneous multiple radar tasks. The rooftop tests were performed on a new facility that was opened by JSF JPD USAF Major General Jack Hudson shortly prior to this milestone. It was estimated that the rooftop trials would take six to eight months to finalise the initial modes required for flight-testing in the BAC 1-11 scheduled for early 2005. The radar would not only be tested in Northrop Grumman's BAC 1-11 but also at a later stage in the Boeing 737-300 CATBird. The delay to the flight-test programme of the F-35 also forced a change in the aircraft in which the radar would be installed. The first aircraft in which the radar is now planned to be installed is the first mission system aircraft, BF-4, due to fly in the fourth quarter of 2008.

The AESA radar is supposed to be an integrated part of the EW system. The EW system is being developed by BAE Systems Information and Warfare Systems of Nashua. On 3 March 2005 one AN/APG-81 array was delivered to Lockheed for radome testing.

On 23 August 2005 one of the Northrop Grumman-owned BAC 1-11s took to the air for the first time equipped with the AN/APG-81, followed by a second flight two days later. Both flights were from Baltimore, Maryland. The photograph released was of the N162W (CN08). The radar, the EW system and the EO-DAS were expected to also help perform a new function – Intelligence Surveillance and Reconnaissance (ISR). This role had been developed for fighter aircraft during Operations Enduring Freedom and Iraqi Freedom. Fighter aircraft were gathering ISR to support the ground war and were thereby fulfilling a 'non traditional' ISR role. This 'non traditional' ISR role was expected to be performed in the future by more non-dedicated aircraft. The F-35 would with the AESA radar and its integrated avionics suite be more capable than any other fighter aircraft flying today.

On 11 January 2006, Northrop Grumman announced that, together with its partners Lockheed Martin and L-3 Communications, it had demonstrated with an AESA AN/APG-77 Raptor radar and a Common Data Link (CDL) that two-way high bandwidth communication was possible. Not only was it possible, but the communication was proved to be possible at two or four times the speed of the 274-megabite per second CDL modems provided by L-3. The development of this capability for this demonstration took two years. This technology was expected to find its way into the F-22A and the F-35. The schedule for integration was not clear at the time. This capability was deemed very important as it would increase the platform's non-traditional ISR capability, a feature becoming more important. It would, however, not be included in the first three block editions. Block 4 is the first block that is still to be determined. The first AN/APG-81 had in the mean time been delivered to Lockheed Martin. By the end of January the BAC 1-11 equipped with the AN/APG-81 radar had made eight flights. Software development for the radar was on schedule. Functions that have to be managed by the software are air-to-air, air–to-ground and EW. The technology would have to be further developed and Northrop Grumman hoped to receive a twelve-month development contract award. So far no requirements were set for such a capability but according to Northrop Grumman it would be just a matter of time. By September 2006 Northrop Grumman had four radars in test facilities including one in the BAC 1-11, which had accumulated sixty-five flight hours, and one at Lockheed Martin.

CHAPTER 19

F-35 UNITS

The Integrated Test Force

The Integrated Test Force was the test unit to fly the F-35 with responsibility for the System Development and Demonstration phase. Paul Metz, previously chief test pilot and the first to fly the YF-23, and also the chief test pilot for F-22 EMD programme, was now vice-president of the F-35 ITF. As Paul Metz explained, ITF will be in a sense a step further than the Combined Test Force (CTF) in use during the EMD of the F-22 Raptor. Besides the contractor pilots, maintenance and support staff (Lockheed Martin, Northrop Grumman and BAE Systems) from two countries and the UK forces (two) and the US forces (three) there will be at selected times pilots from the other participating countries. The ITF was again split into three parts depending on the locations where the flight tests were to be performed: ITF Fort Worth, ITF Patuxent River, also known as Pax River, and ITF Edwards AFB. Paul Metz's deputy, Tom Philips, was responsible for ITF Pax River and ITF Edwards AFB. For ITF Fort Worth John Korstian was the person responsible. The ITF started planning the first flight and the subsequent flights in 2003. The chief test pilot of the F-35

A map of the three main test facilities in the US, plus all the other surrounding facilities that will be at some point used for evaluation purposes. As can be seen, the management of the system development and demonstration phase will be quite difficult because they are dispersed over the entire continent. *Copyright DoD*

Jon Beesley flew the F-35 on its first flight up to 15,000ft, the aim was to fly the AA-1 six times a month. *Copyright Lockheed Martin*

During the first flight the landing gear was not retracted. It had according to Lockheed Martin nothing to do with the trust or quality of the landing system. *Copyright Lockheed Martin*

programme is Jon Beesley. Other pilots that joined the test team in 2003 include Jeff Knowles (Lockheed Martin CV project pilot), Dave 'doc' Nelson (Lockheed Martin Mission systems project pilot – a former F-22 Raptor CTF pilot), Bill Gigliotti (Lockheed Martin test pilot), Lt-Col Dave Sizoo (USAF test pilot) and Cdr Brian Flachsbart (US Navy test pilot).

Jon Beesley first took his seat in the F-35 AA-1 cockpit shortly after the aircraft had its 'flight' out of the construction rig onto its own landing gear in January 2006.

The delay in the programme, although rather small for the size of the project, was long enough for Paul Metz to leave his position prior to the first flight of the F-35 AA-1. He was replaced by Wilbert D. 'Doug' Pearson, a combat pilot and a retired USAF major-general from the USAF. Doug Pearson was no stranger to test flights as he had held the position of head of the Air Force Flight Test Center (AFFTC) until he retired on 1 January 2005. He has flown the only fifth-generation fighter flying at that time – the F-22 Raptor.

ITF Fort Worth

AA-1 was the first aircraft to fly. The first flight was an important milestone as it gave the partner nations a tangible result. For safety reasons it was considered better that for the initial part of the flight test programme that Jon Beesley would fly the F-35. Jon Beesley gave up the best seat in the house on the twelfth mission which was flown by his Lockheed Martin test pilot colleague Jeff Knowles. Jeff was a former US Navy pilot whereas Jon was a former USAF test pilot. Government test pilots were expected to get a chance to fly as early as autumn 2007.

ITF Patuxent River

Although the ITF Patuxent River was the main test facility for the STOVL and CV F-35s, the first aircraft was not due to arrive before 2007. The ITF Patuxent River was supposed to be the last unit within the ITF to receive aircraft. Work, however, was initiated quickly because completely new facilities were being built for the F-35 test unit. The $24 million facilities were handed over in January 2006. The weight problem caused the first aircraft to arrive later than anticipated. The first aircraft, an F-35B, was now scheduled for arrival early in 2008. The first production representative aircraft is due to arrive after initial flight-testing at ITF Fort Worth.

Jon Beesley is welcomed back on the ground after a successful first flight. He described the flight as being flawless. Although the first flight was shortened, Jon Beesley and Lockheed Martin were very wary using the word 'shortened'. *Copyright Lockheed Martin*

The Training Unit

There was a lot of competition as to which base should get the function of training the operational pilots on the Lockheed Martin F-35. In particular, the training helped to secure the base at the time when reorganisation in the USAF was causing much insecurity. The reorganisation was called the Base Realignment And Closure (BRAC). The BRAC was not only because of the approaching introduction of the F-35 but was basically a look at how the USAF and Navy could use their bases better and mainly be more cost efficient. The bases that were lining up themselves to become the home of the training unit was increasing towards the end of the BRAC. In the end the recommendation from the BRAC was that Eglin AFB would be the home base for the training unit. Eglin was chosen because of the nearby range that was already used for weapon testing and was also useful for flight training. The choice of Eglin was confirmed on 10 August, 2006 and people from Luke AFB with experience in training would transfer to prepare the training syllabus and infrastructure for the F-35. The training would not only be for the USAF but also for the US Navy and the USMC and the foreign partners, at least initially.

The training on the three variants was supposed to be relatively simple. The only difference was to be in the take-off and landing part of the flight envelope. The bit in between should be the same as the same avionics, the same systems and therefore the training would apply. There would be one major difference and that was the fact that there was no two-seater and so experience from the F-22 conversion unit based at Tyndal AFB would come in handy as well.

It was not only the base that was confirmed but also the wing that had been selected, the 33rd Fighter Wing. The 33rd FW was now equipped with F-15 Eagles, which would be redistributed among other Fighter Wings. The first F-35 Lightning was expected in 2010, depending on the environmental impact analysis process. The environmental impact analysis process is required by the National Environmental Policy Act and designed to identify and assess potential environmental impacts of the proposed action. The first aircraft to arrive would be the two LRIP I aircraft and they are due for delivery by January-February 2010.

On 4 October 2006 it was further announced that the initial JSF locations besides Eglin Air Force Base, Florida, for primary maintenance and flight training include Nellis AFB, Nevada, and Edwards AFB, California, for flight-testing; and Hill AFB, Utah, and Shaw AFB/McEntire ANGB, SC, in the USA and Kadena Air Base in Japan for operational squadrons. With this announcement, the USAF was to initiate the environmental impact analysis process, which could take up to two years.

UK

A decision by the MoD was made quite early as to where the future Joint Combat Aircraft (JCA) would be based. In fact, the decision was made in 2005 and the main operating base selected was RAF Lossiemouth.

In January 2006 the UK DoD announced that eight British pilots would initiate training in 2007 so that they could participate in the test-flying during the SDD. Another eleven pilots were to follow after the first batch to become instructors for the UK on the F-35. It is not clear in what time frame this should happen. The UK has planned that a total of sixty-four pilots should be trained in the US.

CHAPTER 20

EXPORT COUNTRIES

Export was important for the JSF programme for financial reasons and export countries were contacted early in the development phase, to see if they wanted to participate in the programme. Initially only a few European countries joined as associate members and only the UK joined to become a full member. First of all the UK teamed with McDonnell Douglas as they had experience together working on the Harrier. When it was clear that the McDonnell Douglas team was out of contention British Aerospace chose Lockheed as a partner in the JSF effort after evaluating both the Boeing and the Lockheed proposals.

There were three levels of joining the JSF programme:

- Full collaborative partner (level 1)
- Associate partner (level 2)
- Informed customer (level 3)

During the CDP the US knew it needed more security in gaining export orders and therefore other countries that were interested were allowed to join the programme despite not being able pay the minimum amount required for the lowest level. It was rather obvious that countries that were willing to invest money for information on the programme during development would not like to lose money and at a later stage would also buy the aircraft. Another level besides the already mentioned three levels was created and called major participants.

A full collaborative partner is entitled to the following:

- Full access to programme data and structure, including representative personnel within the programme office
- Ability to influence requirement definition and performance characteristics

The UK was the only participant at this level, committing $200 million for the CDP.

An associate partner is entitled to the following:

- Limited access to data and limited requirements influence
- Representative personnel resident within the JSF programme office
- All aspects of participation could be negotiated with the JSF programme office

Denmark, the Netherlands and Norway formed a group and paid a total of $30 million to participate at this level.

An informed customer is entitled to the following:

- Limited access to programme information and representation within the programme office is negotiable
- No influence on requirements

People from several companies from the partner nations were invited to see the AA-1 take off. All the nations had not signed the Production, Sustainment and Follow on Development (PSFD) MoU but it was hoped that the first flight might help some of the partner nations in making their decisions. *Copyright Lockheed Martin*

Canada and Italy committed $10 million each to participate at this level

The major participants category (level 4) was created after demand was found for other ways of participating in the programme. It is also referred to as FMS or Foreign Military Sales participation or fee for service. Major participants are entitled to:

- Negotiate directly with the programme office for specific JSF programme information (e.g. cost and operational performance trade processes and modelling and simulation studies)

- No representative personnel resident within the JSF programme office

Singapore, Turkey and Israel participated at that level.

The times are changing and one clear sign was that on 11 July 2000 an Antonov An-124 Ruslan arrived at Lockheed Fort Worth to pick up a full-scale mock-up of the Lockheed JSF destined for display at the Farnborough Air Show.

After the fly off of the Lockheed Martin X-35s and the Boeing X-32s the urgency of joining the JSF programme for foreign countries increased. The JSF programme office informed countries that if they participated without delay their industries would get, on a competitive basis, a return on their investment. Buying off the shelf at a later stage was not recommended as there would be no offset deals offered. This was not expected to have a negative effect on future export sales. Joining the JSF programme as a level 1, 2 or 3 partner in the SDD phase was only possible until 15 July 2002.

Country	Date of entry CDP and level	Amount (in million US dollars)	Date of entry SDD and level	Amount (in million US dollars)
Australia	N/A	N/A	31 October 2002 Level 3	$172
Canada	Level 3	$10	7 February 2002 Level 3	$150
Denmark	Level 2	$10	28 May 2002 Level 3	$110
Israel	Level 4	$0.8	Level 4	$150
Italy	Level 3	$10	24 June 2002 Level 2	$1000
Netherlands	Level 2	$10	10 June 2002 Level 2	$800
Norway	Level 2	$10	20 June 2002 Level 3	$122
Singapore	Level 4	$3.5	Level 4	$50
Turkey	Level 4	$8	11 July 2002 Level 3	$175
United Kingdom	Level 1	$200	17 January 2001 Level 1	$2000

The advantages of joining the SDD phase could still be given up. One more document was required to be signed to proceed beyond 2006. It was, however, questionable if all would sign up as some countries were not happy with the industrial cooperation. Participation in the SDD phase allowed countries from the partner nations to compete for contracts on a best value basis. The competition was tough and some politicians had hoped that some sort of offset could be attained. The new document to be signed was called the Production, Sustainment and Follow on Development (PSFD) and Lockheed Martin hoped that all the partner countries (with the exception of Israel and Singapore) would sign by December 2006. In this document the partner countries would commit to buy the aircraft, but strangely they would not be given the final price of the aircraft. If, however, a partner country decided not to buy after signing this document it could be penalised financially. The quality of the aircraft or rather the standard of the aircraft would depend on each nation's Operational Requirement Document (ORD). Commonality was sacrificed. From this it was obvious that the UK would get the same quality of aircraft as the US as it had signed the JORD from the outset. The other partner nations would not. Each partner nation would also need to solve the problems with software coding and operational independence. This would mean that the aircraft could be maintained, repaired and overhauled locally. This was, however, difficult as the US was afraid of technology being transferred.

Signature of the PSFD MoU

Country	Date	Estimated procurement Amount
Netherlands	14 November 2006	85
Canada	11 December 2006	80
Australia	12 December 2006	100
United Kingdom	12 December 2006	138
Turkey	25 January 2007	100
Norway	31 January 2007	48
Italy	7 February 2007	131
Denmark	27 February 2007	48

Australia

Australia was one of the first export countries for the F-18 when the announcement was made on 20 October 1981. The F-18 was replacing the Mirage III in the ground attack and intercept roles. The Australian government was having budgetary constraints and was looking at bringing costs down when initiating its search for a new defence system. The new defence system was not supposed to be just a replacement of the F-111 and F-18 but the entire defence structure, as it was seen as too expensive. From this requirement the AIR 6000 programme was born in May 1999.

The department of future products and technology at Saab was working on different studies regarding the development of unmanned aircraft. In fact, unmanned aircraft were seen as a part of the future Net Centric Warfare. It was foreseen by Saab that in the future the Gripen would work side by side with UAVs capable of bombing missions. This study, which had been on going for some time, was announced by Saab on 2 June 1999.

Different studies were made as well by the Australian Ministry of Defence during 2000 and 2001. The Ministry of Defence requested a total solution in its Request for Information for its AIR 6000 requirement. On 31 January 2002 Saab announced that it had answered the RfI and the solution included the Gripen. Saab offered the new network centric defence structure in which the Gripen and UAVs worked together. The system should be introduced by 2012. Saab pointed out that it was mainly cheaper and safer even during peacetime operations. The F-18 was calculated to be withdrawn from service from 2012 to 2015 and the F-111 was to follow suit from 2015 to 2020. Other aircraft under consideration are the Eurofighter Typhoon, the Dassault Rafale, the Super Hornet, the F-16 block 60, F-22 Raptor, F-15, F-35 and an unspecified aircraft from Sukhoi.

A report about the technical state of the F-111 was the source of speculation that the aircraft would be replaced sooner and that the Australian government had requested Boeing to offer them the F-18E/F. The reports were, however, denied by Boeing, although it admitted that it saw all current F-18 users as potential Super Hornet customers.

The Australian government put an end to all speculation and announced that it had chosen to join the JSF programme by the end of June 2002, thereby ending the AIR 6000 programme. The official view was that the JSF would have capabilities that none of the other contenders would have. The only thing that could change this decision was the demise of the JSF programme but that was not really realistic with all the commitments signed by the other countries. The only thing that remained open was the possibility that the Royal

Australian Air Force would need an early replacement for the F-111 in service because it was doubted that they would reach the planned service life until 2015. The early replacement would be in the form of a lease and the JSF would eventually replace the leased aircraft. The Australian government joined up as a partner in the JSF programme at level 3 on 31 October 2002, and was one of the few countries that admitted that even level 3 partnership meant that it had to buy the JSF. The RAAF was hoping to buy around 100 JSFs. The investment Australia was to make at level 3 participation was US $172 million. Australia was the only country to join the SDD phase that had no prior involvement in the JSF programme.

The RAAF was considering the fact that it would like extended range for its JSF aircraft, so that it would have a similar range to the F-111 that it was going to replace. The RAAF wanted to achieve this by putting a fuel tank in the weapon bays. Another matter under consideration was the fact that cameras and other reconnaissance equipment could be placed in either of the weapon bays. The cost of this development would lie solely with Australia as at the time it was the only country that had expressed a requirement for these facilities. The debate as to whether or not the F-35 was the right choice to replace the F-111 was for this reason quite heated in Australia. It was not known which F-35 version was the preferred option. The CV version with the longest range would be the most logical replacement but the connected cost was the biggest barrier and it was questionable if the relative small increase in range was worth the extra investment.

In the beginning of July 2004 a report was published advising that the RAAF should consider buying two versions of the F-35. The conventional and the STOVL versions would both be required to fulfil the requirement of the RAAF. The RAAF was the second air force to consider a mix of versions as the USAF indicated that it was looking into taking two versions as well. A commitment for the PSFD was due by the end of 2006.

Australia was committed to the JSF programme and saw it as the only real option available but was playing political hardball to get similar assurances to the UK regarding operational sovereignty. On the same day as the UK, Australia committed to the next programme phase when Australian Defence Minister Brendan Nelson signed the memorandum during a ceremony at the US State Department. 'The Joint Strike Fighter is most certainly the correct aircraft for Australia in terms of air-to-air combat and its strike capabilities.' He continued by saying that 'it will see Australia through the next 30 to 40 years.' Only two days later the news broke out that Australian Defence Minister Brendan Nelson was thinking about buying twenty-four Boeing F-18E/F Super Hornets outright as a stop gap in case there were any delays with the JSF programme. The news was confirmed and the contract was signed relatively quickly. On 6 March 2007, Australian Defence Minister, Brendan Nelson, announced that 24 Super Hornets would be acquired for the sum of 6 billion Australian dollars.

The estimated procurement amount of aircraft per fiscal year by Australia as was determined in the PSFD document.

Fiscal Year	2010	2011	2012	2013	2014	2015	2016	2017	2018	Total
Amount	2	6	14	15	15	15	15	15	3	100

The first Australian F-35s should arrive in 2015. The F-18 Super Hornets should remain in service until 2020 or if the Australian government would decide against buying a fourth F-35 squadron, the Super Hornets could remain in service longer. Australia finds itself in a different position from all other partner nations. The government's opposition is not against buying new fighter aircraft, in fact they would like to see the government buy the more expensive but also more capable F-22 Raptor.

Belgium

Belgium was one of the early F-16 buyers. It was also the only country of the original four F-16 buyers that decided against JSF participation during the CDP and SDD, mainly due to budget restrictions. By December 1999 the Belgische Luchtmacht (BLu) or Belgium Air Force had an inventory of ninety F-16s that would require replacement from 2010. From the ninety F-16s, seventy-two were allocated to NATO. The BLu wanted a one-for-one replacement but due to budgetary restrictions this was unlikely, as the number of aircraft that could be acquired was, according to political leaders, closer to forty. Belgium's decision-makers thought that the investment for participation would not pay off and if it did buy the JSF, Belgium would probably buy it off the shelf. Belgium's air force reduction would mean that the total number of required aircraft was also smaller, making the big investment a relatively expensive venture. The other part of the Belgium armed forces had been neglected during the last two decades so all financial investments targeted more urgent material. By the end of 2003 it became clear that the requirement of forty was not far off as the BLu was reduced by 30 per cent. The reduction will be complete by 2015 and by that time only sixty F-16s will remain in service, of which forty-eight will be available for NATO service. The main portion of the reduction was, however, completed before the end of 2004 as eighteen F-16s were retired and put in storage, available to sell to interested parties.

Belgium planned to initiate its replacement programme in 2015 at the earliest, although it was now foreseen that the BLu would first upgrade its F-16 with a so-called End Life Upgrade (ELU) prior to acquiring new fighters. This would mean that the F-16 would be replaced from 2025 to 2030. It would remain to be seen if at some point an investment in a manned fighter was still considered a worthwhile investment as the UCA capabilities would have matured, although many say that a man in the loop will always be necessary.

Canada

For the final stage of the CDP Canada signed an MoU to become a partner on 2 January 1998. Canada paid US $10 million. At the same time, however, Canada made it clear that this was not a commitment to buy the JSF. Canada was the fourth and last country to sign up beside the Netherlands, Norway and Denmark.

Canada was the only neighbour of the US to join the programme and was an early customer of the F/A-18. Canada was ready to replace its aircraft by 2010. Canada, for its size, contibuted a relatively small investment when it decided to participate in the EMD phase on 7 February 2002. Canada was the second country to sign up but the first as a level 3 participant, promising to invest $0.15 billion. Ten companies in Canada can bid for potential work on the JSF.

Canada was more successful than other countries in getting back a return on its investment in business supplied on the best value basis. Pratt & Whitney Canada was awarded a contract to provide the fifth-stage high-pressure compressor integrally bladed rotor by the end of October 2004. As Canada was satisfied with the amount of work returned it had no problems with signing the MoU for the PSFD phase. On 11 December 2006 Canada became the second country to sign up for the PSFD. Canadian Deputy Defense Minister Ward Elcock signed together with his US counterpart Deputy Secretary of Defense Gordon England. Canada plans to replace its CF-18 with eighty F-35A Lightning II aircraft. According to Canadian Defense Minister Ward Elcock, Canada plans to retire its CF-18s by 2017.

The estimated procurement amount of aircraft per fiscal year by Canada as was determined in the PSFD document.

Fiscal Year	2014	2015	2016	2017	2018	2019	2020	2021	Total
Amount	10	10	10	10	10	10	10	10	80

Czech Republic

From the moment the Czech Republic announced it was looking for a replacement for its Soviet-origin inventory it was a target for the JSF programme. The JSF could not be introduced to fulfil the immediate requirement, therefore both new and old F-16s and F-18s were offered, so that they could be replaced when the JSF was available. The strategy was partly successful. When the Czechs made their final decision in 2004 they opted for a ten-year lease for the Saab Gripen aircraft for the Quick Reaction Alert (QRA) NATO role instead of the F-16 and F-18. The lease would end by 2015 by which time the F-35 would be readily available for export customers that were not partners in the JSF programme. The question of affordability remained a question in the Czech Republic as it was not certain that the country could afford the JSF even after ten years to 'beef up' its economy just as it remains a question if the F-35 can fulfil its cost target. Another political problem is that most countries would like to see offsets and the Czech Republic is one of them. This was also one of the considerations in accepting the Gripen lease as Gripen International offered offsets. The JSF programme office and Lockheed Martin have been adamant that the time for offsets is over. Becoming a partner in the programme was the only way of getting a return on investment, although even this stance was slowly but surely disappearing as the competition of the Eurofighter Typhoon became all too real in countries such as Norway and Turkey, even though Norway was thought to be using the Eurofighter consortium to get a better deal out of Lockheed Martin.

Denmark

Denmark was an early customer for the General Dynamics F-16 Fighting Falcon, making it an automatic customer for the JSF. Denmark was suffering like any other western European country from budget constraints and had already lost its Saab Draken in December 1993 without any outright replacement. The F-16s took over the role that was previously performed by the Draken.

The JSF programme office tried to get future export countries involved as early as possible and before the CDP started the office negotiated with the first F-16 customers in the hope of securing commitments for the eventual programme winner. Denmark signed an MoU to participate in the JSF CDP on 10 September 1997 at a cost of US $10 million.

On 28 May 2002 Denmark became one of the select few that participated in the next phase of the JSF programme, the development and demonstration phase. Denmark is to invest $125 million until 2012. This gives Denmark a seat in the JSF programme office and its industry will benefit. It does not commit Denmark to buy the aircraft, but that is considered a sure thing as no country invests so much money in a project to later abandon it and buy some another aircraft. Denmark's total investment including the CDP was US $135 million. Fourteen companies from Denmark can potentially become partners in the JSF programme according to Lockheed Martin.

Although a partner in the JSF programme SDD phase, it did not stop Denmark from evaluating other aircraft. By the end of August 2005 Denmark released a Request for Information to several aircraft manufacturers. Eurofighter reacted quite quickly by inviting Chief of the Royal Danish Air Force Air Materiel Command (AMC) Major General Klaus L. Axelsen to fly the Eurofighter Typhoon. The Danish general visited EADS on 7 and 8 November 2005. The 1 hour 15 minute flight was not just a demonstration flight but an actual scheduled test flight.

Denmark was the last of the countries to sign the PSFD MoU on the 27 February 2007. Danish Minister of Defence, Søren Gade, signed the MoU in the US embassy in Copenhagen. The Danish Ministry of Defence however issued a request for information which was sent out to Eurofighter and Gripen International. The estimated procurement amount of aircraft per fiscal year by Denmark as was determined in the PSFD document. Delivery would be approximately two years after contract signature.

Fiscal Year	2014	2015	2016	2017	2018	2019	Total
Amount	8	8	8	8	8	8	48

India

Although developing its own Light Combat Aircraft (LCA), India had a requirement to replace its MiG-21 Fishbeds and had approached Dassault for Mirage 2000s and Gripen International for the Gripen. Also, considering that BAE Systems had succeeded in selling the Hawk to India, the company already had a foot in the door and a repeat of the South African double was anticipated. India requested, however, a fighter that would be licence-built by its indigenous industry, Hall. An estimated requirement for 120 aircraft existed. The Indian Air Force has a total of 380 MiG-21s but they are building the LCA originally planned to replace all of them, though delays have forced India to think of a new option. The Indian Air Force, however, had also been buying the Russian Su-30. The fact that the trainer aircraft bought were not from Russia gave Gripen International the confidence that dual sourcing was an option with the Indian government.

The aim to replace the MiG-21s was not only noticed by Gripen International. Another big fish with a foot already in the door was Dassault as it had delivered a version of its Mirage 2000 to the Indian Air Force. The Indian Air Force had run into some technical problems with its Mirage 2000s in the autumn of 2004 when three of the type crashed. This was, however, seen as the time to upgrade the aircraft already in service and a chance for Dassault to renew its connections and get, as well as an upgrade contract, a contract for newly produced Mirage 2000s to replace the MiG-21s.

On 17 November 2004 Vice Chief of Air Staff Air Marshal Sunil Kamar stated that the requirement was real and that there would be no restrictions to companies supplying the new fighters. The new fighters would replace the MiG-21 until the very delayed home-developed *LCA* was available. Aircraft that were in contention according to him were the Lockheed F-16, Dassault Mirage 2000-5, the MiG-29 and the Gripen from Gripen International. There was, however, one requirement that every company would have to make and that was that there would be a continuous supply of spare parts even if there were sanctions. This would be quite difficult to promise for Gripen International and Lockheed, meaning that the French Mirage and the Russian MiG had a clear advantage. Selection of a winner was foreseen by the end of 2006/early 2007.

It was not entirely surprising but Boeing was also seeking approval to sell its Boeing F/18E/F Super Hornet to India. India had become a reliable partner in the war against terrorism and was therefore entitled to receive consideration for Super Hornet exports. This was also noticed by the Lockheed JSF programme office, which started pushing the F-35 as an option as well. The F-18E/F would be sold with the full US Navy shipboard capability. The Indian Navy, however, stated that the F-18E/F was not compatible with its ships as they had ski-jumps and the F-18E/F was not designed to take off from such a facility.

Israel

Israel is one of the most reliable customers of the US, buying regularly to update its forces out of need. From the moment that Israel was recognised as a state it was under attack by its neighbouring countries. Israel prevailed in most of these wars. This was not only due to the timely supply of aircraft from the US. The Israeli Air Force has a perfect record and is considered a trustworthy ally.

The Israeli Air Force has vast numbers of F-16s and F-15s that need replacing, and the JSF would be the perfect replacement for the F-16. It took longer than expected before Israel actually committed itself to the JSF programme and when it did it was, surprisingly, at the lowest level.

Although Israel signed up late under the Foreign Military Sales (FMS) programme, it requested something that was not considered by any other countries. Israel wanted a two-seat version of the JSF. This could prove extremely costly as Israel was the only country to request this, but on the other hand Israel had more operational use of their air force than any other country, although the UK and the US were slowly catching up on the experience front, as a result of several no-fly zones and the war against terrorism. The JSF had been deliberately designed and developed from the outset as a single-seat fighter, but it will be interesting to see if other countries will follow suit with this requirement or if the need will arise if new multi-role tasks are required from the JSF. An option is to replace the lift fan of the STOVL version with a cockpit seat instead of a fuel tank. This relatively easy way would still be costly as the outer design would change, as well as the cockpit and structure, and the weight and system distribution would also be affected.

The Israeli Air Force seemed to relinquish this requirement. It wanted, however, to receive F-35s that were fully modified to its requirements, meaning that the aircraft could go straight from the manufacturer to the operator as was the case with the F-16L. After the USAF had announced plans to buy the STOVL version for the CAS mission the Israeli Brig. General Zeev Snir, head of the Israeli Air Force material directorate stated in an interview that the Israeli Air Force was not only evaluating the CTOL/CV version, but was also learning about the STOVL version and its capabilities and interest was growing within the Israeli Air Force material directorate. Studies to integrate Israeli unique capabilities were underway during the first quarter of 2005 at Lockheed Martin. The Israeli Air Force counts with the early deliveries in 2014, which should pose no problem. One special study in preparation was an evaluation of the weapons fit in the STOVL weapon bay. The Israeli Air Force has its own air-to-air and air-to-ground weapons and therefore a funding estimate was requested on 14 March and the proposal with the contract statement of work was due by 28 April 2005.

Israel's dealings with China were considered problematic by the US. The Chinese PL8 missile is based on the Python 3 technology if not a straight copy. The Chinese J10 aircraft has a clear resemblance to the IAI Lavi. It was this that made the US nervous about Israel concerning access to the new technology involved in the JSF. For a short period in 2005 Israel was even denied access to the programme. Only after the Ministers of Defence ironed out the problems and the US was reassured about Israel's export policy was Israel again given access to the programme. Israel had all reason to maintain its high defence requirements even though Syria was now the only Israeli-bordering country that had no peace agreement with Israel. Iraq was removed from the threat map by the US-led invasion in 2003 but Iran was considered a security threat with its nuclear programme. If it was only the nuclear programme then Israel would not be so worried but the call made by freshly elected Iranian president Mahmoud Ahmadinejad 'to wipe Israel off the map' was not taken lightly.

Italy

Italy was interested in joining the JSF CDP perhaps even at a higher level than the Danish, Norwegian and Dutch. The higher-level interest stemmed from the fact that the Italian Air Force had a greater requirement than the previously mentioned states. The main aim was to replace its AV-8B Harriers and its locally developed AMX strike aircraft.

The General Electric/Rolls-Royce JSF team linked up with Fiatavio of Italy shortly before Italy signed the MoU in a move to strengthen their position on the European market. Fiatavio already had good ties with General Electric so the move did not come as a surprise. Fiatavio would be supplying structural components for the Low Pressure (LP) turbine and would further participate in the development of the accessory gearbox. The General Electric/Rolls-Royce team had previously teamed up as well with a Danish, Dutch and Norwegian consortium under the lead of Philips ETG from the Netherlands.

Italy, previously a provider for its own or European industry, made the first step back to the US market when it agreed to lease F-16s as a result of the delays of the Eurofighter. Italy was the sixth country to sign up for the EMD phase on 24 June 2002. Italy signed up for level 2 partnership and planned to replace its AMX, AV-8B Harriers and Tornados. Italy signed to invest $1 billion for an estimated purchase of 100 JSFs.

During the first half of May 2003 Marconi Selenia Communications became the first direct Italian supplier of the JSF F-35. Marconi Selenia Communications had been selected to provide the back-up radio. Italy as well had voiced its unhappiness with the amount of work received so far from Lockheed Martin.

Italy was one of the original Eurofighter countries and had committed to buying 121 Eurofighter Typhoons in three tranches. The first delivery was for twenty-six, followed by forty-six in both the second and third tranches. The second tranche had been signed and paid for but the third became questionable as the Italian Air Force pushed to make a case for local production of the F-35 in Italy. Furthermore, the Italian Air Force perceived the F-35 as more survivable as a result of its more stealthy design. With budgets diminishing throughout Europe, the hope was that the political will for the third tranche in the other nations would be diminishing as well.

Italy, a big partner in the sense that it plans to buy a fair amount of aircraft, left it late signing the PSFD MoU. On behalf of Italy, Under Secretary of State for Defence Giovanni Forcieri signed the MoU on February 7, 2007 in the Pentagon. Italy was close to an agreement for a Final Assembly and Check Out (FACO) facility. Italy also had its own final assembly for its F-104S Starfighters. The estimated procurement amount of aircraft per fiscal year by Italy as was determined in the PSFD document. Delivery would be approximately two years after contract signature.

Fiscal Year	2012	2013	2014	2015	2016	2017	2018	2019	2020	2021	2022	2023	Total
Amount	6	6	14	14	14	14	14	12	12	12	12	1	131

Japan

Since the Second World War the country of the rising sun had been one of the main allies of the US. Proof of this was evident in the inventory of the Japanese Air Force or as it is officially called, Japan Air Self-Defense Force (JASDF). Its inventory listed all the main superiority aircraft that had their origins in the US. The inventory included F-15 Eagles, Mitsubishi/Lockheed F-2s (based heavily on the F-16), and F-4 Phantoms. The F-4 Phantoms were reaching the end of their useful life and needed replacement. The JASDF had received a total of 154 Phantoms, of which some were lost to attrition. An estimated requirement for 100 JSFs exists. It is not clear why the Japanese did not join the JSF programme during the CDP or SDD phases. Some expected the Phantoms to be replaced by the Lockheed Raptor, but the price tag attached to the Raptor might make that option rather expensive.

The Japanese Defense Agency (JDA) officials received briefings on the F-35 and cockpit demonstrations in Tokyo on 13 and 14 October 2004. One requirement of the JASDF might be difficult to overcome – deliveries by 2011. It remained to be seen, however, if the acquisition programme would go through without any of the usual political procurement delays. In April 2005 the F-X programme was launched to replace the F-4EJ Kai (Phantoms) in service. The aircraft in contention were basically all the fourth- and fifth-generation fighters from the western world, meaning the Boeing F-15 (with the advantage that it was already in service with the JASDF), Boeing F-18E/F, Eurofighter Typhoon, Dassault Rafale, the Lockheed Martin F-35 and the Lockheed Martin F-22 Raptor. The Raptor at the time was not freed for export but Japan had been in contact with the US government about the export of the Raptor, according to the JDA. Delivery of the first aircraft would be expected during fiscal year 2008–2009, which made the F-35 a relative outsider. On the other hand programmes of this kind normally have a delay, so even the in-service date could still slip.

The Netherlands

One of the first countries to buy the General Dynamics F-16 (now Lockheed Martin) was the Netherlands. In fact, according to some publications, the Dutch decision to select the F-16 made three other nations follow suit – Belgium, Denmark and Norway. The first F-16 of the Royal Netherlands Air Force (RNAF) arrived in June 1979. The F-16 was bought to replace the older F-104 Starfighter aircraft. A follow-on order made the F-16 also the

The RNAF were enthusiastic about the JSF programme from the start. The Dutch considered there were no other feasible options. *Copyright Lockheed Martin*

Emirates (UAE), which was interested in buying them. Negotiations at the time were going on between Dutch and UAE defence officials. The PVDA, the biggest government party, was in fact against selling the F-16s because they could be kept as a reserve for peacetime losses that the air force was likely to endure during the next twenty years of F-16 use. The following table, again accurate at the time, was created to give an overview of the remaining F-16s.

Year of introduction	Total delivered	Average hours flown per F-16
1981	5	2952
1982	12	2755
1983	16	2677
1984	17	2627
1985	17	2634
1986	14	2444
1987	12	2306
1988	10	2042
1989	12	2015
1990	10	1915
1991	10	1780
1992	3	1727

NATO wanted pilots to have a minimum of 180 flight hours and recommended 240 flight hours per pilot per year if they were to be proficient. Similarly, the RNAF thought that 180 flight hours was enough per year for a pilot to be proficient. Some pilots got to fly more though due to international peace enforcement missions.

At the RNAF open days at Volkel on 1 and 2 September 2000 the unexpected happened. All the competitors for replacement of the F-16 showed up at the show. The Eurofighter Typhoon, which could not even make it to one of the major UK air shows, made it to the Dutch air show days. The Gripen was presented by the 39.186. The Dassault Rafale and the JSF were represented – the JSF with a mock-up. One of the so-called advantages of the JSF was the new stealth technology in which the US had a clear advantage over the competition, but it remained to be seen if stealth would keep its holy cow status as other technologies to detect stealthy aircraft were becoming more and more successful. In former Yugoslavia one stealth aircraft, an F-117, was shot down and another had experienced a near miss. Furthermore, stealth aircraft require a lot more maintenance and that would make the aircraft system again more expensive. However, the above arguments could be easily dispelled by two counter arguments. Firstly The F-117 presented first-generation stealth technology whereas the F-35 would represent fourth-generation stealth technology. Secondly the USAF stated that the F-117 had been following the same route every night, which made it easier for the air defences to shoot it down.

The two prototypes of the JSF programme had taken to the air. The Dutch Ministry of Defence and/or the Dutch government did not make the decision yet. The discussion of whether or not the Netherlands really needed such an expensive system as the JSF was started and the Gripen grew in favour compared with the JSF with some of the Defence officials and politicians. When in the autumn of 2000 both technology demonstrators for the JSF project were flying, Saab-BAE Systems was declaring that the technologies now in development for the Gripen would give it the same if not better capabilities than the JSF. Among other things, an AESA radar system and HMD system were in development for the Gripen.

On 14 February 2001 the new Dutch Commander in Chief of the RNAF, Lt-Gen Dick Berlijn, flew for the first time in the Eurofighter. The flight was flown from the CASA test field at its Getafe flight unit. The flight was made in the DA6 test aircraft and the test pilot flying with the Dutch General was Eduardo Cuadrado.

An important statement was made by the new US President George Bush, who said that it was a fair assumption that the US could not afford to buy the three fighters that the Pentagon wanted to buy. The three fighter programmes he was referring to were the F-22 Raptor, the Boeing F-18E/F Hornet and the JSF. To preserve JSF and US industry, on 14 March 2001 Teal Group recommended that the F-22 and F/A-18E/F acquisition programmes be reduced to 216 and 420 aircraft, respectively. Despite the drawbacks of implementing this programme, it would allow the JSF to proceed after a delay of only about two years, with no major increase over the current level of fighter procurement funding. The Teal Group foresaw a production of almost 3000 fighters between 2001 and 2010. This number was thought to be realistic.

On 21 and 22 March 2001 the Dutch State Secretary of Defence, Mr Henk Van Hoof, visited the EADS Eurofighter facilities after the invitation from the four Eurofighter-producing countries (Germany, Italy, Spain and the UK) to join the Eurofighter programme. Besides Van Hoof, the Commander in Chief of the RNAF, Lt-Gen Dick Berlijn, was present as well. The deal offered included equal partnership in production and design from Eurofighter tranche 3. Eurofighter tranche 3 is supposed to enter service in 2010. The Dutch industry would then become an equal partner in the Eurofighter programme. The decision was expected in late 2001.

On 3 October Van Hoof presented a report to the Dutch parliament with the results so far. In the report he stated that the RNAF, with the support of the TNO and NLR (Nationaal Lucht en Ruimtevaartlaboratorium or National Air and Space Laboratory), had evaluated all the candidate aircraft. The end-life update was found to be an unrealistic option. The Gripen did not fulfil the requirements set. Further evaluation of the Gripen was therefore not undertaken. It made Saab's assumption that the Gripen would be as capable as the JSF also a bit harder to believe. The most important factor was that the Gripen with a heavy weapon load did not have a satisfactory range. According to the report Saab had been informed about this. He further noted that there were three candidates that offered participation, which were the Eurofighter, Rafale and the JSF. The Ministry of Economic affairs had requested the CPB (Centraal Plan Bureau) or Central Plan Bureau, a Dutch bureau for economic analysis that made the report for the Dutch finance minister to put the already inventoried figures of the offers by the three candidates in a more broad cost and profit balance. The figures had been inventoried by the Ministry of Economic affairs with the help of Booz-Allen & Hamilton and the Nederlands Instituut voor Vliegtuig ontwikkeling en Ruimtevaart (NIVR or Dutch Institute Air and Space development) headed by Ben Droste, the former Commander in Chief of the RNAF. In the requested report the difference between buying off the shelf and participation in the various developments was also to be compared. Negotiations with the three manufacturers were continuing. One similarity with all three candidates was that the sooner the Netherlands participated in a programme then the greater the profitability. If the Dutch government decided not to participate and to buy off the shelf, all the options would become available again.

determined in the PSFD document. Delivery would be approximately two years after contract signature.

Fiscal Year	2009	2010	2011	2012	2013	2014	2015	2016	2017	2018	Total
Amount	1	2	0	6	10	12	12	12	12	18	85

Plans to cut the RNAF inventory of F-16 were announced early July 2007. The planned cuts would bring the F-16 force down to 72 from the current 90. Although it was stated that it would have no effect on the JSF, it was very unlikely that the RNAF would replace 72 F-16s with 85 F-35s. The normal way is to say that the new fighter is more capable and therefore RNAF does not require the same amount. For this very reason 85 were thought to be sufficient to replace the 90 F-16s.

Norway

In March 1995, the Norwegian defence ministry took the first step to obtain a next-generation fighter to replace its F-5 Freedom Fighters. The aircraft under consideration were the Eurofighter 2000, Dassault Rafale, the F-16C/D and, of course, the JAS 39 Gripen. The F-16C/D, although not a fourth-generation fighter, was considered because the F-16A/B was already in the inventory of the Norwegian Air Force. Saab retired from this bid pretty soon when it transpired that the Norwegian Air Force at that time preferred twin-engine aircraft. In the competition Saab was therefore thought to stand no or little chance. The Lockheed team remained in the bid with its F-16C/D.

The JAST office briefed Norway on the JSF shortly after March 1996, although it was doubtful that the Norwegian Air Force could wait that long to replace its F-5s. The JSF would, however, be ready when the Norwegians needed to replace their F-16MLUs, which was expected to be around 2010. Shortly after the briefing Norway expressed a desire to join the programme as an informed customer, meaning that the Norwegians would have to invest 0.5 per cent of the total cost of the CDP. Norway was one of the first countries besides the UK to express its desire to join the JSF programme.

The Norwegian government invested, together with the Dutch and the Danish governments, $30 million (one-third each) to become a partner in the JSF CDP. The Norwegian government signed the MoU on 16 April 1997.

The financial crisis had also reached Norway. The Norwegian Chief of Defence, General Arne Solli, announced that the procurement of forty fighters was to be postponed for four years and the requirement due to budget restraints had decreased from forty aircraft to twenty-five. The fighters still in the running are the Lockheed F-16 block 60 and the Eurofighter. The Norwegian decision was expected late 1999.

Another program that had suffered delay was the Indian LCA (Light Combat Aircraft). The first flight was rescheduled and it was due to the economic crisis in the region that further delays could still occur. In fact the first flight of the LCA occurred on the 4th January 2001. No decision had been made by the Norwegian government until 2003.

Norway's political decision to retire the F-5 without replacing it was a big blow to the air force. The Norwegian Air Force remained with fifty-eight F-16s in service. Peacetime losses of the Norwegian F-16 had amounted to sixteen F-16s by the end of 2000. The plan was that the fifty-eight F-16s were to be replaced by forty-eight fighters. As the financial budget was so tight it was deemed necessary to replace at least half of the F-16s in the Norwegian Air Force inventory from 2006 to 2009 and the other half in a second batch in another tender. This would open the possibility to have two different aircraft types again in the inventory. If the plans went ahead as planned then in 2003 all the options would be studied, including the batch 3+ quality (international NATO compatible) Gripen for the first batch. Commander in Chief of the Norwegian Air Force, General-Major Tomas Colin Archer, saw the JSF as the only realistic option for the second batch.

By the end of April 2002 the Ministry of Defence was advised by Defence Staff that the JSF would be the best option for replacement. Earlier there was advice from the National Civilian and Defence Technological Industry Association, which again preferred the Eurofighter tranche 3 offer, as it was thought to have a far better effect for the Norwegian industry than the JSF. The Norwegians signed on for level 3 participation of the JSF programme on 20 June 2002 for US $125 million, expecting to buy forty-eigh aircraft. The Eurofighter consortium, led by EADS, saw that they were about to lose an important customer so they provided a Norwegian company with a big order for the supply of parts for the Eurofighter Typhoon. As the JSF suppliers' contracts were on a competitive basis the offset deals were slow in realising themselves and there were even rumours that the Norwegians would abandon the JSF programme in favour of the Eurofighter around the Paris Air Show Le Bourget 2003. Norway remained with the programme, although voicing on a regular basis that it was not content with the work that it was receiving in return for its investment. A decision as to the commitment to production of the F-35 was expected in 2006.

Norway decided to coninue with the JSF, although this did not present a commitment to buy. In fact, it was looking for similar opportunities elsewhere. Norway was in discussions with the Eurofighter consortium and with Saab about a further development of the Gripen called Gripen N.

Norway was the first country to sign the PSFD MoU in its own country. At the Norwegian Ministry of Defence in Oslo, Norwegian Defence Minister, Anne-Grete Strom-Erichsen signed the PSFD MoU. The estimated procurement amount of aircraft per fiscal year by Norway as was determined in the PSFD document. Delivery would be approximately two years after contract signature.

Fiscal Year	2014	2015	2016	2017	2018	Total
Amount	8	12	12	12	4	48

Norway however made a point of inviting Gripen International and Eurofighter to make similar development deals. Making clear that the JSF had not won the tender yet, even though it was unlikely that Norway would select any of the other aircraft.

Singapore

On 23 February 2003 it was announced that Singapore was considering joining the SDD phase of the JSF programme. This was seen as a slap in the face for the competition as Singapore was expecting to replace its A-4SU Skyhawks by 2007. It was now uncertain if there would be any competition at all. Besides its A-4SU Skyhawks the Royal Singapore Air Force has Northrop Grumman F-5S/Ts, and F-16s. The Singapore Air Force wanted to reduce the number of different types of aircraft in its inventory and therefore the F-16 was thought to be in a very favourable position. The Singapore Air Force was to take delivery of twenty block 52 F-16s from December 2003, giving another advantage to the F-16.

In February 2004 Singapore signed a letter of intent to join the SDD phase of the JSF. Shortly after, on 16 March 2004, Singapore signed up to a bilateral agreement with the US to become a partner in the SDD phase of the JSF programme. The Letter of Offer and

Acceptance (LOA) makes Singapore a Security Cooperation Partner (SCP) and gives Singapore the opportunity to buy the F-35 from 2012. Besides this the Royal Singapore Air Force will be able to perform studies for integration of its requirements. Singapore, however, required aircraft from 2008/9 and it was unclear if Singapore intended to continue and buy an interim fighter, for which it had pre-selected the Eurofighter Typhoon, Dassault Rafale and the Boeing F-15T.

Spain

Although not a partner in the JSF programme, Spain was seen as an inevitable JSF customer for the simple reason that it had AV-8B Harriers in its inventory as well as the F-18 Hornet. Spain was, however, also a partner in the Eurofighter programme like Italy and the UK and budgetary limits could change the situation. It was a big question if Spain's politicians thought that they could afford the STOVL capability in their air force. Spain was briefed by Joint Program Director (JPD) Rear Admiral Craig E. Steidle and USAF Principal Deputy, Office of the Assistant Secretary of the Air Force (Acquisition), George K. Muellner, the previous JPD.

Turkey

Turkey was one of NATO's members that was considered for a long time one of the poorer members and was therefore supported with donations of F-5s from the RNAF when they retired. Turkey, however, was also a customer of F-16s that would at some time need replacement. Besides the F-16 the McDonnell Douglas F-4 Phantom II was also still soldiering on and this could also be replaced by the new JSF. Turkey's air force was indeed very impressive in size and was mainly maintained due to it longstanding problems with its close neighbour Greece.

On 16 June 1999 Turkey signed a Letter of Agreement (LoA) regarding joining the CDP for a total of US $6.2 million. Turkey would join the CDP under the Foreign Military Sales programme similar to that formed for Singapore. Turkey was the second country to join as a fourth level partner and was the eighth country to join the JSF programme in total. The impressive air force development and further stated need to replace the approximately 200 F-4 Phantoms in the Turkish Air Force assured Turkey's participation in the SDD phase. Furthermore, Turkey planned to replace early F-16s with the JSF as well. After the F-4s had been replaced the plan was to have only JSFs and F-16s of the block 40 and 50 standard in the Turkish Air Force. Turkey signed the MoU on 11 July 2002 for level 3 partnership in the SDD phase with an investment of US $175 million. Originally Turkey had hoped for level 2 partnership but this proved too dear. Turkey was the last country to receive its first order in connection with the JSF work. The Turkish government had reason to complain about the return on its investment by June 2003 as return investments were slow in coming in.

Although the work participation improved there was still room for improvement. The Eurofighter Typhoon sales team saw a chance here and tried to offer its aircraft to fill another requirement. If the aircraft was deemed a success then it was possible it would eat away at the JSF requirement. Lockheed had reason enough to be worried by the effort as early in 2005 two Turkish pilots flew the Eurofighter Typhoon in Italy. According to some press reports an offset package was offered to Turkey to counter the offer made by the Eurofighter consortium. The Turkish Air Force was considering several options. The options involved either a force of Eurofighters, or a mixture of Eurofighters and the JSF or just the JSF.

In late October 2006 it was reported that the Turkish Air Force in fact preferred to receive only the JSF. It was now up to the politicians to make the final decision as the date set for the PSFD signature was approaching fast.

Turkey became the second non English speaking partner to sign the PSFD. Deputy Secretary of Defence Gordon England and the Turkish Minister of National Defence Vecdi Gonul signed the PSFD MoU on January 2007. The estimated procurement amount of aircraft per fiscal year by Turkey as was determined in the PSFD document. Delivery would be approximately two years after contract signature.

Fiscal Year	2012	2013	2014	2015	2016	2017	2018	2019	2020	2021	Total
Amount	10	10	10	12	12	10	10	10	10	6	100

UK

It seems strange to name the UK as an export country as it was involved in the programme so early but on the other hand it has only an 8 per cent share in the development cost and about 15 per cent of the production. The JSF is still ultimately seen as a Lockheed Martin product even though BAE Systems has been criticised for joining with the industry of the US instead of Europe (mainly by the French and to some lesser extent the Germans). It was, however, clear that the UK could not find a partner willing to develop a supersonic STOVL-capable fighter in Europe. In fact, Europe had its hands full with the Eurofighter Typhoon, Dassault Rafale and the Saab Gripen. There were declining defence budgets and the political will to fund another major fighter project was not present.

The UK, a partner as long back as the MoU, signed up to join the partnership in the Common Affordable Lightweight Fighter (CALF) programme to study options and technology to replace the Harrier in service. Studies had been performed earlier and even a Harrier III was an option but as the design of the Harrier was almost a forty years' old its growth was limited. In 1990 British Aerospace displayed a model of what should have been the Harrier III. The replacement programme began in earnest in 1996, when a requirement was set and was called the Future Carrier Borne Aircraft (FCBA) to replace the Sea Harrier FA.2, which was planned to begin retiring in 2006. The new requirement was set in staff target (Sea/Air) 6464.

The UK was the only country to become a full partner and contribute US $200 million for CDP, which was budgeted at US $2 billion. On behalf of the UK MoD and US DoD respectively, Dr Malcolm McIntosh, Chief of Defence Procurement, and Dr Paul Kaminsky, Under Secretary of Defence for Acquisition and Technology, signed an MoU regarding this cooperation on 20 December 1995. The UK was heavily criticised by the French as they thought that Europe should keep together and buy European. The French, already nervous, as a result of the success of the F-16, were afraid of a *déjà vu* situation and therefore compared the JSF programme with the Trojan horse for the European aerospace industry, somehow forgetting that Dassault was a partner in the Boeing X-32. Furthermore, Dassault was pushing its CATIA CAD/CAM programme to be used on the JSF.

In 1998 the Strategic Defence Review changed matters for the programme as it was now planned that both the Royal Navy Sea Harriers and the Royal Air Force Harriers had to be joined under one command called Joint Force 2000. The Joint Force 2000 was to be able to operate from land and sea bases; this cost-cutting measure was to ensure commonality between aircraft used on naval ships and land bases. The task of this Joint Force 2000 was to deploy precision strikes at land, sea and air targets. Furthermore, it was to provide air escort for joint assets and provide protection against aggression. It was soon very clear that the JSF or any other contender would be available by 2006, when the Sea Harrier FA.2 needed replacing.

The Joint Force 2000 came into existence on 1 April 2000, when it had changed name to Joint Harrier Force (JHF). The JHF had now in its inventory the Sea Harrier FA.2 and the Harrier GR.7 – two aircraft that were both nearing the time that they needed replacement. The fact that it was now a Joint RN/RAF unit made the name of the replacement FCBA for the Sea Harrier obsolete, which was why a new name for the common replacement was chosen and came into effect in May 2001. The new name reflected better the single need for replacing two aircraft – the Future Joint Combat Aircraft (FJCA) project was born. The plan was now to replace both the Sea Harrier FA.2 and the Harrier GR.7. Shortly afterwards it was decided that the Sea Harrier FA.2 would indeed be retired during 2006. The Harrier GR.7 would be upgraded to the Harrier GR.9 and be operated from sea bases and ashore, improving its capability and lifetime until the FJCA was ready to replace the Harrier GR.9.

It was unclear which aircraft would be chosen and BAE Systems had gambled most on the JSF, but it was not certain that that the programme would survive all the budgets cuts that were contemplated. Within the US even the newly elected Republican President, George Bush, was heard saying that three new aircraft projects could not be afforded and it was to be seen which of those projects would be cut. The JSF was at that time the least advanced aircraft under development and was therefore seen as the programme with the highest risk. This made the UK opt also for a second option, which was a navalised version of the Eurofighter Typhoon.

The Typhoon option had a bigger weapon load, higher speed and, more importantly, a longer range. The commonality issue was pushed as well as the RAF had already ordered 232 Eurofighter Typhoons. The UK, another partner in the Eurofighter partnership, was also briefed on the naval version, as they would encounter the same problem when they wanted to replace their Harriers. Initial studies for the navalised version were initiated in 1996. The studies performed showed some good results and therefore in 1997 another more in-depth study was initiated that lasted twenty-seven months, which looked into the possibilities and requirements that were connected with navalising the Eurofighter Typhoon. Two versions of a navy Typhoon were under consideration – one was with a Short Take Off But Arrested Recovery (STOBAR) and the other a conventional catapult-launched version like the F/A-18E/F and Rafale. The STOBAR version would require thrust vectoring on the EJ200 engine but that was already being studied by the Spanish EJ200 partner (ITP or Industria de Turbo Propulsores).

Another aircraft that came into contention was the Rafale, which had been adapted from the outset for the French Navy's requirements. The Rafale was, however, French and the British home industry would have little or no influence or jobs in the programme. Another option was the Boeing F/A-18E/F, which was about to enter US Navy service. All three of these aircraft, however, lacked stealth and the Vertical Landing capability. Previous cooperation with Boeing (formerly McDonnell Douglas) on the Harrier and the Goshawk made a better opening for influence for BAE Systems but it was still not an ideal option. The best option remained the JSF for the UK industry.

The insecurity of funding gave the British a better negotiating position and the signing was slightly delayed. Finally, on 17 January 2001 the UK signed an MoU with the US to become a level 1 partner in the Engineering, Manufacturing and Demonstration (EMD) phase. It was not made clear which version was the favoured, ie the STOVL or CV, and it was at the time only said that the JSF was the preferred option. Level 1 partnership allowed the UK to be part of the evaluation of the two different designs. The evaluation commenced shortly after on 8 February 2001.

The decision was eventually made to go for the STOVL version on 30 September 2002. The UK was, however, also looking at replacing the HMS *Royal Ark* aircraft carrier. The decision to opt for the STOVL version was thought to have an effect on the size of the aircraft carrier needed. The MoD was, however, looking at the bigger option as it did not like to rule out the use of the E-2 Hawkeye and if there was a replacement for the JSF that did not have STOVL capability then the aircraft carrier would not need to be scrapped. The MoD denied that the reason had anything to do with the uncertainty that the STOVL JSF version was going to be built. Another reason for choosing the STOVL version was that it is more flexible and you can operate it in weather conditions where the CV version would not be able to launch from ships, which can be a major operational advantage. The JSF chosen for the British FJCA became known in the press as the JCA as it promptly lost its 'future' designation.

Problems around technology transfer were present from the start. The problems would all be solved one at a time according to officials from the Joint Program Office. The frictions between the UK and the US, however, were not diminishing. In fact, it seemed that they were increasing. Early in the SDD countries like Norway and Turkey gained most attention because of their dissatisfaction but in 2005 this changed to the UK. Just prior to the Paris Air Show it became known that the integration of the ASRAAM missile was to be delayed, which was a huge disappointment for the UK as it would delay their full weapon capability and the export chances of the missile. The worries were of such importance that the UK Prime Minister Tony Blair had communications about the problems with his US counterpart President George Bush. The technology transfer was considered a big problem and by the end of 2005 the decision to cancel the alternative engine without any consultation with the UK was considered a slap in face. It was something you did not do to someone providing 10 per cent of the funding for the entire programme. The technology transfer problem was, however, considered more serious as it was not certain that the maintenance could be completely carried out by the UK. This was according to some officials of the armed forces unacceptable and would mean that another option would have to be found. As there was no alternative readily available it could end up in quite a loss of capability for the UK armed forces. The MoU planned to be signed in the latter part of the 2006 called the Production, Sustainment and Follow On Development (PSFD) was now in doubt. It was hoped that all partner nations would sign that document and commit to a certain number, but for the UK this would be impossible if it did not receive total autonomy on the technical side. The French made an offer to the UK that they could always buy the Dassault Rafale as it was a fourth-generation fighter qualified for shipborne operations. In fact, as the UK and France were cooperating on the aircraft carrier it would make the requirement they would have more similar in that regard.

The UK new Defence Minister for Procurement, Lord Drayson, stated prior to a visit to the US regarding the JSF in March 2006:

> Whilst I appreciate the concerns of some in the US about the issue of Technology Transfer, the British public expect their Government to equip our Armed Forces with the very best and I am determined to best represent the interests of our national security and our British Service personnel.
>
> The next key milestone in the programme, the signing of the Production, Containment and Follow-On Development MOU will commit the United Kingdom to the whole life of the JSF programme. We must therefore be sure to understand the nature and balance of the obligations between our nations consistent with the principles of the agreements on JSF we have signed to date. Operational sovereignty, the ability to integrate, upgrade, operate and sustain the aircraft as we see fit and

without recourse to others is of paramount importance.

Let me state our bottom line. These issues are important to us because they enable us to make the judgement that the aircraft are 'fit to fight' and we can send our airmen and women into action in that knowledge. This decision has to be one for the UK, indeed the British Government's responsibility to our Armed Forces, and their families, means that this judgement can only be made by the UK. If we do not have the information and technology needed to make that decision, then I shall not be able to sign the MOU. I recognise the consequences that would have on the UK's continuing participation in the programme.

During his visit he was to meet with several influential senators to speak about this, the planned F136 engine cancellation and the interconnected treatment the UK receives. His comments regarding the F136 engine were clear cut:

The F136 inserts an important competitive element to the JSF programme by providing an alternative choice for the aircraft engine both at initial acquisition and, importantly, through life, with all the monetary savings that this will offer us both. There is also the potential growth capability that the F136 offers as a new generation engine. We believe the F136 engine will lead to lower through-life costs and deliver the best outcome for both our war fighters and our taxpayers.

For these reasons and given the importance of the project to Rolls-Royce, we expect, as a level 1 partner, to be properly consulted on decisions of this magnitude. As the Minister responsible for the UK defence industrial base, I still wish to see funding for the F136 included in the Department of Defence programme. This is something that I will be following up with the Administration this week.

Considering that Tony Blair had already lobbied the decision it was not clear what the results would be and if the F136 engine could be saved. If the UK withdrew from the JSF programme at this stage it would mean a loss of face for the US, loss of money for the UK and it would definitely damage the special relationship the two countries professed to have. The lobbying seemed to have a positive effect on things as the Senate reinstated funding for the engine.

On 8 December 2006 the UK House of Commons issued a warning that the UK MoD should be careful not to sign the PSFD until assurances were given regarding sovereignty issues around operational use of the F-35A Lightning II but also be careful not to damage the special relationship between the US and the UK. The UK MoD answered that it would commit only after all the assurances were received that it deemed necessary. Only four days later this seemed to have been achieved and Minister of Defence Lord Peter Drayson signed the PSFD MoU with US Deputy Secretary of Defense Gordon England.

The estimated procurement amount of aircraft per fiscal year by the United Kingdom as was determined in the PSFD document. Delivery would be approximately two years after contract signature. So the UK was expected to sign in fiscal year 2009 for deliveries to start in 2011.

Fiscal Year	2009	2010	2011	2012	2013	2014	2015	2016	2017	2018
Amount	2	3	8	3	2	9	9	12	12	12

Fiscal Year	2019	2020	2021	2022	2023	2024	Total
Amount	12	12	12	12	12	6	138

ABBREVIATIONS

ABL	Air Borne Laser
ACAS	Air-to-air Collision Avoidance System
ACAT	Acquisition CATegory
ACC	Air Combat Command
ACER	Alternate Conformal Ejector Rack
ACES	Advanced Concept Ejection Seat
ACLS	Automatic Carrier Landing System
AEP	Alternate Engine Program
AES	Automatic Ejection System
AESA	Active Electronically Scanned Array
ADS	Air Data System
AEDC	Arnold Engineering Development Center
AFAST	Affordable Fighter Aft-fuselage Structures Technology
AFB	Air Force Base
AFF	Acoustic Fatigue Facility
AFFTC	Air Force Flight Test Center
AFL	Avionics Flying Laboratory
AFRL	Air Force Research Laboratory
AFTI	Advanced Fighter Technology Integration
AGCAS	Automatic Ground Collision Avoidance System
AGE	Aerospace Ground Equipment
AGF	Advanced Gas Facility
AGILE	Advanced Garment Integrated Life Support Ensemble
AGM	Air-to-Ground Missile
AHS	Ammunition Handling System
AIS	Active Inceptor Subsystem
ALAFT	Advanced Lightweight Aircraft Fuselage Structure
ALS	Autonomic Logistics System

AMC	Air Materiel Command
AMLCD	Active Matrix Liquid Crystal Display
AMRAAM	Advanced Medium Range Air-to-Air Missile
AMT	Accelerated Mission Testing
ANG	Air National Guard
ANR	Active Noise Reduction
AoA	Angle of Attack
API	Armour Piercing Incendiary
APS	Auxiliary Power System
ARDS	Advanced Range Data System
ARTE	Auditory Representation of Threat Environments
ART/S	Aerial Refuelling Tank/System
AST	Air Staff Requirement
ASRAAM	Advance Short Range Air-to-Air Missile
ASRR	Air System Requirement Review
ATA	Advanced Tactical Aircraft
ATCS	Advanced Technology Crew Systems
ATEGG	Advanced Turbine Engine Gas Generator
ATF	Advanced Tactical Fighter
ATP	Authority To Proceed
ATR	Autonomic Target Recognition
AVEL	AMRAAM Vertical Ejection Launcher
AVT	Advanced Vectored Thrust
BAA	Broad Area Announcement
BD	Basic Design
BFE	Buyer Furnished Equipment
BK	Bordkanonen
BLu	Belgische Luchtmacht or Belgium Air Force
BOM	Bill Of Material
BRAC	Base Realignment And Closure
CAD/CAM	Computer Aided Design/Computer Aided Manufacturing
CAESAR	Civilian American and European Surface Anthropometry Resource
CALF	Common Affordable Lightweight Fighter
CAS	Close Air Support
CATB	Cooperative Avionics Test Bed
CATIA	Computer Aided, Three-dimensional Interactive Application
CBU	Cluster Bomb Unit

CCD	Charge Coupled Device
CDA	Concept Demonstration Aircraft
CDDR	Concept Definition and Design Research
CDL	Common Data Link
CDP	Concept Demonstration Phase
CDR	Critical Design Review
CE	Concept Exploration
CE	Control Electronics
CFD	Computational Fluid Dynamics
CFIT	Controlled Flight Into Terrain
CIP	Common Integrated Processor
COPT	Cost/Operational Performance Trades
COTS	Commercial Off The Shelf
CNI	Communication Navigation & Identification
CPFF	Cost Plus Fixed Fee
CRDA	Cooperative Research and Development Agreement
CSMU	Crash Survivable Memory Unit
CTF	Combined Test Force
CTOL	Conventional Take-Off and Landing
CV	Carrier Version
DAB	Defense Acquisition Board
DAIRS	Distributed Aperture Infra Red Sensor
DAR	Digital Anti-jam Receiver
DARPA	Defense Advanced Research Project Agency
DAS	Distributed Aperture System
DASH	Display And Sight Helmet
DAT	Digital Audio Tape
DERA	Defence Evaluation and Research Agency
DEW	Directed Energy Weapon
DFCS	Digital Flight Control System
DFRC	Dryden Flight Research Center
DMC	Display Management Computer
DOC	Desired Operational Capabilities
DoD	Department of Defense
DSI	Diverterless Supersonic Inlet
EA	Ejector Augmentor
EAP	Experimental Aircraft Program

EBM	Electrostatic Bearing Monitor
ECME	Electronic Counter Measures Equipment
ECS	Environmental Cooling System
EDMS	Engine Distress Monitoring System
EEE	Electromagnetic Environmental Effects
EFM	Enhanced Fighter Manoeuvrability
EHA	Electro Hydrostatic Actuator
EMA	Electro Mechanical Actuator
EMD	Engineering, Manufacturing and Demonstration
EO	Electro Optical
EODM	Electrostatic Oil Debris Monitor
EOSS	Electro Optical Sensor System
EOTDS	Electro Optical Targeting Demonstration System
EOTS	Electro Optical Targeting System
EPAD	Electronically Powered Actuation Design
ERR	Early Risk Reduction
ESMS	Enhanced Stores Management Set
EW	Electronic Warfare
FADEC	Full Authority Digital Engine Control
FBW	Fly By Wire
FCBA	Future Carrier Borne Aircraft
FCC	Flight Control Computer
FCLP	Field Carrier Landing Practice
FCS	Flight Control System
FDR	Final Design Review
FETT	First Engine To Test
FJCA	Future Joint Combat Aircraft (later JCA Joint Combat Aircraft)
FMS	Foreign Military Sales
FOV	Field Of View
FQ	Flying Qualities
FRR	Flight Readiness Review
FTB	Flying Test Bed
FTC	Flight Test Centre
FTS	Flight Test Squadron
FY	Fiscal Year (in the US a FY runs from the 1 October until 30 September, for example FY05 (01.10.04–30.09.05)
GAO	General Accounting Office
GBU	Guided Bomb Unit

GCAS	Ground Collision Avoidance System
GCLF	Gas Coupled Lift Fan
GDATP	General Dynamics Armament and Technical Products
GFE	Government Furnished Equipment
GLOC	G-induced Loss Of Consciousness
GPS	Global Positioning System
GSCU	Gun System Control Unit
GVT	Ground Vibration Tests
HARM	High-speed Anti Radiation Missile
HDGP	High Drag General Purpose
HEI	High Explosive Incendiary
HFVS	High Frequency Vibration Sensor
HGI	Hot Gas Ingestion
HMD	Helmet Mounted Display
HMS	Helmet Mounted Sight
HP	High Pressure
HQ	Handling Qualities
HTF	Hybrid Tandem Fan
HTU	Helmet Transfer Unit
HUD	Head Up Display
IAF	Israeli Air Force
IBR	Integrated Baselines Review
ICP	Integrated Core Processor
IDA	Infrared Detector Assemblies
IDEFF	Inlet Ducts Edges Front Frame
IDMS	Ingested Debris Monitoring System
IDR	Initial Design Review
IFDL	Intra Flight Data Link
IFF	Impingement Film Floatwall
IFPC	Integrated Flight Propulsion Control
IFR	Initial Flight Release
IHAVS	Integrated Helmet Audio Visual System
IHPTET	Integrated High Performance Turbine Engine Technology
INS	Inertial Navigation System
IPP	Integrated Power Package
IPT	Integrated Product Team
IRST	Infra Red Search and Track

NDP	National Disclosure Policy
NGT	Next Generation Transparency
OARF	Outdoor Aerodynamic Research Facility
OBOGS	On Board Oxygen Generating System
OEF	Operation Enduring Freedom
OIF	Operation Iraqi Freedom
OGE	Outside Ground Effects
ONR	Office of Naval Research
OT&E	Operational Test & Evaluation
PAA	Primary Aircraft Assigned
PBL	Performance Based Logistics
PBW	Power By Wire
PCB	Plenum Chamber Burning
PCD	Panoramic Cockpit Display
PCHM	Propulsion Control & Health Management
PCME	Power Control and Monitoring Electronics
PCU	Power Conversion Unit
PDE	Power Drive Electronics
PDR	Preliminary Design Review
PFR	Primary Flight Reference
PGM	Precision Guided Munitions
PHM	Prognostic & Health Management
PHM	Propulsion Health Management
PMR	Program Management Review
PRDA	Program Research and Development Agreements
PSFD	Production, Sustainment and Follow on Development
PTMS	Power & Thermal Management System
PVI	Pilot Vehicle Interface
PWSC	Preferred Weapon System Concept
QRA	Quick Reaction Alert
RAF	Royal Air Force
RALS	Remote Augmented Lift System
RAM	Radar Absorbing Material
RAS	Radar Absorbent Structure
RCS	Radar Cross Section
RfI	Request for Information
RfP	Request for Proposals

RHI	Right Hand Inceptor
RLG	Ring Laser Gyro
RM&S	Reliability, Maintainability & Supportability
RN	Royal Navy
RNAF	Royal Netherlands Air Force
RVL	Rolling Vertical Landing
RPM	Revolutions Per Minute
RWR	Radar Warning Receiver
SAR	Synthetic Aperture Radar
SAVE	Simulation Assessment & Validation Environment
SCP	Security Cooperation Participant
SDB	Small Diameter Bomb
SDD	System Development & Demonstration
SDLF	Shaft Driven Lift Fan
SEAD	Suppression of Enemy Air Defences
SINCGARS	SINgle Channel Ground and Airborne Radio System
SGR	Sortie Generation Rates
SigMA	Signature Measurement Aircraft
SLO	Supportable Low Observables
S/MTD	STOL/Manoeuvre Technology Demonstrator
SORD	Spatial Orientation Retention Device
SPM	Shots Per Minute
SPO	System Program Office
SRA	Systems Research Aircraft
SRAAM	Short Range Air-to-Air Missiles
S&RE	Suspension & Release Equipment
SRM	Speech Recognition Module
SRR	System Requirement Review
ST	Short Tonne
STO	Short Take-Off
STOBAR	Short Take-Off But Arrested Recovery
STOVL	Short Take-Off and Vertical Landing
SWAN	Stress Wave Analysis Sensor
SWAT	STOVL Weight Attack Team
TAC	Total Accumulated engine Cycles
TACAN	Tactical Air Navigation
TADIRCM	Tactical Aircraft Directional Infra Red Counter Measures

TAF	Thermal Acoustic Facility
TEVEN	Telescopic Vectoring Nozzle
T/EMM	Thermal/Energy Management Module
TFLIR	Targeting Forward Looking Infra Red
TFX	Tactical Fighter Experimental
THELUS	Tactical High-Energy Laser Utility Study
TiMMC	Titanium Metal Matrix Composite
TLS	Tactor Locator system
TP	Target Practice
TPS	Test Pilot School
TRN	Terrain Reference Navigation
TRL	Technology Readiness Level
TRR	Technical Readiness Review
TRS	Transparency Removal System
TSAS	Tactile Situational Awareness System
UDTU	Upgraded Data Transfer Unit
USAF	United States Air Force
USMC	US Marine Corps
USRM	Under Seat Rocket Motor
VAAC	Vector thrust Aircraft Advanced flight Control
VAVBN	Variable Area Vane Box Nozzle
V DC	Volts Direct Current
VFDR	Variable Flow Ducted Rocket
VLBB	Vertical Landing Bring Back
VMC	Vehicle Management Computer
VRS	Voice Recognition System
V/STOL	Vertical/Short Take-off and Landing
WCMD	Wind Corrected Munition Dispenser
WCT	Weapon Carriage Technology
WSC	Weapon System Contractors
WSCD	Weapon System Concept Demonstration
YAL-1 prototype	Attack Laser 1A
3BSM	Three Bearing Swivel Module
3BSN	Three Bearing Swivel Nozzle

TECHNOLOGY READINESS LEVEL (TRL)

Technology Readiness Level (TRL)	Description
1 Basic principles observed and reported	Lowest level of technology readiness. Scientific research begins to be translated into applied research and development. Examples might include paper studies of a technology's basic properties.
2 Technology concept and/or application formulated	Invention begins. Once basic principles are observed, practical applications can be invented. The application is speculative and there is no proof or detailed analysis to support the assumption. Examples are still limited to paper studies.
3 Analytical and experimental critical function and/or characteristic proof of concept	Active research and development is initiated. This includes analytical studies and laboratory studies to validate physically analytical predictions of separate elements of the technology. Examples include components that are not yet integrated or representative.
4 Component and/or breadboard validation in laboratory environment	Basic technological components are integrated to establish that the pieces will work together. This is relatively 'low fidelity' compared to the eventual system. Examples include integration of 'ad hoc' hardware in a laboratory.
5 Component and/or breadboard validation in a relevant environment	Fidelity of breadboard technology increases significantly. The basic technological components are integrated with reasonably realistic supporting elements so that the technology can be tested in a simulated environment. Examples include high fidelity laboratory integration of components.

6	System/subsystem model or rototype demonstration in a relevant environment	Representative model or prototype system which is well beyond the breadboard tested for Technology Readiness Level (TRL) 5, is tested in a relevant environment. Represents a major step up in a technology's demonstrated readiness. Examples include testing the prototype in a high fidelity laboratory environment or in simulated operational environment.
7	System prototype demonstration in an operational environment	Prototype near or at planned operational system. Represents a major step up from TRL 6, requiring the demonstration of an actual system prototype in an operational environment, such as an aircraft, vehicle, or space. Examples include testing the prototype in a test bed aircraft.
8	Actual system completed and flight qualified through test and demonstration	Technology has been proven to work in its final form and under expected conditions. In almost all cases, this TRL represents the end of true system development. Examples include developmental test and evaluation of the system in its intended weapon systems to determine if it meets design specifications.
9	Actual system flight proven through successful mission operations	Actual application of the technology in its final form and under mission conditions, such as those encountered in operational test and evaluation. In almost all cases, this is the end of the last 'bug fixing' aspects of true system development. Examples include using the system under operational mission conditions.

Source: GAO/NSIAD-00-74

PRODUCTION LIST

Serial number/ construction number		First flight	Duration first flight	Pilot	Delivery date	Fate/ retired
CDA		**CDA**	**CDA**	**CDA**	**CDA**	**CDA**
6001	X-32A	18 Sept 2000	0h 20m	Fred Knox	N/A	
6002	X-32B	29 Mar 2001	0h 50m	Dennis O'Donoghue	N/A	31 Mar 2005
301	X-35A	24 Oct 2000	0h 30m	Tom Morgenfeld	N/A	From 21 Nov 2000 on converted to X-35B
301	X-35B	23 June 2001	2–3 secs	Simon Hargreaves	N/A	06 Aug 2001*
300	X-35C	16 Dec 2000	0h 27m	Joe Sweeney	N/A	10 Mar 2001*
SDD		**SDD**	**SDD**	**SDD**	**SDD**	**SDD**
AA-1 2AA-0001		15 Dec 2006	0h 35m	John Beesley		
AF-1						
AF-2						
AF-3						
AF-4						
AF-5						
BF-1						
BF-2						
BF-3						
BF-4						
CF-1						
CF-2						
CF-3						
CF-4						
CF-5						

* The 301 ended up in the Smithsonian Air and Space Museum complex at Washington Dulles Airport and the 300 ended up in the Patuxent River Test and Evaluation Museum. The X-32B (6002) was handed over to the Patuxent River. The X-32A (6001) was delivered in a bad state from Palmdale to the Wright Patterson museum early 2005. The X-32A was being refurbished and readied for display.

MISSION SYSTEM TESTING AIRCRAFT RESPONSIBILITIES DURING SDD

CTOL Aircraft

A-3	A-4	A-5
Internal gun	Integrated avionics	Integrated avionics
Signature	EOTS	Weapon integration & accuracy
Integrated avionics	EO-DAS	Communication Navigation Identification
Radar	Auto GCAS	EO-DAS
Electric Warfare Counter Measures	Weapons accuracy	Reliability Maintainability & Supportability
	Mission effectiveness	RF compatability
		Mission effectiveness

STOVL and CV Aircraft

B-4	B-5	C-3	C-5
EOTS	Reliability Maintainability & Supportability	SS	RF compatability
EO-DAS	Flying qualities	Ship suitability	EOTS
Radar	Chemical biological tests	Ship trials	Integrated avionics
Communication Navigation Identification	Live fire	JPALS	Weapon integration & accuracy
Signature		Signature	Reliability Maintainability & Supportability
Integrated avionics		F136 engine	EEE
Gun pod		Mission effectiveness	Mission effectiveness
UK weapons integration & Accuracy			
Mission effectiveness			
Climatic hangar			

AIRCRAFT DEVELOPMENT AND ACQUISITION CONTRACTS PRODUCTION LIST

	Amount	Order date	Contract value
Concept Demonstration Aircraft	2 Boeing CDA 2 Lockheed CDA	16 Nov 1996 16 Nov 1996	$662 million $719 million
Financial bridging contract until SDD Boeing		6 Apr 2001	$30 million
Financial bridging contract until SDD Lockheed		6 Apr 2001	$30 million
Financial bridging contract until SDD Boeing		25 Sept 2001	$5 million
Financial bridging contract until SDD Lockheed		25 Sept 2001	$5 million
System Development and Demonstration	14+8*	26 Oct 2001	$18.9 billion
Systems update to JPALS	None	24 Feb 2004	$52.44 million
SDD rescheduling contract	1 minus 1**	6 Oct 2005	$6,529 million
SDD Weapons integration change/upgrade		28 Apr 2006	$52.4 million
Long lead items LRIP lot 1 for 5CTOL aircraft	5	28 Apr 2006	$901 million
LRIP lot 1			$
Long lead items LRIP lot 2 for 6CTOL & 6STOVL			$
LRIP lot 2			$

*Of these twenty-two aircraft, five will be F-35A CTOL prototypes, five will be F-35B STOVL prototypes and four will be F-35C Carrier Version prototypes. The remaining eight aircraft are non-flying structures.

** The number of flying SDD aircraft was increased, however, the non-flying aircraft were reduced by one.

Engine Development and Acquisition Contracts

	Amount	Order date	Contract value
JAST propulsion system demos P&W		22 Dec 1994	$5,448,143
Low Cost Nozzles for Enhanced Strike Effectiveness/Turbo-cooler Engine Demonstration for Flexible Thermal Management GE		22 Dec 1994	$3,657,288
P&W Engine design study for Lockheed Boeing McDonnell Douglas	F119-SE611 F119-SE614 F119-SE615	13 Dec 1995	$28,354,675
Contract modification P&W preliminary design engineering support for the definition and development of the propulsion systems		4 Dec 1996	$27,000,000
CDP engines P&W two developmental engines, two qualification engines and two flight-test engines for Boeing and Lockheed each	6 Boeing engines 6 Lockheed engines	23 Jan 1997	$804,046,096
YF-120-FX core development GE		13 Feb 1997	$96,000,000
CDP modification P&W		20 Feb 1997	$29,231,000
Contract modification GE		15 Apr 1997	$10,000,000
Contract modification P&W Two additional diagnostics and health monitoring technology maturation studies		10 July 1997	$6,999,950
Contract modification GE for core spares, high pressure turbine nozzle design and fabrication		25 June 1998	$5,755,000
Contract modification GE test and part manufacturing expansion		20 Aug 1998	$5,991,500
Contract modification GE preparation of requirements for phase III		30 June 1999	$114,830,000
Contract modification GE risk reduction efforts for alternate engine development		14 Mar 2000	$13,981,000
P&W intermediate contract between CDP and SDD including long lead funding		13 April 2001	$72,000,000
System Development and Demonstration P&W	20 + 12	26 Oct 2001	$4,803,460,088
Contract modification GE Pre SDD of the F136 propulsion system		13 Nov 2001	$411,000,000
Commonality trade studies P&W		1 Apr 2002	$12,740,073
GE interchangeability studies for phase IIIb		3 Apr 2002	$14,267,300
Contract modification GE risk reduction efforts		5 May 2003	$27.896.100
Contract modification P&W technology maturation for coatings and composites		10 Sept 2003	$22,961,225
GE risk-reduction efforts for phase IIIb		15 Apr 2004	$14,000,000
GE transition effort from phase IIIb to SDD		3 Nov 2004	$122,155,880
System Development and Demonstration GE	7 + 7 engines	19 Aug 2005	$2,466,258,499
SDD re-scheduling contract P&W		6 Oct 2005	$968,600,000
LRIP lot 1 long lead for six engines		28 Apr 2006	$23,000,000
F135 Gearbox redesign contract modification		01 Dec 2006	$10,000,000
LRIP lot 1 P&W			$
LRIP lot 2 P&W			$

APPENDIX V

AIRCRAFT SPECIFICATIONS

	X-35A CTOL	X-35B STOVL	X-35C CV
Length (w. noseboom)	56.1 ft	56.1 ft	56.1 ft
Wingspan	33 ft	33 ft	40 ft
Wing area (approx)	450 ft^2	450 ft^2	540.5 ft^2

	F-35A CTOL	F-35B STOVL	F-35C CV
Length	15.58 m / 51.1 ft	15.58 m / 51.1 ft	15.64 m / 51.4 ft
Wingspan	10.67 m / 35 ft	10.67 m / 35 ft	13.11 m / 43 ft
Wing area	42.73 m2 460 ft^2	42.73 m2 /460 ft^2	57.6 m2 /620 ft^2
Combat radius	>1092 km / 590 nm	>833 km / 450 nm	>1111 km / 600 nm

Three plan views of the F-35A, the version that will equip USAF and most international partners. *Copyright Lockheed Martin*

F-35A

Conventional Take Off & Landing (CTOL)
Span (ft) 35
Length (ft) 50.5
Wing Area (ft2) 460
Internal Fuel (lb) 18,498

Three plan views of the F-35B, the model that started it all in the early 1990s. If it was not for the STOVL requirement, would there have been such a cooperation between the UK and the US? *Copyright Lockheed Martin*

F-35B

Short Take Off & Vertical Landing (STOVL)
Span (ft) 35
Length (ft) 50.5
Wing Area (ft2) 460
Internal Fuel (lb) 13,326

Three plan views of the F-35C, it represents a return to single-engine aircraft for the US Navy but will probably be the least exportable model, although Australia may take some because of the model's extended range. *Copyright Lockheed Martin*

F-35C

Carrier Variant (CV)
Span (ft) 43
Length (ft) 50.8
Wing Area (ft2) 620
Internal Fuel (lb) 19,624

PRODUCTION REPRESENTATIVE GROUND AND FLIGHT-TEST VEHICLES TEST SCHEDULE

Schedule as of October 2004

CTOL aircraft	Scheduled first flight	Actual first flight	
AA-1 (2AA-0001)	3Q 2006		Airworthiness, environmental
TA-1	3Q 2007		Ground-test vehicle
A-6 (2AF-0001)	1Q 2008		Flutter, flying qualities, propulsion, weapons
A-2 (2AF-0002)	1–2Q 2008		Loads, flying qualities, weapons
A-3 (AF-0003)	2Q 2008		Mission systems, survivability, WDA
TA-3	3Q 2008		Ground-test vehicle
A-4	3Q 2009		Mission systems, survivability, WDA
A-5	3Q 2009		Mission systems, survivability, WDA
STOVL aircraft			
TB-1	1Q 2007		Ground-test vehicle
B-1 (2BF-0001)	3–4Q 2007		STOVL operations, IFPC, propulsion
B-2 (2BF-0002)	2Q 2008		Flutter, flying qualities, propulsion, ship suitability
B-3 (2BF-0003)	3Q 2008		Loads, flying qualities, weapons
B-4 (2BF-0004)	3Q 2008		Mission systems, survivability, WDA, climatic, D-SDD
TB-2	1Q 2009		Ground-test vehicle
B-5 (2BF-0005)	2Q 2009		Flying qualities, survivability, chemical biological and live fire
CV aircraft			
TC-1	2Q 2008		Ground-test vehicle
TC-2	3Q 2008		Ground-test vehicle
C-1 (2CF-0001)	1Q 2009		Flutter, flying qualities, propulsion, weapons
C-2 (2CF-0002)	2Q 2009		Loads, flying qualities, weapons
C-3 (2CF-0003)	2Q 2009		Ship suitability, mission systems, survivability
TC-3	2Q 2009		Ground-test vehicle
C-5 (2CF-0004)	3Q 2009		Mission systems, survivability, WDA, ship suitability

This full scale model was tested for the antenna suite in the Air Force Research Laboratory (AFRL) facility. It was reconfigurable to the STOVL and CV version. *Copyright Lockheed Martin*

The Radar Cross Signature of Lockheed Martins Preferred Weapon Systems Concept was measured with this model during the CDP as a part of the risk reduction and demonstration effort. *Copyright Lockheed Martin*

The paint on the floor shows the effect on the ground of the exhaust of the lift fan in yellow paint and of the main engine in red paint. It is visible that the hot gas does not pass the cool exhaust of the lift fan during in-ground effects testing. The model has holes where canards can be installed. *Copyright Lockheed Martin*

APPENDIX VII

AIRCRAFT USED FOR TECHNOLOGY RISK REDUCTION IN THE JSF PROGRAMME

BAC 1-11 Aircraft Used for Test Purposes

Aircraft	Registration		Operator	Location	Programme/System
BAC 1-11	N161NG	CN067	Northrop Grumman	Baltimore, Washington	AN/APG-81 radar
BAC 1-11	N162W	CN087	Northrop Grumman	Baltimore, Washington	EO-DAS

This aircraft has been used by Northrop Grumman in the CDP as an avionics test-bed and during the SDD for the EO-DAS. The BAC 1-11 flying test-bed prove to be a very useful tool for JSF programme. *Copyright Northrop Grumman*

Boeing 737-300 CATBird

Aircraft	Registration	S/N	Operator	Location	Programme/System
Boeing 737-300	N35LX	23528	Lockheed Martin	Fort Worth	Sensor fusion testing

Harrier

Aircraft	Registration	Unit	Location	Programme/System
McDonnell Douglas TAV-8B	BuNo 163191	Naval Weapon Test Squadron (China Lake)	NAS Patuxent River	IHAVS
McDonnell Douglas AV-8B	BuNo 163854	Naval Weapon Test Squadron (China Lake)	NAS Patuxent River	Ground enviroment STOVL baseline
BAE Systems Harrier T-4	XW-175	DERA/QinetiQ	Boscombe Down	JPALS

Rockwell/MBB X-31

Aircraft	S/N	Unit	Location	Programme/System
Rockwell/MBB X-31	BuNo 164585	NASA Dryden Flight Research Center	Edwards	Tailless

The X-31 shown here with its vertical fin wiped out by modern computer technology. The quassi Tailless programme stopped just short of doing that in reality. *NASA*

This white F-16 is a rare sight at a time when most aircraft are coloured in some variation of grey and the X-35A was unfortunately no exception to the rule. *Copyright Lockheed Martin*

Lockheed Martin F-16

Aircraft	S/N	Unit	Location	Programme/System
Lockheed AFTI F-16	75-0750		Fort Worth Edwards	J/IST/AGCAS
Lockheed VISTA F-16	86-0048	Veridian TPS	Edwards	ACAS/ Virtual HUD
Lockheed F-16D	83-1176		Edwards	AGCAS
Lockheed F-16	83-1120	416 FLTS	Edwards	DSI
Lockheed F-16	86-0359	445 FLTS	Edwards	ERR sensor pod for EO DAS
Lockheed F-16	83-1118		Edwards	ERR sensor pod for EO DAS
Lockheed F-16	83-1119		Edwards	ERR sensor pod for EO DAS
Lockheed F-16 Orange Jumper	6E-35 J-066	323 TacTes Kantoor Test Vliegen (KTV), or Flight Test Centre	Leeuwarden	Ti-MMC/arresting gear

McDonnell Douglas C-17 Globemaster

Aircraft	S/N	Unit	Location	Programme/System
Boeing C-17 Globemaster	T-1	CTF/NASA	Edwards	Propulsion Health Management

Boeing (McDonnell Douglas) F-18 Hornet

Aircraft	Registration	Unit	Location	Programme/System
Boeing F/A-18A	SD110	VX-23 Salty Dogs	NAS Patuxent River	Joint Precision Approach And Landing System
Boeing F-18B	SD325	VX-23 Salty Dogs	NAS Patuxent River	Joint Paintless Aircraft Program
Boeing F-18B Systems Research Aircraft	845	NASA Dryden Flight Research Centre	Edwards	More Electric Aircraft program

Lockheed C-141 Starlifter

Aircraft	S/N	Unit	Location	Programme/System
Lockheed C-141 Starlifter	61-2776	AFFTC	Edwards	Electric Starlifter

Gloster Meteor

Aircraft	S/N	Unit	Location	Programme/System
Meteor T7	WL419	Martin-Baker	Chalgrove	Ejection seat/ TRS

North American T-39 Sabreliner

Aircraft	Registration	S/N	Operator	Location	Programme/System
T-39	N39FS	62-4480	BAE Systems		EW systém
T-39	N11LX	306-75	Lockheed Martin	Goodyear Airport in Phoenix	EOTS

Pitts Special S-2B

Aircraft	Registration	Unit	Location	Programme/System
Pitts Special S-2B	N-597TJ	CN5325		HMD

The idea of the simulated combat manoeuvres was that the pilot would turn and twist his head as he would do during normal one to one dogfight. The HMD during high g manoeuvres should still feel comfortable.
Copyright Lockheed Martin

Squadron Leader Justin Paines was not only involved in test flying the X-35 concept demonstration aircraft but also in the support Vector thrust Aircraft Advanced flight Control (VAAC) programme. *Copyright Lockheed Martin*

Seven of the eight pilots who participated in the X-35 flight test programme. At the back from left to right were Joe Sweeney, Simon Hargreaves, Lt. Col. Paul 'TP' Smith, Tom 'Squid' Morgenfeld, Sqd Ldr Justin Paines RAF. In front from left to right are Lt. Cdr Greg 'Fence' Fenton and Maj. Art 'Turbo' Tomassetti.

APPENDIX VIII

PEOPLE

Lockheed Martin Concept Demonstration Aircraft Pilots

X-35 Test Pilot	Company/ service	X-35A	No. of flights	X-35B	No. of flights	X-35C	No. of flights
Tom 'Squid' Morgenfeld	Lockheed chief test pilot	1st pilot	15	4th pilot	2	4th pilot	8
Joe Sweeney	Lockheed Navy test pilot	4th pilot	1	Did not fly X-35B	0	1st pilot	32
Simon Hargreaves	BAE Systems	5th pilot	2	1st pilot	20	7th pilot	1
Lt-Col Paul 'TP' Smith	USAF	2nd pilot	6	Did not fly X-35B	0	3rd pilot	3
Maj. Art 'Turbo' Tomassetti	US Marine Corp	3rd pilot	1	2nd pilot	9	5th pilot	6
Sqd Ldr Justin Paines	UK RAF	6th pilot	2	3rd pilot	8	6th pilot	1
Lt-Cdr Brian 'Goz' Goszkowicz	US Navy	Did not fly X-35A	0	Did not fly X-35B	0	2nd pilot	7
Lt-Cdr Greg 'Fence' Fenton	US Navy	Did not fly X-35A	0	Did not fly X-35B	0	8th pilot	15
Total			27		39		73

Boeing Concept Demonstration Aircraft Pilots

X-32 Pilot	Company/service	X-32A	No. of flights	X-32B	No. of flights
Fred Knox	Boeing	1st pilot	18	5th pilot	3
Dennis 'Irish' O'Donoghue	Boeing	3rd pilot	5	1st pilot	31
Lt-Col Edward 'Fast Eddie' Cabrera	USAF	4th pilot	12	4th pilot	2
Cdr Phil 'Rowdy' Yates	US Navy	2nd pilot	23		0
Lt-Cdr Paul 'Stoney' Stone	UK Royal Navy	5th pilot	4	3rd pilot	22
Maj. Jeff 'Pig pen' Karnes	US Marine Corp	6th pilot	4	2nd pilot	20
Total			66		78

Joint Program Directors

Period	Name	Title	Remarks
27 January 1994* to August 1995	George Muellner	Lt-General	USAF
August 1995 to August 1997	Craig E. Steidle	Rear Admiral	US NAVY
August 1997 to May 1999	Leslie F. Kenne	Brigadier-General	USAF
May 1999 to October 2001	Michael Hough	Major-General	US Marine Corps
October 2001 to June 2004	Jack Hudson	Brigadier-General	USAF
June 2004 to July 2006	Steven L. Enewold	Rear Admiral	US NAVY
July 2006 to present	Charles R. Davis	Brigadier-General	USAF
	David R. Heinz	Brigadier-General	US Marine Corps

* Brigadier-General George K. Muellner was selected in December 1993 although the office opened on 27 January 1994.

INDEX